SHE WALKS ALONE

Acknowledgements

They say that everyone has a story and so this one is mine from the heart. Some may say it is part fiction and others would say part truth. Well I will leave it up to you to work out but whatever conclusion you come to, you will find that somewhere in this story there will be a passage which will relate to you.

A story of fashion and love but also of trust for this woman WALKED ALONE.

To Keith who encouraged me to do this.

To my family and friends.

To Karen who stood by my side when I gave up on many occasion.

And to Dean who without his help I would still be struggling.

I thank you sincerely for all that you have done.

NORMA

CHAPTER 1

CORRANDER SHARP

CEO OF SHARP INDUSTRIES

That's the title on the door that hits you as you walk into the main office of one of the largest fashion houses in Europe, for she's one of the most talked about women in the fashion world, who came up the hard way from a small town in Yorkshire to be one of the most influential women of her time. Yes, she'd earned that title and everything that came with it as she'd worked so hard to achieve all the recognition that had come her way.

It was now 2010 and she'd the world at her feet or so some people assumed but they didn't know the real woman behind that title, going through all the heartache she'd suffered over the years, suffering and pain not only for herself but also for others that had entered her life.

Born on the 4th August 1959, Corrander Sharp better known to all as she liked to be called, Corry.

As you entered the office it was as just as you'd have imagined should you have met her before, all done out in black and white minimalistic but with an air of warmth and greeting for everyone who entered as that's what Corry was like to everyone who met her.

There were no trappings or any sign of luxuries; the only personal items on her desk were a large photo of her beloved daughter Alexa together with a smaller one of her grandparents and brother.

For those who would meet her for the first time, you could only describe her as 5ft,6, slim with a fantastic figure, long natural blond hair, the most astonishing pale green eyes you could wish for and such a warm dry sense of humour that could either have you in stitches or cut you dead with a sarcastic smile. Her dress sense to say who she was and what she did for a living was very sleek, plain but made a statement that was the height of fashion.

Having such an outgoing personality, those who didn't know her would think she was a very strong minded woman who not only knew what she wanted but also got all her own way, it would also be assumed, she was hard, cold and calculated without any feelings for others, how wrong this assumption would be, for inside of Corry was a gentle, thoughtful and generous human being who'd rather do for others than for herself

Being a workaholic all of her adult life, it was as though there wasn't any time in the day for anything else but the business, even her personal life seemed to be on hold most of the time, that's if she had any personal life at present for she always put others first.

What a weekend it had been for Corry as her only child Alexa had just got engaged to a prominent lawyer in the city, this causing the society pages to have a field day due to Alexa being one of the most sought after fashion models in London, having followed in her mother's footsteps to some extent.

Exhausted, Corry sat in her office that September morning, just pondering over the thought of flying out to Cyprus the next day for a break in what had seemed one hectic party that she'd thrown for the couple at the weekend, well that was before she was interrupted by the company secretary Shelia, who informed her that all the arrangements had been made for her trip whereby a car would be waiting to collect her at the other side when she arrived;

"I've also informed everyone that you will be away a week to ten days, this giving time to sort yourself out when you return".

"You know me better than that, I'll be back in the office the day after I return, and I can assure you of that" she stated;

"We'll, have a nice trip which I'm sure you will, oh' and before I forget, you had a phone call from Jay, he'd like you to contact him as a matter of urgency or so he says" Sheila added with a distrustful expression on her face knowing in her heart it spelt trouble.

Corry's face turned white at this news as she asked;

"Are you sure, it was Jay as no one's heard of him for years let along him being in contact with even his friends.

"Of course I'm sure; I'll never forget his voice for what he put you through, however I did ask if he wanted to speak to Alexa as you were away and therefore not contactable" Corry was just motionless at that statement, when Shelia added;

"But he just said it was you he needed to speak to urgently and not to mention this conversation to anyone else under any circumstance, sorry to upset you, but thought you should know fear you wanted to contact him before you left, I've added his number in your diary".

"No, he's waited this long to make contact, he'll have to wait my time now, why should I spoil my holiday for the likes of him, if it was that important then he should have spoken to Alexa or has he forgotten he's got a grown up daughter".

You could tell by the expression on Corry's face she was fuming, but all the same determined not to get in touch with her ex-husband Jay for whatever he wanted he'd have to wait her time now, he'd not bothered with his daughter since the divorce which had caused much heartache so he'd now have to wait her time and this she was adamant, just who the hell does he think he is she thought after all this time.

Not being able to understand why on earth after all this time, he should get in touch, for it was his decision not to have anything to do with Alexa so in her opinion he could go to hell, as she was determined not to let him spoil her holiday and therefore would put it to the back of her mind knowing that Shelia wouldn't mention anything to Alexa, the only problem was it was hard to put it to the back of her mind.

A couple of vodkas with an early night is what she needed after packing her suitcase so that's what it was going to be she thought, but thoughts don't always go down with feelings as we all know and a restless night was what she suffered

It was still pretty warm when Corry finally woke the next morning, the sun starting to slowly appear out of the mist of cloud and having glanced at her watch thought another five minutes with a shower before dressing and with a last minute call to her daughter, before the taxi to collect her for the airport was to arrive, which would leave her plenty of time to get booked in for the 2pm flight. And yes spot on time, the taxi arrived as she was just leaving the apartment, for this was a thing about her, everything had to run precisely to the minute just as she organised her business;

"Leeds airport is it Miss" the taxi driver enquired

"Yes that's right, thank you", she replied.

"You get in the cab and take the weight off your feet while I put your bags in the back, going anywhere nice" he added

"Just to Cyprus for a week or so" as she replied carefully, lowering herself down onto the back seat gracefully.

Her short plain brown skirt gently draped over the long tan legs finishing off with the highest of heels you could possibly walk in, the pure silk blouse which covered her soft silky skin with a touch of elegance as it showed off the outline of the pert nipples which was a tease to any man who looked closely at this gorgeous female. The long blond hair falling naturally over the end of her tiny shoulders, yes she'd be a prize for any man who could conquer such beauty, but no she had other things on her mind as her thoughts were fixated on the journey she was about to embark upon.

Having doubts already, after the shock of Jay trying to contact her was this the right time to get away from it all or should she cancel the trip when she arrived at the airport. No, that wouldn't be fair, she needed this break and that's exactly what she was going to have, he had always dominated the situation when they were married but he'd no control over the situation now, so why should she change her plans, he would have to wait her time.

Arriving at Leeds airport, the driver was so helpful offloading the cases, packing the trolley, even offered to take the luggage into the lounge as he'd a permanent parking area which was designated to him;

"Are you sure you can manage all these cases all by yourself", he enquired.

"Yes, I'll be fine, I'll get a coffee on the way" she replied handing him a fifty-pound note, not even asking, how much the fare was.

"Just one moment miss, I'll get you some change".

"No, don't bother, treat yourself to a drink on me as you deserve one".

His face was a picture, he never got big tips like that only on very rare occasions, maybe tonight would be the night he'd take the wife flowers home and make her day or even make his night if she was in the mood for a little hanky panky he thought.

Coffee in one hand, trolley in the other she approached the booking desk which had just opened, handing the documents to the desk clerk who subsequently enquired as to whether Corry had packed her own cases, to which she automatically replied;

"Yes", that's fine, now everything's in order and your plane will leave in approximately two hours' time".

"Have a nice journey Miss Sharp" one of the booking clerks stated, as she then proceeded to the VIP lounge, whereby a young bar attendant asked if he could help by getting her anything to eat or drink,

"Yes please, a large vodka and tonic would go down nicely and could you bring it to the large window as just love to watch the aircraft taking off, it somehow has such a soothing effect on me" she stated.

The drink arrived as she settled into the soft velvet easy chair with such a relaxed feeling and an uneasy haunting of the past, not being able to get out of her mind those words Shelia had said not twenty-four hours before. There she was going to a man that worshiped and adored her only to have it spoil by her ex-husband after all these years.

Ordering another couple of vodka's, her mind strayed back to the wonderful days she'd spent with her ex-husband when they first met on the island with not a care in the world, but that was in the past when times were good. It was also Cyprus that their daughter had been conceived and later born, those were the good years. But then again coming down to earth with a bang, she found him to be unfaithful and therefore leading into the start of divorce which changed her world completely, ruining not only her life but also their daughter's.

It's no wonder she couldn't settle, for if it wasn't for the backup from her family in Yorkshire that she had to thank in those early days, yes they'd all been a god send giving Alexa a normal life away from the city, showing her values of homely love as Corry had to work all hours to provide a good living for their future.

Taking into consideration how she had to travel for the company, her family had done well to keep Alexa's feet firmly on the ground with love and stability when it was decided that she would be brought up in the north of England and that's why she'd be eternally grateful.

A normal school instead of being shipped away to a private one where visits to family were restricted to holiday period, no this wasn't for Alexa as she'd have hated it, rebelling rigorously or even turning out to be a spoilt brat wanting all her own way as her father had done, thinking he was better than others.

If only Agnes had been alive things may have been different but there again we can't dwell on the past too much for Agnes, in fairness, adored Corry and gave her the chance to make the success which she'd achieved today, the CEO of the largest fashion group in Europe.

With Alexa, there were no worries at all now for she was to marry a man who worshipped her beyond any doubts, a man that Corry was so proud to call her son in law.

She was so happy for her daughter, if only her own life had turned out like that she'd have been on cloud nine but then again these things happen for a reason and no doubt one day she may have the wish of being truly happy herself without any insecurities spoiling it. Yes, time wasn't on her side but at 51-year-old, there was still a lot of living to do and life was now starting to look up or it was before she received that message from Jay.

Now time to board as the announcement came over the loudspeaker, a little light headed through tiredness together with the touch of vodka she'd consumed, came down to her senses with a roar of the engine on the runway. Walking towards the plane, with thoughts of, well whatever happens I'm going to enjoy this break because when I get back I have a feeling all hell is going to break loose and therefore I'll be ready for it.

This was the story of her life, just when things started to run smooth something would happen to get in the way and alter the course but then that's destiny and we can't change that whatever happens. Entering the plane, she saw a few familiar faces with the cabin crew, as one asked;

"Are you going for long this time on this trip Miss Sharp?"

"No", she replied, "just thought I'd get a week in before the Christmas period was on us, as had a very busy year".

"Well you just have a nice time, you deserve it, and by the way, will you congratulate your daughter on her engagement from all the staff that knows her, we were all thrilled to see the news in the papers yesterday".

"Thank you very much, that was kind of you to say so, I know you all take very good care of us when we fly with you", she replied.

"Not as much as you have done for us over the years" the stewardess stated.

Taking a seat by the window stretching her legs out gracefully as not to draw attention to herself, seatbelts on, she glanced out of the window towards the runway, this was the easy part of flying, sitting back to relax with the world going by without any interruptions. It was always nice to return to the villa, maybe small by comparison of some of the villas near to her but then again, she'd purchased it a few years ago and to be honest, liked it without making many changes.

Thinking back, it was supposed to be a small retreat for her and someone she loved dearly but that never worked out for she panicked at the moment of truth when the memories of Jay haunted her as they'd done so many times before, since her divorce.

It wasn't the kind of place Jay would have considered for it was far too small and he was all for the upper end of the market being rather snobbish to his position as he used to call it, with no consideration to her feelings, but to Corry it was perfect, situated not far from the airport and just further along the beach from where she'd lived when married to Jay.

It comprised of four large bedrooms that opened out onto their own balcony facing the sea, all with en-suites, a large lounge that opened onto the patio, giving the aroma of scented flowers most of the year, the kitchen however was rather large by any standards, for she had an extension built in the early days, so when friends came round they could feel at home.

Ah yes the kitchen, this was something out of a show house as it stocked the finest of foods and wine that anyone could wish for, being a fantastic host when it came to feeding guests even down to the workmen when they did jobs. It was an open but friendly place that everyone felt at ease as soon as they entered the large hand carved front door. And when the property was empty, her close friend Maria would take care of the place in readiness for her return.

The engines roared, the plane jerked, then all of a sudden with a swift thrust, the plane sped along the runway and within seconds lifted its nose for the grand take off which everyone holds their breath seeing the undercarriage lift up as the nose tilts to the sky. Now up in the air and still climbing she could feel a heavy heart going into relaxed mode. Oh boy, did she need this break, having not realised just how weary she felt until now.

The business, although it was running smooth, there was always another project she was looking for, it was as though she was lost in a wilderness and couldn't find her way out, finding new things to take the ventures further, it was as though she was trying to prove something to herself but didn't know what. New ideas came to her fast and furious; putting them into practice was easy for the people she employed were the best you could wish for, but still there was something in her life that was lacking or so she kept telling herself time after time.

Her personal life at the moment was pretty good, she was going to spend a week with a man she thought the world of, but was it love, yes, it was love of a kind but not the kind of love she was searching for, as that didn't exist or if it did it had come at the wrong time in her life which she wasn't prepared to admit as per usual.

This was the third man that had got close to Corry in her life but was he the one or was she holding back for someone that no one knew about, that we will never find out, or will we?

The sound of the engines together with the effect of the alcohol that she'd consumed earlier was now starting to tip her over the edge whereby her eyelids became heavier until finally she dosed off into a deep and wondrous sleep. It was when one of the stewardesses' passed by she couldn't help notice that Corry had fallen asleep in what was to be an uncomfortable position and therefore propped her head up onto a large pillow therefore making her as comfortable as possible, without disturbing the deep sleep that she'd now fallen into.

Corry now in a sound sleep or should we say floating on air as that's how she would remember it when she awoke. For her mind wondered back to the beginning of time when it all began.

CHAPTER 2

THE PAST AND HOW IT ALL BEGAN

Corrander Sharp had come a long way in her life to this present day. Born to professional parents, both she and her brother had been brought up by her maternal grandparents in a small mining village just outside of Doncaster.

Her grandfather Enos was a quiet, proud but educated man, who'd originated from South Wales but now worked down the mines.

Her grandmother Daisy, who on the other hand was the driving force of the family, originated from Newcastle. They'd met one day when Enos had gone to Newcastle looking for work from his home town in Wales, having stopped off at a nearby farm to enquire over somewhere to stay when he met Daisy whose mother also run a small farm on the outskirt of Sunderland and it is understood when their eyes met it was love at first sight for both of them.

Having chattered up young Daisy which resulted in Enos staying to help out on her mother's farm as the relationship blossomed, furthermore resulting in them eventually being married at the local chapel a few miles away in what we would call a small ceremony.

Times were hard and with very little work in those days it was a god send when an opportunity in South Yorkshire for men to come and work in the coal mines arose. And as they were offering not only a job for men that were willing to re-locate but also a small house for their families to live, this giving pride back to those who were not only out of work but those who would take the opportunity to seek a better life.

The main people who came to work there, were from communities up the north of England, even going up as far as Scotland for you had to go where the work was to survive, and so they grabbed this opportunity with both hands moving down to Yorkshire with the promise of a job working down the mines together a house thrown in with it. Yes, life was hard for everyone but they seemed to be happy in their own little world which had given them a decent standard of living together with a roof over their head providing for their families.

Having brought up two boys when the two girls Susie and Nina came along, making a very happy family unit, but sadly after the children had flown the nest Enos had been struck down with emphysema, working in the mines like many others it'd taken its toll on his lungs and consequently he later died in his early fifties.

It was a sad time for all but at least the house they lived in had been secured financially for Enos was a shrewd secretive man who no one really knew, it was only when he died, the family found, he was the illegitimate son of a famous politician who'd left him a considerable amount of money which was enough to buy the house for cash from the coal board which he'd done without telling anyone.

In those days' no one spoke about the secrets that were held in family closets and with no birth control, these things happened, therefore secrets were covered up for ever and a day in some cases, never to be spoken.

Years passed, whereby Daisy was left on her own in what people thought was a big house, too big for her to manage alone, Corry's parents on the other hand were living in rented accommodation with two young children which didn't make sense to Daisy.

So after long discussions it was decided that they move back into the big house and as Corry was now eight and her brother Paul had reached the age of three, it would enable the parents to get better jobs leaving Daisy to take care of the children while both parents worked to bring in a healthy contribution to keep the family in what they classed as luxury.

This was done a lot in those days where the grandparents brought up the children so that the parents could both work to attain a better life style for all.

The only thing was, as both Corry's parents were quite well educated, and to earn the money they deserved, they would be better to move down to London and maybe come back every weekend to help with the children, this was no problem for Daisy and to be truthful she loved the idea as it was like having her family unit back together being mother hen over her little chicks.

Corry's Mother Nina was the first to go to London and get a position she'd applied for as a fashion designer which is what she'd trained for at college, shortly followed by her father George who was a qualified design engineer and therefore walked into a job straight away.

This arrangement worked for years whereby the parents would come home to the children two or three times a month together with all the holidays which were classed as special times where all the family would get together and maybe spend time as a full family unit. The extra money they earned was put to good use whereby the children had things that others couldn't afford and Daisy was in her element for the children was so well mannered and good she never knew she had them at times.

Things worked out well until Corry's mother became very ill having to return to Doncaster. Money wasn't the issue at that time as Daisy had saved most of the money given to her for the children, it was Nina that everyone was worried about, she had undergone many tests but still they couldn't find out why she was losing weight rapidly and in so much pain at that time.

Corry now sixteen, and working in an office for the railways, couldn't settle as she felt trapped but unfortunately this time was a little blurred having to witness her mother deteriorating quite rapidly which was such a worry although she did her best to give her grandmother a break while watching her mother go through so much pain, it was difficult as she was also trying to study to follow in her mother's footsteps with a career in art and design at night school.

Corry's father wasn't much help for he'd only come home when it suited, it was therefore assumed, maybe he'd other interests in London that was keeping him down there but nothing was said and as much as Corry would have liked to have confronted him with this theory, she kept silence to keep the peace fear her mother got wind of it.

Knowing she had to be strong for the whole family at this time but all the same, in her mind knowing her mother wasn't getting any better and it would only be a matter of time before she would leave them all for good as the pain was getting unbearable and with no answers from the medical profession there didn't seem much hope.

And then came that dreaded day, a day she would never forget, her eighteenth birthday when all should have been such a happy time for Corry, but unfortunately that morning as she went in to kiss her mother having done this routinely when she woke, it wasn't the same, for as she bent over, she felt that cold shudder which told her, she had passed away in the night leaving such a peaceful smile on her face.

Ache in her heart but with a sign of relief Corry was pleased that at long last her mother was now free of pain and suffering, as the tears rolled down her face uncontrollably. Sitting on the side of the bed, she stroked her mother's hand and kissed her goodbye, softly whispering,

"I will love you forever, and one day I will make you so proud of me, that I promise you with all my heart".

To this she slowly stood up and proceeded to inform her grandmother who helped break the news to her brother Paul.

The next few hours were a blur which was put to the back of her mind after sending a telegram to her father, it's as though Corry grew up overnight, informing all those that had to be told and arranging everything for the funeral as her father arrived from London but was nothing but a useless ornamental piece as she feared he would be at this time.

It took Corry all her time to even speak to him on the day of the funeral, for it seemed he was more interested in returning to London, and in her mind, she was now sure he had another woman he was returning to and therefore would be glad to see the back of him but for respect to her mother she would keep a civil tongue in her head and not challenge him into a slanging match.

Yes, she'd been right all along for that night, her father returned to London on a late train, after he'd had the decency to make arrangements with her grandmother to send monies for Pauls keep and education.

The one thing Corry never doubted was her father's word to provide a substantial sum of monies for Paul's education being an educated man himself and knowing how important it was for his son to succeed in a good career as he had done.

It was at this time that Corry's determination kicked in to make a promise she'd made on her mother's death bed about making her proud, she would follow in her footsteps by going to London and make a name for herself in the fashion world, maybe eventually becoming a designer if she worked hard enough but whatever, she knew that one thing was for sure, she would never live the lie her mother had lived these past few years with other women in the background.

Oh no, when the time came, for her to fall in love it would be for keeps and would last a lifetime for if he ever cheated on her, she'd walk away for good whatever the consequences may bring she thought.

Everything else had gone pretty well after the funeral although her grandmother did look tired, but there again that was to be expected, she'd lost her daughter without the chance to say goodbye properly.

Now the good news was, Corry had applied to do a night school follow on course in London at a top design school where she'd already been accepted, all she had to do now was find somewhere to stay, and get a little job to top up the monies she'd already saved.

As far as monies to keep the family going, her father had been as good as his word with a weekly cheque to support them all. Thus knowing that Paul's education was a priority.

Although she'd been close to her father when young, it seemed that now, he'd other interests and hardly heard from him at all. There was a saying which was so very true in her case, he would want her before she would want him and that's exactly how it turned out to be. She now had to look out for herself as she wasn't going to be left behind, having had plans, and plenty of them, she'd made her mind up to follow in her mother's footsteps and make a career in the world of fashion.

CHAPTER 3

Moving to London wouldn't be too bad as Corry had contacted an old school friend whose family had moved down there a few years ago and who was willing to let her stay with them until she could get on her own two feet.

She expected things to be difficult at first until getting settled and maybe find a job as part time work was plentiful in those days for those willing to work but knowing she'd fit in with anything going until better opportunities came along. As anticipated, everything went to plan when moving in with her friend's parents who would come to treat her as though she was one of the family.

The meeting with the fashion school had gone marvellous with a placement promised so she'd lean the skills in house so to speak, life really was moving on for her now although it was hard at first to adjust to the silly little things but within time everything would work itself out she thought

It wasn't long before she was on the shop floor learning how things really worked, cutting, drawing, personal skills they never teach you when you're in a classroom, even down to sweeping the floor which is just as important when you're on the way up the ladder, having to work long hours but the benefits, she would receive later on in life, would be compensation for all the work that she was now to put in.

As for men, well you could forget them for she was so hungry for power, they would have to be put on one side until she could achieve her goal in life making a name for herself, ambitious yes, reality well we would have to see about that as the drive to make her dreams come true was the driving force that kept her going.

Getting homesick was her only regret, having been brought up in a small village where everyone knew one another and yet London was so different and strange to her in many ways, it took people all their time to speak if you were a stranger she thought, never mind I'll adapt to their way of thinking in time I'm sure.

No, she could never repay her friend's family for what they had done, treating her like their own daughter, but it was now time to move on and find a place of her own, which she finally did.

Yes, a couple of years had now passed and Corry was starting to get noticed for the work she'd created although it didn't bring in much money but at least it gave her a chance to get her own accommodation, well not her own as it was a small terrace house she shared with two other girls, but to her, it was her way of stating she was now independent.

Keeping her barmaids job, helped pay the bills, but also gave her freedom to enjoy socialising without having to spend any money. It was funny really, for when first arriving in London she was just a face in the crowd, that no one even noticed, but now with her confidence, built over the past couple of years; she found that when she spoke, people actually took notice and listened to what she was saying as it made sense on whatever subjects they were discussing.,

It had even been remarked upon, that this bit of a girl knew what she was talking about in the fashion business, which was an achievement in its self for she'd a habit at that time of listening when people spoke on different topics which enabled her to gain the knowledge, and if by chance she didn't understand, she'd read up on the subject to gain an insight to what was going on around her and the world in its entirety.

Always remembering what her Father had said many a time, that knowledge was power and it was power that made the financial world what it was but having said that, the fashion world was a ruthless place at that time, ruled by influential men that Corry was still up against and although she'd weathered the storm up to press with three years of hard work, gaining a diploma in the art of design, she still had a long way to go for that achievement wasn't enough, for the likes of the big boys at the top who were out to put obstacles in her way being a new up and coming face in the industry for money talks as we all know in situations of power.

The big thing now was to get recognized and apply for a position with one of the big fashion houses, but in fairness, knowing it would be harder for her to manage for she'd no connections and that's how it worked in those days, you had to know someone to get anywhere.

The days were long as she trawled the streets, looking for an opening into her dream world, writing off to all the fashion houses but without any luck, it was as though no one wanted to employ a young girl who was unknown unless she'd got experience but there again how do you get experience if you haven't got a job to prove yourself. All she needed was a break but I'm afraid that wasn't to be at that time, and if it wasn't for the landlady at the local pub giving her extra hours to work she'd have starved as she cried herself to sleep nightly.

Back home, grandmother would send a postal order now and again with the message to treat herself, it was as though she suspected Corry was having a hard time and wouldn't ask for help but that's what families do when they suspect there's a problem, they hold out their hand with a gesture of love which is never spoken about.

It was at this time when Corry couldn't sink any lower in both mind and body that something happened to give her the break that she so desperately needed. Once a week her local, put on a pie and peas night, when all the workers that lived in the area used to come in from work, it was on that night that one of the daily helps came in and asked Corry; in a rather broad cockney accent;

"Do you make clothes to fit anyone as my employer is a lady who isn't too good on her feet and wants someone who can design something special, as it's a rather large society wedding that she's attending".

"We've managed to get her to a few of the fashion houses but I'm afraid there isn't anything to her taste that suits her". With this, Corry could certainly see an opportunity to pay the bills for a few months and delighted as she was answered in a response that even shocked her with;

"Look if you'd like me to go and see this lady, I'll have a talk and advise the best way I can, sorry I didn't catch your name" Corry asked.

"Oh just call me June, I've already told her all about you and how clever you are so if I give you the address, you'll be able to make further arrangements yourself, I really do hope you'll be able to sort her out as she does have difficulties getting what she wants and she is such a nice lady who would certainly look after you financially if you can help at all, I also told her you'd get in touch tomorrow and follow it up with a visit in the next few days, hope you don't mind".

"I can't thank you enough for that" Corry stated, as she looked down at the address written on the piece of paper, St John's Wood, which was a rather posh area of London, yes she had been through that area but that's all, she would have given anything to live in a place like that, if only, but that was only a dream.

Another dawn another day Corry thought as she woke that morning, dressed in a plain outfit with just a touch of foundation, smear of blusher and finish it off with a pale lipstick; yes, she thought to herself, I don't want to give the wrong impression. The address she'd been given was a large apartment in a small block of flats overlooking a large park, the impression from the outside was, only someone with an awful lot of money could afford to live in a place like this and instantly knew that if this job turned out right for her, then maybe it would be the break she'd been waiting for and hopefully her luck had changed.

This lady, oh my God, she forgot to get this lady's name from June, this was when June was talking, all she ever referred to her was, my dear lady' so now was the time to bluff her way she thought quite cleverly, but then again after a little thought she decided to be open and admit the truth. Having arrived at 11am on the dot, she pressed the door bell, to find a soft voice answering.

"Who is there, may I ask"?

"My name is Corrander Sharp, and was informed I would be expected".

No sound was forthcoming as the door opened to a hallway of an unbelievable show of opulence never seen before by her, bringing her down to earth as a softly spoken voice said;

"Miss Corrander Sharp I presume, welcome to my home, we will take tea as it's all prepared and waiting for your arrival".

"Oh please call me Corry as Corrander is such a mouthful and that's what all my friends call me" was the reply.

"Then you will call me Agnes instead of Mrs Hirst, as that's what all my friends call me and I have a feeling that's what we will be, friends before the days over". Corry looked at this smart well-dressed sophisticated lady who stood quite tall but with the grace of a society aristocrat;

"Come on dear, and don't stand to attention on my behalf as I'm nothing special you know".

Nothing special Corry thought, this was a lady of the highest breeding that could command attention from anyone she wished and here am I, giving advice to her on her styling.

The one thing Corry did notice was, Agnes had a limp which would have given her tremendous pain, and maybe this is what June was saying but didn't want to put it into so many words, so as not to offend.

The light that flooded through the large patio windows shone on the mirrors which lit up the room to such magnificence, with soft leather chairs and settee's together with individual small occasional tables set around the floor appropriately, the floor was fitted with the most beautiful carpet Corry had ever seen.;

"Take a seat and make yourself comfortable as tea will be served, I expect that you will be able to manage a large cream cake with your tea so I have got a selection for you to choose from as I can see that you're a growing young lady" Agnes stated as she looked over at Corry's slim silhouette.

Oh boy, there was no fooling this lady as she could plainly see that Corry didn't eat much and had her suspicions that it wasn't through not wanting to eat either, no Agnes was very shrewd, there would be no pulling the wool over this lady's eyes for sure she thought.

Tea was brought in by a quiet but what seemed to be, shy lady who was immediately introduced as Agnes's companion.

"Now help yourself my dear, I would appreciate, if you would be mother and do the honours to pour the tea as I get a little stiff at times as you may have noticed "Agnes said

"Oh that's no problem at all, I think we all have a little trouble of some sort when we get up all of a sudden", Corry replied as to put Agnes at ease.

"Well you have a few of those sandwiches and cream cakes as I think it best if we have a little chat and get to know each other before we get down to business, it's always nice to know something about someone if they're going to be friends and I have a feeling that's exactly what we are going to be," Agnes stated.

Corry felt so comfortable in Agnes's company, it's as though she 'd known her for years and before they both knew it, she'd eaten all the sandwiches and was now starting into the cream cakes as Agnes smiled, knowing her suspicions were right about this young girl not eating.

Corry was so relaxed at this point just babbling on about her parents, grandparent, the struggles that she'd encounter, hopes, heartache and dreams, how she'd love to become a great designer working for herself together with the uphill struggle of the fashion houses that wouldn't entertain her knowing she had not the experience they needed which was in fact a bluff as it wasn't what you knew in those days, it was who you knew for the connections into jobs. Even to the point of walking streets looking for work in anything from shops to cafes just to make ends meet to pay the bills. When, all of a sudden realizing she'd been going on all about herself so much that she'd probably given the wrong impression to Agnes;

"Look I'm sorry I got carried away with talking, you must think I'm very selfish, but you are so easy to talk to, it seems as though I was just spilling my heart out to a motherly figure".

"That's all right my dear, that's what makes the world go round, for we all have stories to tell about ourselves". Corry couldn't believe it, confiding in a stranger, as this was new for her, she kept a lot to herself but for some reason this time was different, it was as though she was talking to her mother but yet again, if it had been her mother then she wouldn't have had the time to listen to her for her mother was more for her brother that her.

You could see that Agnes was not only interested in Corry but something had struck home, when all of a sudden she said "Now my dear, think I will tell you a little about myself and then at least you will be able to judge whether we can at least work together to sort my wardrobe out".

Wardrobe Corry thought to herself, I was under the impression, I was only doing an outfit for a wedding not a full collection. Never the less, it would be nice to hear what Agnes had to say for not only had she been so kind but also a very interesting person to talk with.

"Let's start at the beginning" Agnes stated telling her life story in short;

I had what most would consider an extremely privileged upbringing in the fashionable area of Berlin, which you may know as West Germany. My parents were quite well off or so I understand, as it came to be, that we had everything we ever wanted and more, including servants, and a governess for us children. Our apartment was large and not too far away from the famous Charlottenburg Palace, which is the largest Palace in Berlin, should you know anything about the city for when it was built it was built for the love of what you would call a King for his Queen. We children never knew what our parents did for a living but in those days, children were blind to the fact that their parents did any kind of work at all in my world. We did however know that we all travelled a lot but thought everyone did the same as money was no object.

When the war came, things changed, and to some, it wasn't for the better. Our apartment was bombed like many others in Berlin, therefore the family had to flee to a safer part of the country which was away from the city.

Although I can't remember the details or what was happening, we as children did what was told of us without any questions asked, therefore adapting to the situation that everyone else was in at that time. It was one day before the war ended that it was announced that my father had been killed, to this day, we have never learnt the truth as to what happened to him as a lot of things were swept under the carpet and secrets were hidden away for ever so it seemed.

All we remember was the sight of my Mother crying all the time and not being able to cope with anything as she had never had to do when father was alive. Relatives and friends had all got together at that time to arrange that my brother and I would have to go and live with an aunt in Hanover for we could never return to Berlin again for some reason which again, we never found out.

We as good children never questioned any of this and therefore moved miles away to a lot smaller house in the suburbs of Hanover, Mother on the other hand went to live with other relatives in a little place a few miles away called Nienburg.

Time went by and eventually my brother got a job working for the government, I had already decided that I wanted to study to become an artist as that had always been my dream. After some two years of studying art at a college that my family had managed to get a placement for me, I then became restless and wanted to go out into the world of art. At that time, I had a cousin who lived in London who was pretty close when growing up and therefore suggested that I come to her as she was comfortable and would help support me until I could make a living for myself. I consequently applied for a passport, knowing that my mother would be taken care of by my brother and the family, realising this was a big step into an unknown world I had to admit I was a little frightened but then again we sometimes have to take that leap of fate to become who we are, so with bags packed and the monies I had saved, it was, off to London to live with my cousin who had lived there for some time.

London and all that it brought was not what I had anticipated, for I really struggled and although I was fluent in the language that was all, for the ways and customs were somewhat strange to me at that point but I must say my cousin was an angel for she wouldn't take any monies for my keep as she said there would be time for that when I was successful in obtaining full time employment.

In those early days any job that came along however challenging, I did it, from ironing for the rich to looking after children for the wealthy, you name it and I did it just keep my head above water even though hard work didn't come easily to me, it was however a learning point where I now appreciate people from poor backgrounds and do what I can to help.

Yes, I could have contacted my family who would have only been too pleased to help financially as they were doing pretty well back in Germany at that time but pride got in the way for I thought I had to do it for myself if I was going to achieve anything. I knew deep down if they'd known my circumstances they would have said well I warned you not to leave Germany but then again I always had a determination to succeed.

Pausing for a while as she looked into Corry's face for a reaction to the story so far Agnes stated;

"You see, that's why I fully understand what you are doing and how hard it is for you to have the break you so desire, you will have that break I can assure you, there is no question about it, just as I had the same break as a struggling artist".

Corry looked in awe at what she had heard, but looking at Agnes's face, she had not finished telling the story as yet.

Agnes smiled at Corry as she said "Have some more tea my dear and I will tell you how my break became to the fore"

Corry wasn't particularly worried about the tea, it was listening to this fascinating life this grand lady had lived, even though she did seem a little eccentric, she was so mesmerising in what she had been saying so far that Corry just wanted hear the end of the story and how she had gone from more or less rags to riches so listening intensely as Agnes commenced;

"My break came about one day when I was sat on the pavement with a couple of drawings I'd done earlier, eating a sandwich while waiting for my friend to finish work. Thinking my mind must have been in a bit of a dream mode when all of a sudden I noticed an elderly gentleman leaving the building at the side of me, due to him being a little unsteady on his feet, he tripped on the uneven pavement, consequently taking a fall to which I instantly rushed forward to help him up visibly knowing he was badly shaken;

Are you alright I asked as I could plainly see he was distressed, look don't worry if you tell me your address I'll take you home.

No it's alright as I have a car coming to pick me up in a while this gentleman said in a softly well-spoken voice.

At that moment I turned around to pick up the drawings which had dropped on the pavement, scattering all over, when all of a sudden this gentleman commented;

Oh dear, you seemed to have dropped your prize possession my dear, smiling to himself as by now he'd regained his footing.

To this, we both laughed as it was the way he said it,

Let me have a look at those sketches, did you do those yourself or do they belong to someone else he asked.

No Sir, I did them myself I replied, but there not very good for I wasn't concentrating on anything in particular, more of a doodle than anything while I was waiting for my friend to finish work

How talented you are my dear and so young at that, to get them just at the right angle, a different prospective to what others would have done, yes I like that very much, he said.

I couldn't see what he was looking at to be honest they were only sketches of nudes or maybe it was something that only he could see for at the end of the day they were only done roughly.

Have you done any other work of this kind or attempted to paint he asked.

Of course, I studied art and have loads in my flat, but no one seems to like them, I only work with feelings and not what others see.

I was amazed what happened next for this kind gent turned and said, bring some of your work to my house and I will take a look, little did I realise he had an interest in a large art gallery in the West End of London, and therefore handing over a business card told me he would be expecting a call from me later to arrange a meeting sometime next week as he turned bidding me good day and thanked me for my kindness. I was so shocked at what happened as a large car rolled up helped the gentleman into the back seat as he rolled the window down and shouted;

Now don't forget, I will expect to see you before the end of next week with your drawings my dear he politely stated.

I just stood there in amazement, not daring to believe what I'd just experienced from a total stranger. Yes, this happened to be my break, for when the phone call was made and subsequently the meeting followed; I was totally amazed to find that he was the largest art dealer in London unbeknown to me at that time. What a wonderful gentleman he turned out to be as not only did he give me my first showing of the paintings but he also introduced me to his only son whereby it was love at first sight leading eventually to marriage some four years later.

As I'd been introduced to the art world by someone who truly believed in me, I then went on to fame and fortune well above my wildest dreams with the man I loved by my side. We had the most wonderful married life you could ever wish for, our love and devotion for each other was endless till the day he died We were never parted from that wonderful day that we met; God had surely rewarded us with such love for each other.

Our only regret was, we weren't blessed with a child of our own as it was found, I couldn't have children due to a childhood illness when I lived in Berlin and although we lived life to the full with riches beyond our dreams, all that mattered was, we had each other until some four years ago when he sadly passed away with cancer.

I thought my life was over at this time, then I realised there must be a reason, he'd been taken away from me so soon, so in my grief I prayed to God in the synagogue for the answer, yes I had changed my faith to his due to the war and rumours of the Nazi's.

A few weeks later I saw a child crying, this small child had an air lip that was infected rather badly, and so asking the child's mother why she had not done something about it, the answer was quite sharply, we haven't the money and the hospital says it's not important in someone so small.

So there staring me in the face was my answer, for money wasn't an object to me, I had plenty in the bank, far more than I needed, the next day I contacted my Lawyers and arranged for this child to have the operation, with the understanding they didn't divulge my name and that's why I try and give a little back".

"So you never had any children then". Corry asked;

"Oh yes, we had a son, very good looking and so talented" Agnes replied.

"But you said that you weren't blessed with any children or did I miss-hear you" Corry asked politely,

"No that's right; we weren't blessed with any, my cousin's daughter died in childbirth, her husband was so distraught he committed suicide soon afterwards, as my cousin wasn't in the best of health after all the trauma she'd suffered and in no fit state to bring a young baby up which you can well understand.

The family got together and after a heart-breaking decision, it was decided that the best thing for all concerned was for my husband and me to give the boy a good home and make it official through the courts by adopting him legally. It was hard at first as we had to cope with my cousin's loss and eventually she had a nervous breakdown and was admitted into hospital for she couldn't accept her daughter was never coming back, blaming the child for her death.

This was the same cousin who'd helped when I arrived in this country looked after, fed and housed me when she herself did without knowing her husband was a gambler and struggling to keep her head above water. Yes, I owed her so much for what she'd sacrificed and therefore it was my duty to pay her back but, unfortunately she died of a broken heart in the end grieving for her daughter".

What a wonderful story Agnes told and what a noble life she'd led from the war torn years in Germany to living in this beautiful apartment laced with all the memories that came with her to make this life possible She was still a beautiful woman for her age even though she had a disability, therefore would have been such an outstanding beauty in her youth Corry thought.

Corry still mesmerized by what she'd heard when all of a sudden she was brought back down to earth by the lounge door creaking as it opened slowly and to her surprise, in walked June, the same lady that had introduced Corry to Agnes by recommending her for her outstanding talents.

"I just thought I'd see if everything was alright and if Corry would be able to sort things out for you" June asked with a broad smile on her face knowing the answer before a reply.

"I can't thank you enough, I'm sure that Corry and I are going to get along fine and just by looking at the outfit she is wearing today, I've every confidence I'll be the bell of the ball at the wedding, don't you think".

"Yes" was the reply sharply, for June couldn't help but laugh as Agnes's sense of humour was so dry at times, even though she never let it show through that she was in so much pain daily;

"Well, I think you need that pot of tea topping up so I'll run along and get you both a fresh one and if there is anything else, just let me know" she said politely.

"A fresh pot of tea would go down wonderful together with some more of those special cream and marzipan cakes that we have in the larder" Agnes said as June turned to leave the room.

The meeting with Agnes had gone beyond Corry's dreams as not only had she met this wonderful lady but she also came away with an order for six outfits on a made to measure basis and could see with the money that she would make, it would enable her to get on her feet and perhaps look to the future enabling her to start her own little business.

The outfits designed for Agnes's were all in fine silks which was becoming for such a noble lady, a special one for the wedding was a pale green slender fitting plain dress, capped sleeve with a bolero edged in fine cream lace. Not only did it look so striking, Corry also designed a matching hat which again was in fine silk but alternated by doing it in cream silk with pale green lace, this was finished off with little satin covered shoe buttons on the brim which set it off perfectly.

When Agnes saw what Corry had done, she cried Yes she thought this girl's going to go far and I'm going to do the best I can to make that happen for if anyone deserved it, she did.

Attended by all the gentry and therefore reported by the tabloids as the wedding of the year for not often did you get a Duke marrying a Showgirl and so this was the start of Corry's new career, the break she'd been waiting for, thinking she would now be offered a design post with one of the big companies.

Unfortunately, that wasn't going to happen for Agnes had realised Corry's potential and offered to back her financially in setting up her own company; she coming in as a silent partner and therefore not interfere with the running of this new found company.

CHAPTER 4

Again, Agnes was as good as her word, she'd called her lawyers who'd arranged for a transfer of money to be invested in the opening of a small exclusive shop whereby Corry would be able to do her own thing as far as designs and it was also thought with a little help, would be able to get her financially on her feet, as for forward planning, Agnes allocated a reserve amount to back up the project having faith in Corry's ambitions.

It's funny how things come together all at once for that's just how it happened. Corry still thought of her father from time to time as idolising him when growing up but that was as a young girl who puts her father on a pedestal, knowing in her heart he wouldn't give her a second thought as he'd always been selfish even as a child or so her grandmother had said.

Having said that, he was as good as his word in sending monies back to her grandmother for the keep of Paul, that's one thing she'd be grateful for, therefore less to worry about for she seemed to take thing to heart when it came to others.

Sending monies back whenever possible to help out although nothing had been mentioned about this matter to her father, in her mind it was a matter of duty being the eldest, and in a position to help out wherever she could. Her main worry was Paul should get all the help she could give him as his big sister. Maybe she couldn't be there when he needed her by his side but financially she would stand by him for whatever he trained to do in the future.

Time passing now and Corry still had not made it up with her father but then again she wasn't asking for a miracle, knowing it would take him all his time to return to visit Paul let alone get in touch with her. And with these thoughts in mind, she maintained he'd want her before she wanted him but sadly that wasn't to be the case, for it was just after the big society wedding that Agnes had attended when all the financial paperwork had gone through for Corry's business venture was informed that her father had passed away. Apparently he'd been ill for some time and so weak, he'd be admitted to hospital with pneumonia, the woman that he'd been living with, had left him and so he was all alone. No one knew who to contact as there was no indication of his family when he arrived on the ward and being so ill he never regained consciousness fully until it was too late.

Staff at the hospital was very good in trying to contact his next of kin but to no avail with no one visiting him and it was hard for them to track down anyone. As time passed he got weaker and therefore either couldn't fight or he just gave up the will to live and therefore passed away in a hospital bed with no one by his side. He did however leave a will that surprised everyone, for they didn't realise he had anything left to leave.

The will stated that he was sorry for the way he'd treated everyone but he really did love Nina with all his heart even towards the end, it's just that it wasn't in his nature to show feelings and no one could understand that, he was a private person who was alone in not only his thoughts but also his feelings, being an only child himself who was spoilt beyond recognition by his family who'd given him an education that only the privileged class had gained the opportunity of attaining, which to his credit had worked out to his advantage.

He also asked to be forgiven for all the heartache that he caused, to all concerned. In the will, he stated to his children, although he'd never been a good father to them, he felt sure they would achieve recognition beyond their dreams and therefor his wish would be to help them achieve this in the only way he could and that was to make this bequest and let them know he loved them dearly.

Finally, He stated, he should thank Daisy for all the help she'd given the children in making them strong to go out and become better people, something that he could never have done, had he been left to bring them up alone after Nina had died

He then went on to give one thousand pound to Daisy for all her kindness, together with the sum of ten thousand pounds to be split equally between Corry and Paul. Now ten thousand pounds was a lot of money in those days and would go some way to help both of them on their way to succeed in their chosen careers.

Daisy couldn't get over the fact that George couldn't save money let alone have been able to save such a large amount as that, but was pleased that at least he'd made good with the children, giving them a start in life financially.

Now at least Paul would be able to start his own business and with Corry starting her own little empire so to speak, there would be less worry for Daisy as a grandmother. Corry, on the other hand took it badly as although she'd lost touch with her father, she loved him deep down and always put him on a pedestal when she was younger being a daddy's little girl and worshipped him with all she had.

It's funny how we judge people, for some can't show feeling and others show the wrong ones as it looked in George's case, maybe if we could see into people's hearts then it may be different, maybe this is what Corry was doing when helping others, we'll never know as things aren't so transparent as we would like them to be.

As we view each other, we see the light but when we look into the dark, where are we

This was rather a sad time for Corry but on the other hand she'd been waiting for this break to come for a long time and couldn't afford to let it go by with sadness in her life. Having now inherited five thousand pounds together with the financial help from Agnes, this would take her one step further to achieve her ambition and therefore wasn't about to let it slip through her fingers.

Now time to search all the properties on the open market, eventually finding a house that had been converted into a shop in a little back street, and with her eye for design thought it would make a grand place for her business, which with a little help would house the equipment together with the facilities to go forward. It also had the advantage of an attic which would come in at a later date for maybe a bedsit to rent out.

Therefore, being no time to loose, put in a bid for the property straight away for she wasn't one to let the grass grow under her feet as this was just what she was looking for, an opportunity to make things happen.

Having secured the property, she moved fast and furious to start moving things in which she acquired from anywhere possible, second hand dealers to factories who were throwing things away that may become useful and not one to slack, she got help from a few of the regulars in the pub, they helped not only with the heavy work but sprucing the place up with a mixture of decorators to joiners, they all got to work and within a month you wouldn't have known the place for it was like something out of a magazine done all out in monochrome.

Word got around, and it wasn't long before she received a few offers to help back her financially but being stubborn she thought no one wanted to help her before when struggling so would do this alone as she was determined to succeed and therefore no one was ever going to take it away from her as she'd worked so hard to start this venture.

Agnes was a darling for she came to visit a few times not interfering at all and although she'd ploughed so much money into the project, was an excellent financial backer in every sense, for without her help she'd never have furnished her dream to what was looking to a bright future. Everything from the sewing machines to the light fittings Corry had either acquired or purchased second hand knowing how to be thrifty where money was concerned.

Now the ceiling in the shop was pretty high which seemed to be a problem and therefore to make an impression when clients walked through the door she had to come up with an idea which would suffice until one of the society ladies she'd done a few garments for, donated a large crystal chandelier.

And oh how smart the fitted royal blue carpet was as you entered the shop which had been donated from Agnes's spare bedroom.

What had been a small cubby hole was now an elaborate changing room with large expensive mirrors, again these had been donated by friends of Agnes who'd followed her advice and brought custom for designed garments that was just that little bit different.

Corry was aware that such an establishment wouldn't attract the upper class so would have to think of something different which would appeal and tempt them to the new found premises, and therefore coming up with an idea, where she played an ace card; asking Agnes for advice as to maybe a picture on the wall, but no, Agnes had a better idea, she asked a local painter to design a mural of tranquillity such as a sea view that was relaxing to look at.

With a bit of redesign between the painter and Agnes, they came up with a Mediterranean view which looked outstandingly peaceful, but that wasn't the end of it for Agnes then signed it on one side, this made it special for as a well-known artist as she was, clients would flock in knowing that only the upper class frequented this establishment. I'm afraid that's how it worked in those days for you had to either know or be somebody to get on with the upper class.

The second floor was fitted out to take a cutting out table together with two machines, fittings, and cupboards together odds and ends leaving just enough room to fit the materials into one corner.

Now was time to sort some staff out, it was decided that if Corry could perhaps persuade a couple of the art students at the collage down the road to come and work for her while keeping up their studies at night, for she'd make it worth their while.

The two girls that she approached were from rather poor families but were very gifted, apparently according to the tutor they were so ambitious they would work for peanuts, knowing this Corry jumped at the chance and having a word offered them the job stating there was only a minimum that she could pay them to start, but if her ideas took off then she would do everything in her power to help them on their way to further the career they aspired to.

By this, they saw an opportunity of a lifetime and therefore welcomed it with open arms, knowing the money wouldn't be much but by getting a little job to compensate they would manage and gain the experience to further their career. They appreciated they'd have to do everything from sweeping floors to making tea for clients but none of that mattered as they'd eventually be doing something they 'd aspired to for a long time and had faith in what Corry had promised about paying them when the business had got off the ground knowing one day everything would come to fruition.

This girl really is going to go far Agnes thought to herself as she looked at Corry, not only is she artistically clever but she's a shrewd way of financially achieving what she wants. Everything in place when Corry opened the doors for business, a little slow at first but then Agnes stepped in again putting the word round she'd gone into a joint venture with a young talented dress designer who was not only different but wasn't afraid to make elegant garments for women that would make a statement in one off designed pieces.

Now this was Corry's dream and she wasn't going to settle for anything less than perfection. It wasn't long before word got around about this little boutique style designer shop and within months they were so busy that Corry had to start making appointments to keep up with all the orders for her personal services of couture designs and with this in mind made a decision to buy two more machines therefore taking a gamble by setting a couple more of the girls from the college on, for by now she'd be in a position to pay a little higher wages. She couldn't believe how well everything seemed to be falling into place, and although tired at times, thought it would all be worth it in the end.

Within another six months not only had she rented the shop next door with an option to buy it later, but had also made another sewing room to accommodate all the orders that were coming in for special occasional wear that she'd specialised in to start off with for those that attended such outings as the races at Ascot. Don't get me wrong, Corry had worked day and night together with her dedicated staff to achieve such a clientele but now it was really starting to pay the dividends for all concerned.

The girls were excellent in how they handled the clientele and word got around about their professional qualities for not only could they converse with the upper class but some even found their outlook was changing, they wanted a better way of life and was willing to go for it at any cost, Corry had sent two of the girls to night school as she'd acknowledged they were good at figures and therefore thought it a good idea to offer them a chance to study in book keeping which again they jumped at with such excitement.

This would be an advantage should the business keep growing as she couldn't keep up with everything and it'd also save money in the end with not having to pay the accountants so much whereby they'd do most of the book keeping in house so to speak.

The next idea was to dress all the girls in some sort of uniform to make them look smart to the clientele, this idea was born out of the fact that a couple of the girls dressed a little shabby due to not being able to afford good clothing. Having a word with the girls, Corry let them decide what colours they wanted and in the end was grey and white dresses with the two original girls to be dressed in navy and white. Now the two girls that had been there since the beginning was Betty and Kath who would become supervisor dressed in navy and white.

"Should you have any problems then they're the ones you should see first as I'm sure they'll be able to sort things out for you". She remarked

Both Betty and Kath stood mesmerized at what Corry had just come out with for they knew nothing about what'd been said. Taking them both on one side Corry stated they would be in charge of the girls from now on and their wages would go up considerably to compensate for this service. The looks on both of their faces said it all as they'd never dreamt this would happen. Yes, Corry had been good as her word when she'd promised to look after them. This would enable them to look after their parents and give a little back for what they'd done for them, for families were so close in those days

This was an enterprise with a difference, once you were accepted and worked well, the company looked after your interests and was prepared to listen to what you had to say, giving you the chance to go further in your set career. Corry was always on hand and the hours she put in to make this work was unbelievable, therefore between all of them pulling their weight and with the determination to succeed this venture of loyal soldiers was going to win as they would say in Yorkshire. But Kath who was still in shock after hearing about her new promotion uttered the words;

"I think this will be my job for life as my parents will never believe it when I get home and tell them the news.

It was then that Betty also chirped up with a comment of her own;

"Do you know, the first time I saw Corry I just knew we could trust her, she was the sort that would never let us down, we've not only passed all our final certificates but have been able to gain valuable experience by learning on the job from meeting clients, to doing some of our own designs, that would never have happened should we have gone to work in a factory".

This was a time of unrest in the country whereby strikes were happening on a regular basis and therefore money was tight amongst the working class, therefore every penny counted and it was important that you had a steady job which you were grateful for at any lengths.

Now word started to get around fast about a new girl that had captured wealthy clients with her unusual designs; this again was ignored by those in power in the fashion industry not wanting to believe such noticeable changes that were on the way although in some quarter's alarm bells had already started to ring. The one or two top designers that was on their toes were in fact a little shaky, but there again they were so conceited, they'd put it all down to a flash in the pan that would soon go away if they ignored it and oh how wrong they were for as time was going by, Corry was moving from strength to strength and would eventually regret their arrogance towards this young up and coming northern girl they 'd often remarked as, no breeding to make it to the big time in their arrogance and snobbery which was now becoming quite blatant from them.

Then one day a well-known designer stepped into the shop and asking to see Corry whom she knew full well was definitely becoming a threat to the industry for this lady not only presented herself in such a friendly manner but also offered to buy Corry out, offering her a position as a top a designer in charge of a team in her own company. Now this was something new, for this lady was very shrewd and had everything worked out before she ventured into anything being such a strong and smart businesswoman it was rumoured who was not only ruthless in business but also quite a tyrant to work for.

Corry could see the fear amongst some of the staff that day as they were obviously frightened for their jobs, but soon put their fears to rest as she turned the offer down immediately to the disappointment of this woman who wished her all the best, adding she admired her courage on what she was attempting to achieve as a new comer in the city.

What the staff wasn't aware at that point, Corry had it in her mind that if the orders kept rolling in as fast as they had done the last few weeks, then she would have to obviously employ extra staff to cope, and also consider following her ambition which was to enter the famous London Fashion Week

Now this would hopefully open more doors for her, knowing she'd only be a small part of it didn't deter her in the least, for the main aim would be, get her name out there showing the public a different light to fashion where it could be for the everyday person and not just for the elite. The driving force had really set in with her by now and had no intentions of sitting back and letting it run away for she was in this for the long run.

Now, having to come up with an idea that'd wipe the smile off the faces of the smug fashion moguls that run the top fashion houses would be a challenge she was prepared to take on, as rumour had it whereby they'd called her a little girl with ideas above her station and would soon be a name of the past, well they were definitely in for a surprise as you never take a Yorkshire girl on and win the battle for they are made of a breed that will fight to the bitter end.

The one thing they couldn't understand was where she was getting her money from as the banks weren't backing her so in their minds she would soon be out of business. As weeks went by Corry's mind was a blank only concentrating on how to bring in new business, don't get me wrong, she was doing extremely well but that was never enough for her, she was always looking for new ideas if not in designs then in ways to expand. Then one day when walking down the road to the little coffee bar she often called off at, when the girl behind the counter said;

"You look nice in that dress it really does suit you, wish I could afford a dress like that, but on my wages, I'd have to save up for six months to buy one".

"Oh how very nice of you to say that, you've just made my day and given me an idea I've been praying for" she replied.

"Look, I'd like you to call in the shop; as you've just earned yourself a new dress which I'll design personally for giving me an idea that I've been looking for these past few weeks, it will be of your choice and colour so don't worry as it's with my compliments".

The girl looked at Corry as though she was having a bad turn or something for she'd never seen her acting like this before. Corry finished the coffee rather sharply and spoke to the girl again before leaving,

"Now don't forget, call in the shop and I'll arrange for them to take your measurement for the new dress I've promised, this'll be my gift to you for the idea you've given me."

The girl was still bewildered thinking all her dreams had come true but wasn't quite sure if Corry meant what she'd said and so, the next day when she visited the shop on the off chance, she was somewhat surprised to find not only did they take her measurements for a new dress but they designed two new outfits for her with Corry's compliments.

Now Corry on the other hand returned to the workshop studying just how she could make a few outfits on a ready to wear basis at a fraction of the costs but still using good fabrics only to come up with an idea, if she was to buy her fabrics in bulk, it would be cost effective. The same with the designs, if they produced a sample and then copied say twenty to thirty pieces, this again would cut costs and time, having thought seriously about this, they could probably go into production straight away on a trial basis.

Looking at these calculations alone, the idea would be viable and therefore could supply the big department stores with a special range created by her company. Her biggest fear was, should the top designers find out before-hand; they may attempt to steal the idea and market it for themselves, even attempting to put obstacles in her way and therefore decided to discuss it with only a few close colleagues whereby separating her workers, so they didn't realise what was going on for the time being.

The fashion industry at that time was such a close knit unit there was even talk of trying to run her out of town or buy her out, but then she was a Yorkshire girl though and through with guts of steel and this wasn't going to happen, she was going to give these high powered men a run for their money.

Each night studying just how all this would work and how the couture designs would be kept separate as they were her bread and butter and therefore couldn't afford to lose at any cost.

And with such influential clients that had stayed loyal to her in the past when there'd been big society occasions on the red carpet. Yes, she'd seen her designs on not only the nobility but on one or two royals but those had to be kept secret as she wasn't a big name and snobbery in those days was rife amongst all the upper class wanting to be something they weren't really, but all the same having a very good try in the right circles, no she couldn't afford to upset these people.

Word spread quickly about her success which brought in orders from the film world as young starlets wanted to be trendy and therefore fed up with all the old ball gowns that were around at that time, it's as though, those designers at the top of the ladder wanted to keep women looking as though they were in a glass cage. But since a new designer had come to town and was trying to get away from all this old fashioned look, it seemed, it was now opening to a new younger style which would make women not only presentable but with an air of elegance as more and more women entered the high powered jobs but also kept their femininity.

With reasonable and serious thoughts Corry approached Agnes with her ideas asking for help in expanding the business by renting a small warehouse so as to take her new project forward, hoping beyond hope that Agnes as a businesswoman would see what she could for see, and after long consideration, Agnes came back with her full approval to take the idea forward knowing it'd be a success for Corry seemed to have the Midas touch.

Time was moving fast now as she found a small warehouse and with the help of friends, converted it to a factory for the ready to wear production to commence immediately, leaving the shop to attend to the couture lines which needed the personal touch.

In just over two years Corry had gone a long way, a lot was due to the help of Agnes and friends that'd stayed loyal to her but for the hours she'd put in and the effort, there was no surprise in her achievement for she really loved her work, and never took anything for granted both in her personal life or with the people she employed, her motto was, I am only as good as the people who are backing me and loyalty is the key to all my achievement for she'd respect not only for herself but all those who came into contact with her.

Yes, she may have been of a young age to command such a powerful position but having said that, she was the driving force behind everything and would be eternally grateful for those who'd helped her succeed and that's how she looked at life. Those who worked for her treated her with such respect even though a lot of them were her elders, they recognised just how gifted she was, turning her hands to anything from sweeping the floors to designing the most beautiful clothes you could ever wish to wear.

Her clients regarded her as something special for when she designed especially for them it was something that her heart and soul had been put into with an individual detail that brought out their special requirements.

Now the problem was, Corry had a hunger for perfection and therefore wouldn't give in until she'd satisfied that goal, not even for a relationship which those that were close to her tried to encourage but to no avail for her ambition to succeed was all she cared about.

The money her father had left together with the finances Agnes supplied had gone a long way whereby every penny was accounted for with no room for adjustments. She'd been brought up to look after finances and therefore was very frugal in what she spent, with no room for luxuries at this time, on the other hand the contribution from her faithful friend and founder, well that was a different matter.

Corry's one regret was; her mother had not lived long enough to see her achievement, but these things happen for a reason and there would be regrets somewhere along the way as life isn't plain sailing as were all aware of.

There is always a price to pay somewhere along the line, for that we should all recognise but what she wasn't aware of at that time was the biggest regret of her life was to come one Christmas in the near future, as that regret would affect her for the rest of her life.

Chapter 5

ISSA

By now Corry was really starting to go places on the fashion scene in London, she'd visited Paris and Milan on several occasions now and was looking forward to going to New York next but something was holding her back from that for some unknown reason, the American market was so big and many a young designer had fallen on their back by going over there too soon. Having thought about this very hard as London was her real scene and knowing the market place well, she started by visiting the big Department Stores to study their labels and reconsidered her options.

Perhaps if she went further into the market by promoting her ready to wear designs and attach them to the upper society, that was one option, the second was maybe to attach shoes and handbags to the ready to wear, lowering the prices by combining all three together.
The modelling of course was easy as she could cut costs by getting the workforce to model the clothes or even barmaids and shop girls as they were the up and coming customers of not only today but the buying force of tomorrow. The more she thought about it the harder it became. Until one day when walking through London, her head up in the air so to speak, her mind on other things, as she walked across a road not looking where she's going, a hand shot out, pulling her to one side while shouting;

"Watch where you're going, you're going to get run over, that car only narrowly missed you".
Corry, half shocked and taken back at this young voice, looked up to see a young girl approximately sixteen or no older than seventeen at least, dressed in a little shabby frock, her face with no makeup and a little dirty at that. Honestly she thought to herself, this young girl is so thin, I don't think she's eaten for about a month, well Corry wasn't far wrong with that estimation;

"What's your name and where about do you come from? Corry asked in a quiet voice as not to frighten the young girl.

"I'm sorry if I frightened you miss, but I thought you'd get run over by a car the way you're walking into the road not looking" came a timid reply.

"What's your name and where do you come from". Corry repeated

"Sorry, my name is Issa and I come from Newcastle originally"

"And what may I ask are you doing down in London, are you with your parents".

"No, I live here in London, by myself, well sort of, why am I in trouble", she asked in an uneasy manner.

"No not at all, quite the opposite, would you like to accompany me over the road for a coffee, my treat" Corry replied, as she looked at this young girl who had 'the most beautiful elf like face she'd seen, while sensing the girl was a little uneasy at the situation in hand.

The girl looked a little puzzled at that request as no one had ever been so kind as this to her for a long time, and therefore mystified as to why a stranger would want to help her, before replying;

"Yes if you don't mind, I'd love to but I haven't got any money for a drink."

"That's alright, as I've said, the treats on me, you did save my life so that's the least I can do" Corry stated

Walking a little further along the road past the coffee shop and entering a restaurant, Corry could see the young girl's embarrassment as she looked down at her shabby clothes

"Look if you're worried about how your dressed, then don't, as the people who come in here aren't stuck up at all, they'll understand and to be honest I think you look lovely".

"Thank you miss but this place is so expensive, you can't afford to buy me a coffee in here when the place down the road will be a lot cheaper",

"That's alright, I've decided I'm a little peckish right now and seen as it's my idea, then I insist you join me for a light lunch as I can't eat alone, don't worry about the expense, as to be honest I get meals here quite often and they give me a discount".

Sitting down at the table, the young girl looked around in amazement noticing quite a lot of influential people eating and no one even noticed her, this putting her more at ease being in such a posh place she thought to herself. Corry realised how uncomfortable this girl looked and to make her feel more comfortable, she added.

"You must order what you want as the treat is on me",

"I'll just have a plate of chips" was the reply.

"No you won't, you'll have a proper meal as it looks as though you haven't had one for some time now", she said quite sternly.

Looking down at the menu, Corry noticed her favourite dish was on the menu which was steak and kidney pie, fresh vegetables, mash potatoes and gravy. "Look, I'm going to have the steak and kidney pie as it reminds me when my brother and I were growing up, we'd come in from school to my grandmother's cooking".

The girl looked at Corry her tongue nearly hanging out at the thought of a slap up meal like that brought tears to her eyes as she asked;

"Would it be possible for me to have the same as you, for that was our favourite when my dad was alive?

"Of course it will" she replied knowing full well she was now starting to break the barriers down slowly with an ease of conversation that flowed between the two of them.

It wasn't long before the meal arrived to such a delightful look on the young girl's face for Corry knew only too well that was the first decent meal she'd had in several weeks and to watch her enjoy it, gave a warm feeling of satisfaction.

There was something very different about this girl when she started to eat for her table manners were impeccable, this wasn't someone who'd been dragged up or even come from a rough family, she was someone who seemed to have had quite a good upbringing although she did eat the food a little too fast but then again, maybe the reason for that was because she'd not eaten a good meal in such a long time.
Having cleaned her plate to the satisfaction of the waiter as he came to collect it, Corry then asked for the menu for a pudding.

"Oh I just love pudding don't you" Corry enquired, looking up at the girl's face, which by now was beaming with such an expression of glee over that question.

"Now I'm going to have some chocolate fudge cake, how about I order two lots and have ice cream put on them just to spoil us."

But before there was any kind of answer, Corry had already shouted the waiter placing an order for them, together with a couple of coffees. Having finished the pudding, the girl looked at Corry and said;

"Oh that was lovely, I thoroughly enjoyed it and can't thank you enough for what you've done for me today".

This young girl's face was so full of gratitude, you could see it in her expressions, it looked as though she'd died and gone to heaven as maybe that's what she was thinking at the time for no one had treat her like this for a long time and she would never forget this kindness as long as she lived;

"Look let's have another cup of coffee and maybe a nice big cream cake would go down nicely."

"Don't you think you've spent enough money on me today, as the meal alone must have cost a fortune and all I did was pull your arm saving you from oncoming traffic fear you lost your balance which is what anyone would have done in the same position" was the reply.

But Corry wasn't taking no for an answer as she shouted the waiter with an order for two large pieces of his finest cream cakes together with coffees. It was as the waiter delivered the order that Corry asked the young girl; How on earth she managed to be in London on her own at such a young age and who was she running away from, for if she could help at all she would. The girl looked at Corry with such gratitude for what she'd done already and decided to tell the truth and then Corry would be able to judge for herself and so with a few tears in her eyes said;

"Look I'll tell you everything on the condition you now start calling me Issa instead of looking at me as though I haven't got a name".

"Well Issa it is, I quite agree, it was rude of me to treat you like that as you do seem to be quite an intelligent young lady and if I can help you in any way possible, then that's what I intend for everyone needs help at some point in their lives and I know that better than anyone" Corry said, with a little sadness in her heart.

As the coffee arrived served with what you would call a very large portion of fresh cream cake, Corry realised what a rough time this girl had somehow suffered and was therefore ready to hear just how she'd got to this stage

"Now, you tell me a little about yourself and then we'll see just what I can do to try and help," she said looking straight at Issa.

"Now this is going to be hard for you to fully understand so I'd better start from the beginning" was the reply that Corry never expected;

"Being an only child of a serving soldier on tour in Ireland, I'd a pretty privileged upbringing until one day when a knock on the door came informing us my dad had been blown up and was therefore being sent home to spend four months in hospital before being pensioned out of the army.

It was when we finally returned to Newcastle things went from bad to worse as the only thing he enjoyed was his music which seemed to give him some kind of peace from the mental pain he suffered, however, my mother took this in her stride for a while before starting to drink heavily not being able to face up to the horrendous scarring on his body.

Then one morning I went into his room to kiss him before leaving for my little job, when I noticed such a beautiful expression on his face that spelt, he'd passed away in peace, away from a tormented body of pain, and although the death certificate stated; Natural causes, we were told it was Post Traumatic Stress
I'll never get over the pain of seeing him being buried as he'd a full Military funeral attended by hundreds due to the fact that he'd saved three soldiers being blown up in which we only learnt of that day.

It was then mother seemed to go off the rails, out every night with a new boyfriend every week as money wasn't a problem with the Army pensions which were adequately contributing to our financial daily living. Yes, she'd always played away from home when dad was away but not to this extent, and to be honest, I think she blamed me for having to get married so young taking her youth away and that's why we probably weren't close at all. Yes, she was my mother and I wouldn't wish her any harm but her nights out were many and maybe a little worrying at times,

But then all of sudden things changed when she met Tony for she seemed to settle down a bit, him being smart with a good job who tendered to give her all the attention she thought was lacking. And so after a few months she asked if I minded him moving in, which I was agreeable to as he was someone I could get on with for he understood how much I missed my dad".

Taking a short break, Issa finished her coffee and looked Corry straight in the face with such a sad expression that Corry knew there was a lot more to this story, and therefore had a feeling it wasn't going to be too pleasant at that but there again it had to be said so that she could understand how Issa got to be where she was at this moment. Perhaps when it all came out, then Issa would be able to build bridges and maybe start all over again with her life;

"Are you alright my dear", Corry asked with a sympathetic smile.

"Yes I'm fine" whispered a softly spoken Issa as she then prepared to carry on

"Well as I've said before, Issa continued, I had a little job which got me out of the house and to be honest just kept me busy not having many friends or wanting to do the normal things like date boyfriends, all I wanted to do was study and work hard with thoughts of probably getting an office job and maybe save enough money for a place of my own, a bit ambitious I know; but then the unspeakable happened" she said as tears rolled down her face

Corry froze and with fear in her face handed Issa some tissues before asking her what she meant, feeling an uneasy pain in her stomach

"It was one afternoon when I'd finished work early, came home made a sandwich and coffee I went to my room to study as my mother was out for the day. Yes, this was the day that Tony came home and raped me".

"What did you say, Oh My god, you poor little thing"

"It was after he'd finished, he said;

I've wanted to do that for a long time, you have a very beautiful body that turns me on immensely, your smooth youthful and tempting skin, where no one has been before I'd guess, yes definitely a virgin, sorry if I hurt you but it will get easier the next time I can assure you.

I honestly couldn't fight him off however hard I tried, it seemed as though I was in a dream and couldn't get out of it and with so much pain inside of me, it was unbelievable, maybe if I'd have screamed it'd have helped but I tried and yet nothing came out of my mouth" she said with a frozen look of fear.

At this point Corry felt sick to the stomach, all she wanted to do was wrap her arms around Issa and try to take some of her pain, but I'm afraid this kind of pain stays with you over a lifetime so it wasn't possible. You may be able to sympathize with someone over circumstances such as these but I'm afraid you have to suffer them to understand and not many women have, thank goodness.

It was a couple of hours later when my mother returned from Newcastle with her friends, a little merry to say the least but on the whole still sober which was a nice change. Taking her on one side I managed to tell to her what'd happened with Tony but to my amazement; she looked me straight in the eyes and said;

You're a liar, your just jealous', she screeched at the top of her voice.

No I'm telling you the truth; please believe me, I would never lie to you about anything like that". But no, my mother wasn't having any of that as the fire of hate was in her eyes. I don't want to ever hear any more of this nonsense and lies again, so I'd suggest you shut up before I throw you out of my house, he's a good man who takes care of me which is more than your father ever did' she screamed.

Starting to plead my case so she'd listen but to no avail, for when I tried to tell her what happened, she really lost it big style and slapped me hard across the face, leaving her handprints quite visible.

By then her friends had politely left knowing they didn't want to get involved in a family argument which was understandable but all the same they'd heard and to be honest, wouldn't have thought they'd be impressed due to the kind of people they were. It was no good trying to say anymore, as she couldn't see any wrong in Tony therefore the only safe place for me in the future was my bedroom when they were together

The next morning arrived which I was simply dreading, but lo and behold, as I entered the kitchen to grab a quick bite to eat before leaving the house for work, there they were, all over each other like a rash as though nothing had happened the day before, I just couldn't believe it, but there again nothing would have surprised me after what had happened.

Sadly, mother looked me in the eyes with a smirk on her face as she said;

"Whatever has happened to your face honey? Have you slept a little awkward on the pillow, as it's all marked and a little swollen, you need to put some cream on it as it looks a little sore"?

The cheek of it, when she knew only too well what'd happened, it was her that hit me with such force having taken my breath away, there was no answer from me just a look that told her I didn't want to speak and on the other hand,

Tony just smiled at me with an expression of satisfaction for whatever I said, no one was going to believe me.

Now a couple of weeks past as I tried to put it to the back of my mind, in which time I kept out of the way of both of them or if I did come into contact with Tony, I made sure my mother was there knowing he wouldn't dare make a move in front of her.

Still feeling humiliated as to what'd happened that day, even though it wasn't my fault, I couldn't get it out of my mind what this monster had done. The smell of his aftershave lingering on my body, his breath and perspiration that'd filled the air just wouldn't go away even though I soaked myself with perfumes after each shower, no the thoughts of Tony made me feel so nauseated.

Weeks passed by as things started to return to normal as possible with Tony keeping out of my way; when I again arrived home early, made a light lunch and with a drink in one hand and books in the other, started to make my way up to the bedroom for a little studying The house quite with no sign of movement until I climbed the stairs, where I could clearly hear the shower running, not thinking anymore of it other than it must be mother as she'll be going out with her friends into Newcastle drinking as usual, although she'd not mentioned anything that morning which wasn't like her.

Not thinking anymore about it as I proceeded to my bedroom where the temptation to lay on the bed and read was a comforting thought and with soft music in the background, coffee on the side of the bed, a book in my hand, it seemed peace was on my side as I lay there, but alas that wasn't so, as I sensed the door open with amazement, for as I looked up to find Tony walking towards me with just a towel draped round his waist and a look in his eyes which said it all.
Before I could make a move to get out of the way, there he was looking down at me with a perspiration of anxiety running wild from my body where he could sense the fear as he said;

You will enjoy me a lot better this time as I'm going to take it more slowly for you, as he then dropped the towel to the floor exposing his erect penis with a pride that shouted out a million words.

No I won't, I shouted, get out of my room, but before I could move out of his way, he pounced on top of me with a strength which I couldn't eject, just as he'd done the time before, pinning my arms to the bed whereby I'd nothing to fight with. Looking down on me with a fire in his eyes and a wanting in his body, as the next words he uttered in defiance;

I told you before no one will ever believe you, I'm going to take you again and if you put up a fight then you'll regret it as I need to fulfil my desires with a satisfaction your mother can't provide. And to this he repeated to rape me with a lust and hunger I'd never known. Only this time he wasn't going to get away with it as I came to my senses with a new found adrenalin racing throughout my body, which made me angry, yes angry enough to lash out at anything or anyone, I thought who is this man who thinks he can violate my body whenever he wants as a red mist appeared in front of my eyes.

Looking around the room not even thinking what I was looking for, when I noticed a pair of high heel shoes on a rack at the side of the wardrobe door and without thinking of the consequences moved slowly towards the shoes, picked one up and drove the heel straight into Tony's shoulder as he tried to defend himself, but I'm afraid it was too late, for the heel had already cut into the flesh rather deeply, with blood now starting to drip downwards towards the towel which he'd regained from the floor where he'd dropped it;

YOU BITCH you'll pay for that in more ways than one he screamed

For by now his shoulder bleeding quite heavily, as he made his way to the bathroom., giving me chance to get away and so running downstairs just as mother was walking through the front door;

What on earth is going on, what's all the noise, you could hear it outside.

Well if you ask your precious boyfriend who's now in a pool of blood, he can tell you how he's just raped me again, now are you satisfied was my reply.

The horror in her eyes said it all as she ran upstairs shouting, what on earth has she done to you darling. No, she wasn't bothered at all about what he'd done to me as long as her precious Tony was alright, that was obvious. For the next I knew, mother was grabbing the keys to her car shouting that she'd sort me out when she got back from the hospital.

No that wasn't going to be the case under any circumstance for I wouldn't give her the satisfaction of pushing me out of my own home for a no good monster like Tony as there wasn't anything left for me anyway, I was going to pack everything I could and leave before they both returned

It was then I heard a knock on the door only to see one of my best friends standing in the porch way, apparently she'd heard a lot of shouting and screaming as she'd tried to visit me earlier and so left, only to return when she saw my mother's car pull away. Rushing down to let her in, I begged her to help me get away, explaining just a little of what'd happened but not in its entirety fear she took it the wrong way but to my surprise she agreed knowing I wasn't happy also aware of the neighbourhood gossip about my mother, for not many people liked her, only to feel sorry for me".

One of things I made sure, I wasn't leaving behind was my dad's army medals he'd received for bravery for they were so precious to me, no way was she having them, she only mentioned them to others when wanting sympathy and people realised that. Struggling to get out of the house before mother and Tony returned, we then proceeded to my friend's house who, incidentally only lived at the bottom of the road.

Her mother was brilliant for she welcomed me into her home without any hesitation; not even to ask any questions at all. She could plainly see how upset I was, seeing the marks on my arms that Tony did while he was holding me down. I don't know what I'd have done if it weren't for her at that time, they were a real family and treated me with respect, not enquiring what'd happened at all, instead just making a comment that if I wanted to tell them, I would do so in my own time, if not they were only just too happy to help me get through whatever I was going through.

These people weren't blind; they knew what kind of life my dad had and the suffering when he was alive and therefore settled for the knowledge they had. These were good people who were willing to take me in and help through a difficult time, therefore I plucked up the courage to confide in them but also begged that they didn't go to the police as they'd wanted to, all I wanted to do at that time was get away from Newcastle, forget the past and start a fresh, feeling the shame that'd come down on me although it wasn't of my own making.

Mother on the other hand knew where I was staying but never made any attempt to enquire how I was going on, well good luck to her I thought, for as far as I was concerned, she was now dead to me and that's how I wanted it to stay".
Looking at Corry, who'd tears in her eyes by now, while Issa added;

"I bet you think I'm a bad person to think that about my mother but I'm Afraid I can't help it, she killed all feelings I'd got for her after that, I'll never forgive, there's an old saying that my dad always used to say and that was; What goes around comes around and boy will I be there when it comes around to her.

Corry was so choked at that remark she couldn't honestly answer but just shook her head instead, pausing to let Issa carry on with her story.

Again taking a deep breath Issa continued.

When I'd saved as much as I could and felt it was time to leave having the offer from an old school friend who lived in London to stay with, these kind people gave me a new purse as a leaving present with five hundred pounds in to start a new life.

Now this is the kind of family I'd hope for all my life but am afraid it wasn't to be as it wasn't my family but someone else's and that I couldn't infringe any longer, with their wonderful kindness which I'll never forget, It was a little upsetting leaving there, but again I'd to fend for myself sooner or later so as my friend Sue offered to put me up in her one bed flat in London, I'd to take a chance and leave, yes it was small but quite manageable and it would give me time to look for a job.

Sadly, this wasn't to be, yes it worked out for a few weeks as Sue had promised but then she herself was offered a job as a trainee nurse and therefore accommodation was provided, the landlord was very good and understood my circumstances but after a month I'd to move out as I couldn't afford the rent and didn't have a proper job.

After then thing went from bad to worse, staying with one or two friends that I'd already made, doing little cleaning jobs but still couldn't get a proper job because I had not anywhere to live, my only option was to stay with friends who'd put me up for a few nights at a time, leaning on their generosity which I was so grateful for.

The landlord of Sue's flat said he'd keep my things while I got sorted out and if he heard of any work going, he'd get in touch, which to be honest, he was as good as his word arranging that I cleaned his other properties as they became vacant, also odd cleaning jobs for his friends which again was good for this helped me with a little money for food, so that's my story up to date Issa finished off but also adding;

I can't complain really, it's a lot better than living at home and having made quite a few friends in the same position, the thing is when you live like this at least you learn to share the good fortune when it comes along".

Corry looked at Issa with such concern before asking.

"Where are you staying at the moment and have you ever taken drugs"?

"I'm staying for a few days with a girl I met the other week, her mother 's gone up north to see relatives so she offered to put me up at their place until her mother returns, as for drugs, I know a lot of people take them but I never have and don't intend to as a couple of my friends' back home have really got hooked and that's not for me at all", Issa stated in a stern tone

"Good" Corry replied, as she'd listened to Issa's story so intensely, feeling her pain as the story of her life had spilled out with a sadness and feeling that only a woman could understand, and now she would turn this young girls' life upside down by presenting her with an offer she couldn't refuse.
How would you like to come and work for me, I'm offering you the chance of learning a trade in the fashion business, starting at the bottom, paid only a small wage but enough for you to live on and I'll also provide you with a small but comfortable place that you can sleep".

I'll also kit you out with a few new clothes so you won't feel out of place with the rest of the girls, the work is hard, with long hours but I think you'll be fine once you're settled in and make new friends as I don't think you're the type that's frightened of hard work".

The expression on Issa's face was astonishing, nothing like this had ever happened for her in this way and it would be a dream to work with posh clothes she thought as she suddenly came to her senses.

"I'd love to, but are you sure after what I've told you," she asked pausing for a few minutes before adding;

"I'll never let you down you know".

"Yes I know that, you will however have to stay with me for the present, while we do the room out on the top floor at the shop, but at least you'll have a nice warm bed to sleep in and three meals a day provided by me".

"There are only two things that I ask; the first being, you get in touch with your mother telling her you're safe. The second thing, you must get in touch with the police in Newcastle informing them of your whereabouts as they may have you on the missing persons register".

"Do you understand and agree with what I've said", Corry asked.

Issa was overwhelmed by what she'd heard, and in a daze agreed whole heartedly, not believing this was happening, maybe she'd wake up and find it was all in a dream but no it was real enough.

"Fine, I'll get in touch with the police straight away but where mother's concerned, I'll write her a letter but won't enclose the address if that's alright"

"If that's what you wish then its ok by me" was the reply.

Issa paused for a moment before asking;

"Please tell me, why you're doing all this for me, a complete stranger until a couple of hours ago"?

"The answer to that question is, because you're an exceptional person whose gone through a great deal and come out of the other side, everyone needs a break somewhere along the way, all I'm asking, is you don't let me down. For when I was down and thought there was nowhere to go, someone came along and gave me the break that I so needed for which I've been forever grateful and maybe you will do the same for someone else in time".

To that Corry paid the bill, and getting up to leave saying;

"Now you're ready, we have to go and collect your belongings".

Corry felt so good about what she'd just done for Issa, this was really the start of how she intended to pay back for all the kind things that people like Agnes had done for her. Not only that, but she'd a feeling that there was something in this girl that was very different to anything she'd come across before, not knowing what it was at the time but how right she was and it wouldn't be too long before others found it for her.

Slowly heading back to Corry's apartment having called for Issa's belongings which were a few bits of clothing but most important of all some personal things that had belonged to her dad, a few photos of them together when she was young with medals that she treasured and rightly so, for they meant he'd always be with her. It was now a new beginning for Issa, one to look forward.

Although Corry's apartment was on the small side there was just enough room to put Issa up for the time being and wouldn't be any trouble as she'd be working most of the time. All they had to do now was smarten Issa up and that would be quite easy for the girls to run up a few little outfits. Corry in turn would allow Issa to display her dad's photo's so she wouldn't feel out of sorts staying in a strange place.

What Corry didn't anticipate was the fact Issa was so creative and tidy; the flat would always look immaculate, not like when she herself lived in it alone for she wasn't the tidiest of people, and it really was pleasant having her around.

Everything had to be sorted out rather quickly with the fashion show on the horizon so kitting her out was a rush job with no time to waste being business as usual, for the show must go on and designs had to be drawn up with samples for the it.

Issa, poor thing was caught up in quite a world wind of procedure for the time being but everything had to be planned in that line of work and she fully appreciated this fact and so just fitted in where she possibly could, being so grateful for what everyone was trying to do to help her.

Corry in turn, introduced her to the se
wing girls who instantly took a shine, showing her all the ropes to start this wonderful career off. Well when I say the ropes the first thing they showed her was how to pick up a sweeping brush to sweep for everything had to be kept clean for the delicate fabric in which they used for samples before the decisions were made as to how they would look before going into full production.

It was also duly noticed she was highly intelligent therefore it wouldn't take long to teach her about the fashion industry from scratch. And on Corry's part, she would take time out training her as she'd been trained, starting with the fundamentals, such as listening to client as they were the ones who were paying for time and expertise, treat them with respect at all times, even if you disagreed with what they wanted. As with experience, you could persuade them what would flatter and what fabric would look best made up to create a garment that would outshine all their friends.

But most of all never tell lies to a customer should she ask about the fitting of a garment as a perfect fit was the secret of elegance. Issa had only been at Corry's a matter of weeks and not only had she re-organized everything but had also gone to town on the apartment as well, for everything had a place and was so tidy the girls couldn't believe it.

The girls in the workshop had taken Issa under their wing and taught her so much in such little time but then again she was hungry to learn which impressed everyone, whenever they asked her to do something there were no questions, she just got on with the job, if she didn't understand then she asked for it to be explained until she'd grasp what they were talking about. The clients on the other hand were a little more suspicious for they knew nothing about this girl but in time, they warmed to her, like everyone else that came into contact, they not only accepted but loved her for her bright and warm personality.

But since that first day Issa had entered Corry's life, she'd had a nagging feeling about her but no matter what it was she couldn't work it out, yes this feeling just wouldn't go away and kept coming back like a reminder of something was going to happen. Months had now gone by with Issa still living at Corry's, but to no avail as she was a little god send for nothing was too much trouble and also a workaholic which kept everyone on their toes.

With work coming in so fast, it was by mutual agreement that now was the time to go in for a showing at the famous London Fashion Week. Corry was a little nervous over this decision as it was a big gamble going in against the big boys that were at the top of their creative career but with a little push from those around she would jump in with both feet first. This was a big gamble and very ambitious but Agnes had suggested that it was possible; therefore, everyone should put their faith in it and literally go for it.

The big boys of the fashion industry just laughed this off thinking it was a joke that a little back street business would be a challenge to the likes of them.

Oh boy, how wrong they were because Corry's plan was to design a new style of outfit with accessories to match, this had never been tried before, so was a little unsure, thinking deeply about it, she knew it had to be something that would knock the smile off their silly arrogant faces but with no ideas on the horizon was at a loss to take the idea forward at that moment.

Her clients together with Agnes backed her all the way at that time, money wasn't any object for Agnes had so many influential friends that bankrolled the deal, and therefore it would be plain sailing. All she had to do was come up with the ideas which again she struggled with at the moment as the hours were long and the sleep was in short supply, some days struggling to even manage five hours but her goal to achieve this dream was so strong, sleep had to be sacrificed

With top names the competition was fierce and with this in mind, she'd to pull something out of the hat that was so very different with her designs, when all of a sudden she hit on an idea to lower all necklines, even taking some down to the waist, this was a risk but not only was she to take it, she went that little bit further, lowering the back to show the shoulders off. Her showpieces were to be the wedding dresses and with a secret weapon there would be no way of stopping her at this stage as the adrenalin ran through her veins.

Corry had to have all her wits about her for the next few weeks knowing if any of the plans got out they could be sabotaged for this was the kind of competition she was up against even though it was her first year.

The experienced designers in the city would love nothing more than to see her fall flat on her face, but I'm afraid that wasn't going to happen for she was in this for the long run and if they wanted a fight on their hands they certainly would get one from her, for she was made of stronger stuff than they ever thought, a true Yorkshire girl. And without much sleep, it was thought a day off to catch up on things that'd been put on one side such as an appointment with her accountant which would become a priority, therefore dropping Issa off at work and arranging to collect her later on for an early night, which to be honest was what they both needed.

And so first thing the next morning Issa was dropped off at the workshop with arrangement to collect her later after meetings she'd already arranged with both new clients and the accountant together with fitting in a new model who would be the star of the show in the wedding creation for the finale.

In the meantime, the girls back at the workshop got together and decided they were going to make Issa up and using her as a trial model for the outfits that were already made. Starting with the face using the barest of minerals to make her look like a porcelain doll, a touch of eye shadow that covered the eyelids showing off the deep brown eyes, a velvet smear of blusher over the high cheek bones, a natural pout of the lips in a sleek pale peach, her hair trimmed to one side of the face in a semi bob which on a glance would show off her elf like features to perfection.

And to complete, they dressed her in a short plain dress that not only showed her trim figure but also her long shapely legs. Someone had taken a pair of shoes out of the winter collection that was to be shown together with a fur stole which complimented the whole outfit perfectly. It was as Corry arrived back expecting to collect Issa, she was met with an astonishing sight of the future model of the year as that was the vision that fit Issa, she knew there was something about her and now it had come to light, all this time she'd kept racking her brain and in less than eight hours the girls had found what she'd been looking for.

"Oh my God, she gasped not believing her eyes, is that really you Issa" while one of the girls piped up,

"Well you did tell us to sort the outfits for the show and we hadn't got a model so decided to improvise using Issa as she's just perfect for the job and having taken a vote we came up with the idea that she'd be perfect as the new face of fashion for the company".

"With her looks, style and the way she holds herself, we could teach her how to walk together with all the tricks those stuck up models that haven't got any personality to show off their talents, instead of paying a fortune to air their tantrums when something isn't to their pleasing" one of the girls piped up with.

Well Corry couldn't argue with that as they cost a fortune and the tantrums on the day which they often displayed was ridiculous she thought. It was all coming together now, for what she'd thought in the beginning about Issa was now coming to the fore, if the girls had pulled this off in so little time then she couldn't doubt them when they offered to teach her the ropes and maybe a star would be born.

The room was left in silence when one of the girls piped up;

"Well, what do you think about our suggestion?".

"I think it's brilliant and I'm willing to go with the idea" Corry said smiling.

Issa was silent for a moment not being able to take it all in, me a model she thought, no way, but having second thoughts knowing if she did this, it'd be one way of paying Corry and the girls back for all they'd done for her. Everyone made her so welcome, teaching her with pride on how to accomplice a goal that she'd never even thought achievable. But now accepted as one of them, she felt part of their little family.

It was now time for Corry to start putting things in motion with no leaks to the press as to what she'd be planning whereby bringing an un-known girl to wow the fashion scene as she hoped it'd turn out to be.

Swearing them all to secrecy, and knowing if this was going to be pulled off with military precision she'd keep Issa at her place and not bother with the rooms above the shop. The dress which was the star of the show had already been locked away, this being a wedding dress that would wow everyone and with a little tweaking, would be sensational on Issa.

"Now all that's settled, I think it's about time we called it a day, a very productive day at that may I say" Corry remarked looking rather tired.

Having both reached home, it dawned on them what'd actually happened, not only was it financially viable to save on a string of temperamental models but they 'd also gained a new star of the show that no one had ever seen before, this in its self would make the headlines in London. You see in those days' models were from the upper class so was used to getting their own way, Issa was fresh, new and with a youthful spark that everyone could relate to;

"think that deserves a large coffee with a fresh cream cake I brought in don't you", Corry stated as she kicked her shoes off, absolutely shattered.

What a treasure this girl has been, firstly saving me from a vehicle knocking me down, then turns out to be my secret weapon for the house of fashion and design and to top it all goes ahead makes me a great cup of coffee, what a treasure Corry thought.

A treasure beyond belief as it turned out to be for the future to come as she sat back falling asleep with exhaustion that had actually caught up with her finally.

Chapter 6

The next few weeks were horrendous for everyone as it was now late August, the city buzzing with tourists that were arriving from abroad, not only to see the sites of the big city but also a couple of weeks stay before the big fashion houses started their showing. Corry didn't know if she was on her head or her feet in that time, what with trying to keep everything under wraps so word couldn't get out about her plans, but with this in mind she was truly satisfied everything else was running on schedule with all the garments finished and therefore it was only a matter of the accessories that had to be organised, but at this point her nerves were starting to get the better of her.

Having put all her faith in the girls as they'd worked so hard pulling this off, and knowing she couldn't let them down, therefore got in touch with her grandmother with an invite to the show thus knowing if anyone could give her the support she needed, it definitely would be her.

The best way to approach this would be to actually go back up north and visit, taking Issa which would be a short break for both of them away from the bedlam of the city.

No time like the present and so the next morning bright and early with just enough time for a quick breakfast, they boarded the early train from Kings Cross station to Doncaster before all the rush hour workers, and although it was only to be a short visit, never the less it was one that she'd enjoy as she missed her home town immensely at times. Yes, it definitely would be a short visit but one where she'd return re-invigorated and ready to take on the task in hand with the help of what she called her band of angels.

Upon arrival grandmother looked Issa over and as expected, gave her opinion in just one look before coming out with;

"I think you ought to feed this one up as she's all skin and bones, a good plate of stew and dumpling wouldn't go a miss".

Well what would you expect, coming from Yorkshire folk, and that's exactly what they got waiting for them good old fashioned stew and dumplings, to put meat on their bones as the saying went.

Although only an overnight stay but a lot was put into that time whereby Corry explained everything what'd been happening recently together with the full story of how she came to find Issa, going further into it, stating she was like a little sister that she'd never had, her background and right up to the fashion show where she was going to use her for the final glory to close the show.

Grandmother just listened to everything with a look of sadness in her eyes as seeing what this little bag of bones as she kept on calling her had gone through together with how proud she was of Corry in helping her, for that was the kind of thing that she'd have done herself in those circumstances.

Although it was a short stay, it was also a very pleasant one as they were both made to feel the warmth of the northern hospitality together with a love and protective feeling that you only feel from a family member in those circumstances. Having said their goodbyes, the next morning it was a parting with such sadness as although Corry had grown to love the big city with all the hustle and bustle where there was always something going on, her heart would always belong to her home town and the family who brought her up, nothing would ever change that.

Heading back to London, it seemed a big burden had been lifted from her shoulders as though what ever happened now was going to work out for them both, and that's why the trip to Doncaster was so important, away from the pressures of the city that'd brought everything into prospective.

With less than a week to go when the well-known designers would start their shows, the pressure would also be starting to build up for everyone, not at least for Corry, but then again she had a little breathing space for as it was her first showing, she'd be fitted into one of the last days with all the little unknown designers that was also hungry to be discovered like her.

Nerves were really starting to mount as they put the finishing touches to everything for only perfection and originality would do, checking everything over and over again. It'd been planned for Agnes to take in a couple of the shows by the top designer on the first day of showing and then report back to Corry about the competition but that wasn't any good really as she was bias having such an invested interest in Corry's organisation.

Day One, and this was the first day of the showings where all the celebrities together with the aristocracy, would be seated at shows like Norman Hartnell, Vivienne Westwood etc. Knowing they were the designers who created the look for London every season. The city was aghast at their designs for they were the ones that made the headlines, it was the little unknown designers that had to work hard to even get a look in, but none the less Corry had made her mark by showing her determination and therefore do her upmost to show them she wasn't to be run out of town or intimidated by them so easily.

Now was her chance to prove them all wrong when they'd called her a little nobody and a flash in the pan, adding, no one will even remember her this time next year? How wrong they would be, for she was going to make them eat their words after her showings which would be small but impressive in her eyes.

As the big shows came to an end with stories hitting the papers of how successful London fashion week had been and with a selection of after parties where all the big names of society had attended, it was plain to see how people like Corry felt, left out in the cold, so to speak but with a determination you couldn't put down. Yes, there was a lot of money flying around at these events so much so that many hotels couldn't keep up with the bottles of champagne they were supplying their guests, but then that was what London was all about with the elite.

The dawn of the last day of the fashion week, which was Corry's showing;

Now this was her chance to finally prove to the city she wasn't an overnight wonder but had enough fight in her body to make an impression, and they'd have a fight on their hands. Rumours around the trade speculated where the money was coming from to back her as it was a complete mystery, but that was to be kept quite amongst her backers so as not to upset the apple cart before she made it big, as these good people were behind her 100 per cent, knowing this little girl from Yorkshire would be a winner someday soon with her outstanding talents.

Most of the people that attended Corry's show were friends, financial backers, and others that ware fed up with the parties they'd enjoyed for the last few nights. Coming up with an idea that the first two front rows next to the stage would be by admission only and that the others would be of a free courtesy to those of the public that couldn't afford such luxury was a brilliant idea, for this gave an opportunity to the working class, a chance to see how the other half lived affording things they'd never experienced before.

They weren't really bothered whether she was a top designer as long as they could go back to their friends and say they'd been to a showing at the London fashion week.

And to her surprise, there were half a dozen of the press, which was brought in by Agnes's influence, for she wasn't going to let an opportunity pass by, to let her golden girl get onto the front pages of the tabloids.

The lighting was minimal to start with as the show opened:

The music loud with a beat that got everyone tapping their feet as the first model walked out onto the catwalk followed sharply by two others, this wasn't going to be a stuffy sombre stroll of models like the other shows, it was to be a vibrant show of determination with a modern feel of youth, something that hadn't been attempted before.

The audience was quite shocked as they diverted their eyes from one model to the other for they hadn't quite expected such down to earth girls.

All three models were dressed the same only in different colours, now some people would describe the outfits as boiler suits but no, they may have looked a bit like them but in fact they were, well what can I say, boiler suits made in the highest quality satin cotton twill, neatly fitting over the body and held in at the waist with a broad belt.

Then followed, three more models as before dressed all in different coloured fitted skirts this time, down to the knees with bomber jackets to match.

Yes, this was the theme all through the first half of the show and no one could believe their eyes for this kind of thing didn't happen in London as it was all too sophisticated for women to dress like that. Whispers went round the room like wild fire, was this a new trend we were getting into, actually dressing like the forces that were proud to serve the natation, maybe so was one comment that was heard from the front row, not knowing if they liked it or not.

Approaching the second half, which was a little more relaxed as Corry had brought out some pretty pastel dresses that could be worn through the day but this again wasn't what you would expect as they were more of a sundress that was a little lower cut at the neckline than had been worn in the past.

Yes, she'd gone for a more daring look but then again she wanted to be different and show women they could be feminine and flighty as well as sophisticated. Still the audience wasn't quite sure at this stage and to be honest a lot of them had only gone to look at the fashion, knowing they couldn't afford a designer dress.

Slowly, drawing to the end of the show was the best of all for everyone, as this was the bit where something special was always the highlight of the evening and in this case, there wouldn't be any disappointment as the lights dimmed to a low smoky scene while everything went quite.

Silence in the room was deafening when all of a sudden out walked the belle of the ball so to speak, yes it was Issa, and as she took her first few steps onto the catwalk the spotlights came alive shining down on her magnificent presence. Her angelic look was only matched by the wedding gown that she wore.

A heavy pure white satin gown which fitted straight down to below the knee then trailing away in a soft sweep of a fish tail, the top part of the dress, fitted just under the bust line and encrusted with tiny seed pearls, a sweetheart neck that sat nicely but then trailed off to small cap sleeves. Finishing off with a puffed up flower that had been made from the same material as the dress, this again was covered in seed pearls to match the top of the dress and therefore didn't need a veil at all to sit on her head.

As she walked down the catwalk Corry had dressed four little girls in ballerina dresses to follow, these were made up in the same shade as Issa's flowers which were of a deep burnt orange that took on its own glow of the evening. The audience went wild for they'd never seen anything like this before, the noise was astounding with the sound of the audience's roar of approval together with the flashing of the lights coming from the cameras.

Now the closing of the show, when Issa entered the catwalk for the last time followed by the team that'd made everything a success, but still the roar and applause that filled the room was quite deafening. It was a good few minutes before the noise started to die down, when Issa managed to get hold of a microphone to give a speech of her own appreciation of the night, waiting a few moments before she said;

"I would like to thank Corrander Sharp for giving us all the opportunity to share in tonight's success, not only is she talented but she is the most wonderful person you could ever wish to meet and I know this will only be the start of her mark as a fashion designer in the city" taking a few minutes before adding;

"Now ladies and gentlemen I would like to introduce you to the person who was responsible for tonight as you will no doubt give a big hand for what you have seen, a new revelation of fashion which we hope will sweep the country.

Corrander please come and take a bow as you've earned it tonight".

What more can I say, as Corry walked onto the catwalk in a flood of tears and thanked everyone, for this night, she would never forget as long as she lived as it was the start of something that would change a lot of people's lives for the best.

Corry did however manage to stop in at another show which started just after her own show had finished, this was a show of the finest knitwear you could ever see, made up in all fine wools and silks. Her mind racing, she thought to herself, now this has real potential and as a new designer like herself if she could combine these materials with her designs there may be another avenue she could pursue, but for now she was just on a high for the night had gone so well.

The next morning was a shock for the city as according to all the newspapers, a new star had been born and her name was Issa, the woman behind the scenes was none other than a young unknown dress designer from the North of England. As nothing was known about this woman the press was eager to trace all avenues to find out more but one thing for sure, they had all stated she was not only talented but with new ideas and ranges of clothing that delighted all that saw the show, yes, a breath of fresh air for the industry they printed.

With her ability to create clothing like they'd never seen before together with the delightful model that would no doubt be the sensational find of the future, Corrander Sharp and Issa will take the city into a new beginning with their ideas of fashion.

Chapter 7

The show had taken a lot out of Corry both in nerves and exhaustion which was now evident, looking extremely tired and run down, yes, she'd achieved a lot with the reviews and hard work they'd put in, and now felt it'd be beneficial to get away from all the back lash of sniping men that run the big fashion houses in the city, maybe take a few days away in the sun which would hopefully do the trick, and so upon her return, would be at least refreshed and willing to fight another day.

Yes, everything had gone to plan and now it was up to the staff to run the place while Corry took that well-earned break, as to be honest, she was totally shattered having given it all she'd got so to speak, her head now out of the clouds she realised this wouldn't go amiss where she'd be able to put her feet up for a while, as promised, she'd take Issa along for not only company but to show her gratitude for helping make the show such a success.

Corry realised all the hard worked that Issa had put in and therefore wanted to reward her in a way she thought appropriate, not realising at that time how big an impact the girl had on that catwalk that day of the show, eventually to become such a famous model in her own right whereby she'd be able to name her price and live a life of luxury on her gains one day.

With a little forward planning she phoned the travel agents down the road and have them look a for a cheap quick holiday for both of them;

"I need to book a week for two people, no longer than maybe a four-hour flight, a nice hotel near the beach, good food, good wine and a relaxing atmosphere, although it'll be just the two of us, we'll require a double room each, I don't care where, as long as the weather is warm, so If you can sort something out I'll be eternally grateful as desperately need a break" she said laughing.

"Oh I'm sure we'll be able to find you something as there is a fair bit coming up at the moment in Spain and Cyprus, so will phone you back when I get some details, oh by the way when would you like to travel" she added.

"Tomorrow if possible, but will leave it with you" she jokingly replied.

"By the way, your show was absolutely fantastic all the girls from here went to see it and Issa especially, she looked just like a super model" the voice on the other side of phone stated.

"Why thank you, that's very kind of you to say so, I'm pleased you enjoyed it", was Corry's last words before putting the phone down.

Having told Issa about the holiday they both decided to pack in anticipation while waiting for a call to say the travel agents had found something for them but alas they hadn't got that long to wait before that call came to say, it would be a seven-day holiday in Cyprus with an early morning flight the next day. Yes, the agents had done them proud, for they'd booked them into a four-star hotel situated five minutes from the beach just outside of Larnaca, which was a busy town although it also had a beautiful beach, white sands with nice shops, restaurants and lively night life should they want it.

"Having never been to Cyprus, but heard it 'was really beautiful, so looking forward to it, I'll pop down with a cheque while you sort the paperwork out as we've already packed and ready to go", Corry replied

Early to bed and early to rise for that's what they both did that night, with the memories of the past week drifting away to the tune of exhaustion

Day 1
A little hectic the next morning to say the least having arranged for a taxi to pick them up for Gatwick airport, but quite excited getting in the swing of everything as they boarded the plane, it seemed that all the stress was starting to drift away. The next seven days was going to be such a relaxing time and also an enjoyable one or so they thought, but little did Corry realise this holiday was going to change her life forever.

The plane full of travellers and the voices mulling in the background made a nice change where Corry could sit back with no cares in the world to worry about for seven whole days, what heaven she thought. It was a really smooth flight as flights go and seemed to pass quickly, now all she was bothered about was how long it would be before they reached their destination for she'd be able to sit back and let the world go by for seven whole days, relaxing after such a hectic schedule leading up to the show or so she thought but things never run to plan as we all know by now and this was no exception to that rule either.

The smooth landing of the plane brought them down to earth with the reality of arriving on terra firma and heading for the airport terminal, when Corry noticed that one or two passengers kept looking at both her and Issa but couldn't for the life of her understand why until one of the passengers came up to Issa and said;

"Aren't you that new super model that all the papers were raving about from the London fashion shows?"
Issa stood and stared, she couldn't believe what she'd heard, me a super model,

"No, I did one of the shows but I'm far from being a super model I can assure you, nothing so glamorous" she replied with a smirk on her face.

This woman turned to her friend and said;

"I know she's wrong, I never forget a face and just look at her she is absolutely beautiful, that's her alright."

Issa just smiled, said "thank you for those kind words" and walked over to collect her baggage from the carrousel.

"Now wasn't that kind of that woman to say that" she asked Corry

"No not t at all, you just don't realise how beautiful you are, I said you'd be a star, a face that teenagers would relate to and older people would appreciate your serene beauty".

Issa, just simply smiled and turned away, knowing she could always rely on Corry to buck her spirits up when feeling down, making her feel good in herself just as her father used to do when she was little. Having collected their cases, it didn't seem too long before boarding the coach which would take them to their hotel with thoughts of dropping their bags after booking in and catching a bite to eat.
About three quarter of an hours ride to Protaras which was as the travel agent had stated and although it looked to be a small place, she wasn't wrong, it looked quite, but very beautiful with the beach front that led down to the most wonderful secluded bay. Corry also noticed, on the way to Protaras they passed an Army base which looked quite lively, not knowing much about the forces but had seen a fair few army vehicles guarding the roads to the camp.

It ran through her mind, with that being the case, at least they wouldn't have a problem with the language as the local people would be able to speak enough English for them to get by which in those days' people never learnt a second language at school as they do now.

Time passed quite quickly since leaving London and it was now drawing close to lunch so after unpacking, they enjoyed a quick snack together with a couple of hours by the pool relaxing with a couple or should I say a few martinis' thrown into the bargain, before they organise what outfits to wear for the evening. There was no dressing up for dinner at this hotel only smart to casual so after a quick shower and a casual dress they proceeded to dinner.

The smell that greeted them, was of tradition good wholesome food that your grandmother made when growing up, it was some sort of lamb stew with vegetables which to be honest, they hadn't a clue what they were but certainly tasted the real deal, this was followed by strawberries and homemade ice cream together with a freshly made coffee and biscuits to finish off leaving their plates clean as you could image with food like that

A walk along the beach promenade to help digest that wonderful meal and maybe call for a couple of drinks at a local bar on the way back to the hotel, for with this in mind it would help them sleep on their first night in a strange bed, which was always difficult at the best of times so to speak.

"Now that was a great idea" Issa replied for even she was exhausted from the past few weeks. It was now starting to dawn on them what a rewarding and successful week it'd been and therefore would have to replenish their bodies before flying back to the lime light that was to follow.

Leaving the hotel that evening, the warm air was quite refreshing, maybe a bit too refreshing as they started to relax in the warmth of the night, therefore a walk along the sea front would be lovely, and maybe on the way back they'd call at the local bar they'd spotted earlier on, a couple of quite drinks would do the trick before their heads hit the pillow, it would be asleep in no time, well that was the plan anyway.

The sea air and warm breeze touched their faces with a relaxing change from the last six months, no working to a clock as they'd been used to seven days a week not realizing how it'd taken it out of their bodies getting ready for the show. Both dressed in little white linen dresses which was appropriate for that evening, they looked the picture of health, all they needed now was a good sun tan to go with it and they would be set to take on the world so to speak.

Oh this is the life just to relax and do whatever we wish with not a worry in the world, Corry thought to herself as they'd walked at least a couple of miles by now and not even realised it.

Walking another mile when hearing loud music coming from a rather large bar situated just set back from the main road;
"I know it sounds a bit rowdy but let's go in as it sounds fun and the sleep has disappeared from my body already just listening to the noise" Issa asked.

"Go on then, you may be right and it does sound rather good", was the reply.

Oh my god they thought as they walked through the main entrance, this was really living, the music loud, the atmosphere electric and the place was full, mind you it was full of soldiers who were off duty for one thing, and secondly, they'd never experienced this kind of thing before in London.

Walking up to the bar, obviously seemed to be the centre of attention, mind you, there weren't many females in the place except the bar staff and maybe a couple of older females with their husbands, so all eyes were on them being two attractive females. but when reaching the bar to order the drinks, a voice out of the crowd shouted

"I'll buy those two ladies a drink, get them whatever they want barman".

And as Corry turned round, to her surprise, stood this very attractive man looking at her, he was about 6ft1 fair hair, dressed in, grey trousers and shoes to match, white shirt showing his tan to perfection. There were no words to be spoken as yet just a magnetism when their eyes met, this hunk of man just glided over to Corry before stating;

"Hi my name is James but they call me Jay for short and what's your name"?

"It's Corrander but I get Corry for short, and by the way thank you for the drinks, it was very kind of you".

"Not at all, would you care to come over here where it's a little more peaceful so we can get better acquainted", he asked in a very well educated manner.

It's at this point Corry turned around to check on Issa as she was left at the bar with a considerable amount of service men around her. Corry on the other hand had other things on her mind as she thought to herself what a dishy fella this Jay was, glancing into his deep brown eyes, it was as if time was standing still between them for he was as mesmerized as she herself was. But having second thoughts about her friend, Corry, excused herself from Jay, approached the bar to check if Issa was alright.

"Don't worry, she's in good hands we can assure you, the problem is, are you?" they asked with a shrill in their voice

As for Issa, well she was so wrapped up in all the attention she was now receiving for she'd not notice what anyone else was up to. As long as she's safe, that's all that mattered to Corry for she wasn't what you call street wise although she may have thought differently.
Having joined Jay, Corry couldn't hear half of what he was saying with the music being so loud and to be honest she wasn't entirely bothered as this guy seemed to be the genuine good guy and with such a fit body, he could probably charm the birds out of the trees if he tried she thought.

Well the night went on and on, everyone in such a great mood, the music loud, as Jay moved closer to her, putting the world to right as they say, telling each other a little about themselves as best they could in the surroundings but none the less, enjoying each other's company as the magnetism between them was so evident to those around.

She working with fabrics and clothing but not telling him the full story about how big a designer she was and with a northern accent not having the advantages that he'd been privileged to, him, well he was a Captain in the Army, stationed out in Cyprus for another three years, he was single and not committed to any relationship at that stage as she was in the same position. They swapped stories as though they were old friends who'd just met up again after years and getting to know each other on the way;

"How come you lot are out until all hours and it's not even the weekend" Corry had asked.

"Well to be honest, all the lads have just come back from a two-month mini tour at the other end of the island, having no time at all off as they'd to put a seven days a week in, and so they've now been granted seven days off, and that's why we're all out celebrating" he replied.

"Now tell me, what's your excuse to come to Cyprus is" he enquired."

Being a little cagey at this time Corry answered with caution,

"More or less the same as you, we've been working seven days a week for the last few months and now the company we work for has booked us a week here as a reward for all the hours and hard work we've put in for them".

Both explanations were true although a little far stretched, but what the hell who was to know the truth anyway, knowing they'd never meet again and people never tell the truth on holiday anyway, they just make it up as they go along Corry thought. It was gone three in the morning when the party started to disperse, some of the crowd at the bar had already gone back to barracks which left six of them to walk Issa back to the hotel and because they'd been drinking steadily all night, they were quite capable of escorting her, she on the other hand was a little tipsy but still aware what she was doing, but after saying that, they're good lads who were just out to enjoy themselves while trying to impress an attractive female.

Jay being an officer and a gentleman walked her back to the hotel, kissing her goodnight on each side of the cheek, as he asked politely.

"I'd love to see you tomorrow if that's alright with you?"

Alright, Corry thought, you must be joking of course it's alright but with a hesitance in her voice she answered,

"Yes I'm sure it will be".

"Pick you up at ten then, have your swimming gear packed and I'll take you for a ride round the island as it looks as though your friend has ideas of her own".

That night both Issa and Corry slept like a log only to wake to the sound of birds singing their hearts out at six in the morning as the light broke through their open windows. It wasn't long before they were sitting on the balcony drinking coffee, swapping stories from the night before, both apologizing for making individual dates for that morning. Issa, to spend the day seeing the island with a young soldier called Rob who would incidentally pick her up at 10am the same time as Jay was to pick Corry up, which seemed such a coincidence in their eyes, obviously arranged.

Realizing this was just a short holiday romance but what the hell, this was what they needed, just to laugh and a good time.

To this, Corry thought to herself, although he seemed to be one of the lads, Jay was far too posh for her and had obviously been privately educated, therefore definitely out of her league for it stood out a mile and then there was that remark that one of the lads had made the night before, so he must have been one for the ladies

DAY 2

10am on the dot as arranged the night before, both girls were picked up by their individual escorts, dressed appropriately, in tiny shorts and tee shirts with their bikinis underneath, they set off on their individual dates in different directions.

While Issa and her new found friend went down towards Paphos which was at the south side of the island, Corry and Jay headed towards the north, near enough to the Turkish border but at a safe distance as there was still a small amount of friction on the island between the Greek and Turkish communities at that time.

This part of the island was very beautiful and finding a small bay down by the border of Famagusta where only a few tourists ever came, they had more or less, the beach to themselves, which was very convenient as they started to get close in their friendship. The water still warm at that time of the year as the sun shone down with a warm breeze, the mood was quite romantic as you would expect with two people on the island of Aphrodite the Goddess of love, what more could they ask for.

Swimming all morning, with a little sunbathing, then a spot of lunch in a little beachside café that Jay knew, and while it didn't look all that good from the outside, it was as they entered Corry was somewhat surprised as the place was immaculate with the food being superb, owned by a Greek family who'd known Jay since arriving on the island, and in fact, made him feel like one of the family.
The meal was just starting to settle when fresh coffee came to the table served with ice cream and fresh strawberries, how did they know that was one of Corry's favourite or was it just a co-incident, and not being able to resist them cleared the full bowl before leaving;

"That was fantastic" she sighed;

"I'm pleased you enjoyed it, we'll have to come here again seen as you like it so much and anyway I've every intention of bringing you back" he said with a smirk on his face.

The afternoon was just as good, lying on a white sandy beach with no care in the world while watching waves slowly hitting the shore line, now and again Jay wrapped his arm around Corry to gently kiss her neck in such a romantic way making shudders shoot through her body.

And as the sun reached a mind blowing heat, he would tenderly cover her so as not to let her burn by the intense heat of the day, what a thoughtful man this was, not only good looking, charming thoughtful but also good company to be with. Yes, they'd lots of things to talk about but not touching on their family life, for not knowing each other that long it wouldn't have been appropriate and again, that would come in time should anything else develop between them.

It was just nice to lie on a beach watching the world go by, now and again a few cars would pull up, people would get out for a stroll along the breakwater but that never seemed to bother them as they just carried on with whatever conversation they were having at the time and to be truthful were in their own little world or so it seemed. As the afternoon drew to a close, Jay threw a towel over her and with a look of contentment and said;

"I think it's time we made a move back to the hotel to change as I'm taking you dancing tonight".

"Dancing, how do you know I can dance" was her reply being a little flabbergasted at such a comment.

"Well if you can't, then I'll have to teach you, so no arguments there" he answered laughing.

"There's a lovely little place I know which is set on the sea front, in Larnaca the food is superb and we can enjoy the music as a local band plays, I think you'll like it, in fact I'm sure you'll like it" he said in a rather commanding voice.

Standing up after that comment, Corry seemed to lose her footing whereby the towel happened to drop on the sands, but before she could attempt to grab it, Jay had it in his hands to save her modesty, but with a roving eye he also noticed just what beautiful legs she had. Legs that he would never forget in a hurry, as coming to his senses quickly before handing over the towel while saying;

"Put it in your bag and we'll call for some strawberries on the way back seen as you've such a passion for them".

Oh this man really knew how to treat a lady Corry thought, this was obviously his upbringing whereby men were always in charge but having said that, times were changing for the working class as a new generation were coming up and women were now making the decisions, but for the time being she was on holiday and with the breeze on her face as they drove back to the hotel, her thoughts were on other things and it wasn't strawberries I can assure you.

It was just after five thirty when they finally reached the hotel and seemingly a little busier than it'd been the previous evening at that time, must be bingo night she laughed to herself;

"Don't forget your swimming gear, you'll need to dry it out for tomorrow as I think we'll go somewhere a little different where maybe the sea will be calmer", he stated as though something had already been arranged that she knew nothing of.

"Oh" she replied, a little taken back at what he'd said, "We will, will we, now that's news to me", was the reply.

"Well you know what news is like, it travels fast, that fast, that sometimes you don't always pick it up, and don't forget that I'm picking you up at seven thirty on the dot, by the way, did I also mention, Rob will be taking Issa dancing tonight, so there's no need for you to worry about her".

What more could she say to that as in less than 24 hours this man was taking over her life, although at the moment she wasn't complaining as she was a little smitten by him already. Arriving at her room to be met by what you would only call a commotion, she heard Issa shouting at the top of her voice;

"Come out onto the balcony, I've something to tell you",

Now what was so important that all the building had to overhear, Corry thought? But it wasn't long before she was to find out for Issa sounded as though she'd explode with the impatience she was portraying, therefore it was the balcony as her first stop before anything else;

"Rob's taking me to Larnaca; apparently it's a port a few miles away and the saying goes, it's pretty lively at nights with restaurants and dancing on the sea front", taking a few breaths before she dared to ask in a concerned tone thinking her friend may be upset at the arrangements that'd already been made

"Will you be alright with that"?

"No that's fine, Jay's already told me about the arrangements, apparently they'd been made earlier this morning, as were also going to Larnaca for a meal at a restaurant on the sea front that also has dancing" was the reply.

"Oh that'll be nice, I think you've got a soft spot for this Jay, I've seen the way you look at him, mind you, I have to admit he is handsome, maybe not as handsome as my Rob but there you go, you can't have everything can you" she laughed.

Corry never replied to that comment, as Issa carried on mumbling to herself, adding;

"Were going to some big fish restaurant up by the market, it's supposed to be very nice or so Rob recons, but will let you know what I think tomorrow as never been a big fish lover".

The shower was quite cool on Corry's warm body as the water trickled down to the shower base, you could see the bronzing tan starting to take on a glow of radiance over her silky soft skin, now a couple more days like today and she'd be really dark for having an olive complexion, she caught the sun quite quickly, in fact some would say she'd that foreign look about her after returning from holiday.

Yes, she thought, that was quite refreshing as she stepped out of the shower, but all the same she'd have to get a move on to be ready to be picked up on time.
Now came the hard bit as to what she was to wear that evening and so with a quick glance in the wardrobe Corry chose one of her favourite outfits, taking it off the hanger she admired the pure white soft satin cotton which was such a simple design, shoe string straps that would hang over her tiny shoulders, the bodice clinging softly to her firm breast and floating down past her tiny waistline, the skirt with just enough material in it that if she swirled around, you would just about see her thighs together with her firm shapely legs which had a tan from the glow of the sun that'd already caught her that day.

A white and silver pair of high heels with clutch bag to match finishing the outfit off perfectly and with an afterthought she reached into the bedside drawer to pull out the briefest of white knickers, slipping them on while adding the palest of lipstick to her face, she was now ready to eat and party the night away to her heart's content.

Just like all servicemen, both Jay and Rob were waiting downstairs with military precision for their girls to arrive. Firstly, to approach was Issa, dressed all in white that showed off the tan she'd managed to get that afternoon, a silk top you had to look twice at as it showed the shape of her nipples slightly caressed against the sheer material.

The pure chiffon skirt that complimented her tiny waist, hanging tightly onto her neatly tight bottom, finishing off the outfit with high heels and an envelope purse; she definitely looked the part of a top model in anyone's eyes. Corry followed shortly behind not wanting to make a grand entrance as that was how she was; a little shy at times until coming out of her shell but when she did, there was no stopping her. Approaching as Jay grabbed her hand and whispered;

"You look gorgeous even good enough to eat but then I'll leave that until later" he said laughing with a cheeky smile.

It had been decided beforehand they'd all go down into Larnaca by taxi with no drinking and driving as that would be the most sensible thing to do if they were to have a good night. The taxi was already awaiting as they strolled out of the hotel although Corry looked a bit bewildered at this but never said anything, Jay on the other hand picked up on this straight away and stated;

"It's alright, were going to leave those two when we arrive down town as the restaurant they're going to, is at the other side of the port from ours".

"Not a problem" Corry replied with a sheepish look.

Larnaca was only a few miles down the road therefore it wasn't long before arriving, the breeze now coming up and swirling around Corry's shoulders as she got out of the taxi first but still this didn't bother her as it was a warm pleasant breeze that drifted towards her. The restaurant, set back on the sea front had low lights, romantic music, with a warm scented aroma which came drifting through the air when sat at a table that had been reserved especially for them, yes, Jay had thought of everything to impress she thought.

How romantic could you get, this is what story books write about although you'd never dream of experiencing it yourself. Am I dreaming Corry thought, dining with this romantic, attractive man who seemed to have everything at his fingertips and yet when he spoke, people just looked, smiled and seemed to obey his wishes without question, with an awareness of his authority or was it because he was an officer in the British Army? Whatever the answer was Corry was certainly putty in his hands so to speak.

Dressed in a nice cream pair of designer slacks, shirt to match with tan shoes he looked every part of the officer and gentleman that he was. The meal again, was superb as they glanced over at each other all through the evening, their eyes rarely leaving one another, hands slowly crossing the table every now and again to make a little gesture to each other, what had this man got that was drawing Corry into what seemed to be a spider's web.

They laughed, flirted and gently kissed as the coffee arrived, the restaurant by now was quite full with lots of the diners having finished their meal was getting up to dance to the slow romantic sounds that filled the air. When all of a sudden Jay stood up, grabbed Corry's hand pulling her towards him with all the intentions of a man in charge, leading her to the dance floor, she in astonishment just followed with not a word to be spoken to his silent command.

It was when Jay wrapped his arm around her waist, she'd such a comforting feeling inside with just a little giddiness on the side, here she was dancing with what anyone could imagine to be the man of their dreams as he draws her closer and closer to his body, and what a body for the firm torso was in such good shape, being a keep fit junkie who worked out almost daily.

The music soft and gentle even though it was a little groovy, yes Johnny Mathis could put anyone in a romantic mood she thought but this wasn't the music that was making her heart skip a beat, for she'd have to admit it was something a lot stronger than that, so strong her stomach was churning with a feeling that excited her whole being.

They seemed to dance the night away only stopping to visit the bar on occasions while the night had a mood of its own although the wine didn't hinder the situation for Corry wasn't really used to drinking, only the odd glass of wine.

Coming up to 2am, the night was still young, and with romance in the air, whatever could two young lovers do in those circumstances but with a suggestion of leaving the restaurant and maybe walk along the sea front for a little fresh air. Walking for little while hand in hand, seemed to be heaven, as the soft breeze filled the night air caressing the aroma of nearby flowers that was caught in the night, a magical moment in all lovers' eyes where their thoughts were of a distant gaze into a time beyond the future.

A time that was passing and yet stood still with the cooler air drifting across the seafront, for these two lovers wouldn't notice as by now their bodies were on fire for each other. A fire that was erupting so fast and yet not a word to be spoken before grabbing her arm, swinging her round full circle as she landed in his arms for that one awaiting kiss that would seal the evening.

Well when I say a kiss maybe that was an underestimation for there was a few more to follow as the fire had now started to burn in both of their bodies to a tune of excitement that wasn't going to be dampened, which left only one conclusion and that was to return to the hotel where the bar would be open for residents and drinks would be served all night long or was that a song that came to mind as a taxi was called for their return journey.

The journey back was quite rewarding for the taxi driver, as at this time of night his passengers were usually rowdy to the point that when he reached their destination, he knew the words to the song they'd been singing all night with maybe a few words that didn't even fit the melody and so looking in the mirror at this young couple was a pleasure to see the holding of their hands and a little kiss from time to time.

Entering the hotel reception, which to be honest was quite busy seen as it was early hours of the morning when everyone should have been in bed and although it'd been a long day, never the less both of them weren't in the least bit tired, quite the opposite as you could imagine, as Jay stepped up to the bar and asked for a couple of vodka's with a splash of tonic to round off a wonderful evening with even more wonderful company as he put it. With the drink in one hand as he reached out for Corry's hand with the other he asked;

"You did enjoy yourself didn't you" with an authoritarian voice that Corry had now come to accept as his manner.

"I don't think you need to ask that question do you?" was the reply.

And so, with the vodka barely touching the sides of her throat as she knocked it back in one large gulp, which left a burning sensation going down at such a speed, she stood up.

"Won't be long, little girls room needed urgently".

Watching Corry, a little unsteady on her feet as she returned, and being a gentleman, he walked towards her with an outstretched hand so she wouldn't slip, for if she'd lost her balance in those heels she definitely would have woke in the morning with a few more bruises she'd got when leaving the hotel for the night, as he whispered gently;

"You, young lady, are going to bed and I am taking you" not realizing just what he'd said, but to that statement, no argument was entered as they both walked into the lift.

Knowing full well she wasn't in any fit state to probably find her room, his arm wrapped around her shoulder with a gaze that told a thousand words. It was now a matter of seconds before the lift arrived at her floor, both walking to Corry's room, sliding the card into the security lock while opening the door, still unaware as to what was going to happen between them as the door closed silently behind them.

Jay's intentions at that stage was to undress Corry, putting her to bed knowing she wasn't in any fit state to attempt anything else, but you would be surprised how quickly a mood can change when a situation like that arises for as he started to undress her, she came to life with a look in her eyes that something inside of her body was smouldering for more than the tender touch of the man she'd been with all that evening. Reading the signs as he looked into her eyes was something you would never repeat coming from a lady when grabbing her shoulder, he proceeded to push her onto the neatly laid out bed, whispering;

"I've wanted to do this all night, you just don't realise how much you turn me on, the way you look, the way you smile, the softness of your beautiful hair, the smell of your skin, your body that came close to mine this evening and last but not least the clothes that's coming off".

To this Corry just laid there in total shock, not knowing if this was real or was she dreaming, as he knelt down to remove her shoes throwing them onto the floor beside him, and with a firm grip of her ankles pulled her somewhat further towards him. It was now that she started to gather her senses and asked rather stupidly,

"What the hell are you doing to me?"

"Patience is a virtue my dear, just stop talking and you'll no doubt find out, in good time" he replied.

But before she could get any further, Jay's left hand had shot up to remove her skimpy undies which by now was quite damp with excitement, his right hand just as quick when it shot up between her legs, parting them on the way and thrusting two fingers up inside of her with such force that she screamed out with both pain and excitement;

"Are you alright" he whispered with a tender loving gesture.

"Yes, fine, it just caught me by surprise" she smirked looking longingly into his eyes.
"It was no surprise to me, as I've wanted you since the first time I saw you in that bar last night," he replied with a fixation of what was coming next.

Pulling his fingers out of her gently, taking them up to his lips with a kiss; "That's exactly what I thought, a sweet wet pussy waiting for me to stroke it".

Corry was shocked at this statement, for she'd never heard a man talk to her or anyone else in that manner, maybe that was because he was an Army man who working with men all the time, used that kind of language, but all the same it did turn her on as she'd have to admit, when a thrill ran through her body.

Standing up, as he stared down at Corry's body with such a hunger in his eyes, she on the other hand couldn't understand what was going on in his mind for she'd never met anyone like this before.

Firstly, kicking off his shoes, then the shirt and lastly dropping his slacks to the floor, with not a stitch of underwear to be seen as he stood naked in front of her, with a large erection being highlighted with the glow of the moonlight shining through the window;

"Don't worry about marking your beautiful dress, as that's now coming off", he added looking down at her sleek tanned body with a growing desire for satisfaction.

By now Corry was quite calm as all the effects of the drink had dwindled from her body completely; she'd never experienced anything like this before and the excitement that ran through her was uncontrollable. Glancing down at her momentarily, he then bent over, tugging at the dress which slid over the shoulder, throwing it onto the floor, slowly moving towards her lips, brushing them with a slight kiss, at the same time his tongue reaching into her soft warm mouth. No, he wasn't shy at this point she thought enjoying every moment with anticipation for the next move to come as he moved down her body biting her skin on the way, his hand firmly on her, so she could hardly move.

Reaching her mound of thick pubic hair, he pushed her legs wide apart, working his tongue into her clitoris, his teeth now circling the same as he'd gently bite now and again.to experience a sensation which would run wild through both their bodies;

"Oh my God" she cried out loud,

"Am I hurting you yet" he asked.

"Not sure but I'm getting some kind of ache from it "she muttered.

That's fine he thought as that will soften the pain that she'll experience when I enter as she's rather tight for me.

Struggling at this stage, and with an erection that was throbbing Jay didn't know how long he could master his control, realising he was being a bit rough with her, but it'd been a while since he had sex and his body was now going into overdrive with such a huge throbbing member that was positioned between his legs. Corry on the other hand never noticed that he'd slid his hand onto the floor and reached for a sheath from his trouser pocket, for she was now in oblivion. When all of a sudden he stood up both in statue and with such a huge erection, pulled the sheath over his penis, and entered her with such a mighty strength taking her breath away, this was quite painful at this point for her but enjoyable at the same time even though he was a little rough.

Having a small frame, she was built quite tiny inside and therefore his enjoyment was mounting very quickly with every stroke he took to combat his eagerness.

I must make her come now before I explode he thought so without any hesitation he pulled out, and grabbing her by the hips, spun her around like a rag doll before entering her from behind, grasping her clitoris with his finger and with such a movement he knew he would make her come as he thrust into her repeatedly knowing they would come together as the final scream of delight would explode for both.

Standing up, Jay looked down at Corry with an apology of;

"Sorry, I was a little rough but it's been a while and I don't know what came over me, it's alright because I'll be far gentler with you tomorrow night, I promise".

With no hesitation, he then dressed, kissed her, started to walk to the door and with an afterthought, turned round and said;

"Be ready in the morning and I'll pick you up at around 11am, I'm taking you up Mount Troodos, think you'll like it up there, it's totally different to the coastal area and you can look down over the island, the fresh air will do you the world of good and make you sleep tomorrow night. Got it all planned so don't worry about anything, we'll stop on the way for a little lunch, be back in time for a shower and then out again tomorrow night, so be ready" he commanded.

Corry couldn't believe what was happening, who does this man think he is, see me tomorrow, I haven't agreed to anything she thought, but still the words wouldn't come out of her mouth as he left.

Oh what the hell she thought as she walked into the bathroom for a shower, teeth cleaned, and finally bed, what's another day, it may be quite interesting and would also have to admit the sex was maybe a little rough but all the same was quite enjoyable. As her head touched the pillow in those early hours, her mind was wondering in some far land until falling asleep, and sleep she did as total exhaustion engulfed her body.

DAY 3

The morning mist with a new fresh day on the horizon as both Issa and Corry awoke, and with the sun slowly appearing from the clouds but still the mist of the morning dew was in the air, with windows wide open as they both sauntered out onto their individual balconies, a coffee in their hands, each starting to swap stories of what happened the night before.

Issa, on one hand had danced the night away with her and Rob hitting the town's bars in all directions, yes, one of those nights although they didn't have much to drink and what they had, wore off with all the dancing they did, although couldn't remember what time they'd got back to the hotel but it was about two in the morning she thought;

"Rob is quite the gentleman you know, he never tried it on at all, well not really, only his hand would wonder a little but that's men for you isn't" Issa commented",

"That's good, but don't forget to take precautions if you do" Corry reminded her.

"Oh by the way, will it be alright if I spend the rest of the week with Rob as he wants to take me all over the island in his car, and did say something about Jay would be spending the same with you.
I told him I'd consult you before I made a decision as it was only fair, but I do like him and he is such good fun to be with".

"No that's alright, you go off and enjoy yourselves, but remember what I said about protection should it get that far, we don't want you pregnant when you've become such a big star back home do we". Corry said smiling.

" Yes I know, you keep telling me and to be honest I've got something in my bag for that occasion should it arise" was the answer to that smirking all over her pretty little face.

They both talked for a couple of hours before going down to catch a little breakfast, little breakfast Corry thought, now that wasn't true where Issa was concerned as she could eat for England and then some, but never put an ounce of weight on. Breakfast for Corry was just a couple of poached eggs on toast with orange juice and a coffee, Issa, well she finished off the cereal, a full English breakfast extra toast, marmalade, fresh juice, coffee and croissants, where on earth she puts it heaven knows as knowing her the way we do, she'll be starving in a couple of hours.

Breakfast over as they both walked back to their rooms wondering what they'd wear, something simple like a pair of jeans and a warm jacket as it had been mentioned the night before about Mount Troodos being cold when you reached the top, even in the summer months.

Remembering what Jay had also told her the night before about taking something fancy in which to change into as he had arranged an evening meal, and getting back would be late or not at all, he added, so if need be, he would arrange accommodation for them both.

On time as usual both Jay and Rob arrived within minutes of each other to collect the girls, both setting off in different directions as they had the day before. Corry having the last word as they departed, shouting out to Rob;

"Be careful how you drive and take care of her as she's to be back at work next week in one piece."

Driving up along the winding roads to the mountain was an experience, and to say it was beautiful was an understatement, passing through the little villages as they went along, Corry couldn't believe her eyes how quant it all was, stopping for the occasional fresh coffee, the scenery was so breath-taking that she couldn't take it all in at once, even the local people was so pleasant with time to spare for strangers. Having come to one small village, Jay pulled up and proceeded to get out of the car, walking round to her side, opened the door, put out his hand in such a gentle way while saying;

"Now there is something special I want to show you down this street."

To Corry there wasn't anything she could see out of the ordinary, so what on earth was it she thought, but as they eventually reached the end of the street. There stood a little house, door open, with a chatter of young voices and as they entered, Corry was taken back, for there were about nine or ten young boys all working wildly with what seemed like tweezers in their hands;

"What on earth are they doing, I can't make it out for the life of me" Corry asked.

"They're making fine jewellery out of gold wire and it's called Filigree," he explained.

"But they're only young boys "she stated in astonishment.

"Yes that's right, but the works are so precise and concentrated, that when they reach the age of fourteen their eyes aren't as strong and therefore can't manage the delicate work".

Glancing down, Corry picked up a few pieces of the jewellery to admire and especially one piece that took her eye; this was such a simple but delicate broach in the shape of a rose.

"Oh this is beautiful and so delicate; I've never seen anything as lovely as this",

"Now come on, put it down and let's get off as we'll be here all day" Jay commanded.
Oh that's men all over she thought as she walked back down the street towards the car.

"Oh my God, I've dropped the car keys in that house, you head back to the car and I'll fetch them, sorry about that." Jay said rather apologetic.

It didn't take long before they were driving away, Corry not giving it another thought as she was more interested in all the lovely little houses and how friendly the people were.

Troodos was a beautiful surprise and to her amazement some parts of the mountain even had snow, but what she didn't realise was up near the top, a ski resort which had been built by the British Army, proudly portrayed by the Royal Engineers skills.
Drawing closer to the top of the mountain she started feeling a little cold and breathless therefore asking Jay to stop the car so as to change into her jeans and jacket. Well to this he couldn't resist the fact that he'd told her previously it would be rather cold when they reached the top, oh boy was he smug at times she thought. Not saying too much at that stage as she also had a headache coming on which was unusual for her as she wasn't prone to headaches.

Glancing over he noticed Corry wasn't looking too good at that stage and said in a comforting gesture;

"Look, think we'd better start down the mountain as you look pretty grey to me, it's alright as mountain air affects some people that way, it's the altitude up here and the air is so thin but nothing to worry about, you'll be ok when we reach the bottom again ".

The rest of the day was filled with walking further down the mountain, calling for a little lunch and generally exploring, they talked, laughed about silly little things, he picked flowers for her, she chased him over the rocks and before they knew it, the sun started to drop with a warm breeze coming in as they descended to the bottom of Troodos;
"Now what we're going to do, is call at a friend of mines villa, take a shower, dress for dinner, and head off to a nice restaurant that I know."

"Sounds great, but what will your friend thinks, about us turning up at his place with such short notice "was the reply.

"Oh don't worry your pretty little head about that as he won't be bothered due to him being back in England on home leave and there again, I've got the keys to the villa when he goes away."

He'd definitely thought of everything she muttered to herself. It didn't take long before they'd both showered, dressed and heading for the local restaurant which incidentally had been booked in advance to Corry's surprise; this man was so cock sure of himself she thought.

Leaving the car at his friends, where they would walk down to the restaurant it being such a lovely night and to be honest it was only a stone's throw away so wouldn't be a problem in getting a taxi back if need be as again unbeknown to Corry, it had been pre-arranged with his friend that they would stay the night in one of the four spare bedrooms. The restaurant was set in a little bay down by the waterfront with the smell of exotic perfume arising from the flowers drifting down from the trees set back amongst the white painted houses situated in the back streets, these being what the local people lived in. It was really quant and peaceful with nothing but the sound of the sea lapping onto the shore giving such a romantic feeling in the air;

"Now I've been here many times and the foods outstanding, but really you must try the lamb and goat's cheese as it's the best on the island, this restaurant is renowned for this dish "Jay commented.

Corry looked and thought to herself, is there anywhere this man hasn't been, but as usual he was right so what more could be said. What a romantic night, as they both talked all night about silly little things in both of their childhoods, also touching on things about families but not to the extent of parents for some unknown reason, it had been discovered that Jay was an only child, attended boarding school then going onto university where he made up his mind that an army career was the life for him travelling the world with nothing to tie him down.

Corry at this stage got the impression that he'd got all his own way, being spoilt into the bargain, which obviously he had. She also gathered that he'd been telling the truth about not having a girlfriend or wife in the background, but all the same was a ladies' man at heart, that could pull them whenever he wanted getting his own way with an attitude of love them and leave them into the bargain, for surprising how quickly you can sum up someone after a few drinks.

Jay on the other hand, assumed that Corry had a basic education, worked from leaving school very hard to achieve her way in life, being from the north of England and was very close to her family with the only living relatives being a brother and grandparents but that was only an assumption as she never came out and said it to be factual.

He did however wrongly presume she worked in a little shop or department store now as she mentioned fashion quite frequently but never delved too deeply, as to be truthful they mixed in different circles and he was a bit of a snob if all facts were known.

As the candles across the table in the restaurant flickered as the night set in with a full moon glowing out across the water, their eyes meeting now and again with such wantonness for each other. Their relaxed mind and bodies slowly being taken over with the wine gently flowing, no not merry but just a warm soothing feeling they both experienced, it was as though they had been friends forever talking the night away, both comfortable with each other as their body language showed to any outsider that saw them.

Another night of wonderful food and company what more could she have asked for, if Issa had enjoyed her day as much as she had then this was worth all the hard work they'd put in through the year Corry thought.

It was as Jay paid the bill, when she nipped into the little girl's room to add a little lipstick to her glowing face, standing in front of the mirror, she couldn't help but notice the little pale blue silk dress hung tightly to her figure showing off every curve, with a hint of tightness around the nipples, wondering whether that was the right thing to wear for the evening or was it far too sexy an outfit as Jay may get the wrong idea and she didn't want that at all. But then again this was only a second thought due to the alcohol they'd both consumed, for it didn't really matter as the night was young and awaiting surprises of another encounter.

Leaving the restaurant hand in hand, the moon shone down as though lightening the way for a special kind of love that night, the stars twinkled in the sky as though dancing to the mood that was between their excitements of each other. It wasn't too far from the restaurant, so it made sense to carry the mood on and walk slowly back to the villa talking about anything that came to mind.

While laughing like crazy teenagers as they walked along, not even knowing what they were laughing about at times, the mood was in such high spirits so they'd not got a care in the world at that point, it was just one of those crazy nights when everything went to plan and in the mood of teenagers with no thoughts for what would come next, as that's what they felt like, teenagers.

It was upon Reaching the villa, Corry enquired as to what the sleeping arrangements would be for the night;

"Oh don't worry your pretty little head about them" Jay assured her putting the key in the door to welcome his lady in.

Locking the door behind him, taking her hand, heading in the direction of the large bedroom in which he used when staying with his friend, slowly guiding her to the king sized bed, seating her comfortably as he walked towards the veranda doors flinging them open to let the warm breeze ventilate the room, walking back as he kicked off his shoes, removed his trousers and shirt and then carefully placed them on a chair at the side of the wardrobe, leaving Corry sat on the side of the bed being rather bewildered while doing all this which only seemed to take a few minutes anyway;

"Now young lady, I'm about to disrobe you out of that sensual fitting dress that's been teasing me all night when your nipples were sliding up and down the silk, do you realise what effect they gave between my legs, I could hardly stop myself from coming all over them, so now you're going to pay for that" he stated with such a sweet grin at the side of his mouth.

Pulling Corry up from the bed while lifting the dress up over her body, which then revealed the tight breasts that were glowing in the moonlight, as he proceeded to carefully slide the dress over to the chair, placing it on top of his clothing which was what all soldiers were trained to do with pride of their appearance. Standing back he could see the wonders of her body, slim with neatly arranged breast and tight nipples, with her smooth tanned legs, starting

from the high heeled shoes up to the mound of pubic hair which was covered with the smallest of under wear.
Now moving forward, encircling his hand around her back, and gently guiding her down to the bed, pushing her legs over onto the sheet while removing her shoes with expert prosaicism;

"I hope this isn't going to be like last night whereby you were like a bull in a china shop" Corry asked?

"Not at all, tonight I'm about to make love like you have never been made love to before, with all the passion I can possibly give" he replied.

All of a sudden Jay left the room while Corry in a world of her own just lay there thinking what the hell now, but it was only a brief moment before he returned with a bottle of champagne, two glasses and an ice cooler, romantic she thought, well get on with it, yes, the Yorkshire girl was definitely showing her spirit now.
Oh he wasn't going to spoil this night and rush as he'd done the night beforehand, no he was to make love to her as he'd promised, for he'd the experience to make all her dreams come true in that department.

Proceeding to pour the champagne into the glasses, handing one to her, taking a drink himself out of the other, "now drink that up" he ordered in a commanding voice.

Surprisingly, she did as she was told, putting the glass back down on the side table. Jay looked down at her with such a longing in his eyes as he moved beside her, his fingers running up and down her body with softness of a feather, turning towards her face, the look in his eyes was of a distant feeling but still she couldn't read his thoughts as he pulled her towards him kissing her slightly on the lips, then his tongue rolling up to her ear, around the neck as the shivers shot through her body at maximum speed. And as they lay there just gazing at each other for a while, Corry wishing she could read his thoughts, but there were no inclination as to how he was feeling, before turning her body to press slightly on to his, but it was still a thoughtless look on his face as though he was in another world, wrapping his arm around her pulling tighter into his body with a warmth building up inside of them both although still no emotion showing, just a faint glow, no reaction that you would expect in that situation.

Had he been hurt in the past she wondered, maybe he was one of those people who were cold and yet everything about him showed how hot blooded and thoughtful he was in other ways. When all of a sudden he caught hold of her face, looked deeply into her eyes and kissed her so tightly she thought she'd never come up for air. What brought that on she wondered as her fingernails slid down to the arch of his back, whereby he shuddered, and then braking away started to kiss the back of her neck, moving his tongue to her tightly formed breasts, while biting the nipples with tenderness;

"You like that don't you" he asked,

But no reply was forthcoming as she was enjoying the moment with thoughts still running through her mind of the night before. She couldn't understand just how gentle he was tonight; very different to how he'd been previously.

But by now Corry was so excited with the touch of him on her nipples, the thrill racing through her body was picking up at such speed, he could feel the excitement as he sucked them so tightly but on the other hand with a firm and gentle touch, knowing the response she'd be experiencing the same, slowly he moved down her body kissing it all the way until he reached his main objective, clasping his teeth around her clitoris, he sucked to his heart's content as the fluids dripped from her heated body.

And although she tossed and withered with a desiring ache inside that was an unbearable pleasure, he'd stop now and again for a couple of seconds, knowing her body would calm down, only to resume the action yet again till she moaned with delight;

"Don't worry, I've no intentions of letting you come yet, I told you earlier you'd suffer for what you were putting me through in that dress, and suffer you will by the time the night's over "he stated

How on earth could she last at this pace as every time he sucked her dry, he would then move to her clitoris and entwine his tongue round it bringing her into spasms yet again, driving her insane with feelings she'd never experienced before, taking her to heights she didn't know existed although wanting him to pause but all the same praying he wouldn't. Yes, she had to do something to calm these feeling down or she'd explode, when all of a sudden he paused, moved his head to one side to nibble the top of her leg, now this was her chance as she wrapped one leg around him into a simulated headlock thus moving him to the other side of the bed then slowly released her grip, twisted her body round and grabbed his thighs.

This was an opportunity to give her some leeway as what she intended, for now she was in control moving down his body with her lips kissing passionately against his tanned skin. Insight was the target she was heading for, an erection that would do any man proud, just standing to attention, waiting to be put down but with plenty of fight left to save the day.

Definitely inviting, and so pushing his legs apart with both hands, her tongue darted towards the tip of his penis, twirling round it slowly and then with her teeth gently caressing until taking one mighty suck to bring the whole of it within her mouth.

Now it was her time to suck quite gently to start with and then stop altogether, but to his astonishment he pleaded for her to carry on, this had never happened before as he'd always been in charge so to speak, this carried on for a while as his plea's got louder and louder but then she wasn't having any of this, ignoring them altogether.

Moving her head up his body, spreading her legs apart while positioning herself on top of this almighty stallion, then taking him fully into her awaiting body as she rode him like a thorough bred, galloping at the start while eventually picking up speed until he could no longer hang on; the race was coming to its final finish as he screamed;

"Give it to me baby with all that you've got, just give it to me".

And as a good little girl, she obeyed his every wish as he came with such an almighty finish but with her as the winner to collect the trophy.

"Oh boy, you really did excel yourself there didn't you? He said, to which she ignored the comment rolling over and falling to asleep in his arms.

DAY 4
There was nothing like a hearty breakfast in the morning to get the adrenalin flowing and with talk of what they would do for the rest of the day.

After a little discussion although it was a one sided discussion on Jay's part, they would just chill out on the beach in the morning after finishing breakfast, a little light lunch when the sun came up to its highest, and maybe have a drive into Nicosia later

Now Nicosia was the capital of Cyprus and therefore contained a lot of history which was not only fascinating but very interesting as the island was now split in two halves. One side was occupied by Greek Cypriots while the other was occupied by Turkish Cypriots, as they couldn't get on politically, this wasn't the reasoning of local people but as usual, governments have different issues which therefore affect the lives of all those around. I'm afraid there had to be a dividing border which was guarded by the United Nations at that time, this was all so sad, as it was such a beautiful island and one of great history, splitting many close ties between family and friends

Yes, Nicosia was all that she'd expected, steeped in history, architecture and the grandest fashion shops, shops which Corry found interesting due to her mind never being very far away from her profession but all the same trying not to bring work into the conversation. Wondering around the city she sensed a little sadness as on nearly all the streets, soldiers were keeping a watchful eye fear trouble broke out but there again, they were doing their job to make the city safe for all those that lived there.

Everything fell into place as they planned that day, a little sea, sun and sand, lunch with a trip to Nicosia which they really enjoyed, it felt so relaxed in each other's company, and it was as though they'd known each other for years instead of days. Like two lovers, holding hands, chasing each other down streets in somewhat of a playful manner, even sharing a large drink with two straws, this was a side that no one had ever seen in Jay, they were just two happy people who were enjoying each other's company; like you read in fairy stories.

But it was upon the return from Nicosia; Jay thought he would show Corry the Sovereign Base at Dhekelia where he was stationed. Now this was situated on the sea front and with a view that you could only describe as being in a magazine, a large garrison that the army occupied on the island but to her it looked as though it was a small town, not knowing anything about the forces and how things were.

It was as you approached the entrance to the garrison, Jay pointed out a couple of very large buildings, these housed some of the single soldiers he informed her giving an insight to his occupation of a senior ranking officer. On the opposite side, a small road which led off down to a beautiful private cove where the shallow water was of a lovely shade of green, this again was for the use of service personnel and their families, and overlooking this cove stood an estate of what you would call typical English houses that service personnel and their families occupied.

What amazed Corry, was not only a brand new school but a very large hospital which took pride of place at the very top of the hill, this stood so tall, that should you reach the top of it, you would be able to see Turkey over the water on a clear day. It was just like having your own personal guide in Jay as he drove around pointing out what everything was and with that he finished off by saying;

"We'll now head back for your hotel as you've been shown the grand tour of where I live and work that is".

"Oh I forgot to tell you, we're going to a big dinner and dance in the officer's mess tomorrow night, and don't worry if you haven't anything to wear, I've arranged with a little boutique that I know in Larnaca to fit you out with a new dress and again, no arguments, understand".

Somewhat shocked at what he'd said, she just replied "yes, fine, whatever".

The garrison wasn't far from Corry's hotel and so with that, it didn't take them long before they reached it but as he pulled up outside of the main entrance he added;

"Right get out, go and freshen up and I'll pick you up 7pm as usual, we'll drive along the coast road and find a nice place to eat, nothing elaborates just nice".

Who the hell was this man who'd just walked into my life, turned it upside down, giving me orders as though he was the boss, here I am on holiday for a rest after such a tremendous season with my first ever successful fashion show, which is more than I could have ever dreamed of, and yet I'm letting him tell me what to do, Corry thought.

Being aware he didn't know anything about her personal life or that she had her own company and that is how she wanted to keep it, just as she didn't know his circumstances either, but for some reason it seemed she was now

succumbing to his every wish, not even putting an argument up, as she usually did with other people, being an independent woman that had to fight for what she wanted.
What was happening to her she thought as this wasn't like her at all, she was so independent in every way and had been for years, well it was only a couple more days before leaving the island and hated to admit, it was an enjoyable attention she was getting so would go with the flow.

Walking past the reception Corry noticed Issa's key still behind the desk, her lovely friend had actually found a boyfriend who would love her for who she really was not only good on the outside but also on the inside which was rare and the only worry was, she wouldn't get hurt for Rob seemed such a good man with true feelings and that's what she deserved, being quite smitten with him as he was with her from the very first moment they met.

Corry had always told her that if she met someone she cared about then to be open and tell him the truth of her background as it would only catch up with her in the end and surprisingly enough Issa had done that already being quite confident in the man she'd met therefore told him on their second date which he accepted not having had such a good childhood himself being put up for adoption at an early age. And with this the two bonded in a unity that would flourish in time bringing happiness on both sides.

Entering the lift, there seemed to be a funny sound coming from somewhere, but as other things were on her mind Corry never took too much notice, as all she wanted to do was shower, nice little dress on, do her hair and be ready for the evening out with Jay as no doubt he would be on time as usually she thought.

The shower, being just at the right temperature as it hit her hot sweaty body, washing the grime and tiny bits of sand from her while leaving a glowing tan that by now was starting to build up to a deep bronze. No, she'd not got too long before Jay was picking her up, so had to get a move on.

A little red number she thought, yes a sleek silk bright red dress that clung to her body like a second skin, red knickers and shoes to match was the outfit of the evening. Her long flowing hair dangling over one shoulder down the back and in a mass of natural curls as it dried in the warmth of the air, big round sparkle earrings with a bangle to match made the outfit, just stunning to say the least, upon completion.

Still no sign of Issa, so with that, she scribbled a little note, pushing it under her door as she passed on the way out, going down the lift to meet Jay she noticed it was still making that funny sound that it made when she first came up, but it was maybe a bit of sand that had got in one of the cogs making it sound worse than it really was she thought. No, she wasn't wrong about Jay, for as she walked through the reception, there he was waiting impatiently;

"Come on you, or we'll be late, I've booked a table down the road at a little restaurant, seen as it isn't very far away, I thought we'd walk and maybe after something to eat, can take a stroll along the front for a nice steady walk back, Oh by the way, you look absolutely ravishing tonight my dear" he added.

"Why thank you, kind Sir, you don't look too bad yourself" she replied in jest.

As the man had stated, a little restaurant down the road it was, this being just a short walk away, and a small charming white building which was lit up with pretty blue lights.

Approaching, you could smell the most beautiful aroma, a cross between honeysuckles and jasmine, it almost sent you in to a sensual mood, and that was before the evening had begun. What was it about the perfume smells on this little Island Corry thought, and then she remembered, this was the island of Aphrodite's the Goddess of love, maybe that was it. Never the less it really set the scene for the oncoming evening and that's all that mattered for she was slowly to expect all of these things when being with Jay as he loved all the little details that made the night a night to remember;

"A seat by the window, so that you can gaze onto the waves flowing in from the sea" the waiter had said in a quiet voice as he guided them to a table.

"Yes that would be fine" Jay replied with such a commanding voice.
"Oh by the way, we'll both be having the special fish dinner tonight" he requested as they took their seats by the open window, overlooking the moonlight casting a shadow down over the deep blue sea in the bay.

Here we go again Corry thought, he's ordering for me without even asking if I'd like to choose my own, just who does he thinks he is, but still no words came out to argue and so just let it go as she had on previous occasions now.

The meal came and Corry would have to admit the fish was superb and couldn't fault it at all, again Jay was right but she hated to admit it. Even for the sweet, he'd taken over and ordered fresh strawberries with fruit sauce, ice cream, fresh coffee, and a liquor which went down nicely.

Well as all good things must end they thought, leaving the restaurant after such a beautiful night out, but then it wasn't to end entirely as they strode along the beach road. Such a romantic setting as the moon shone down over the sea, you could hear the waves splashing against the rocks as the tide hit the shores.

The night was so tranquil, little stars shooting above, which looked as though dancing in the sky to heavenly music, the mood so peaceful there was nothing to be said between them but obviously there must have been some serious thoughts running through both their minds as every now and again Corry would catch a slight glimpse of Jay and a broad smile that came across his smooth lips that hid a mystery that she wasn't aware of

Only wishing she could read his mind, was he thinking of her or was his mind just a blank as he never gave anything away and when it came to romance, well he never let his feelings be shown to her at all. He was so cold and yet on the other hand was so hot blooded inside, no she could never work out the thoughts behind him, with nothing ever fazing him.

Having walked for about a mile or so, this being the long way back to the hotel, when all of a sudden they heard laughter coming from a little bar in the distance, only to decide that's where they were heading, as the music filled the distant air of the night. Well there was no doubt after that, and so to the bar it would be, where they'd join in with the frivolity of the evening, a few drinks and karaoke with the thoughts of only a short distance to walk back to the hotel being the intentions of finalising the evening

But to their surprise as they walked through the open door, it was great to see Issa and Rob both sat on the bar with microphones singing along to all the Elvis melodies.
I don't know about return to sender but it was thought they should have returned a long time ago for not only were they out of tune but for some reason the words had been changed as well, although it was rather doubtful if anyone would have realised with the amount of alcohol that was freely flowing and who cared anyway at that time of night.

The music loud, the alcohol giving out a merriment of the night, the singing well what could you say about that, other than it would have made a wonderful cats chorus in an alley but what the hell, these lads had been stuck in camp for months without leave and now letting off steam in a pleasant way, just who could blame them.

It wasn't until Jay approached the bar that Issa noticed them but even so with the attention that Rob was giving her it wasn't surprising as he watched every move she made, taking care of what he used to call his girl, but having said that, eventually Issa did make a bee line flinging her arms around Corry and in a slurring voice said;

"Do you know if it wasn't for my friend here I would be living on the streets of London now for having had nowhere to live she took me under her wing"?

To this Corry grabbed hold of Issa, and without any hesitation asked;

"Aren't we going to the toilet now", as Issa just looked bewildered but all the same followed as Corry led the way.

Now taking Issa on one side Corry warned her not to say anymore.

"Just keep quiet about our lives back home, we don't want anyone to know, we'll never see these people again and so what goes on in Cyprus stays in Cyprus "she added.

Issa now coming to her senses agreed with this and apologised adding in a tearful voice that she wouldn't say anymore on the subject where others could overhear.

Back in the bar no one was any the wiser that both girls had just been to the toilet and the banter just carried on until nearing 2am when Corry and Jay decided to return to the hotel, leaving Issa in Rob's safe custody.

The walk back to the hotel was a refreshing change to the rowdy noise the last couple of hours had been, just a simple cuddle and kiss along the way before Jay reminded her he would be going back to camp due to arrangements for the next morning adding;

"You haven't forgotten I'm taking you to the Ball in the Officers mess tomorrow night and will be returning to camp after I've seen you back to the hotel tonight have you?"

"No not at all she" replied rather sheepishly.

"Don't worry, I'm collecting you around lunchtime, taking you for a light lunch in the morning so you won't starve," he said laughing.

Again Corry thought, this man never ceased to amaze, having it all pre-planned out in advance without any thoughts of consulting her first.

Arriving back at the hotel, the lights dimmed, while the receptionist enjoyed a coffee break with the night porter when they both walked through the doors, it was fairly quite as you could imagine being 3am and therefore Jay would escort Corry to her room and with a good night kiss leave, being the gentleman he was or so it was assumed.

Quietly, they sauntered over to the lift, entered and pushed the button for Corry's floor when all of a sudden the lift started to shudder thus making such a noise that it was deafening, a large bang was then heard, as all of a sudden and without any hesitation Corry was thrown to the floor;

"Are you alright sweetheart", Jay asked being concerned should she be hurt.

"A little dazed but other than that I'm fine," she replied.

"Now come on, let's get you on your feet again, you look a little silly down there" he said as he tried to reassure her.

But as he went to help her up, his hand caught her dress accidentally knocking the strap down over one shoulder, and as it slipped further down her body, he caught sight of her heaving breast, the softness of the material made the dress slip even further until the fullness of her breast was revealed, for there in sight stood to attention was one nipple just begging for attention.

This he couldn't resist, taking one hand he gently lifted it up towards his mouth and taking one mighty suck of it with the tip of his teeth, to which Corry gave out such an expression of wanting desire. It looked as though they would be stuck in the lift for some time now he assumed as the sound of the lift breaking down had sent off the alarm notifying the reception desk, so he may as well make the most of the situation in hand he thought.

Yes, the movement of his lips and teeth had the desired effect alright as he pulled out the other breast, again the nipple standing to attention, waiting for the heat of his mouth to tease and suck like there was no tomorrow, knowing that when his hand moved down between her legs, she would be so wet, she would beg for him.

Right enough, as when his hand went down between her legs, he could feel her juices dripping down; pushing his two fingers up inside of her, it was like a running tap that couldn't be turned off. She was his girl alright he thought to himself as he then proceeded to push her to the back of the lift, while taking one hand, grabbing her thighs, pulling her towards him, kneeling as he sucked her clitoris as though he was going to swallow it.

The pain and excitement engrossed her body as she came with such a forceful moan, it was now time to finish what he'd started and so standing up undoing his trousers at the same time, swinging Corry around so she was facing the back of the lift, putting one hand on the back of her neck forcing her to bend at an angle and entered her from behind with such a passionate force that run wild inside of her heated body, while at the same time putting two fingers on her clitoris working the G spot as he hammered his full erection into her with the strength of a mad bull in a china shop.

"Don't worry baby you're going to come more than once as I haven't finished with you yet and then I'll suck you dry, knowing you're waiting for the pleasure of my tongue to give you the satisfaction to carry you over till tomorrow".

The more she came the bigger he felt inside of her until he just exploded with his own juices of the night. And as promised, he pulled out of her wet pussy, bent down between her legs and sucked her dry bringing on yet another orgasm, well she had to look presentable for when the lift started to move and they'd not that long to wait I can assure you for all of a sudden there was a large bang with the shudder of the lift cables, and before they knew it, there were a couple of engineers waiting for them as the doors opened;

"We are sorry for that sir, and do apologise for any inconvenience, is the lady alright." one of the engineers asked politely;

"Yes fine, and accidents do happen, things like that are beyond our control at times" Jay stated in an understanding tone, as they both departed from the lift to Corry's room.
"Well that's enough excitement for one night my darling, I'm sure you'll sleep well after it, see you, tomorrow

DAY 5
Still early and with sun belting down from the sky, it was definitely going to be one scorcher of a day, yes, she'd slept well as you can imagine after an explosive intimacy. But sleep wasn't her favourite pass time as four to five hours was maximum for her, after that she would just wake, shower, dress, snatching the odd coffee and toast for what she called breakfast and be off, so felt this was just like any other day, only difference was she was on holiday.

Coming up to 7am; as Corry sat out on the balcony drinking her second coffee of the morning when Issa appeared;

"Don't, worry" she said, "I've already made a large coffee for you together with a plate of toast, knowing you'd be starving as usual this time in the morning, I honestly don't know where you put it at times for you never stop eating and don't put an ounce of weight on".

Issa just smiled and thought, well yes that's right.

There was no need to move from the balcony for the sun now belting down on them as they talked about what they'd both been up to the last few days, when all of a sudden Corry came out with;

"Be careful Issa, I think you are getting far too close to Rob and we're going home in a couple of days, the path that you're taking will only end in tears, without a doubt, hoping against hope she was wrong but then again, for warned, is for armed so the saying goes.

"No don't worry, we're going to write to each other, he's coming home on leave at Christmas and we've arranged to spend time together, he's even told his mother about me", she replied.

"Just be careful, make sure that he wears protection, we don't want any little Rob's running around the workshop do we?" Corry said jokingly.

I think that's enough said on that subject Corry thought to herself as Issa was no fool, with what she'd been through these past few years. It wasn't long before they heard Rob knocking on the door to take Issa for a drive to the other side of the island;

"You don't mind us leaving you all alone do you" Rob asked in a courteous manner.

"Not at all" was the reply as Corry knowing it wouldn't be long before getting ready for lunch and snatching a couple of hours of sunbathing on the balcony;

"Look, just go and enjoy your selves" she said as they were already heading out of the door, while she herself was sprawled out in the sun for the next couple of hours.

Quick shower, pair of shorts, tee shirt, sandals and ready to go, just in time yet again as Jay walked up the corridor to meet her;

"Are you hungry as we're eating early due to the dinner and dance in the officer's mess tonight", he stated.

"I'll settle for a sandwich, ice cream and strawberries, together with a long cold drink", Corry replied.

"Well that's settled as that's what we'll both have", was the reply.

The lunch was just what the doctor ordered so to speak, light but tasty as they sat out on the patio of one of the local cafes, Corry finishing off the fresh strawberries that she seemed to be getting quite a liking for every day;

"Come on, let's stroll down to the bay at the bottom of the road as it's one of the best on the island, just everyone has heard of Fig tree bay, with it's clear blue waters and secluded white sand, people come for miles just to look out over the ocean from here", Jay said with pride in his voice.

And sure enough, it really was what he'd described; you could feel such a tranquil feeling in the air as you stood looking out over the sea she thought. The afternoon went quite quickly soaking up the sun, now and again they would take a walk along the sea front to cool off with bare feet in the cool waters which brought a relaxed feeling that both of them enjoyed; no pressure or time to worry about.

And with a slow walk back to the hotel, stopping only to look into one or two shops, as they went along, Corry buying a couple of presents for friends' back home with not having time to do any shopping since she arrived. The sun now at its highest peak and therefore a quite drink in the bar which they found quite busy when returning to the hotel, and so it was a couple of lagers on the terrace they settled for before Jay returned to camp knowing he was picking her up around 7pm. This giving her plenty of time to shower and dress, for what sounded like a boring evening, in Corry's opinion.

Having brought an arrangement of dresses, she'd have to study very carefully which one would make the best impression on these people, apparently it was rumoured that some of the higher rank's wives were said to be a bit toffee nosed and looked down on those whom in their opinion, didn't fit in.

This definitely wasn't going to happen tonight she thought, they may have their ball gowns but she also had a flair for something different as she would show them. In the end she chose a long slinky satin midnight blue dress that fit just about where it touched on her slim body, silver sandals, purse to match, her underwear of the night was a minute G string, and I mean minute, her long blond hair flowing, she looked absolutely stunning. It was when she came down through the reception area, everyone just turned around in amazement at the sight, with one commenting;

"Some lucky man that will be tonight my dear", yes a typical comment she thought laughing with a thought of, you don't know half.

Here was this man, approaching with such pride on his face that no one could doubt;

"You look outstanding" jay commented, "mind you always have, since the first night we met".

"No ordinary vehicle for you tonight, I'm afraid it's a staff car that awaits your pleasure he stated, don't worry about getting back as I've arranged you stay with me at one of my friend's houses as he's on home leave".

"You could have warned me before hand, then I'd have brought a nightdress" she answered.
"It's alright as you won't be needing one" he replied with a smirk all over his face looking straight at her body that left very little to the imagination.

It didn't take long before they arrived at the Officers mess, rather grand she thought, as they walked through the main entrance, with a feel of eyes watching every move, looking her up and down, as she overheard a comment of;
"Who on earth is that he's brought with him".

If this was anything to go by, she wasn't going to enjoy the night at all as in her opinion, they seemed quite aloof and stuck up snobs but she knew in her heart that wasn't going to deter as she'd beat far greater competition than that.

The meal was quite formal with Corry now getting to know a small amount of people who tried to make her feel a little more comfortable as the night went on although her first impression was right about them being snobs, never the less it was the reaction from the men that brought a smile to her face as they couldn't do enough to make her feel welcome. She was no fool, and knew she didn't fit in with these people but on the other hand also knew the dress she was wearing, was of course, catching everyone's eye, as not only was it a one off but it was also designed by herself.

Well it was either the dress or what was in it as she brushed all the negative thoughts to one side and with a positive reaction decided she going to enjoy this night as in a couple of days it would be back with her kind of people, never to see these snobs again.

As the night moved on and with all the champagne starting to relax, whereby in the end she would have to admit thoroughly enjoying herself. And It was when the last dance was announced that Jay swept her into his arms, that she realised just how close she was getting to him, her heart pounding, body weak, this was not a good sign as she'd never felt like this before and to be honest, didn't know how to handle the situation, maybe it was the softness of the music or the heat of the night that was now getting to her, whatever it was, she had to stay strong knowing that in a couple of days she'd be returning home never to see him again.

The last dance now over, it was goodnight or should I say morning as they headed towards Jay's friend's house for what was to be a night of passion A short walk, with both of them laughing and joking along the way when he stopped to say;

"Come on girl I'll race you, it's only that house at the end of the road, come on slow coach, you can do better than that" as he started to run in front of her. Well that was a challenge so off came the shoes as she started to run, having no intentions of letting him win, for that's exactly what happened, a little out of breath but none the less the winner was Corry to his amazement, as you could see the look on his face, it didn't go down too well for he'd always been competitive and didn't like to lose at anything.

"Well my dear I think the night went quite well, you looked stunning as usual, kept your cool with all those wives who no doubt, were so envious that their men just couldn't keep their eyes off you, but as you've been teasing me with those nipples all night, I think It's my turn to show my appreciation for such a wonderful evening" as he picked her up in his arms, heading towards the bedroom while kicking his shoes off on the way. Corry couldn't argue with those comments, as the evening had gone better than expected and in fairness she had risen above the snobbery with a graceful air.

The moonlight so bright, shining through the window didn't warrant any other lighting as Corry glanced across the room, but it was what was in front which was really amazing, a large bed with the sheets carefully pulled back, rose petals spread all over them while on one of the pillows lay a red rose, this had certainly been well planned beforehand she thought, in which her breath was simply taken away with all the trouble he'd gone to.
"What a beautiful rose she muttered out loud",

"Not at all my dear the beauty is in the thorn that is going deep up inside of you shortly" he commented out loudly.

Gently laying her down on the bed while slowly removing her dress and shoes as the moon shone down on her beautifully tanned body, while not making a move and thinking to herself if this is what it's going to be like tonight, then you can do all the romancing yourself as you're doing a pretty good job so far and wouldn't want to spoil the moment for this will definitely be a night to remember for the scrapbook.

Caressing that body as though it was so sacred to the touch, the shivers ran wild inside of her but she showed no emotions at all until pulling her head to one side and passionately kissing those sensual lips, rolling his tongue to the side of her face, down the ear, along the neck and shoulder, now this was starting to get the adrenalin running wild not knowing just how long the resistance would last while gritting her teeth, and yet showing him she was going to put up a fight against his advances and not let him dominate her body as he had done in the past.

His hands found her breast which made her nipples respond immediately, his tongue reaching out to the tip and then passionately taking one nipple at a time into the suction of his awaiting mouth, first of all gently sucking and then increasing the pressure as he knew she wouldn't be able to fight as any resistance would be futile.

Her body now heated with passion, and shuddering inside, due to him being so close to her; she could feel his penis up against her with such an arising strength, his hand finding a way down between her legs, knowing just how to gravitate the situation to his expectations. But tonight was going to be a night of resistance on her part as why should he dictate even with rose petals she thought. Well that was the idea but like all ideas, they seem to disappear somewhere along the way as she was showing signs of giving in far too quickly with her emotions getting the better. Showing how wet she had now become, it seemed she was losing the battle, and couldn't hide her feelings, knowing that he'd the advantage as she turned swiftly, pushing him onto his back with one hand while the other grabbing hold of his penis, moving down the body her lips entwined the end of it with a suction he couldn't fight;

"Take me, take me fully in to that cove of madness" he groaned.

No way she thought, whereby ignoring his pleas, a little at a time she worked her magic both with the tongue, then to excite even more her teeth took over grating on the tip, just enough for him to come near to ejaculation as she would then pull away. Knowing what madness was going through his head and therefore would keep him at that point until she was ready as he started to calm his body down, she lowered her mouth over him with one mighty suck which he couldn't hold any longer and ejaculated down the back of her throat;

"Oh my god, where on earth did that come from?" he asked rather apologetically and somewhat embarrassed.

"Well if you don't know then why should I tell you, all I would say is, don't ever try and dominate me in bed again or I will always return the favour" was the reply that wasn't anticipated.

Now this was a challenge he thought grabbing hold, pushing her back down onto the pillow, proceeding to force her legs wide apart. Pushing them up into the air, over his shoulders, his mouth resting on the sweet wet juices that by now was flooding from her pussy so fast it was turning him on to a savagery emotion that he'd never experienced before as he sucked her dry over and over again until he was feeling his own erection strong and firm.

Now this wasn't a moment that he'd turn away from so easily, as he mounted her like some raging bull, pushing his huge erection in as far as he could go inside of her, the screams of delight were overpowering as be rammed his penis into her a few times and then would stop thus making her wait as she'd done to him, it seemed she wasn't the only one who could play games and to that he was going to show her just who was the dominant partner as he'd always been with others.

Her inner muscles now contracting so strongly around the tip of him that she knew he wouldn't be able to resist for much longer, he on the other hand knew she wanted the same release as he was going to give and therefore pushed into her so hard and wild that they both found complete satisfaction together.

Rolling over, and with a lasting comment of "should you want me again in the night, don't hesitate to wake me, as I'm sure I'll be able to oblige with satisfaction as required yet again"

Who does this man think he is, when he can get what he wants she thought as sleep found them both a few minutes later.

DAY 6
As the heat of the day was dawning and the sun shone down brightly into the bedroom, Corry woke to find she was alone in bed, what's happening she thought, but it wasn't too long before she heard Jay's voice singing in the distance of the kitchen.

"Come on sleepy head, time to get up and enjoy your last day as I'm going to take you back to the hotel so t you can start packing, that's after you've had a good breakfast, which by the way is already on the table waiting, don't worry, you can have a shower after you've eaten" he added. Oh my god there were no limits to his talents she thought, mind he was a soldier and they were known for being self-sufficient on all occasion.

Breakfast went down nicely and with fresh orange was just what the waiter ordered so to speak, now a shower to wash away the thoughts of the past week that had gone by so quickly, not realising that Jay had arranged previously with Issa, to put a change of clothing with him, so that Corry wouldn't have to return to the hotel in just a flimsy satin dress which would have been a bit conspicuous to say the least.

A nice clean towel in her hand Corry stepped into the large bathroom, dropped the towel on the side while entering the shower, the water being just right as she began to lather her body with soap, when all of a sudden the door opened with company she'd not expected,

"I think you need a hand in there my dear" Jay remarked.

Before she could utter anything otherwise, he was accompanying her in the shower with, soap in one hand and sponge in the other as he started to wash her silky smooth body down, it was no good objecting, for he was already showing his manhood to the maximum length, her nipples were so taught, there was no question as to what she wanted either.

Being so erect and swollen, as her eyes glanced upon him, the desire she felt made her want him there and then. How could she resist such a tool of delight, not even having to guide him into her treasure trove, as he would be able to find his own way by now, just looking into each other's eyes they both knew what they desired?

No words were passed between them as he dropped the soap and then the sponge, his hand catching the back of her lower bottom, pulling her towards him as he thrust into her, time and time again until they both came together.

"I knew you needed help my dear was the comment he made getting out of the shower, now get dried and hurry up, we're going back to the hotel so you don't leave all the packing until last minute as you women usually do".

And with orders like that she jumped to attention or should I say that's what he would have liked but then again she wasn't the type to take orders lightly.

It was now early afternoon by the time they arrived back at the hotel which was time for Corry to meet with Issa, make arrangements to get everything ready for the flight home the next day. Apparently unbeknown to both the girls, it had been arranged they would all share a quite drink down at one of the local bars, being it was their last night.

It had also been pre-arranged that instead of a coach picking them up the next day, a staff car would take them to the airport, which just goes to show it's not what you know but who you know that counts for these privileges. Being pretty organised It didn't take long to get sorted out for the journey home, leaving just a little white dress out for the evening together with clothes in which to travel so they could go out for a last drink on the island.

Tonight was going to be special as the feeling of romance was in the air, not so special, as this was the end of the road for Corry and Jay but on the other hand Issa had made arrangements that Rob was going to join her for Christmas. Corry was as pleased about that decision, as Issa had gone through so much heartache since her father had died and with this being her first real boyfriend, she would have a sense of belonging to someone if it all worked out for that's what she was hoping for.

The night was young, the mood being so romantic, as both of the girls were picked up from the hotel and taken to a little restaurant down the road.

Both wearing white linen dresses with strappy sandals as still very warm, a corner table overlooking the sea, soft music that filled the air sitting down and enjoying the meal in such a relaxed atmosphere. It was nice to catch up on what they'd done over the last week with funny stories and places they'd been, enjoying every moment of it.

In true style, Corry had to have her last helping of strawberries and ice cream on the island to finish the meal off before leaving and joining in the merriment that was going on a few bars away from the restaurant. Although the music

was loud it was also enjoyable with both of the girls knocking the drink back as though there was no tomorrow, but never mind they thought as their plane was not due to leave until late in the afternoon so a lie in was definitely on the cards.
The night passed quickly in fact too quickly as before they knew it, the clock had turned midnight and time was running away with the memories they'd built over the last week;

"I think it's about time we were getting back to the hotel as the girls need some sleep before tomorrow" Rob said, being a little concerned for Issa's health.

"Good idea "Jay replied turning to look at the expression on Corry's sad face.

It had been one of the best weeks of his life, but knew it was only just a holiday romance for both of them; they would have to come down to earth sooner or later for he was a serving officer in the armed forces and she was probably only a shop girl. They'd not really got into conversation as to what their backgrounds were but with a little indication of what she did, it was obvious that he couldn't get mixed up with someone beneath him, for when all said and done, he could have his fun with her but that was as far as it could go for she would never be accepted into his world as an equal.

It was the warm breeze of the night that brought them down to reality, sadly as they strolled back to the hotel, arriving in the reception was like any other early morning, subdued lighting a porter and receptionist sat half asleep in the easy chairs behind the desk. Softly treading as not to make any noise, they all made their way to the lift, Issa and Rob going towards one room with Corry and Jay to the other.

There was something different about tonight Corry thought, a cold silence in the air, yet a warm feeling between their minds as though Jay had something to say but the words just wouldn't come out, maybe he didn't want to spoil the mood being their last night together but then how would she know for he was a dark one, as far as feelings were concerned. Once in the room, they both undressed, slipping between the sheets together, drawing her close and whispering;

"I want this moment to last forever, but I'm no fool and realise, you will be gone tomorrow and the dream will end for the both of us".

Corry was silent as a cold shiver ran through her body; she knew he meant every word of what he'd said as he held her so tightly sensing a strange feeling that ran between them. The deathly silence filled the air around as he turned her head gently towards him with a kiss of such passion as he had never done before, but the only words that she longed to hear never came as he started to kiss her body with such warmth and feelings.

Cupping her breast for a while but still in silence, she could feel how erect he was up against her body but to her this didn't seem the same person that she'd spent the last six days with, even his kisses felt different, it was as though he wanted to shout out loud but then nothing was materialising between his brain and vocal cords as he slowly entered her.

His hands firmly on her bottom as he pushed into her slowly but firmly with a timely rhythm, stopping shortly to gaze into her eyes before gathering up more speed. He could feel her inner body's firm grip around his penis and knew she was as ready as he was to explode and with a lump in his throat asked;

"Are you ready darling", knowing that this would be the last time he would experience the explosive expression in her face that was screaming out for that final burst of energy.

Yes, she was ready alright as every nerve in her body was at such a height it was going to explode any minute now and with sadness in his voice he began to whisper;

"Come on baby lets light our final fireworks together" to which the final eruption of all eruptions which blew their minds away followed.

It wasn't long before sleep petered into each other's bodies as both knew this was going to be the end of a most exciting chapter of their lives, a memory they would never forget. As mid-morning approached and everyone had showered, dressed, packed for the oncoming journey, it was decided they would have coffee, book out of the hotel, pack the car with suitcases, drive down to the airport, stopping on the way to have a light lunch.

There was plenty time to say all their goodbyes in the airport lounge before departure but sadly the feelings were now starting to show as they all tried to put on a brave and sombre show but this again didn't stop the tears flowing from time to time as it was merely impossible to control such feelings they all had. And with such feelings arising, that broke the silence that exchanged between them, over memories that the past week had brought. From then on, everything went to plan, the drive was great as it washed all the cobwebs out of the air, the lunch was light which was just enough to tide them over until evening, arriving in plenty of time to book in, leaving their farewell to the last minute.

Booking in was straight forward as they proceeded to the private lounge where they could say their good-byes in peace having pulled a few strings with Jay being a ranking officer, but it was when they reached the lounge that emotions had now started to explode as he glanced out of the corner of his eyes, noticing the sadness in Corry's face but all the same was equally hurt for the lump in his throat seemed to be choking when Corry all of a sudden stood up with tears rolling down her face, tuned to Rob and said;

"I hope everything works out for both you and Issa, and if you do get home at Christmas, then we'll have a night out together, show you a bit of the big city that we call home".

Turning quickly, she walked away only to notice Jay following, catching her arm; he swung her round and said;

"I'm truly sorry but this is how it has to be. We live in two different worlds so to speak, I could never adapt to your way of life and it would be unfair to ask you to accept mine, I will never forget you no matter how hard I try".

His face however told a different story as he reached into his pocket, pulled out a package, handed it to her with the instruction not to open it until she boarded the plane.

In a trance and with tears flowing down her cheeks, she accepted the package, walked towards the boarding desk, not even daring to look back and with her heart pounding boarded the plane with Issa trailing behind. Taking their seats but still no words passed between them, Issa knew how much Corry was hurting and therefore left her to come round in her own time knowing what she must be going through. For how many words can describe what you're going through at a time like that, your body feels so empty, knots in your stomach, lump in your throat and with the tears of pain rolling down your face?

I think most of us have been there at one time or another but not all of us like to admit it, for in some ways we feel it's a moment of weakness that if truth be known, we can't handle and therefore something inside falls to pieces and then makes hurtful memories. When all of a sudden the sound of the engines roaring as the plane taxied to the end of the runway, a swift take off and they were in the air.

Issa looked at Corry's face which was now a little calmer before asking;

"Aren't you going to open that box he gave you or do I have to open it for you"?
 Corry swiftly turned not realizing that the box was still in her hand.

"Oh I expect it'll be a small charm to remind me of the island", was her reply.

But Issa was more curious than that and wanted to help her friend change the mood as she insisted this was how it was going to be.

"You're either going to open the box or I shall open it for you." she demanded.

And knowing Issa wasn't going to let the subject drop and would carry on all the way back to London if need be, therefore to shut her up, she was prepared to give in revealing the contents of the box. But then it was to Corries amazement, staring up at her was the gold filigree rose broach that she'd admired so much on the day both her and Jay visited Troodos Mountain. Well you could imagine the expression on her face as she turned to Issa and commented in a defiant way;

"Now are you satisfied?"

The look on Issa's face said it all for she knew in her heart that everything was going to be alright, for there was a strong feeling something would happen that would change Corry's future for the better.

Not wanting to go into anything further at that moment, Issa sat back dosing off knowing that time is a great healer and her friend would be alright as she was a fighter. Knowing also, when they arrived back in London, it would be so busy preparing for the next season's collection that Corry wouldn't have time to think back about Jay and again she had other admirers that would go that extra mile to even have a chance of being seen with her friend.

Chapter 8

Work, work, work, that's all Corry and Issa had done since the return from their holiday.

The orders had literally poured in as a result of the last show and to be honest they were literally run off their feet with the only solution being, to hire more staff in which to cope.

To her surprise, Corry had also received invitations to meet buyers from all over Europe as they were also interested in her designs for the upper class market. Word had spread to America that there was a new designer in London who was taking the market by storm, not wanting to miss out, they had also sent some of their top buyers over to capture the creations before anyone else, these being for their wealthier clients.

Things were really starting to look up for the business and in fact there were times Corry didn't have a minute to herself, which was a good thing when you're trying to get over a holiday romance.

With work coming in so fast and starting to get out of hand, the first thing she did was to hire a secretary who would be able to deal with all the correspondence as she just didn't have time, but there again even with that help, it became impossible as it seemed the buyers only wanted to deal with Corry herself on a personal basis.

Issa on the other hand had decided to move out of Corry's apartment and therefore found a nice little one which she could afford in Kensington; this was to accommodate Rob when he was to visit at Christmas, as they could be on their own which was understandable. The apartment was rather luxury but that didn't bother Issa as she could well afford it by now, with a contract she'd just signed with Vogue as their top model in the magazine. Excited as she was, her thoughts were never too far away from her friend but at the end of the day she had other things to look forward to now as couldn't get Rob out of her mind and the apartment would be their little love nest for the time being.

It was one night as Corry returned from work, sat down with a much earned coffee, literally shattered, thinking to herself how much longer can I keep this up for all I seem to do is work and sleep and it wouldn't be fair to expect any more work from the girls as they're in the same boat as me with so many orders to cope with.

The only way she could see out of the situation was to have a word with the accountant to see what he suggested, maybe if we could afford to hire a couple more staff on a part time basis, for the time being, at least that would help she thought. Knowing the girls were in the same position, it was starting to tell on them and if she wasn't careful they may look for jobs elsewhere, so had to think of a way to solve the problem before it became an issue.

Having mulled the idea over in her head, maybe if she opened small premises away from the shop, then it would be viable to delegate a team who could run the design studio while she herself would promote the ready to wear clothes she had in mind. Knowing this was a little ambitious to say the least but then again was confident that with help, she could achieve it for knowing the staff would back her up to the hilt as they'd done in the past.

Corry would discuss these ideas with the staff first as she liked to get everyone involved, appreciating their backing at all times, then it would be up to her to make it happen as that was the driving force inside of her. Strolling into the accountant's officer the next day, she was quite confident he would agree with what she called a small request for help with the business, knowing they seemed to be going from strength to strength with the supply of orders to new customers.

Having sat down with him, Corry went through all her ideas and to her amazement he not only agreed with her but suggested that she take on even more staff than she'd anticipated;

"Oh my god, I can't afford to take that many staff on surely?" she asked"

"I'm afraid you can, and if you don't, then you may lose all the backing from the buyers, having checked your books over this last month it seems as there screaming out with new orders, I don't think you realise just how popular your fashion styling is".

To this Corry sat looking at this man in somewhat bewilderment and therefore added;

"You want to concentrate on this ready to wear promotion, well there seems to be a big opening in the marketplace for this at the moment, and that's what you should concentrate on as that's where the money is" he suggested.

Shocked at this proposal as she didn't think she'd ever achieve anything as grand as he was suggesting.

"Now you've listened to my advice, I think you deserve a well-earned coffee to think things over, maybe with a couple of chocolate biscuits thrown in to help your train of thoughts" the accountant said with rather a serious expression on his face.

Now this was something new which Corry didn't expected; and having to give serious thought to such an expansion of the business wasn't going to come easy with the worry of how would she be able to manage all this as it was a massive job to get her head around, but without any hesitation she jumped to her feet and said;

"Right we'll do it, but what about the financial part of all this structure?".

"Don't worry about that as I've got that in hand already, I've also put in a proposal for a general manager to run the ready to wear items together with the special design couture range, all of them taking orders directly from you which will alleviate the pressure of the daily running of the business off your shoulders should you agree", the accountant replied.

"You really have thought about everything haven't you?" asked Corry.

"Well that's what you pay me for isn't it" was the reply.

"Not only do I pay you for it, but I would make a suggestion that I pay you a lot more as you become a Director of the company, for I couldn't have done all this without you and to be honest, you have always been there safeguarding my interests, so will that be a yes I hear" Corry asked?

Well what more could be said to that outstanding proposal.

"Thank you, I would be delighted to accept your offer, and may I say you'll never regret this" was the courteous reply

"Hope not otherwise I'll charge you for the sign that'll be made for your office today when I get back,

PETER COOK FINANCIAL DIRECTOR.
"Sounds good doesn't it" Corry remarked laughing.

Peter just smiled but that smile said it all, for Corry was a woman of her word and oh boy was this woman going places in the fashion business which he'd no doubts at all about.

Chapter 9

PETERS STORY

As for all the legal contracts to appoint him, he knew very well they would be on his desk within the next week or so as that's how she worked, on the ball all the time, never letting the grass grow under her feet so to speak.

Yes, Peter Cook had worked extremely hard for that position and it was well deserved, for Corry couldn't believe that in only two months' since she'd gone to him to manage her accounts, he'd turned the business round to the extent of two more factories in the pipeline which would be ready to go into production in the new year.

Finance had been arranged, premises had been found, staff had been hired, machinery and tools together with equipment were on order, and suppliers had received approval for all the new fabrics to be delivered.

This man was a marvel, and this Corry knew from the first day she'd set eyes on Peter for the potential was there, as he had such a driving force which was unstoppable. It was only when she really started to get to know him intimately that she discovered what it was that drove him to the maximum.

Apparently, he was born to two loving parents that were both blind at birth. Having had a normal childhood, not knowing that anything was different other than having social workers that would come to the house every few days together with helpers that would also check on things on a weekly basis. But to him, that was a way of life as he never even questioned it, other children around him never mentioned it so it was something that was just accepted by everyone that his parents were just a little different and needed help with some of the odd jobs.

It was only when he started secondary school that things started to change, for others would tease him about why his parents weren't what they regarded as normal. This bothered Peter as often he'd go home and straight up to his room while crying himself to sleep, not letting on to his parents what was the matter for fear of upsetting them as they loved him so much, and being an only child the strain would be devastating for them.

After school he would do all his chores and then concentrate on his schoolwork for he was determined to show these bullies, he was better than them. Night after night locking himself in his room where he could study to his heart's content on his favourite subject which was maths. Figures had always been his best subject and with the help of a favourite teacher who took an interest in him, he was now on the way to getting an apprenticeship with a firm of accountants.

Then came the day when he left school and started on a pittance of a wage at the local accountants, his parents being so excited that their son was going to make a mark in the business world for they were so proud of how well he'd done taking into account of the disabilities they had in life.

Should all this work out as they hoped then at least their prayers had been answered in that a fine career their son would be able to achieve, making a professional mark in life. Peter worked hard to learn his trade from the bottom for he realised not many boys from his background ever got the opportunities that had come his way and so he wasn't going to waste them for he wanted his parents to be proud of his achievements.

It was as Peter started to earn good money, gratitude for what his parents had sacrificed for him had come to mind as his saving started to grow whereby with rewards and bonuses he would give a little back in the way of a deposit for a nice little house in the countryside where they could enjoy the fresh air away from the inner city.

Returning home one night after work he informed them of two surprises, the first being that he'd met a nice girl from the office he worked in. The second was an even bigger surprise, it was that he'd already put a large deposit down on a little terrace house in the country that friends had offered to rally round and adapt specially to accommodate someone who had disabilities such as theirs. The house had a large garden in which his father could work his magic with green fingers and pottering around as that's what he enjoyed.

This was a big step for Peter but then he had faith and judgement in his decision, knowing his parents would be over the moon with a little more independence for them to manage their own lives, living in a property which they actually owned and not under the strict rules of Social Services.

All he wanted, was to bring a little sunshine into their lives as they'd done for him growing up for no one could have wished for better parents than he'd got in his opinion, and to him they had no disabilities at all, they were normal for that's the values they'd taught him to understand, blindness wasn't a disability it was an act of god that made them special and in which they could develop other stronger abilities to cope.

Peter's mother was so shocked for she couldn't get over how much he'd saved in such a short time, getting enough monies for such a large deposit for the house which sounded wonderful, these were dreams beyond their comprehension and therefore delighted at such news.

Now the girlfriend was another matter, she was such a quiet little thing, nicely dressed long dark hair, plain but pretty, with such good manners, and to be honest, her name suited her down to the ground, my little Anna they all called her. It was after the first meeting that Peter's mother stated that Anna would make a fine wife and warned her son, he had better look after her as she was somewhat special, having a motherly instinct about these matters.

Don't worry mum I intend to take care of her, she means so much to me already, but as we've only been seeing each other for a short period of time, I think marriage will be a fair way off at the moment he replied to the delight of both his parents.

It was after completing his apprenticeship, Peter being loyal to those that had given him the opportunity, stayed with the same firm until the owner past away, but to his astonishment, the very firm that gave him his chance to shine with feet firmly on the ladder, was to be his alone for the owner having no living relatives, made a will leaving everything to Peter.

After the funeral, solicitors had called the employees together and apart from individual requests to a few, had left the entire business along with a small detached house to Peter on conditions that he should carry on the business as usual but adding a small clause.

This clause was to be, that he would take on a young apprentice every two years, giving them the same chance that Peter had been given.

It wasn't very long after that period that Peter proposed to Anna with the wedding which followed shortly after, to the delight of not only his immediate family but also the employees who held him in such high esteem for all the hard work he'd put in since he'd inherited the firm. Some two years later Peter was happy to announce that he was to be a proud father but as we know things don't always run to plan, for when Anna went into labour, she was left too long before the birth and their son was born with a hearing defect.

Although they were devastated, Peter knew he had to be strong for his wife as she sank into a deep depression not wanting to know anyone.

This was a difficult time for all concerned as they loved the little boy but still he had to carry on with the business to provide not only for the family but also had an obligation to the staff. It was at this time, he made the decision to get his parents to move in with him and Anna knowing with their experience of dealing with the unexpected situations it would leave him to concentrate on the business. It took quite a while for Anna to get over the depression, in fact it was some four years before she finally accepted that her son was deaf, but when she finally did come to terms with the situation, tragedy struck yet again.

It was one hot humid day as Anna decided to take the car for a drive into the country and so asked Peter's parents if they'd also like to accompany her and her son Anthony. As Peter had loads of work to do and wasn't feeling too well himself, he would stay at home inevitably trying to catch up with things from the office.

Anna being considerate to the last, thought a little peace and quiet would be just the time he needed to himself on this occasion and therefore bungled everyone into the car. They'd only been gone about an hour or so, driving through a small village when a lorry headed towards them out of control, smashing straight into the car.

Anna had no recollection of what happened after that as she came around in a nearby hospital bed some two days later. All was a blur and what seemed a crowd of strange faces, was in fact medical staff who had nursed her for the last couple of days in which she'd been unconscious.

But her first reaction was to scream, my baby, my baby, I want my son.

Don't worry Anna, your son is safe, in fact he hasn't even got a scratch on him, would you like to see him as he's been asking for you, the last couple of days and won't shut up talking about you and the car, a young nurse had said. But to that comment Anna was rather confused, asking what the hell was going on as Anthony was deaf.

But no the nurse was adamant for she had spoken to him herself upon arrival.

Not believing anything that was being told to her, the only things she would settle for was to speak to her husband who would tell then all they were wrong.

Just then a doctor walked into the room to see what all the commotion was about only to tell Anna that her husband would be along shortly for he was just sorting some arrangements out to do with his parents, not being able to remember all the facts.

What do you mean arrangement to do with his parents, why were they in the accident as well she enquired, not being able to remember?
The doctor looked a little blank at this question but all the same answered it with a sympathetic concern saying;

I'm afraid they had to be cut out of the car as the lorry that you collided with, smashed into the side of your car when you obviously tried to avoid a head on incident.

It was at this time the young doctor lent over Anna and gave her an injection putting her to sleep just as a nurse entered the room with the words;

May we all offer you our condolences for the loss of your parents?

In a trance, Anna lay there, not making any sense of what was going on and definitely didn't understand what the nurse was on about as she slowly drifted off into a deep sleep as the injection had finally taken its course. It was a couple of days later before Anna came around properly and by this time, Peter was by her side and to be truthful he looked as though he'd not slept for a month;

Peter, what's going on, please explain for nothing seems to make sense, first they tell me Anthony can not only talk but also hear and then someone says something about their condolences, I realise I've been asleep for a while but what's everyone going on about, Anna said rather mystified while looking Peter straight in the eyes.

Looking down at his wife he answered with sadness in his voice,

Don't you worry darling, everything is going to be alright from now on, the doctors have checked Anthony over and say both his hearing and speech is fine, they themselves can't explain what's brought everything back, they say it's just one of those things that mystifies medical science.

The tears in Anna's eyes said it all but still she knew that wasn't the whole story as Peter was keeping something back.

Carry on, I know that's not the end of it, what else haven't you told me, she said in such a stern voice.

Unfortunately, both my parents didn't make it, apparently as the lorry came towards the car, it seemed my mother grabbed Anthony, opened the door and threw him out onto the grass verge which saved his life before the other vehicle hit the car.

Yes, it had always been known that although you may be blind, your other senses seem sharper which obviously happened in that case. And with tears rolling down Peters face as he continued;

It was my father who took the full brunt of the crash and when the fire crew arrived to cut him free, they stated that he'd died on impact and therefore never suffered which was a relief.

There was no words Anna could say to console her husband as she knew how he would be suffering, only time would heal such a devastating blow that had been dealt this wonderful man, it was bad enough to lose one parent but to lose two was unbelievably cruel to say the least on such a loving family. The main thing now was to thank god their son was alive and look forward to the future hard as it may be, for they had been given a miracle in that their only child had survived, it was now their turn to show their gratitude by pulling together and doing good for others. It wasn't long before Anna came out of hospital to complete their little family again but time had now changed and they had different views on life.

Anna' would cherish what she had for the rest of her life asking for nothing in return but the health of her family while Peter made a promise to himself that he would work till the day he died to prove how grateful he was, and whereby at least one miracle had come out of such a tragedy. And therefore keeping to his promise that he'd take on an apprentice every couple of years, word got round what an outstanding firm that he'd created and should you want a good accountant in London, then you no longer need to look any further than Peter Cook's business……..

As Corry was up to her eyes in paperwork at that time and couldn't manage without help, she made an urgent appointment with his office, meeting him the next day.

Her first words to Peter was, "I need an accountant and understand that you're the best in London or so I'm told".

Peter took one look at Corry, grabbing her by the hand, marching her into his office and said;

"Well you'd better take a seat and tell me a little about yourself firstly, oh will that be black or white coffee and no sugar as I can see your sweet enough?".

"Yes that would be nice and make that black please" was the reply.

From that day on they got on like a house on fire so to speak, being such firm friends both inside and out of their professional relationship.

Yes, this was a friendship that would last for a lifetime.

She not only trusted him with her life as well as all her business interests as knowing he'd never let her down and had been a god send to her when her back had been against the wall with financial issues, sorting all the priorities out for the new factories as they came up.

A devout family man, Corry made it a priority to get to know his family which worked out quite well in the end as she became very close and would be regarded as part of their family. Having learnt so much from Peter in such a short time but most of all she trusted him completely, he had been through so much and yet you never heard him complain for he just got on with it, which is why he was much respected, both in his private life as well as his professional one. Now with Peter by her side there was no going back for it was onwards and upwards so he'd often say when she felt unsure on things.

The factories would be ready and in full production in time for the spring collection and knowing this would be cutting it fine therefore had to have Peter's assurances to make this happen. However, a little unsure about the ready to wear line although all the designs and hard work had been completed, she was still on edge having never attempted anything as brave before, yes, it was a gamble that she was ready to take but with the Christmas so close at hand knew that without Peter it would have all collapsed.

So with this in mind, Corry had to find time to organise a little shopping spree.

Still not believing her luck as to what was happening, thinking she'd take another look at all the plans whereby, not only the new factories with the delivery of machinery which was due any day, but also the fittings and fixtures had already been installed. Peter had even organised for the new staff to be interviewed earlier that anticipated leaving no stone unturned. The whole scheme was coming together nicely, and by New Year everything would be full steam ahead.

Corry however was a little concerned over the production of the new range and therefore organised a handful of staff to work on the samples before the holidays knowing that if there was going to be any teething problems, then they would be able to correct them before going ahead with the lines, for at the end of the day she was a perfectionist.

Now although Christmas was on top of them, Corry still couldn't rest until everything was sorted and to be honest was staring to get under everyone feet with last minute nerves which in one way was understandable until Peter decided to make her see sense that everything was under control by saying;

"For goodness sake will you get lost and do some Christmas shopping, I've told you everything's in hand and none of us can do any more at the moment so go or do I have to throw you out. I can manage without you getting under my feet for at least a couple of days and look at all the shopping you've got to do including my present from Santa".

To that she turned and walked away, when Peter shouted',

"Oh by the way, what are you doing for Christmas, would you like to come and spend it with us or have you already made arrangements".

"Thanks all the same but I thought I'd spend a few days with Agnes seen as I seemed to have neglected her since we came back off holiday and to be truthful it would be nice to catch up and have a few days of peace and quiet".

"Fine, but if you change your mind, then the offer's always open and you'd be very welcome to stay" Peter said.

To this Corry took the hint and headed towards the shops to start the festive shopping.

Chapter 10

Now to the serious shopping as Christmas was only a matter of a couple of weeks away, so time was definitely of the essence as she'd not made any definite plans to go up north and stay with family.

Having thought long and hard about Issa but there again with Rob coming home for Christmas any day now, it was out of the question spending time with her for even a catch up and drinks, being their first time together since the holiday for they would want to be alone as lovers do and really the girl deserved a little happiness.

Knowing Agnes would be by herself although she had many friends that would be in and out visiting, it really would be nice to have some time with her as she felt she'd neglected her since she'd returned from holiday, and therefore it would be nice to spend the holidays with someone that was now regarded as part of her immediate family. Having informed Agnes of her decision, it was full steam ahead to make sure all the presents were sorted for the immediate staff and close friends and then she'd have time to pack a few things and then be on her way.

Two days before Christmas, the city was buzzing with the excitement of office parties which was a magical time of the year when everyone was in high spirits, dressing up for the occasion lifting the moods of everyone, even Corry took a few hours off to let her hair down, joining close friends for drinks which was a first since her holiday.

Yes a few drinks and a few more as she ended up on a bar in one of the pubs singing her heart out to her friend's delight, she was definitely back to her usual self so Issa thought, when all of a sudden a camera man appeared, taking a photo of her in full party mood. Never mind, they all thought, as it would be publicity for her new collection hitting the morning papers after the news got out.

Now who could blame Corry letting her hair down once in a while especially at Christmas time knowing that New Year, she'd have to pull out all the stops to get everything into prospective so with this, her last chance to have a little fun for all the work she'd put into making the business a success so far and with Issa joining her for a pre-Christmas drink, everything was now perfect.

Sure as eggs were eggs, the next morning in the papers, the headline in the society page read as follows;

SHE DOES IT AGAIN

The fashion industries secret weapon looked radiant on a night out at her local bar with her fellow workers, dressed in a mid-night blue velvet dress; Miss Corry Sharp actually let her hair down and showed us all what a good boss she was, holding a party for close friends and staff.

This kind of thing was big news in those days as everything Corry did hit the papers after she'd taken the autumn fashion show to new heights with bigger write ups than Paris, which was surprising for that was the fashion capitol of the world at that time.

One thing Corry did know for sure was the next morning, her head was aching that much it proved she'd really had a good time as everyone had told her. Slowly pulling herself together, a slice of toast, with a much needed black coffee, shower and then dressed in something simple but also making a statement fear the papers would have another go, being the night after her partying on the town so to speak. Having packed a few clothes in a small overnight bag, was then ready for the journey across London to spend the next few days with Agnes.

By now looking forward to the well-earned break and catch up with her dear friend who she knew would help her through this stressful period of a new venture which was coming to fruition. It didn't seem any time at all before she arrived at Agnes's apartment; even the traffic wasn't that bad to say it was Christmas Eve and therefore the last working day before the holidays, a time where most people had broken up from work and already started the festive season in advance she thought.

Having arrived to such a warm welcome it was just like coming home as that's the feeling Agnes showed towards her, she wasn't a guest, she was made to feel like the daughter that Agnes never had;

"Oh my dear, it's so lovely to see you, I've a feeling this is going to be a Christmas to remember for all of us and you've still got that lovely colour from your holiday which you'll have to tell me all about. Now put your bags down and we'll have a fresh cup of tea and cream cake, then you'll be able to tell me what you got up to, as you were pretty vague when we spoke on the telephone" Agnes said.

"Forget the cream cakes, I've brought you some of those marzipan squires that you love together with the cream cakes from that little bakery down the road from me, knowing the kettle would be on when I arrived" she replied.

The apartment looked lovely trimmed up with all the old fashioned decorations, some even being from the days when Agnes was a young girl in Germany and standing in one corner was a large Christmas tree which took pride of place, yes it was just like returning home when Corry was young;

"Now come and sit down, tell me all your news and gossip, don't leave anything out as you know I love to hear what's been happening, not been able to get out as much as I'd like to nowadays", Agnes stated.

"Well first of all the business, this is doing really well, we're planning to open two new factories in the New Year, one for the special designs along with couture and the other one will be to produce the ready to wear lines which orders are already flooding in".

Secondly, we've taken a new Director on, who I'm sure you will definitely approve of, he is to oversee everything from hiring, budgeting and financial affairs on my behalf and is officially the Finance Director.

Thirdly, he's already sorted everything out for the new ventures and we're running on time for the new collections, if you remember, I did get your approval before finally making this decision, he's even hired two managers for the new factories."

"Now that doesn't sound too good as this man is an outsider, what do we really know about him", Agnes chipped in at this point having a strong financial awareness.

"No, you don't have to worry as the two managers are from the little shop and I trained them myself from college", Corry replied.

"Female managers, now that's a new one on me, do you think a woman can do the job, I know it won't go down too well with the industry but there again, you know what you're doing and I have every faith in you my dear. What about the financial side to all this, do you need more capital investment from me as you know only too well, you only have to ask", Agnes enquired.

"No that's fine as it's all been taken care of by our new financial director Peter, he's been in touch with the banks and they are only too happy to back the venture". Corry assured Agnes.

"Well I'm impressed; he really must be all that you've said at this rate" Agnes commented.

"Oh he really is, trust me, you're going to get on famously with him when you meet" was the answer.

"Now let's get to the important bits, how was the holiday, I understand Issa met a nice young man who's coming to stay with her for the Christmas. And what about you, did you meet someone nice? I do hope so, I wish you'd meet someone who'd look after you so you wouldn't have to work so hard", Agnes said with such feeling.

Just then Corry heard the door open and close, looking rather mystified she asked;

"Are you expecting anyone"?

"Oh no, it's only my son that's come in, he's come to stay for the Christmas as not seen him for a while, he arrived last night and popped out to pick up a couple of things, don't worry, he won't get in your way, as expect he'll be out most of the time, he's a bit of a party animal not like you at all my dear".

Party animal, yes Corry's mind wondered back to a couple of months previously as that's what jay was but there again that was in the past which was still a little raw at times when she thought about it, bringing her back down to reality as Agnes broke her train of thought;

"Sorry my dear, I forgot, you've never met my son have you, I think you'll get on quite well together and maybe he will be able to take you to meet some of his society friends while you're here as in my opinion, you need to mix more with people of your own age instead of being stuck with old fogies like me".

"Oh Agnes, stop it, I won't be his type anyway from what you've told me about him, you made him out to be a bit of a snob and I'm far from that as you well know".

"Never mind about that, just tell me about the holiday and drink your tea up while you're at it", was the reply.

"Well to put your mind at rest, I did meet someone, thought he was wonderful, spent most of the holiday with him, took me all over the island and it hurt when we parted" Corry stated with a tear in her eyes.

Agnes looked a bit bewildered at this stage as she asked

"What island was that, I thought you were going to mainland Greece"?

"No it was Cyprus we went to in the end as that was the only place they could get us for a last minute booking" Corry replied.

"I wish I'd known that as that's where my son lives, I could have arranged for him to take you sight-seeing while you were there, show you a bit of night life instead of you meeting someone who didn't appreciate what a good person he had the chance to be with".

"Now give up Agnes, it was only a fling on his part for I wasn't good enough for him, we mixed in two different worlds as he kindly put it, but then again at least I have one thing to remember him by"

Agnes looked in horror as she asked the fearful question;

"I hope he didn't make you pregnant my dear"

"No nothing like that, it was a filigree rose gold broach which I will always treasure and memories I will never forget as he was someone special in my eyes".

"A gold rose broach", came a voice from the hallway.

And with that Corry froze at the sound of that familiar voice, as surely not she thought, when seconds later in walked Jay as large as life with an expression on his face of such bewilderment. The silence was deafening, who was going to speak first, as words wouldn't materialise from either of them, it was Jay's face that said it all and poor Agnes just couldn't believe what was happening in front of her very eyes.

Fear, excitement, happiness, whatever, as all hearts were pounding by now and the look on all their faces couldn't explain the situation. It was Agnes who broke the ice as she stood up, walked to the door and stated;

"I think I should leave you two together to sort this mess out by yourselves while I go and have a lay down to rest; for I've a feeling I may need it by the day's over with explanations needed from both of you", as she then departed to her bed.

"What the hell are you doing here, and how do you know mother," Jay enquired.

Corry wasn't going to be put down with the tone in Jay's voice and so replied;

"I may as well ask you the same question".

"Well as this is my home in England, I think I have the right to be here" was the reply Corry received.

"And so do I as this is not only my friend but also my partner in the business" as Corry's anger erupted in her expressive action.

"So you are the special one my mother keeps referring to in her letters, the one who is not only talented but a raving beauty that she keeps talking about, I thought you were just a shop girl when I met you, as never did you mention anything about owning your own business, maybe things would have been different between us if you had" Jay said as his voice started to soften.

"Different in what way Jay', you could have told me a little more about yourself and maybe then I'd have known, instead you kept it all bottled up".

There was a very strained look that passed between them both as it was an awkward situation to be in, with none of them wanting to make the first move to re-ignite what they'd shared some months ago having stubbornness on both sides. By this time Corry's stomach was churning like mad as Jay's heart was beating ten to the dozen, each not knowing what was going to happen next as the look between them was so magical until the electricity in their bodies couldn't hold out any longer and started to merge as fate took a hand, with Jay eventually putting out a hand, pulling Corry towards him and kissing her as never before.

Oh yes, the feeling of passion was still there as he looked into her eyes longingly before attempting to say;

"Why didn't you tell me who you were, we've wasted all this time when we could have been together, it really hurt seeing you get on that plane, walking out of my life as you did. I never stopped thinking about you from that day on. I know one thing for sure, I'm never going to ever let you walk away again" he stated with strong emotion.

Corry stood there, not knowing what to say and even if she did, the words wouldn't materialise, as thoughts of she must be dreaming.

The love between them filled the room and time just flew by not realizing what was happening until Agnes entered the room with a gleeful expression on her face muttering;

"I can't believe the two people that mean so much to me will now make my dreams come true for I know you're meant to be together as this is fate. Now we've got all the excitement out of the way, I think it calls for a toast and maybe something to eat as dinner will be ready shortly and you two lovebirds will probably want to be going out, celebrating with your friends."

Now the expression on Agnes's face said it all for this had been a dream beyond dreams that these two people would meet, but not wishing to go further added;

"But before that we will have dinner as I've arranged for a few friends to come over and therefore would appreciate you staying for a couple of drinks at least, as these people are quite influential and will help Corry in the business".

"That's fine" Jay replied, as it had been arranged beforehand that he was to meet up with both Issa and Rob for drinks, then go on to a party.

Oh boy won't they be surprise when he turns up with Corry on his arm he thought. Dinner was excellent that night as Agnes had arranged for something special to be done on her son's first night home and it was a couple of hours later that the guest started to arrive. Now being all close friends of Agnes's it was fairly informal drinks, running buffet and a good old catch up on the general news amongst friends before handing presents out, which happened every year, this being a German tradition whereby presents are given on Christmas eve.

Agnes was there to greet everyone, accompanied by Jay of course this year with him being on home leave, one or two of the guests had already met Corry but only in the capacity of her being a business partner in one of Agnes's many ventures and so it was quite an informal gathering.

It was as the guests mingled that Corry made her grand entrance and what an entrance'.

Dressed in a midnight blue velvet figure hugging dress, cut quite low at the back and which showed her slender back and shoulders off to perfection, finishing off with a pair of high heel dark shoes, carefully chipped with rhine stones on the front, her hair tied back in a ponytail, which showed her to be plain but surprisingly beautiful. Yes, all eyes were definitely on her as those who knew her had never seen her looking as radiant as she did that evening. In fact, one of the guests even commented;

"Any man would be so proud to be seen with her whoever she is".

Overhearing this comment, Jay piped up with;

"The only man that will be seen with her from now on is me I can assure you; now please let me introduce you to my fiancé Corrander Sharp or Corry as some of you may know her".

There was such a look of astonishment that went round the room as Jay had never been serious about any woman and really they were only a means to an end in his opinion. That statement not only took the wind out of everyone's sail's but it was also an almighty shock for his own mother as well. It has been said that love can bring the best out in you but that saying is double sided and can also bring out the worse. I'm afraid in Jay's case it brought out the worse side as Corry was later to experience.

The shock of the proposal now over, with everyone mingling, it wasn't long before Jay and Corry said their fond farewells to everyone before leaving to join their own friends where no doubt a bigger shock was in store for them at such news.

Upon arrival, it was Jay that made the grand entrance with Corry just a way behind him, but as soon as Issa saw the two of them together, she let out one almighty scream that everyone stopped dead in their tracks wondering what on earth had happened, thinking the worse, perhaps she'd hurt herself.

Where, What, How, When, the words wouldn't even come out, she couldn't string a sentence together, trying to make sense as she went along but to no avail;

"Wasn't aware you knew where she was or even been in touch with her let alone meet", Issa said in an excitement that outshone all other sounds in the room.

"Long story, we'll go into it later" Jay replied smiling like a Cheshire Cat.

Issa just couldn't let that remark go as she pulled Corry to one side, asking in an impatient voice';

"Well tell me more what's happened, I can't wait till tomorrow not knowing if he'll hurt you again like before".

"All I can say at the moment is that it was a shock to me, it turns out that Jay is Agnes's son", was the reply.

"I can't believe it and all this time none of us knew" Issa said.

"Don't worry, there wasn't anyone more surprised than me when he walked in and Agnes announced who he was, just as I was telling her about the special person who'd bought me the gold rose broach".

"Well what's going to happen next, you going to see him again or is this just a one off night "? she asked.

"Not sure really but one thing's for sure, I don't think I could go through the hurt of him walking away again, but the funny thing is when we had a few drinks with Agnes and her friends this evening, he introduced me as his fiancé" Corry's replied.

"He what, what's he playing at, has he mention any more about this since then"?

"No, but he's very deep, so I'm going to leave it until were back at the apartment or even tomorrow" was Corry's answer.

"Now let's go and party".

The party went on till the early hours of the morning before someone decided it was now Christmas day and so would all make their way home for an early breakfast.

The entire apartment was peaceful and quiet as they returned, which was nice for they could relax having a coffee while talking things through as it had been impossible with everyone around asking questions all the time. Talk, well that was a joke for when they'd finished coffee, Jay stood up, looked at Corry with a certain wanting in his eyes and said;

"After you, young lady, you're coming with me now as I'm never going to let you go again and anyway my bed is a lot bigger than the one you have."

Corry being a good girl just did what she was told as he led, she followed. There was something different about that night as Jay was a lot softer than she could remember him being in Cyprus but then again he actually showed feelings towards her this time.

It was as they entered the bedroom, he swung round to undo her dress, carefully placing the it on a side chair; she in turn kicked off her shoes as he laid her down gently on the king sized bed, having removed his clothing, he moved to lay beside her with a lingering look as much to say, oh what a fool I've been to get so close to losing this woman. Placing his arm softly around her smooth body, turning slightly to kiss her soft mouth slowly, as the excitement arising in both their bodies was now at a rapid speed and couldn't be contained much longer as he entered her with a gust of emotion raging inside, until they both came together.

It was quick, soft and passionate but with such emotion which was more of a need than anything else for both of them.

Jay had never been like this before, this was a new side to him, kind but considerate to her needs, putting his arm around her exhausted, until asleep overcame them both.

The morning frost was now starting to bite with the sound of birds at the window in a chorus of harmony which broke all peaceful dreams as they awoke. Funny how you go to bed all warm and cuddly and yet when you wake up in the morning it's so cold that everything is freezing, well it must be as there was something digging into her back so hard and solid and it had no intention of melting under the covers as Corry turned to face Jay only to see the warmth in his face;

"Did you sleep well sweetheart", he asked, moving towards her shoulder, placing his lips with passion then rotating towards her luscious breasts which were starting to swell by now, as his warm sliver touched her delicate skin, he could see her nipples rising outwards begging for his undivided attention as he then moved his hand down her body in a slow taunting movement with a velvet touch of the outer breast now and again.

"Do they give milk this early in a morning" he enquired as his mouth clasped round the nipple sucking vigorously.

"No but I can feel something that will" she replied which excited him even more.

"Well as I haven't got a bottle, I'll have to find somewhere to store it then, any suggestions he smirked.

By then the sucking had increased to such a point that her whole body was all over the place aching with desire, the desire of the man that had brought all her expectations to the fore on an island that gave her so much pleasure and now was to experience that pleasure yet again with an extravagance you wouldn't believe possible. This wasn't going to be all about him she thought moving her body suddenly, pushing him backwards and mounting him like a race horse in the Grand National.

"Go sweetheart ride me like only you know how to "he said panting to the rhythm of her body, yes she rode him to a beat that increased her body suctions to a height that only she would cross the finishing line first with him being a very close second.

No, nothing had really changed emotionally between them only the softer side of Jay was starting to rise to the fore; this was a side that she'd never experienced as he was so dark in his thoughts, it wasn't impossible to read his true emotions.

Time to shower, dress and look presentably ready for the big day, after all it was Christmas and although Agnes was brought up a little different whereby the German tradition was to celebrate with presents to be given out on the 24th December, he had always been brought up to celebrate an extra gift on Christmas day as well. Agnes however did a little mixture as she celebrated Christmas as in the country she lived in but she also kept to her traditional celebrations of birth as well.

To see the expression on Agnes's face when both Corry and Jay emerged together holding hands was a vision of happiness, as this was going to be the best present that anyone could have given her she thought and therefore she intended to saviour the moment of the two people who had been closest to her heart for a long time.

A hearty breakfast was the order of the morning. Again, this was later followed by the traditional Christmas dinner with all the trimmings, which was a fair sight for anyone to feast their eyes upon. Now for the presents, as thoughts of them had slipped out of everyone's mind the evening before with all the excitement that had presented itself. Corry had bought Agnes a beautiful cashmere shawl, Jay on the other hand had designed a filigree ring for his mother from the same little place the rose broach came from in Cyprus.

Agnes bought her son a Rolex watch inscribed on the back with love; she had also got the same for Corry who she'd looked on as a daughter from the first day they met. But the biggest surprise of all was that Agnes had given both Jay and Corry an equal share of the art company that she owned in Kensington.

What a day Agnes thought to herself, she had never seen her son looking so happy and content as he did at this time, he was a good boy who had brought her so much love and contentment in her life and now that's all she wanted for him, contentment, knowing Corry as she did, she had every faith knowing she was the right one to stand by his side and fulfil this wish of hers.

That night Agnes had arranged for just a few friends to come for drinks, these were people that couldn't attend the night previously, it would only be for cocktails and bites nothing elaborate just a small gathering which was nice really not being able to get out as much as she'd have like to with her legs playing up from time to time. It was a well-known fact that she loved to party but through circumstances it wasn't possible so she used to frequently hold dinner parties and then join friends when they went to the theatre on special occasions.

The day went to plan with everyone in a relaxed mood after all the food, a few games of cards, board games and with the Queens speech thrown in which was another thing which was traditional to listen to in houses all over the country followed by a little nap which was exhausting for all before getting ready for the evening.

Corry as usual dressed in a lovely little red satin dress looked beautiful as she mixed with the guests that night, although these were a lot older people than the night before, she had such a great personality, everyone just took to her instantly, also being nice for Agnes to show off her new daughter in law to be. Drinks went down very nicely as they all mingled to Agnes's delight and it was only when her dear son Jay asked everyone to be quite as he had an announcement to make, the unexpected happened;

"On my Mother's behalf, I would like to thank you all for coming here tonight, as very dear friends of hers I understand that you are always on hand to keep her company and due to the fact that I'm living abroad at the present moment in time and therefore am not close enough to be here very often. I would also like to thank you on a personal note as I appreciate this immensely".

Now taking a deep breath while he'd everyone's attention, he paused before adding;

"I may also add that I have an announcement of my own to make for those who weren't here last night, as I would also like you to meet my future wife Miss Corrander Sharp, some of you may know her already as Corry, who is in fact a leading fashion designer here in the city, but it is tonight that I am the one who has the designs on her as my future wife".

Yet again the silence was deafening as they knew Jay was nothing but a spoilt playboy who Agnes had ruined all his life, yes, it was well known he'd had his flings and it had been rumoured in the past that he'd got a couple of girls pregnant and paid them off to have abortions which his mother knew nothing about, but to get married, that was something different even for him. Corry on the other hand was in total amazement, that being the second time Jay had made this speech in less than twenty-four hours.

Did I hear it right she thought, did I miss something, am I dreaming as guests came up to congratulate.

But It was then that Jay walked up and whispered;

"It's alright darling we'll go and pick out an engagement ring of your choice in the next few days before making arrangements for the wedding, which I thought would be sometime in April, that will give you plenty time to get the spring collection over with".

Oh yes, he'd thought of everything, and yes, she was madly in love with him, and yes, she would have accepted his proposal if he'd bothered to have ask, but still, did she somehow miss something, as not for the life of her could she ever remember him asking her any part of this she thought.

Although the room was quite noisy by now, but still in shock when looking over to Agnes, who by then was taking everything in her stride with a smile that said her son was happy and therefore nothing was going to spoil it, for she was ecstatic at this news.

Nothing more was said on the matter as they mingled with everyone and seeing Agnes who was just over the moon at that announcement was heart-warming in itself. It wasn't until later that night when everyone had departed, that Agnes not only gave her blessing to the announcement but said her little piece whereby it was her dearest wish that they would have met and fallen in love as it had been with her own marriage, this truly must have been fate she insisted.

Fatigue was now starting to set in as the last forty-eight hours had been a little too much for Agnes and it was now starting to tell although she wouldn't admit, but having noticed this Jay stepped in and thanked everyone for coming remarking that his mother was now starting to get tired and maybe in pain so would kindly bid good night to everyone which they all understood, as she retired to her bed leaving the young lovers alone.

Taking the moment in hand. it was now that Corry ceased the chance to have a good talk to Jay in which she hoped to clarify a few things;

"What was all that about us getting engaged and the wedding being in April", she enquired.

"What do you mean darling "he asked? with a sympathetic expression

"I mean two proposals in two nights, which I didn't know anything about and which came out of the blue" she answered.

"Why out of the blue, you do love me and you will marry me won't you"?

"Of course I love you and yes, I'll marry you but it would have been nice, to have been asked before you made any announcement" was her answer.

"Well I'm sorry but I never thought, I was just so proud of you and wanted to tell the whole world that you were mine, can you forgive me darling" he asked as he rolled his big brown eyes towards her.

"Of course I can, you know darn well I can, but in future I would like to be consulted first in these matter that concern me ".

"Don't worry sweetheart, I'll make it up to you in bed seen as I've been such a bad boy in your eyes" he said sarcastically.

And yes, he was as good as his word, for Corry wasn't going to let him off with a promise like that for she wanted his body just as much as he wanted hers. The night was still young as both lay down together kissing passionately while holding each other so tightly, for Cyprus seemed such a long time away and they were about to make up for all the passion they'd missed in the time they had been apart. Oh how he'd missed the warmth, her touch, the feelings that aroused him whenever she came near, yes, this desire he had for her was a longing that never went away whenever he thought about her, but still he couldn't tell her for then it would show his true feelings for he'd be breaking a lifetime habit if he did.

Moving down to those beautiful breasts that was now back in his life forever and taking those pert nipples that he loved so much into his mouth, and between his teeth as the excitement grew in his loins, nestling like a baby enjoying its first feed of the day from its mother's milk, yes, he'd missed this longing sensation while they'd been apart.

How could he have ever thought that a woman could have produced such a feeling as this throughout his body, in the past it had been just an urge that ran through him to attain his own satisfaction but this was different for he wanted to give satisfaction to Corry more than the satisfaction he received.

Her breasts heaving as she panted to the suction of those tender lips around her nipples which drove her crazy, but still she couldn't move for he had full control and was enjoying her body so much, while not wanting to disturb, she pushed her knee between his thighs knowing his erection would come into contact and the arousal would intensify even greater.

Now two could play at this game she thought, and knowing that he would position himself at an angle where her toes would play with his huge balls which was now on lustful fire, for she would be in the driving seat to command the next move. No, she was no fool, knowing he wouldn't be able to resist taking that sucking action to a more favourable spot that was now flowing with her juices wildly.

Her creamy clitoris now aching for the pleasure of what those nipples had experienced, he succumbed to her silent wishes with no thought for himself as the dripping sperm slithered down his inner legs to the arousal of both their bodies. Sucking her juices vigorously as this body screamed out silently for more which was his way of apologising for what had happened earlier that evening but he was a man of needs himself and with his balls on fire, his penis dribbling at such a pace he knew he wouldn't be able to last much longer. And as he grabbed hold of the back of Corry's ankles pushing her legs up into the air and over his shoulder while entering his huge manhood inside of her wet vaginal canal with such an insertion that she screamed with delight for a rhythm that carried on until they both came to a satisfactory conclusion;

"Now am I forgiven for what I've done then" Jay asked laughing as he laid Corry into his arm for a night of slumber.

Corry wanting to have the last word replied;

"Maybe, I haven't made my mind up as yet; you may have to do a re-run of tonight before I think about forgiving you

It wasn't until the next morning when Corry phoned her friend Issa to say what had happened the previous night that everything started to sink in, again Issa let out a shrill of excitement that came down the phone in a deafening tone.

"I can't believe what's happened, one minute you are pining for this man and the next, you're not only getting engaged but he wants to set the date for the wedding, oh boy, when he makes up his mind he really does move quickly", Issa stated.

From that day on, it was a load of social events for both Corry and Jay together with the purchase of a ring that came first and foremost which was a three carat diamond solitaire set in platinum, not really what Corry wanted as she would have preferred something a little smaller maybe Victorian setting but no, Jay had to have the best as he'd had all of his privileged life with him having his own way as usual and Corry giving in to his wishes.

Was it going into the officer's mess up against all those stuffy wives with competition that he was far better than them, for that's just the impression he gave at times.

She wasn't good enough when he thought she was a shop girl but now he knew different, and she owned a successful business, something of a rising star in the city, who was his equal both financially and talented, it seemed it was a different ball game altogether, but then again she didn't mind too much for she loved Jay and as the old saying goes, love is blind and in this case it definitely was for the time being. It must also be said that Jay was head over heels in love with Corry for when she left the island to fly back to England he couldn't get her out of his head, like most men, he didn't realise what he'd got until she was gone.

Power had always ruled Jay and it wasn't any different now, he was used to calling all the shots with everyone, people thought it was the army training that had done this but I'm afraid that wasn't so for he'd been like it since a small boy, he only had to sulk and Agnes would give into him.

Her husband on the other hand had been the strength in the family putting his foot firmly down reminding his wife; she would regret it one day giving into the boy every time and to this, Agnes would look and think to herself that they'd been blessed with her niece's child to care and nourish as their own so that was her excuse for spoiling him.

Having been the best academically pupil in the school and so competitive at everything he put his mind to, when passing all exams before going onto university studying business and finance. But although he'd been offered a job in the city, decided that wasn't for him as he wanted a career with excitement and travel therefore entered the Army whereby he applied to go to Sandhurst and become an officer achieving and surpassing every obstacle on his way up. Yes, the pride on Agnes's face when anyone asked how he was doing, lit up the room.

On his twenty first birthday, Agnes bought him a Volvo 1800 sports car which in those days was rarely to be seen on the roads in England, for one they were classed as a very fast and furious vehicle and secondly, no one could afford such luxury

It seemed anything Jay wanted, his mother would appease her son's wishes and for this he never brought any trouble home or disgraced the family name like many young people that had everything at their fingertips.
It was the same with the woman he'd meet, after a couple of weeks wining and dining, maybe bedding them as well, he'd finally get bored and replace with another available candidate eliminating the relationship with no feelings just to move on to the next as he put it quite bluntly.

But for some reason Corry was different, with her there was a contented look about him whenever she was around, something he'd never experienced before. He did in fact adore Corry from the first moment he set eyes on her in that bar on the island, he wouldn't have let her go then but for the status factor of his position in the Army.

It was just one of those things that in his position he would marry into a wealthy family, although he was wealthy in his own right for it was a matter of status, but there again there's a saying that money goes to money and how true it was, unfortunately there was a new generation coming up who was so ambitious, things were to change.

There was a move to have more women in powerful positions, ambitious women who were thirsty for power, women who had more drive for they knew what they wanted, not to be just housewives bringing up children but to be in the workforce earning their own money to spend how they wished. They would dress with a sexy, sensual look which was to please their taste and not to please others.

Times were certainly changing alright; with a Queen on the throne it wouldn't be long before there were more women in power, maybe running the country. Now Corry was aware of all this and wasn't going to drag her heels as she wanted to be a part of this change, to be the modern woman of the world who would reach the top of her profession and be recognised for her achievements.

Jay on the other hand would never accept that Corry was his true equal in that sense and therefore at times would attempt to put her down, but she put that down to his army training and therefore overlooked it for the time being, but that wouldn't always be the case as he would find in time, she was a very shrewd businesswoman who knew exactly where she was going and he wasn't going to step in her way at any price.

There was a lot of work to be done before the wedding but most importantly was the fact they would have to visit the family up north letting them know personally before word got out for as you know what Chinese whispers were like, exaggerated to the hilt and if the family got wind of the wedding before she could tell them herself is would feel like an act of betrayal.

So as time was of the essence, this would have to be done before the New Year and therefore arrangements were made for both Corry and Jay to travel to Doncaster on an early morning train, stay the night and return the next day after breaking the news to the family in a relaxed way over perhaps a nice meal in the countryside.

Having made a few phone calls everything was set to go and to be honest, Corry was looking forward to the break although short, it would give them both a little time to be together as a couple. There was also another matter she wanted to discuss with the family and that was news of two new factories that were to open in the New Year, for it was her intention to present her brother with a share of the company as a silent partner in the near future.

As always, the excitement of returning home to the family filled her with a somewhat peace of mind for at times she felt a little guilty, she couldn't spend as much time as she'd have liked with them, but there again, tried her best to compensate by making life easier financially and with this in mind an introduction to the man she'd fallen in love with was to come. A little apprehensive at breaking the news but all the same Corry knew in her heart they would love Jay as much as she did, when they saw how happy he made her.

Chapter 11

The train now was leaving Kings Cross at approximately 6am,
arriving in Doncaster shortly before 8am, having pre-warned the family of their flying visit, staying at a hotel overnight making arrangements for them all to go out for a meal as they had news but not to worry as it was good news.

Corry's grandmother wasn't too worried as she'd a feeling it was something of a personal matter but on the other hand her brother Paul was a little panicky for this was a bit unusual for his sister to carry on like this on the spur of the moment. Never the less they would all meet about six that evening for a family meal whereby the bombshell would be presented, that a wedding was to be planned for just after the spring fashion show.

By the time they arrived in Doncaster, everything had been set into motion whereby a taxi was waiting to take them to the hotel and having arrived at the hotel, Corry decided that after a little breakfast, maybe shopping was on the menu, not as though she needed anything but it was always a good excuse to see the town that she loved so much and maybe catch up with a few friends. Yes, London was great but then again Doncaster was her home town that she'd grown up in and therefore it was just nice to wander around familiar surroundings.

It was late afternoon before they returned to the hotel, and sure enough there was a message waiting, stating that Paul had already made arrangements for dinner at a restaurant just outside of town, knowing how much his sister loved the Swiss Cottage so had taken it upon himself to book a table, a fine restaurant that was always a little special, expensive but his sister was well worth pushing the boat out so to speak, not being able to see her as often as he'd have liked.

Having told the family, she intended to bring up a friend, they obviously assumed it to be Issa that was accompanying her, having taken to this girl in a big way.

Early evening came, as Paul arrived at the hotel to collect his sister and her friend having already picked grandmother up first, and with Corry dressed in a little black cocktail dress, shoes and handbag to match, with a fancy shawl wrapped around her shoulders, looking stunning as usual, Jay dressed in a smart suit, white shirt and tie to match looked just the part of an Officer and Gentleman which was in fact true, in every sense of the word.

Now there was something about Corry that night they thought, a beaming face, a happy relaxed posture, but not being able to put his finger on it, he now had his suspicions there was bound to be something of a surprise coming;

"Hi Sis" is everything all right as your phone call got us a bit worried", he asked.

"Stop panicking for goodness sake" was Corry's reply laughing as she said it.

Paul looked a bit bewildered but all the same didn't read too much into that remark as knowing his sister, she had a dry sense of humour.

"Come on you two, its cold outside and Nan's in the car waiting, so we'd better be off", but as they jumped into the car, Corry added;

"Oh by the way, I hope you didn't mind but this is my friend Jay whom I met in Cyprus" nothing else was said although Paul did glance over to his grandmother with a smirk on his face and a thought running through his mind, what's she been up to now.

Having exchange pleasant conversation for a while, they were soon to reach Swiss Cottage, with Corry thinking to herself, this was going to be harder than anticipated, breaking the news that I'm now engaged and to be married before the summer, a bit difficult but then again nothing ever came easy for her, so why should this be any different, as the car pulled into the beautiful grounds of the restaurant.

Ah yes, this was how I remember the place, very expensive and not the kind of place we could ever afford when growing up, mind you, times change and this time, it was for the better;

"Now madam, may I take your coats" the waiter enquired as he approached their party in a professional stance.
"We have a nice table near the window which was reserved for you as requested, the menus are all set out, and the wine waiter will be with you shortly to take your order, if there's anything you would like that's not on the menu, then please don't hesitate to ask and I'll send the chef over to see you personally".

"That's fine "Paul muttered as they took their seat.

"Excuse me, could you order me a bottle of champagne please", Corry asked as the waiter turned to leave.

Well that was a surprise as she never even liked it, let alone order it to their knowledge, for her tipple had always been vodka and tonic and therefore seizing the moment Paul couldn't resist piping up with;

"Have you gone mad sis, or aren't you telling us something, oh my god, you're not pregnant are you"?

"Oh for god's sake Paul, stop panicking. and no I'm not, but as I've just got engaged and intend to get married shortly after the spring showing, I do think this calls for a celebration don't you" taking a deep breath as she added, "Oh by the way this is my fiancé, Jay".

"You're a brave man taking my sister on aren't you, but having said that, we wish you all the best as she deserves someone in her life to look after her, right Nan" was Paul's answer to the news as he looked towards grandmother. Grandmother just looked in amazement as her eyes filled up with happiness, before saying;

"Welcome to the family Jay, you have one of the best there, so look after her as she means so much to us, you know."

"Oh I intend to don't you worry about that "was the reply in a courteous manner.

Yes, grandmother liked this man, she could see straight away that he really loved her granddaughter but having said that Paul wasn't too sure, there was something very dark about Jay he thought but putting that aside he wished his sister all the happiness but all the same he would keep an eye on the situation as instincts told him he wasn't all he seemed in his opinion.
.
Now for the meal which was a garnish of vegetables accompanied by the largest steaks you could image, followed by apple pie and custard, Irish coffee and small chocolates, well you were in the north of England not like those small bird like meals you got in London, but there again that's what you paid for in those days, in such a high class establishment.

How would you describe that night, well it was one of those nights that everyone got on well together with the conversation flowing from one subject to another but like every enjoyable evening it became time to return back to the hotel having gone through all the childhood memories as you would on such a happy occasion and as time was passing quickly, they would have to call it a day. But never the less promised to get up sometime in the future before the wedding where they'd be able to spend a little more time getting to know each other.

It was shortly after midnight when they arrived back at the hotel after saying all their farewells leaving Corry's grandmother in tears at such a short visit, and after reiterating what had been said before, about a return, a kiss farewell followed by talk of all the wedding arrangements that would be forwarded on as soon as they were finalised. Knowing it wouldn't be too long before they'd be able to meet up again when discussing full arrangement for the wedding.

Feeling a little sad leaving the family but that's how it had to be, although this time it was especially sad for behind all those smiles, her grandmother's thoughts would have been, if only Corry's mother was alive to see her daughter walk down the aisle. Yes, this was every mother's dream, to see her daughter walk down the aisle on her wedding day full of happiness, but alas this wasn't to happen on this great occasion.

And with an early to rise the next morning with a little sadness about leaving the family, both Corry and Jay headed towards the station for the 8am train back to London, the journey being straight forward after having enjoyed breakfast on the train, so it wasn't too long before pulling into Kings Cross station.

Having jumped into a taxi, Corry thought to herself, this would probably be the last time she'd manage to go home before the wedding but didn't want to tell the family, and therefore would bring them to London instead. It was a shame really as she just loved the thrill of returning home, for Doncaster would always be her home, a northern girl at heart. Going back to the flat with Jay by her side, seemed a little awkward as the only person she'd ever shared it with was Issa, but none the less she would have to get used to it as Jay was her life now that she was about to be married.

New year's Eve and everyone was out to party the night away but first of all a meal had been booked to take Agnes, Issa, and Rob to a cosy little restaurant which both Corry and Jay had chosen especially, after the meal they would then put Agnes in a taxi taking her back to her apartment, that being her wishes, not wanting to spoil the fun of the party.

The meal was superb with all the trimmings which you would expect from a high class restaurant in the Kensington area, but it became noticeable after the meal, that Agnes was in fact looking a little tired by the end of the night so after wishing her well for the New Year, and putting her safely in a taxi home, the remaining four sauntered off to meet their friends in a local bar, which had a running buffet to take the old year out and welcome the new year in, which in other words was, a good old knee's up.

The night was something out of a wild story book for unbeknown to most of them, John the landlord had arranged for a local band to play, and what a band, well more of a rock group than a band for by the time they finished, all the street was up and dancing, not only in the bar but overflowing into what you would call a modern day street party. For that's how it was in those days, everyone contributed when music was the life and soul of the community, ending up as one big party.

Having turned 5am by the time everyone returned to their homes shattered but none the less with a sense of enjoyment, letting in the New Year, it was now time for the young lovers to return to Agnes's place with one or two New Year resolutions of their own that they'd made on the way.

As a result of the evening there was to be no love making that night for as they climbed into bed, the only thing they were about to do was sleep as their heads hit the pillow.

The next week passed so quickly, both Corry and Jay trying to sort out arrangement for the forthcoming wedding, he wanted the wedding to be in April while she was adamant she couldn't manage it before the spring showing, so after a lot of discussions between everyone, it was decided, as Corry's mother wouldn't be there to see her daughter marry, then they would do the second best thing, in her honour, and make the date for the 23rd July, the wedding day which would have been her mother's birthday and also the one Corry was determined to have put in place anyway.

Jay wanted it sooner but fully understood how much this meant to Corry after discussing it with his own mother and so went along with the idea as to be honest it made sense. For choosing the later date, it appeared, Corry would then have sufficient time to organise the spring collection as her priority without any pitfalls.

Nothing lasts forever as the holiday season was now over and time for the boys return to Cyprus, leaving Corry and Issa to get on with the preparations for the spring show, as it seemed the next few months were going to be so hectic, and in any case there wouldn't have been much time to have arranged the wedding anyway with all the designs not fully completed and with the new factories to open, it seemed everything had come at once as this usually happens in life.

Now the priorities were the designs, although they'd been done to perfection she wasn't sure about the colours, these were a little weak in her opinion, and therefore pondered on an idea that would knock the socks off the industry, but what, she just couldn't concentrate with everything that had been going on and that was the problem, she needed new ideas. Perhaps after the boys had returned to Cyprus, her inspiration would also return whereby allowing her to concentrate a little better, not having anything to divert her attentions elsewhere she thought.

Oh how time flies when you don't want it to and therefore It soon came round to that day when both Jay and Rob received notification of their flights which was always a sad time for their partners to accept, not being able to guarantee when they'd get leave again. But that was the army for you, you were a serving soldier that had committed to an organisation which demanded all your time, being twenty-three hours in a day with only one hour's grace as they drilled into them.

A meal at a local restaurant the night before they were due to leave was on the cards but even that was tinged with sadness realising it was their last night together before their return to barracks. And so Corry had decided that Jay would spend the last evening at Agnes's apartment due to him wanting to spend a little time with his mother which was understandable in the circumstances but at the insistence of Agnes she herself was also to stay, being a couple now and therefore after a couple of drinks it was to their bed that they retired.

The silence was deafening as they lay, holding each other for a considerable time, but as time went by so did the urge of contentment as Jay pushed Corry onto her back, pushing open her legs with the force of his knee before sliding down her body to that wonderful nest that was awaiting his call like a homing pigeon. Sliding his tongue into the deep wilderness of mystery as he muttered something about having to take one last tour round the new home he was going to settle in for the rest of his life.

Sucking with strength of a hurricane as her river of waves flooded to the point of releasing her peace and tranquillity, that he wanted to remember until his return and without a trace of wanting a satisfaction for himself, which had never happened before, as sleep then called to them both.

Morning came and with the flights back to Cyprus which was to go in the afternoon but like all RAF flights, personnel had to be at the airfield for a set time and getting to Lytham was sometimes a bit difficult, so an early train had to fit in with their parting.

Yes, there were tears all around as a lot had happened in such a short time, a lot of things you could only dream of, but in fact those dreams became true for some, but for others they would have to wait for that date in the future.

As the train pulled away with both Rob and Jay on, to the sight of two young ladies crying for their lovers, a sight that would become only too familiar in the near future as that was what forces families came to expect, the tearful parting of couples, also the happy delights when they were reunited. Well, there was nothing more to do in a situation like this but for the girls to throw themselves into the mountains of work, knowing that it wouldn't be too long before the nearness of time would bring their arms around those they loved yet again.

This is exactly what happened, the next couple of months, working all hours to get the preparations finalised for the spring collection, but still Corry's mind was a blank as to a new idea that would Wow the show, and therefore put it down to nerves of the oncoming wedding which she'd got in the back of her mind. And with the city buzzing over what all the other designers were attempting to do, still no idea as to what she would come up with, therefore knowing if something didn't materialise quickly, she would be losing not only face in the industry but also money for her backers and that wasn't good at all.

Then in a fit of desperation decided, maybe taking Issa to lunch would be a good idea and then perhaps between them they could come up with something, but it didn't stop there as it was lunch and a few drinks, the result was obvious. Therefore, a walk to clear their heads had to be on the cards before calling it a day, meanwhile with a wild suggestion that Issa had never been to the Zoo, that was the place to go.

Stupid idea maybe but yes, that sounded about right when you've had a few drinks, the animals would be able to make fun of then in their giggly state of mind. But then again that idea was the one that brought Corry to her senses for all of a sudden, she stopped dead in her tracks as a couple of tigers came into view and with a screech of;

"GOT IT, that's what I'm going to do, all this time and it was right under my nose, I just can't believe it she muttered".
"What you on about', have you gone mad" was the words that came from her friend "noticing that passer-by's were looking at them to the extent that they were on something

No, No, No, that's it, the zoo, black and white prints, spots, zig zags, stripes all animal colours, that's what we're going to do for the collection something no one would ever dream of doing, the collection will be of a wild life theme" Corry said loudly

In the end Issa thought, she'd gone mad at first, but yes it sounded great although a bit risky, with a wild idea like that but never the less it was wild ideas that worked at times.

"Are you sure, no one's ever attempted anything like that before because if they have we'll be a laughing stock, mind you at least we'll give the public something to talk about".

Corry smiled to herself, and thought, well if the industry is talking about me now, they'll definitely talk about me when I've finished with this collection, as I intend to give them all a run for their money.

Having run the idea past Peter for both new factories to concentrate on the lines of a safari collection, knowing she could adapt the designs already completed to fit the fabrics she had in mind and with this idea, Peter would back her to the hilt. These would be kept under wraps for the big showing of couture and they would also be adapted for the ready to wear market, going into the department stores immediately after the shows.

Although this had never been done before and therefore a big gamble to say the least, never the less you have to take some gambles in life to succeed she thought, for if this paid off, they could flood the market with ready to wear clothing, it would however make a dent in the couture market but on a financial aspect it would double or treble the benefits.
The small workshop would still design for special clients as that had been her bread and butter so far and didn't want to let those valued clients down, but having thought about it, she would make the end of the show for couture

designs followed by the big finish of the bridal wear, yes, that's it, that's what we'll go with Corry thought.

Putting all this to Peter, well just to see the smile on his face was enough, as he remarked;

"I think we're going to make a lot of enemies but, oh boy are we going to make a lot of money if you pull this one off.

"Well that's the idea, and that's what we're going to go with", Corry stated adamantly.

The next few weeks were so hectic; Corry never had much time to contact Jay although he was never out of her thoughts for long, she had a driving ambition to put her ideas into practice even though she was exhausted, nothing was going to stand in her way now she thought.

The ready to wear simple designs that showed off the figure, knee length skirts with tops to match, dresses that just flowed with a little imagination when it came to showing off the curves in the right places. Everything just fell into place without any effort now, as for time, well even that wasn't a problem as they were well ahead of the schedule with the help of Peter's ideas.

And by now, Corry was on a roll and therefore decided to take yet another gamble, that was to go with the same theme when doing the special couture line, only this time she would team up tribal prints with bold plain colours, this making a statement, a plain fitted dress with a tribal jacket and vice versa.

Knowing this was yet another gamble but all the same willing to go with it as if you don't take chances when they arise you'll never get anywhere she thought, for even the elite liked a little imagination when showing off to their friends, The only thing she was a little hesitant about this time was, if colours were too bold for the upper class market they could ruin her reputation as a one off creation, so would it be viable to proceed this way, but then again being on a high, thought, in for a penny in for a pound so to speak.

As usual, the three wedding gowns which would take centre stage would also be another gamble for Corry, as she'd decided that instead of going with a traditional white wedding gown, it would be an ivory shade of heavy satin and although It had always been tradition that you wore a white wedding gown because you were a virgin, times were now changing and in many cases that didn't follow.

Peter however, did have reservations about the couture line but then having thought seriously about it, knew just how stubborn Corry was when her mind was made up and so went along with plans as she'd presented them.

Another idea was to put a flower girl on the cat walk to accompany each bride as she took centre stage, a little girl dressed in a frilly dress throwing petals from a basket as she walked, which would also catch the audiences imagination as to how they'd look on their wedding day. No one had used children on a catwalk like this, but if it paid off, then that would be another line she could probably go into at a later date she thought.

The city was all of an excitement leading up to the major shows, these being for the top names, although Corry was starting to be recognised amongst a few celebrities, but still wasn't a front page name and therefore couldn't pick and choose her slot. Having to rely on luck for what was allocated, being such a small name that most people didn't yet know, and yet again it would be on the last day of the fashion show that her slot would be allocated, when all the top designers had shown their creations.

Now this wasn't a threat to the big designers or so they thought, well in their mind she was just a silly little girl who'd come up from nothing, had a showing in the last season, and made a bit of a name for herself which had gone to her head.

These men in the city thought Corry was a ten-day wonder who'd burn herself out at the showing, and therefore with no threat to them at all, a young girl who had ideas above her station as some put it, never the less they hadn't anticipated what a strong determination they were up against.

The arrogance of these money people who'd been brought up with a silver spoon in their mouth was blatantly obvious in their attitude towards a newcomer, especially a woman as this was seen to be a man's world, with one even making a comment about, men were the brains behind designs and women were there to sew the garments up.
Oh boy, were they in for a shock this time, they'd got away with remarks so offensive in the past but Corry was now out for war. She may have an unknown model in Issa with very little experience, but that unknown model was now starting to get talked about which was earning her a lot of money.

Being allocated the final day of the week wasn't so bad for at least the general public would have chance to see what the upper class could afford and then there was the bright side where Corry was to bring a new trend to the city being affordable designs.

The week had started on a high with outstanding celebrities bringing colour to the city and, with the press raving about London being the fashion capital of the world with couture that couldn't be matched even by Paris standard, there was still an open opportunity for maybe a newcomer to the scene.

As the last day of the week was now upon them, it was announced in the morning, an unknown Japanese knitwear company would be presenting his designs into the country, again, no one had any knowledge of this man, but to the surprise of the audience. This was a big hit that had everyone talking, the models again were unknown, apparently they'd been taken from the technical college that was studying fashion, all young students that was only too pleased to earn a little money doing something they only dreamed of doing.

Dressed in sweaters, cardigans and even little shift dresses, they looked a picture of youth which was so very different from the highbrow fashion models that had supported the cat walk in the past week.

Being so professional looking as they modelled the elegant knitwear showing it off to perfection, yes it was very different to what women wore in England and yes beauty instilled, luxury and practicability.

It was after their show had finished, that Corry went over to congratulate them all on doing such a fine job, she also had a bigger motive in mind, and that was, if everything went as she hoped with her show, maybe she could persuade the owner of this knitwear company to have dinner and talks which would be advantageous to both of them. The advantage may be beneficial in a way that combining both companies which would give an opening into the British market for this unknown talented man, for it was hard enough for new comers like herself but a foreigner at that time was impossible.

The Japanese had the markets for the purest of silks which would help her summer designs and for the winter, she could work around the pure cashmere garments, these again would tie into a range that would work well for both of them should it come to fruition.
Yes, in her mind it was another idea looming, although she would of course consult with Peter but at the end of the day she'd set her heart on it, another factory maybe?

Having said her pleasantries to everyone concerned, it was now the time for her showing as this was scheduled for 2pm.

Walking slowly into the tent that had been erected for the showing, she went back stage to check on all the girls that had kindly offered their services to model that day. These being her own staff that knew the clothes better than anyone, for they were the ones that had put their heart and soul into every last detail in a hope that the show would be a success.

Yes, they were good girls and weren't too bothered about big money to model the outfits although Corry did pay them well, they just wanted the acclamation for what they'd achieved. And with this, the show was about to commence with all those who had been back stage on tender hooks.

First of all, it was the sombre music of the jungle sounds as Corry peeked out onto the catwalk to the sight of the first couple of rows only to see the audience looking in disgust at each other and yet bewildered, as in their minds she knew what they'd thinking', has this girl gone mad, this is London not Africa.

Then all of a sudden, the first three models appeared wearing fitted dresses in tribal print material, with jackets in plain bold colours, chunky heeled shoes and little clutch bags, as all eyes were on the outfits in amazement, but before the audience could get their breath, another three models followed, but these were in dresses of plain bold colours with tribal printed jackets, chunky heels and the same clutch bags.

There were no hats in sight, for the models just let their hair down naturally, now the upper class of London was used to a lady wearing a hat at all times, but Corry was determined to change this idea, she wanted them to look smart but casual as hats sometime made women look far too formal.

As the music picked up more to the beat, yet again three more models appeared in dresses off the shoulder, showing a little cleavage as they entered the catwalk; yes, a total of 15 girls paraded the catwalk with similar outfits thus coming to an end of the couture lines.

Now, was to be the time of deliberation as everything went silent with the lights appearing at full blast to end the first half of the show.
It was at that point a woman who was sat in the front row, stood up and shouted;
"Bravo, Bravo, "someone has actually made us look and feel like real women".

To this statement the audience reacted in agreement; the press went even more over the top which surprised Corry, for they were so stick in the mud or so she thought in her past experience of them, but that night they were totally in full agreement it seemed.

It was some 20 minutes later when the second half of the show commenced, which was to be the biggest gamble, for these were all ready to wear garments that would be dispatched to the shops immediately after the show and therefore the tension was surreal.

Knowing the time had come when it would either be sink or swim, she stood at the side of the stage on tender hooks as the music commenced, again, to an African feel with drums in the background together with animal sounds which filled the air.

Now on this occasion, she had arranged for grass to be spread over the stage creating a feel of the jungle. This was a little different, for as the drums started to beat, out came 10 models, one after another, dressed in bright colours with tribal designs all over them, they were short shift dresses this time which came just above the knee, shorts and tops, flowing casual blouses, sundresses that wrapped over the body and tied round the waist, and with girls walking with nothing on their feet to give a feeling of freedom of spirit in the open air.

Slowly walking back into the dressing rooms to change, they re-entered the catwalk again in clingy dresses this time. The theme had now changed to black and white zebra prints together with a leopard print to compliment the whole African feel.

The audience was aghast with excitement as no one had ever been as daring as to create such a style or even a showing such as this, and with the whole thing screaming out', look here, we've come and yes here we are to stay, and be noticed.

In those days' young girls left school got a job, met a nice boy, got married and then had a family, very few trained for a career and so was quite happy just being housewives with maybe a few hours working to help with financial outgoing of the household. But things were now changing where more and more women worked full time by choice and therefore could afford these extra luxuries for themselves.

Corry knew instantly by the expressions on the face of buyers that sat in the front row what a winner this show was turning out to be and that was before the showing of the new range of bridal wear, garments which she was confident, would wow the socks off them all at affordable prices that everyone could afford.

Gone was the old fashioned homemade clothes that everyone had to make themselves for special occasions, this was a new concept she hoped would flood the department stores which was springing up in all the big towns by now. Yes, it was still a good thing that people made their own clothes as they couldn't afford to buy new ones all the time, but for the special occasion, it would be nice to save up and purchase something that was a bit special.

The ready to wear models slowly lined up one by one in their finest of clothes, stopping to pick the grass and bits up off the catwalk as the drums got louder, when all of a sudden the music changed to the sound of birds singing in the background as the models started to descend one by one.

The lights dimmed to a near darkness with only the sound of birds singing. The audience seemed to be transfixed by this time as to what was happening next, then lo and behold, the bright lights came on with a twinkle as though set in a midnight palace. When out walked the first of the models showing off the bridal wear which was;

A soft ivory heavy satin dress fitted down to the waist which flared fully down to the floor, a small coronet placed firmly on the model's head accompanied by a three quarter net veil studded with tiny diamante's, yes it definitely was outstanding, plain but with a statement.

The second model wore an ivory dress which was fitted from the neckline to under the bust in what they called the empire line, which again tapered down to the floor; in this case, the dress had long fitted sleeves all in heavy satin. The train fitted to the back of the dress, which flowed for approximately three yards long and trailing magnificently, again a small diamante coronet was fixed on the model's head with just a small net veil that would cover her face, the only detail in this dress was all the edges were cut in a scalloped finish, plain maybe, but all the same outstandingly beautiful.

The third model again wore ivory heavy satin, but this was a sweetheart neck with fitted bodice into the waist, flaring out into a net skirt which finished just past the knees in a ballerina style, stitched into the net was sequins which shone like diamonds in the light as a detailed point, again the headdress comprised of a satin skull cap with a net veil attached.

All brides wore high heeled satin shoes to match the dresses and carried prayer books with a ribbon attached; at the end of the ribbon was a cream rose which dangled down beautifully in front of the dress.

Then out came three young girls who were no older than seven or eight, these were children of employees, each had silk ivory dresses which nipped in at the waist and floated down to their ankles. On the skirts, you could just about see the little embroidered butterflies which had all been sewn on by hand.
Each child carried a basket full of flower petals in which was thrown from side to side as they walked to the end of the catwalk and back. Now for their shoes, which were such a novelty, ivory satin with little butterflies sawn on the front of them and in each butterfly little scattered crystals shone as the light hit their matching their little dresses.

All of a sudden the music changed to the bridal march when out walked the star of the show in everyone's opinion.

For standing under an arch of roses, Issa paused to the delight of the audience, a beauty of perfection in anyone's eyes;

Her dress was of a heavy white satin with the willow pattern running through the material in silver thread, now the willow pattern for all who aren't aware, is a Chinese love story so as the lights hit the silver thread, it was the most wonderful vision you could wish for. Issa had the perfect body shape and therefore it had been created to fit her with perfection. There was no other detail in the style only a plain fit from top to bottom with a fish trail at the back, this was finished off with a cap of plain heavy satin in the shape of a flower fitted snugly onto the crown of her head, as she carried an arrangement of ivory roses.

Walking slowly to the end of the catwalk with a twirl so all could see, the audience couldn't believe their eyes, as magnificent wasn't the word for it, never had anyone seen anything so outstandingly beautiful before, this was a vision that all young girls would dream of for their wedding day,

It was thought that the whole show would be talked about for weeks at this rate as the lights dropped and on walked Corry in a simple little animal print dress, this was to be her style for a long time to come she thought being not only smart but also very comfortable to wear.

The show now coming to a finale as the lights started to rise, when Issa spoke up and said;

"I would now like to take the opportunity to thank Corry for what she has shown us tonight, as I think this will be a new beginning for the fashion world as we know it".

To this the crowds just let out such a roar of approval with cheering that could be heard a long way off as the evening drew to a close.
And as Corry's was the last of the shows for the week, the press had not taken her show seriously and therefore many had gone home as she was only a small fish in a big pond so to speak or so they were meant to believe from an outside source's
But with only a handful of photographers left to work their magic at the finale these would be the lucky ones of the week for this show would take London fashion week by storm in all the national papers and magazines. And yes they would be the ones that had the last laugh for this was the most outstanding show of the week. They would also be able to command a better price for their articles in the magazines, this had worked out nicely for them and they would never forget how Corry had looked after them with special seating arrangement she'd organised personally.

The star of the show was Issa, there was no doubt about it, and it was Issa that everyone wanted after the show, but that's not how it worked out for she was so loyal to Corry, the praise had to be put all on her for the wonderful artistry that she'd accomplished. Bringing out a burning desire in women that was to unleash the fashion industry like it had never been unleashed before.

The next day the papers were full of the new girl on the block who was about to turn the fashion industry on its heels, it was put nicely by one reporter that women were now making a stand in society after the showing of Corrander Sharp 's untimely fashions.

Yes, the headlines gave preference to her show over the rest of the week, it being the talking point on everyone's lips and to be honest, the big boys of the industry didn't like it one bit, this slip of a girl was getting far too big for her boots it had been said in some quarters.

The one drawback with all this was, she had some mighty powerful backers and therefore they'd have to watch their step very carefully, for money talks and they'd lose face if they made one wrong move, that's how it was in a city like London, it's not what you know but who you know as the saying goes and a very truthful saying indeed.

Corry was really starting to move in the right circles by now and with the backing of some powerful money, it was going to be hard to knock her down a peg or two was the rumours that circulated, but that was water off a ducks back as far as she was concerned for she now had real fighting spirit in her body which was going to show, she was now going places.

It was thought that her crazy ideas about bringing out a ready to wear line would just fade away like a bad dream, but no, that wasn't to be for the department stores had latched on to the idea and orders were flooding in so fast that the staff could hardly keep up with demands. Therefore, knowing she had a strong backing force in her staff she made sure they were looked after as they'd done the same for her in the beginning.

Everything had gone to plan and therefore the next step was to start with the wedding plans or so she thought.

It was a week or so after the show, being full of the joys of spring when walking into her office, only to find her secretary Shelia, in a flood of tears, although trying to hide it, she instinctively knew something was drastically wrong. Trying to ignore the situation for a little while before asking Shelia;

"What's the chance of you getting two coffees and chocolate biscuits as we may be able to have a catch up with events of the last week or so before the wedding plans begin"?

Sheila knew only too well that meant one thing, Corry wanted to know exactly why all the tears were and wouldn't give up until she'd told her, for that's exactly what she was like, always thinking of others before herself;

"Now what's the matter and don't tell me nothing, I just won't believe you having never seen you cry before".

Sheila had worked for Corry from the beginning, well, that was since she'd taken a few of the girls on from the college to help in the shop part time, but as it proceeded with the orders and everyone wanted a piece of Corry, then it was essential that she needed help not being able to manage everything herself.

And therefore Peter had suggested, one of the girls, who worked in the shop, was in fact a trained secretary and therefore knowing the industry as she did would be ideal to do all the office work and with that, offered her the job as an assistant to Corry. And to be honest it worked out well taking a lot of responsibilities off Corry's shoulders at that time, but obviously, as things got more and more hectic, Shelia's work became more demanding.

She was a quiet, timid 23year old young girl, always smart, well-spoken and altogether helpful, nothing much was known of her being a pretty private person both in and out of work, who it was understood, lived with her mother. Now, it was a complete surprise to see Shelia crying, obviously there was something drastically wrong for she wasn't the type who would knowingly let things get to her so easily.

Corry wasn't having any of the attitude you give when you're trying to hide something, the vacant look which says leave me alone but behind the sadness in her eyes, you could see it was a different matter for as they sat down for their coffee, Shelia couldn't hold her composure much longer, before she blurted out in one gasp of air;
"My mother's been taken into hospital for a serious operation and I can't really afford the time off when she comes home, they've said, she's to have constant care for a month after the operation for the fear of infection and as an only child and no other living relatives to help out, I just don't know which way to turn; can't afford to take time off as there's only my money coming in and to be honest we haven't any saving as we only just get by as it is".

"Oh for goodness sake, I thought someone had died, you'll take the time off and don't worry about being paid as we'll cover your wages until you're ready to return, now let's have less of this and go and take the rest of the day off, organize what's to be done at home and we'll see you in the morning, don't forget to call by Peter's office and let him know the situation before you leave and I'll sort the rest out with him "was Corry's last words on the subject.

Sheila couldn't believe her ears, for in those days' no one, helped you with your wages in situations like that, but there again Corry wasn't just a normal boss, she was one of the few people that cared and that's why everyone respected her so much.

Now as for Sheila's mother, she went on to have the operation with Corry sending both flowers and toiletries, while Sheila taking the time off to care for her and returning when all was well.

Like Chinese whispers, the rest of the staff heard what had happened, resulting in an almighty respect for their boss.

In the meantime, Corry had a wedding to plan, knowing as time was short, the only person she could rely on completely, was her faithful friend Issa so therefore with all hands to the deck so to speak they got down to designing a wedding dress. Being a rather private person, they proceeded to plan a small wedding with no fuss, only a few friends and family, a small church, and then a reception to be held at one of the local restaurants, well that was the plan as she wasn't a fussy person and hated all the attention that was made on these occasions.
The church would be booked and with a nearby restaurant to follow as the reception, the day was all set in her mind as she only wanted a small affair, in her opinion if you were in love, you showed each other as you'd no one else to prove anything to but yourselves.

But unbeknown to her, Jay had already arranged everything including the church and reception which was to be held in a far grander manner leaving Corry's job just to sort her dress, bridesmaid dress for Issa and the two small pageboys out. Yes, one of the girls who'd been with Corry from day one, had twin boys of seven, so Corry thought it would be nice to have them join in the celebration having known them since babies.

The dress in mind would be fitted, Ivory heavy satin flowing away to a fish tail at the back, it may be plain but that was just what she was like, plain and simple with scallop neckline, short sleeves and to finish off would be, a Veil of fine voile, dotted with tiny seed pearls all over, held on by a diamante tiara.

Now the flowers she'd set her heart on would be a bouquet of gold roses, for they were her mother's favourites.

Underwear, she'd already bought together with the ivory Italian leather high heel shoes.

Having sketched the dress already, it wouldn't be a big job for the girls to make and then all she'd have to do was add the finishing touches.

Issa's dress would be in heavy gold satin, fitted to show off her slim figure, gold shoes and an ivory prayer book as that's what she wanted to carry for the memory of her father.
The page boys again, would be in ivory and gold little satin suits with waistcoats.

Yes, she had all this figured out in her mind and therefore nothing should go wrong or so she thought, yet when contacting Jay, sparks started to fly for his idea of the wedding was drastically different to hers, as he'd wanted the big society thing with all the trimmings and therefore gone ahead and pre-booked it all when he arrived back at barracks without the courtesy of consulting her what so ever

This upset Corry as she wasn't the type to put on a big show of herself so decided to have a quite word with Agnes asking for advice, knowing full well if anyone would be able to talk to Jay, it would be her and therefore hoped a compromise may be in the best interest to solve what they both wanted.

Having talked it over with Agnes, was now surprised what the outcome was to be for she could see Corry's side knowing her well enough to realise that a big elaborate affair wasn't her thing and therefore making her feel so uncomfortable.

But on the other hand, knowing her son as she did, he had to have the best but on this occasion he couldn't have all his own way as it would backfire on him altogether, and so not wanting this to happen Agnes decided to have a word with Jay and maybe talk some sense into him before he lost her altogether, all because of his pig headedness.

Corry was a flamboyant woman in business but that didn't roll over into her private life as that was always kept away from the public and that's how she liked it. Now this was going to be a little awkward. But never the less it had to be done, as knowing her son and his stubbornness he wouldn't listen to Corry, just going ahead with what he wanted, therefore driving the love of his life away and that wasn't going to happen if she could at least prevent it.

Leaving it with Agnes for the time being, expecting she'd come back to her after speaking to Jay, she therefore put the plans on hold for the time being but as time was of the essence Agnes had other ideas and therefore contacted her son immediately before it was too late to salvage anything. And after a long conversation with him, it seemed she'd made some headway, whereby he listened, but didn't like what he heard, however if it meant keeping Corry, he would have to give in to her this time although wasn't happy to do so, knowing his mother was right he then went ahead and cancelled the big wedding he'd already put into action;

"I only want to keep Corry happy" was his last words on the subject.

None the less, Agnes could only imagine the look on his face when he said those words for he never liked the word NO.

Well, the wedding plans went ahead just as Corry wanted, a small wedding, everything running smoothly before Jay and Rob was to arrive home on leave.

Arranging those coming from Yorkshire would arrive a couple of days before, stay at a nice little hotel while Jay and Rob were on their way home, and with this, Issa decided she would kindly meet the family at the station, taking them onto the hotel which was situated not far from the church where they would have time to settle in before the wedding. Yes, Issa, as she just loved to be involved with her extended family as she now referred to them.

It was fantastic as everything went to plan; the meal, the evening, small talk, everyone just got on with excitement about the forthcoming morning, the party broke up early as expected, each going their separate ways after such an enjoyable night and yet looking forward to the excitement of the days to follow which would make them all happy seeing Corry step into a future of fulfilment.

Hectic wasn't the word the next morning but then again, as planned, everything ran exceptionally smooth and as for the wedding dress which everyone was inquisitive about, the only one that had seen the dress had been Issa, having helped with the design

Now was the time to leave for the church as the car arrived, it was last minute nerves that started to set in but alas they were only to be for a few moments as this was the day she was to marry her Prince Charming, being swept away in his arms for a future of ideal bliss, but that only happens in story books so she thought, therefore coming down to earth in a haze of calmness her journey was to begin.

Arriving at the church she could plainly see Issa and the pageboys awaiting her attendance, while stepping onto the pavement to the words of;

"You look absolutely fantastic".

Those words spoken by a few as she stepped out of the car, who stopped to see what was happening and therefore amazed to see just who it was,

"Corry Sharp, well I never" one said,

While another commented;

"I've never seen anything so beautiful in all my life, she looks amazing, just like a princess out of a story book".

And yes, there was no doubt about it; she really did look amazing, walking slowly to the church and down the aisle, her dress so simple but so becoming as the fish tail slid along the floor in a sweeping glory that everyone couldn't take their eyes off.

A fairy-tale bride in all her glory, a picture that would have brought tears to her mother's eyes had she still been alive, oh yes she was right to have gone with that style she thought for it showed off her figure to a tea.

Even Jay couldn't keep his eyes off her as he'd never seen her in this light before, the love in his face was something that even Agnes had never witnessed before that day, was this the beginning of a new chapter for her son, for if it was, then her wishes had come true she thought to herself as the vows were taken to seal a love story that would last a lifetime or so it was thought

He would at that moment in time be pleased that his mother had persuaded him to go along with all of Corry's plans, for the day was perfect, small with only family and close friends but none the less, having all he'd ever wanted by his side and that was the woman that only men could have dreamed about. For his love for her was something that everyone witnessed that day, he seemed to have changed from the hard hitting personality who wanted all his own way to a softer side that was so becoming with a tenderness he showed which was unbelievable to all those around that knew the real person he'd always portrayed.

Corry's grandmother wept as the vows were said for there were thoughts of her own daughter's wedding and how the wish of, if only she could have been here today to see the happiness on Corry's face.

The restaurant put on a reception that not even Jay could complain about; everything had been organized with a personal touch for they knew Corry was a special person with such a tender heart that would go out of her way to help others and with this in mind, made a point of showing their gratitude in giving a little back for what she'd done to help local charities around the area, which again wasn't known generally.

Now speeches were short and simplified, one coming from her brother, one from her grandmother who cried all the way through, one special one from Agnes, one from Rob and last but least one from Issa.

But then after some ten minutes Jay stood up to give his grand piece; well, he always did like to be centre of attention so why change on this special day as he started with his speech of tenderness;

I would like to express my thanks to all who have attended this special day and made it the most perfect day that I will remember for as long as I may live".

"My mother who brought me up to realise that perfection comes in different shapes and sizes, who has worked hard to give me an education and a way of life that most people only dream of, friends that have stayed by me in a true sense not asking for anything in return but most of all I thank god for giving me the opportunity to meet the most beautiful woman in the world who has now become my precious wife, whom I not only adore but will stay true to for the rest of my life, as she is the only one that will ever hold my heart".

Well what more can I say, the whole room was flabbergasted, Agnes sat there with tears streaming down her face, being so proud at what her son had said for he'd never shown emotions like this before, it was as though he'd been struck with a bolt of lightning. The others couldn't believe how this man had shown such love and care towards his new wife, and Corry, well she was so in love there were stars in her eyes as they started to enjoy the rest of the afternoon.

It was now approaching 4pm with guests starting to depart; having wished the happy couple farewell, Agnes on the other hand had arranged that Jay and Corry would stay the night at the Grosvenor House hotel as that was one of Jay's favourite places due to the splendour and elegance as you walked into the light of crystal chandeliers which adorned this magnificent old building in the centre of the city.

The goodbye's' were all said and now it was time for the happy couple to depart for their first night together being man and wife. It would only be a short stay as they were due to fly out to Cyprus in a couple of days spending their honeymoon on the island of love as it was written in Greek mythology.

Arriving at the Grosvenor House was something of splendour being the place to stay for the upper class in those days, as the manager was on hand to welcome them with a bottle of champagne.;

"Good evening Mr and Mrs Hirst, may I congratulate you on your wedding, should there be anything that you wish, you only have to ask, and may I take this opportunity to say what a lovely couple you both make".

Corry and Jays thoughts were of a different meaning as they wanted a room, undress out of wedding clothes and relax, for it'd been a long day, so with that, they accepted the pleasantries and departed to the room for the rest of the evening.

As this was the bridal suite everything was as you would have expected it to be, decorated all in white and gold with flowers adorning the room and a large bottle of champagne with two glasses positioned on a table by the bedside. What a perfect setting for their first night of wedded bliss they both thought;

"A glass of champagne Mrs Hirst" Jay enquired as he started to pour from the bottle and with thoughts of, yes this will be the first of many as only the best for my wife handing the glass over to Corry with admiration in his facial expression

"Oh that was good" she said taking that first sip, while slowly putting the glass down by her side.

But jay had other ideas and it wasn't the champagne that was good, moving over to his bride and carefully starting to unzip her dress.

"I think it's about time this came off, for I'm going to make love to you like you've never been made love to before, now you're all mine for the rest of my life, so finish that drink and let me show just how much I love you".
And with a swift motion placed her onto the bed while standing back to admire her body for what seemed like minutes but was in fact seconds, positioning himself by her side, stroking her hair so gently it felt like velvet caressing it.

Moving his fingers to her mouth, parting her sensual lips before moving towards them, the softness of his kiss sent shivers through both their bodies as he then proceeded to caress her neck and shoulders in a massaging motion that sent tingles throughout her body, and with a burning fire inside both of their bodies by this time resulting with an urge that was uncontrollable. But this was their wedding night and the first of love making as a married couple, so it had to be a special performance, one they would never forget.

Jay had a special thing about Corry's breast, for if he had his way, he would suck on them all night long; her nipples were so pert he couldn't resist lingering over them with such a suction that would drive her wild, maybe this was because he wasn't breast fed as a child and therefore making up for lost time, who knows but at that moment in time, who cared.

The erection that was arising so close to her leg with moisture of excitement while trying his best to control, knowing the thrill that was entering every nerve of her body with juices flowing in abundance to his command and therefore sending signals to the brain whereby further action would be forthcoming erupting into an almighty explosion of fire but no wait. This was his wedding night where he would take her for better or worse and therefore show his true feelings of desire, making her orgasm when and if she wanted to, at a pace where he wouldn't dictate.

Corry on the other hand seemed to want that feeling of fulfilment whereby her body could release her fluids showing the true love she had for him. But with no other thought for himself, he slowly worked his way down her body bringing her pleasures that any good man could promise bringing an exotic bliss to the highest of expectations.

Well if you couldn't enjoy your wedding night, then there wouldn't be any memories to look back on over the years he thought.

Her breath now becoming rapid as the first real orgasm came, but still he took no notice only to suck harder on those luscious nipples with a grinding of his teeth in a twirling motion, knowing it would arouse her inner feeling yet again. Moving slow and lovingly up and down her body, he then pushed her legs wide apart, shooting two fingers up inside of her abruptly as she screamed a pleasurable pain which she'd now come to expect when he was dominant;

"Come on baby, let it all go again as there's a lot more to come yet", her body torn and withering as her feelings went with the rhythm which was now out of control, and while opening her legs wider apart to descend into the heart of her mount, grasping his teeth around her clitoris, sucking her dry until she came again like a tap over flowing.

Her body now aching for more and more having never experienced the likes of this before whereby every time she came, the ache inside of her screamed out yet again, with such delight, he had never met a woman like this before that could go all night as his appetite demanded of her knowing her drive was insatiable.

Having aroused her, it was now starting to take effect on parts of his body which was actively yearning for his own ejaculation, but then he would save the best of it to come inside of her while being turned on with the pleasure he was now receiving as he enjoyed the fruits he was providing to accompany the love he had for her. It was as she attempted to move, he'd push her back down and suck her a little harder until she was dry again, but eventually tables were about to turn, for this was a two-way street and she wasn't walking alone.

Now thinking he was alone in this situation, and knowing it was time for his own pleasure to erupt and so would drive a hard bargain into the walls of her G spot making an impressive entry due to thoughts that he was now to enter the tightness of her vagina and therefore send him over the top in all expectation of his own needs.

It was as he entered, her inner muscles clung to him like barbed wire for he'd no control and yet still wanted the release that he so longed for, but now it was her turn to take control of the situation, making him wait her time for every time he got near to offloading his juices she would grip her muscles tighter knowing, he couldn't finish what he'd started.

Yes, she was definitely in full control making him suffer as he begged;

"Please Corry; let me go before I go out of my mind"

But this plea was to fall on deaf ears for she was in full control and he would have to dance to her tune now as she had danced to his in earlier times, yes, this was definitely payback time in such a satisfying way on her part.

It was a few more minutes of pleading from Jay before Corry would let him have his own way as she finally gripped the end of his throbbing penis with her controlling inner muscle, knowing he'd have to dance to her tune to complete his desire.

"You bitch" he screamed as she finally let him come inside of her with an overflowing waterfall of delight.

The smirk on her face said it all as she looked up at him and said;

"It takes two to tango you know, so don't ever forget that and as for being a bitch well you'd better believe it as that's what it said on my C.V, when I applied for this position".

No, I don't think he ever would forget, he'd definitely met his match in bed, for he'd taught her well and now she was coming back with her own brand of medicine.

The one thing you can say about a woman is, you may have the upper hand or so you think but a woman's revenge is sweet and no matter how long she has to wait, she will definitely wait until she gets it.

To fall asleep in each other's arms, it was the end of a perfect day and the beginning of a new chapter for the time being.

Chapter 12

The wedding now over, but the memories would last forever, everything had gone like a dream but there again dreams sometimes turn into nightmares as the years would show.

But for now they were just young lovers heading away to the island of love to embark on two wonderful weeks that had been set aside for their honeymoon, before returning to London for a couple of days whereby they'd sort a system out for Corry to travel. This had been arranged before getting married as it seemed the most sensible thing to do in the situation, Jay wouldn't always be at home and so she would try and work around him as much as possible, travelling between Cyprus and London.

Having arranged to hire a fully furnished bungalow which was set back just off the shore on the outskirts of Larnaca, it was quite large but there again that was Jay's style, he had to have everything to impress whereby Corry on the other hand was quite happy to settle for something that made her happy and content.

Two weeks alone on the island which they regarded as their honeymoon, was relaxed, chilled and really a time to get to know each other, this being such a short period of time since they met, but that was wholly to do with circumstances.as his work dictated.

And like most couples on honeymoon, getting to know each other's likes and dislikes was a trial period and so putting everything together and spending time with each other, they started the process whereby a shopping trip was required to get all the essentials to make the place of their liking, although the furniture was of a high stranded, it was the personal touch that was needed to make it a home.

But to an outsider you could see they were just two people in love, acting like teenagers, doing all the silly things and making love at every opportunity they managed to get which was quite a lot in their case for they'd a lot of catching up to do as it was often remarked.

It was at this point that Corry did start to notice one thing though, when anything was to be decided, it was Jay that did it, for there was no consultation with her what so ever, and although she didn't agree, she did however go along with it for the time being as she knew he'd always had his own way. But also knew she'd change him gradually for it wasn't a man's world, women were coming to the fore and therefore decisions were to be made on an equal basis. There was a saying and how true it was: Rome wasn't built in a day so it would take time but there again that wasn't her contract otherwise it may have been, she thought laughing to herself.

Nothing lasts forever as the honeymoon was now coming to an end with Jay returning to work which would result in him having to fly out to Malta for six weeks training exercise.

And with Jay gone for that length of time, it would give her the advantage of returning to London to start arrangement for the winter fashion show. And as she'd made preparation for the designs a little while before the wedding, at least she'd a head start and with the help of Issa filling in while she'd been away, there would be no stopping her or so she thought.

What wasn't anticipated was, the ready to wear garments which had been purchased by the department stores had been such a success, that production just couldn't keep up with all the new orders and therefore it would be one hell of a race to get things organized in time

So with Jay returning to work and Corry now heading back to London with the intentions of catching up, for when all was said and done it was her business and although the staff were loyal and wouldn't let her dawn, it was up to her to keep the business afloat and find the solutions to the problems of supply and demand. It was as the plane touched down, at least one of her problems drifted, when she caught site of Peter waiting for her, now the others would only be hiccups she had to sort or so she thought.

It was upon hearing Peters suggestion of a board meeting with the investors for their backing of an expansion due to the orders coming in which they couldn't fulfil on time blew Corry's mind altogether as she never expected that one being laid at her feet when she arrived and therefore looked quite alarmed;

"Have you gone mad, it's only been a few weeks since I left and not that long since we opened the new places, even if you're right they won't agree to such a request as it's not even a full season of garments that's been produced, therefore we haven't the figures on hand to the financial position were in surely" she shrieked.

"Look I think we should go for a meal where we'll talk it over sensibly as I've done all the figures, checked the orders, worked out all the finance and put a planned meeting for the board to listen. If we don't move on all of this quickly then someone else is going to come in, steal the idea and therefore make a killing,

At the moment we're just holding our heads above water with the orders but that won't last for long as the girls are tired and working every hour god sends just to keep up, that's even with overtime, and that's before the next season even starts to go into production so it's your call at the end of the day. Look I know you've a lot on with the fabrics that haven't yet been ordered and although I realise you'll have something up your sleeve, but I think we should go for that meal now and talk it over".

Corry could see where he was coming from and therefore agreed with all the suggestions that were proposed for it would then be up to the board to sanction these proposals knowing she would have the time to help carry out what was necessary on this trip to alleviate the problems that had arisen looking into the situation more deeply having time on her hands to concentrate on a solution.

For this visit, she'd also decided to stay with Issa as not only would it be nice to catch up but she'd also missed the company of her faithful friend.

The next few weeks were horrendous to say the least, it seemed that all she did was have meetings with buyers together with her backers although the backers were no trouble at all as they seemed to just go along with what was suggested, whatever it was, it was bringing in a good capital return and that's all that mattered to money people.

It was with everything mulling around in her mind and not being able to sleep having missed Jay so much, that an idea then struck like lightening.

Perhaps if they could possibly open two factories in the north of England, this would not only alleviate the production for the ready to wear orders, but would also save on transport costs. Now if this could be done, it would make sense that arrangements be made for someone to go to Yorkshire and check out the most viable place for this idea, and having discussed this with Peter the next day, therefore suggesting he should be the one to go,

But to this suggestion, I'm afraid she was in for a surprise as he wouldn't hear of it at all with a response of;

"If you think about this seriously, the answer is right in front of you".

Looking a little mystified she asked "what on earth are you on about".

"Well you come from Doncaster, doesn't it make sense that if we open two factories there, we have easy access to the north for Doncaster is on the A1 road that goes straight up to Scotland, therefore cutting costs a lot further, and there is also a rumour they're to build a motorway straight through the town, which will be even better as there won't be any problem getting planning permission, it'll bring more jobs to the area together with the fact, it's a main rail link to the borders and Scotland".

Oh boy she thought to herself, this man is great, just what would I do without him. He thinks of everything as well as watching my back, if I go a little too far.

And so it was decided to call a meeting, arrange for someone to check out the empty premises in the town, lease two factories, get everything sorted out in just one month, now that was some going but with drive and determination they could pull it off.

Knowing time was of the essence, they'd have to act quickly and so pull in all the favours possible, but the advantage there would be that Corry still knew a lot of people in her home town and therefore with a little help from Issa they could perhaps spend a couple of days up there sorting staffing levels out themselves, hoping to be able to spend a little time with her family.

Although it had only been a couple or so days since Corry returned to London, she'd not only nearly doubled the workforce, arranged the winter fashion collection, seen the buyers who by now were all backing her to the hilt and that's before the new collection came out, it was also rumoured that she was now a force not to be recon with in the city.

By mid-September, everything had been finalized, the factories set up, staff hired, machinery in place together with a production starting within the week. She'd brought new jobs to the town, the local officials had done everything in their power to help push things through and besides that; she was a bit of a hero, as they thought of her as local girl making the headlines.

Corry was no fool, hiring only people she knew and trusted to run both factories, ones that would work every hour god sent just to make a go of this new venture for her. Having come up with the idea that perhaps women could work flexible hours to fit in with their families she'd be able to put in a shift system which would help women return to work after having children.

This helped with their financial responsibilities and family life, which she herself treasured so much when growing up. Her idea to offer the workforce a pay deal with good bonuses when required for their hard work, this would also instil a loyalty that would go far with her workers down in London and if it worked, then it would also be put into practice throughout the company.

The big boys of the industry started to get very troubled by these ideas for everything she touched came off with such a grand success, it was as though she had the Midas touch where everything turned to gold and they were very nervous over this position.

With everything going to plan in the north of England, it was now time to return back to London where all the last minute problems would have to be sorted quickly as time was running out whereby she was to return to Cyprus

The big names were having their shows first as usual but that never bothered her as she had such a good relationship with the press by now, for they always went that extra mile to accommodate her with the finer things.

Her thoughts were, you should treat people how you would want to be treated yourself, that was her motto for getting though life which served her well over the coming years as she headed for the top of her profession, but there again this was a woman of principles who valued everything that others did to help and therefore knew by experience that nothing in life was given freely.

The last few months had gone so well, even she couldn't believe how quickly everything was happening, it seemed as though everything was falling into place, knowing how hard the staff had worked to make all this happen, and this she would never forget as a proud woman at the helm of her own company, the achievement was all down to her determination.

But with a late call to inform Corry that Jay had to stay in Malta another ten days or so there was no time to rush back before the week of the shows and so it was decided that a meeting would be called for some of things that needed to be changed and therefore would have to be discussed with her backers yet again.

One thing that weighed heavily on her mind was the fact that, Peter was doing too much and needed to take some of the responsibilities off his shoulders to share with others or she could foresee a breakdown in his health and that weighed heavily on her mind, therefore an urgent meeting was called whereby Corry was to chair such discussions;

"I'm sorry about this, but I'm afraid this meeting was called to clear the air on some of the matters that have to be sorted out as a matter of urgency" was her opening speech.

"First and foremost, I would like to thank all concerned for all the hard work that's been put into making this such a success, I would also like to congratulate you for the time you've put in to sort out the two new factories that are now in full production with all the new lines, these as you're aware, are situated up in the north of England. Should any of you wish to work for a few weeks at these new factories, so that the staff up there may familiarize themselves with the company policies, I would appreciate you feeling free to either have a word with Peter or myself where it will be arranged.

I may also add, excellent accommodation will be available and I'm sure you will have a great time as they are a fantastic set of people who will look after you, showing you the northern side of hospitality.

I would also like to inform you, that I've been in touch with the Japanese company who had such a marvellous display of knitwear at the last fashion show, and the owner of this small company a Mr Malcomb Chow has now kindly agreed to talks in respect of merging his company with ours and therefore becoming a Director.

This will be a fantastic opportunity to move forward as we will not only have a knitwear collection but also be able to branch out into much finer silk wear which I've every intention of using in the winter collection should we receive the fabrics in time.

Now Corry secretly had a word with Peter over this after the last showing when she couldn't get over the finery of the work that they'd produced but wanted to keep a lid on the news until everything was in place to hit the market with one explosive bang.

Peter on the other hand, hadn't held out much hope on this score for the Japanese had always gone it alone, never the less, it seemed that she had yet again pulled the deal off whereby charming the lovely Mr Chow;

I would now like to formally introduce you to Mr Malcomb Chow, who will be Director of knitwear and accessories.

To this Malcomb Chow stood up and with a courteous bow to everyone in such a gentlemanly fashion which was so impressive, to everyone's amazement.

I should also like to propose that we take on another Director who will assist Peter, this being a personal friend of mine.

He comes from the north of England the same as myself, started a small building company, and made it a household name in less than three years before selling it out, he has the touch of not only class but everything he does touch, turns to gold which will be good for all of us as a company; I may also add that his motivation is boundless.

You may not have heard of him, being a pretty private person who tends to keep in the background, his name is Mr David Thomas, I would add that David won't be joining us for a short time yet due to sorting out some business deal of his own before moving down to take his seat on the board, but again I'm sure you will all get on famously with him as although he's a private person he also has a great personality combined with a dry sense of humour which you will no doubt get to understand in time.

Next I propose that we take a back seat with the couture lines, handing it over to the girls that have made it a success from day one, I will of course still oversee this but will let them have a free run of everything, their wages will now become on a salary basis, as they've earned it for what they have done for this company.

We will also concentrate on the future as I see it, the ready to wear is the future and that is where we are now heading as a first in the market and one to be reckoned with should anyone stand in our way which I'm sure you will agree, is a step forward for all of us as I have every faith in what we're trying to achieve and will continue to back you in every way possible spending as much time as needed in London.

Now with a look around the room at everyone's expressions before adding;

I would now like to close this meeting and would appreciate your vote to take these ideas forward, should you object to anything, then please state that objection now, as time is running out and we have a show to put on next week".

Well the look of astonishment that went round the room was amazing, there was also a short pause before everyone stood up and with a cheer that was simply deafening, gave the answer that Corry had hoped for, yes that was the backing of everyone.

It was Agnes who spoke in the end and said without any reservation;

"Well I think I speak for all of us by saying, you have never let us down in the past, so think we can trust you with everything that you've put forward today.

We as your Directors, Backers and Friends, are with you all the way.

Realizing the changes, you have already accomplice which have brought benefits and therefore trust you to take the company to the highest limits as I'm sure you will for if you can pull all of this off, we will then be the largest fashion group in Britain".

To this, everyone stood up and applauded yet again for Corry as a leader who would not only fight to get ahead in the industry but would also look after the interests of her company.

Meeting to an end, Corry had done her homework and now with the extra help she was getting, would be able to spend more time with Jay and maybe go in for a family of her own, well that was the plan but then again, plans never run as you would like them to

It was only after the meeting that Corry had another thought and that was she'd forgot to mention to Peter something which was a quite important decision and so must take it up with him straight away, knowing she was on a roll and therefore unstoppable, therefore rushing after him shouting';

"Let's have a drink in the pub down the road and maybe a bite to eat before we get carried away with all the work in hand".

Peter knew only too well that Corry wanted something more than a talk, for this was her way of getting all his attention without any interruptions.

"Go on then, but what do you think you're up to now?" he asked.

Looking kind of sheepish as she did when she wanted something her answer being;

"I think we ought to let Issa have a bigger stake in the company to make suggestions or even organise the running of the models agency".

"What Model Agency" he replied rather sharply.

"Now that's what I was going to suggest, we run our own model agency from our premises, training young girls to work as a team with a different view to the toffee nosed ones that's costing us a fortune to hire for the shows".

"Oh my God, do you ever give up. Just when did you come up with that bright idea", Peter asked.

"I've been thinking about it for a while now, the ones we don't use, we could keep on the books and organize work for them with other companies or even the department stores and with Issa running the team, she has such an eye for that kind of thing and again with our own agency, it would save us a hell of a lot of money", she finished off all in one breath.

"Oh my god, it wouldn't be any good arguing, as if I did, then I'm afraid I wouldn't get any lunch at this rate, so I'll look into it and have a talk with Issa myself" Peter replied.

She knew very well Peter would sort it out; otherwise he would have put up an argument there and then, for he was a shrewd cookie where money was concerned.

Having the last word as usual, she added

"Come on then slowcoach, I'm going to treat you to lunch before we both starve".

Peter was aware that Corry had got her own way yet again but having thought about it, she was definitely right in what she'd said, it made perfect sense as far as he was concerned.

Again the city was buzzing with everyone arriving for the start of the fashion week; the top designers were on form with all their pieces that were priceless, modelled by only the elite model agencies which could demand what prices they wanted for their models.

The after parties that continue through the night were simply aghast with the dresses but then again they could afford the best as money was no object to in their circles.

It had been arranged for Corry's showing to be the last one of the week which suited her, in fact she was delighted, hoping to pull off the same surprise as last season.

Again, her show followed the Japanese company which although was very small in comparison to the others, was however, very different as well.

Plans had already been set up with Malcomb Chow to come on board and join her little empire but had been kept under wraps from the press for the time being, for it's always an element of surprise that makes the headlines. No one really trusted the Japanese in business in those days as they wanted to move in on the British market but that didn't bother Corry as she was used to all the controversy.

The day of the show arrived with the entire front row being taken up by VIP's and of course, the national press with twice the original amount of reporters than the last showing. She was well aware of this and so in turn made special arrangements that they would be allocated the best positions on the front rows and should also be looked after and treated like VIP's.

It had been noticed at the last show, a cameraman who had a club foot and found it difficult to manoeuvre like the rest of them, and so Corry remembered this incident and making sure this man would get preferential placing, this giving him a better position than the rest of them to his amazement.

Everything went quite as the show was about to commence and with the anticipation that ran through the room, the feeling was quite electrifying as the lighting dimmed to a low sombre fusion

First of all, out walked five models all dressed in slate grey, with accessories of pink, these ranged from tight fitted skirts followed by tailored fitting suits and dresses, no she'd not gone mad like the other shows, quite the opposite for they'd gone with the idea of a season whereby women would turn towards the fancy dress look for the winter season.

Corry on the other hand had gone for the fitted tailored look that made a woman look not only smart and sophisticated but with high heel shoes that had been ordered in from Italy, thus giving them a sexy leg appeal. No hats, gloves or handbags were on show, just the sleek, sexy style that made a statement when a woman walked into a room, a sort of wow, look at me impression.

That was the look she wanted to achieve, to turn the industry round, whereby they would look at women in a new light, for Corry had dreamt of giving them a new roll altogether, they weren't just housewives and mothers; they were women to be desired and listened to. Knowing others wouldn't take lightly to this, but again, times were changing and it had to be acknowledged that women had a place in the workforce as well as the home.

Out came more and more of the models in similar outfits all with the shades of greys and burgundy as the audience looked on in astonishment for they'd never seen anything like these clothes before and to top it all, they were to be available in the department stores at reasonable prices that everyone could afford, which again was something new to them.

Adding a selection of pure wool coats and bomber jackets in grey and burgundy which would just slip over the shoulders as casual attire. It was now that the audience knew the show was coming to an end as there would be only the couple of bridal gowns to be seen before it finished.

Yes, they were right in one way but never take anything for granted, for as it turned out the unexpected was to change everything and yes in this case it did, for Corry stepped out onto the catwalk with an announcement of;

"I'm sorry to say, there will be no bridal wear in this show at all, realising that some of you will be very disappointed with this decision, so have replaced it with something a little different to end our show this season".

"To start this off, I would like to thank all our models for participating in this new venture as I will now take a back seat and introduce our own special collection, hoping it will delight you all.".

Well if you could have seen the expressions on the various faces, you would have died, for shock wasn't the word at all you'd use.

Out came the first of the models in a black lace bra, French nickers, garter, hold up stocking and wearing high heeled shoes

The second model followed, dressed in a red, bra, panties, suspender belt, and stockings together with red shoes to match.

A total of 6 models paraded around the catwalk in the finest of brief underwear before Issa appeared in what would be called a magnificent sleek black sheer voile nightdress; this was held up over her shoulders by two fine straps attached at each side by a small diamante pear drop, underneath the gown she wore a sheer thong to cover her modesty while her small but shapely breasts gave an outline of revealing splendour.

The crowd didn't know whether to applaud or walk out in disgust as this had never been seen before, you lived in an age where modesty was the buzz word.

After the silence broke the audience just went wild, Corry had done what no one else could have done, the cameramen seemed to have a field day as not only had they got the scoop of the fashion week, they also had a front row view of everything that was on show. It would take an awful lot to put Corry in her place now, for she would be able to stand her ground and change the narrow minded old fogies in the industry to take notice of that slip of a girl as they used to refer to her.

The show over and with the departure of all concerned, it had been a tiring day with the result of not only achievement but a calling of sleep to all those that had participated in the run up to the show which they rightly deserved, the audience however had other ideas being a weekend, some wanting to carry the celebrations on, went out on the town celebrating. Now while that wasn't Corry's scene at all for all she wanted was, a clean bed and a hot cup of chocolate until an early wake up call for the reviews in the morning's papers.

Papers out, and boy oh boy, there she was on the front pages of all the top newspapers, the press had done her proud again, mind-blowing but all the same proud. It was the same with the magazines; they were full of the underwear pictures that had been on show as this was new to them at a big event like fashion week. It was definitely the start of something new which would be in the shops at a reasonable price for the likes of everyone and not just the rich and affluent.

Oh, there would be a lot of people who would criticize flaunting women's bodies on a catwalk like she'd done. But there was an up and coming youth that was starting to demand more recognition for themselves and that's the market she was counting on because the youth of the day demanded more power and would voice their opinions to achieve it.

This would make women aware that their bodies weren't to be hidden away like in the past but to be adored in every way for the future, not like some who thought it would be a seven-day wonder and disgusting but then, come round to a different way of thinking in the end.

To wear a nice tailored dress and sexy underwear for women would be a turn on for any man that was the thinking behind her decision and it worked for the demand for a sleek and sexy look came to fruition as the sales went wild.

Having another week in London before she returned to Cyprus and therefore knowing she'd have to move fast if things had to be sorted out for Malcomb Chow to join the company along with the other Directors as she'd arranged, but there again it was only a formality with Lawyers paperwork holding things up.

As Malcomb stayed over in London for a couple of weeks after the showing, it was decided that everything would get drawn up for his company to merge while she was there to oversee the progress. This had to be done fairly quickly as when the press got wind of it, rumours would fly and there would be a lot of speculation as to what was going on and Corry didn't want them to know before everything had been settled.

The city already knew about the expansion of factories up north but wasn't quite aware they were to turn out ready to wear garments in such great quantities and so that was another thing that had been kept under control until after the fashion week for you never give the enemy an advance on your intentions was her way of thinking.

They were still getting over the shock that Corry had branched out into the production of sexy underwear as they now called it, so introducing a knitwear line, designed by the Japanese and then eventually pure silk under garments. Well that would never go down with old men that were running the fashion industry in the capital, the shock would send them up into a dizzy height or maybe a heart attack she thought.

Negotiating with Malcomb was a piece of cake for Corry as she could see the look in his eye every time she glanced at him but there again it was a good deal that had been agreed so it never phased her at all.

MALCOMB CHOW

Malcomb, although shy, was a very handsome man, born in America, his mother a well-known Japanese singer, his Father an American airline pilot, they met one day in Japan as his father stayed at a hotel where all the pilots stayed between flights, fell in love at first sight, married, moved to live in America but unfortunately she died in childbirth while having Malcomb.

Obviously in shock over the death of his wife Malcolm's father tended to reject the baby, this caused a lot of heartache within the family unit and therefore the wealthy American grandparents stepped in to bring the child up as their own while his father carried on with his career, having the finest of education; he then went on to study fashion at a famous design school in America.

With the help of his grandparents and a trust fund left from his Mother, he opened a small factory in Japan. This was a new beginning for design as he knew it and so he learned the craft of the traditional Japanese and made it his own.

After a period of hard work and study he applied to do his first show in London and from that show he never looked back, for that was when he first met Corry. Applying for a visa he then moved to London making it his home for that was where everything was based, Paris on the other hand was so far out of his reach and to be honest he felt more comfortable in England being able to speak the language. To join Corry in her journey, would eventually take him to the heights that he had never dreamed about, making him one of the most talented respectable bachelors of all times.

His only regret would be, to fall in love with her at a later date, but that's how men felt as they got close, for she had this wonderful charm that melted their hearts, it was like being a spider in a web that they couldn't escape from. But then again did they want to.

Finally, everything was tied up so Peter could get on with his family life, it was a good job Anna was an understanding person for the hours he put in at work was horrendously long but never laborious in anyone's books.

Now the only other thing that had to be organised would be, the modelling agency which would run parallel with the running of the underwear lines which Issa had already got in hand.

Putting all of this together wouldn't be a problem with her personal life as Rob was still a serving soldier with the regiment in Cyprus and didn't expect to get anymore leave granted for at least another three to four months, yes, all of this was coming together nicely but then she never doubted as Peter was a wizard at controlling the company when she wasn't there, her only problem was the thoughts of it being too much but then again he thrived on work.

David Thomas on the other hand was still in negotiations with business people up the north of England, therefore couldn't officially accept the position of a Directorship until the New Year although he had accepted it verbally, now this again would work out better than they all thought for then she would be able to assist Peter with an official introduction.

Corry had achieved a lot in the short time she'd been home, but the one thing she'd not got round to, was to look for a bigger place for her and Jay when they returned to England but that wasn't a priority at the moment, the business was, their bread and butter and therefore the priority.

Now time to make her return to Cyprus as she said her tearful good byes to everyone before heading off to the airport. Tired and weary from her time in London, her only thoughts were to get back to the man she loved for it would only be a couple of days before he was to return from Malta due to the fact that an extra month had been added on to his initial couple of months which was in her favour as that was what enabled her to accomplish everything in London

Having arranged to take two weeks off when he returned, they would spend a little time together as a short but sweet second honeymoon. This is how it was when you were married to a soldier, you had to make the most of the time together as you were parted so much.

Jay was so happy that Corry had sorted everything out in London, well for the time being, as now they had a little time to themselves and it was wonderful they were away from the entire mad house as he often called London and her business knowing she worked so hard to build the business and admired her professionalism immensely but it was now time for him to spend time with his wife without being interrupted with work from both sides.

The next two weeks spent together was like an eternal honeymoon, as time passed so quickly when love was in the air and you hadn't seen your lover for some three months. And so the first week went by making love as they couldn't get enough of each other, after that, they settled down enjoying the silly things that new married couples do together and just acting like teenagers again with no thoughts for anyone but themselves, unfortunately things had to end when Jay return to barracks as work was then calling.

After a few weeks when the newness of being married into this kind of life had started to wear off, Corry found It hard adapting as she wasn't the type to lounge around doing coffee morning with cocktails, discussing trivial things mixing with a circle of women she found alien to what she'd been used to.

Therefore, setting up a design studio in a spare bedroom was such a great idea; this enabled her to work while Jay was in barracks, thus concentrating on the couture lines as they're the ones that needed more concentration than the ready to wear range for the next season.

Keeping in touch with the London office on a daily basis, she soon got back into a system that worked for her; Jay had his work commitments which he never brought home as when they were together, it was just a normal enjoyable married life like any other couple.

It wasn't until Jay arrived home one evening with the news of, it was expected of her to entertain the officer's wives at certain social functions, that she felt out of her league, but there again never having to do this before, it would only be like having a cocktail party with maybe a few friends around where they'd all be seen to help with everything knowing she was new to all of this.

How wrong she was, for when she did organise a social gathering of the wives, it turned out to be a disaster as in her opinion they were mostly toffee nosed snobs who'd never done a day's work in all their lives and wouldn't have entertained her if she'd not been in what they called their social circle.

No, this wasn't Corry's scene at all but at least she tried for the sake of Jay, but after holding a couple more of these gatherings realised it wasn't for her and therefore her work was far more important being a businesswoman with drive and flair for her own company and therefore made it quite plain to Jay she wouldn't be able to accommodate what she called a wives' again.

Although that statement didn't go down well, he did however accept it was a truthful admission, for her own business had to be a priority, well that was making far more money than his salary and was no fool where financial gain was concerned. He also had to consider how fast the company was growing and jobs depended on Corry's ideas and designs, also her loyalty to the company in which he admired immensely, knowing his wife would never let the staff down.

Christmas was all parties in the officer's mess but as Corry and Jay had already arranged to return to England, this wouldn't be an issue as the only one event they would have to attend, would be the regimental dinner and dance which was a compulsory black and white do, and therefore couldn't get out of it however hard they tried for it was one of those do's that was expected of them. Well if they had to attend such a dinner and dance in the mess at least

Corry would go in something that was at least outstanding she thought, which she'd designed herself.

And to this she would show her talents off as not only a designer but a lady of style and eloquence t both walking in with a perfection of;

Jay dressed in a black dinner suit, Corry in a long straight black velvet fitted dress which was slit up the back allowing her to walk and with a diamond necklace, earrings and bracelet to match, diamante high heeled shoes, her long blond hair swept up in a Grecian style, looking the perfect couple and an envy of everyone they came into contact with.

The Christmas dinner and dance was just what you'd expect of a regimental do which to Corry was boring to say the least, cocktails, five course meal, small talk, men retiring to the bar while the women made conversation about children, houses clothing and holidays after dinner. No surprises there Corry thought as she silently left them to their own devices and joined the men at the bar which didn't go down too well at all, it wasn't a done thing with ladies of their standing, or so they thought which in her opinion was a little too pompous to say the least.

Now Jay was getting used to this kind of behaviour with Corry and let it ride over his head knowing full well she'd only do what she wanted and anyway he loved her to be different as she attracted all the attention away from the others. Men admired her and women were jealous of the attention she was receiving.

Making all their apologies as they left early due to the situation of their flights being brought forward the next morning, it was a relief for both of them to leave and get an early night. Now for the flight home to spend the real Christmas and New Year where they could let their hair down, mixing with the real people.

Spending their first Christmas as a married couple with Agnes, which was a Christmas to remember, for all their friends were there and it was such a different atmosphere than the stuffy officer's mess that she'd experienced in Cyprus. Corry now feeling more at ease with just normal working class people while Jay had to live up to a different breed altogether when he was at work, for in some ways he would love her to change and accept a new way of life but when they were alone together she was like a breath of fresh air for they deeply loved one another and then again if she did change, would that love still be the same he thought.

New Year came and passed by with Jay joining his unit in Malta yet again only this time he would return back to Cyprus early April. It was decided that Corry would stay in England to sort things out with the business and would also have time to welcome her new Director David Thomas on board.

YES, DAVID THOMAS

Now she had known David for some years now as having gone to school with some of his brothers, he was a strong willed man who knew what he wanted out of life and wasn't frightened to go out and get it, having been brought up, one of five boys who lost their parents when he was a teenager, he had entered the building industry at the right time, made a lot of money and then sold the business on.

Rumour had it, that after selling his business he'd met this girl from a family who was wealthy in their own rights, and as the rumours broadened, it became that apparently this girl was nothing but a spoilt brat who wanted all her own way, not stopping before getting it.

But there again we all know what rumours are like and this wasn't quite the case at all for in some ways this girl had experience a lot of heartache in her childhood. Never the less, it was said that she'd set her mind on David and through hell and high waters, was determined to get him, spoilt or not, David was the right person to tame her if anybody could' for he was such a down to earth and grounded person which she obviously needed.

As Corry hadn't met this girl or even knew her name, she'd make up her own mind when the time came, knowing that people were always too ready to judge and be critical when it suited them or was this story a little bit farfetched.

Time seemed to be flying past by now and already early February by the time that everything was in place with David on board, knowing very little about the fashion world, he'd taken to it quite quickly but there again he had the Midas touch and was there to make money for the company assisting Peter wherever he could to lighten the everyday running of things.

Malcomb on the other hand had settled in well, bought a place just outside of London, got a team together from a local art school and was making quite an impression on the staff by his new venture being such a relaxed character that just everyone loved working with him. Not frightened to get his hands dirty like some, he just got on with the job in hand and therefore it showed in his artistry to the business. It was said in some quarters that he was a little effeminate as he'd never bother with women but that wasn't the case at all, he just loved his work and that was his priority.

Issa, well she was in her glory with her new position as Director of the modelling agency together with running the underwear section which was doing so well they couldn't keep up with the orders, women were just going wild for what they regarded as sexy underwear, yes this was a brand new world for them, a world of freedom to show how sexy they were.

To say the gentlemen of the city were shocked by such sheer sexy items, not at all for they were going mad to purchase the same for their wives, girlfriends and mistresses. Yes, the press had really done Corry proud with the publicity they had created after that shocking launch of underwear that had been presented.

Flying back to Cyprus, Corry knew she'd have to try, putting her feeling aside and fit in with Jay's career, this was going to be hard but at least she'd try her best no matter how hard it was going to be for when it comes down to it, love is blind and reality goes out of the window when cupid fires that arrow.

As it had been some four months since she'd seen her husband, this being usual in the army when soldiers have to go away from time to time, it was expected they would have a quite night in. But afraid not as he met her off the plane with a surprise of, taking her out for a romantic meal on the town that night, just the two of them, adding it would be a night to remember that he'd already planned, all she had to do was put on her best finery and look stunning for he'd missed her so much. Yes, she was definitely up for some of that as she'd missed him also and just wanted them to be alone together to catch up on the closeness that they'd both missed.

Yes, that night was definitely going to be a special night as they left for a beautiful meal in a little restaurant situated on the sea front in Larnaca, Corry dressed in a little gold silk outfit teamed up with black accessories looked absolutely stunning.

The meal of lamb was superb as for some reason the local people cooked it in herbs that she'd never even heard of which gave it a taste that you couldn't describe, soft music playing in the background and wine flowing which made such a relaxing time for both as Jay looked lovingly into his wife's eyes, even though she was getting a little tipsy by now. For anyone could see the love was in abundance in her face, yes it was so nice to see her in that way for he knew how hard she'd been working since he'd been away in Malta. The night was drawing to a close when Jay softly said;

"Time for home darling, the taxi 's waiting, so come on as the travelling has now started to catch up with you and I don't want to carry you home".

Having entered the front door of their home; Jay turned swiftly, picked her up into his arms carrying her to the bedroom where the aroma of the rose petals that covered the neatly white bed linen was something more than a romantic gesture.

Although a little tired Corry could feel the burning rising inside of her as she kicked off her shoes, gently falling onto the bed as Jay removed her dress and panties with a lust that couldn't be controlled.

Looking down at her slender body, he dropped his clothing where he stood in anticipation.

"Tonight is yours and yours alone he whispered", to her tenderly, with a lust in his face.

Starting by Kissing her feet while working his way up between her legs to the ever awaiting clitoris that he knew so well, then sinking his mouth into the wet sweet sticky fluid that by now was flowing from her like a tap, his tongue started to work its magic like only she would experience as she swayed to the rhythm of her withering body, her mind racing as her body on fire with a heat that was now growing uncontrollable for the suction from his mouth as she climaxed for the first time, letting out one almighty scream which could be heard throughout the house.

"So you have missed me" he stated with an air of satisfaction

"You know darn well I have" was the reply.

"Sorry but you're going to miss me a lot more before the nights over my dear" as he went in further to roam around her clitoris again, knowing well that it excited her so much, still dripping like a tap, she wanted it more and more as he then proceeded to move two fingers up inside her with a delight that excited both of them.

"No baby, you're going to have to wait as my balls are on fire, and if I enter you right now I'll lose control and will come too soon, when all I want to do is pleasure you over and over again, making up for those months we've been apart".

Corry wasn't having any of this as she moved her foot between his legs, she could feel the erect penis swelling out of control and therefore if she positioned her foot to a certain angle, knowing her toes could rub against his huge shaft, this causing more arousal than he anticipated.

Oh yes' this was doing the trick alright as her toes were wet with the sperm leaking from that great stiff member between his legs, knowing he wouldn't be able to last long and how right she was, for he moved up positioning himself on top of her body, entering her with such vigour and thrust he couldn't control and therefore giving way to all his pent up emotion, shooting his sperm right up inside of her to the heights of eternity.;

"I hope you're satisfied with what you've done now, I wanted it to last a lot longer so you'd experience the heights of ecstasy" he said

"Very satisfied" she replied with a smile on her face.

"I wanted to make it an all-night session therefore making up for the time we've been parted, knowing you would have wanted me as much as I've wanted you," he said with an expression of fulfilment on his face.

"Oh come on, you would never have lasted all night as you were gagging for it she replied adding;

Anyway darling, there will be other nights as the old saying goes, practice makes perfect so you've a lot to learn before you succeed, for tonight was just a trial run wasn't it" she asked in a sarcastic tone although he knew she was joking.

Other nights indeed, for six weeks later, Corry broke the happy news to Jay that she was in fact pregnant.

This came as quite a shock to him, he never expected her to catch on so quickly although they'd not taken precautions, he just imagined it would be some time before they thought about a family but really, they couldn't keep their hands off each other so it shouldn't have been such a surprise

After the initial shock, Jay settled down and seemed to be pleased as punch at Corry's pregnancy, it seemed he couldn't do enough for her, there wasn't anything she asked for that was denied, even their love making whereby Corry couldn't get enough of him, for the pregnancy brought out such a craving of intimate closeness in their bodies.

Travelling back and forward to London was no problem for her as the pregnancy was quite easy and as she'd made up her mind to carry on working until the last minute, Jay let her get on with it knowing it was futile arguing with her at that stage.

In England everyone would look after her so that she didn't overdo it and back in Cyprus Jay would take over and just spoil her. which pleased her immensely. Agnes was over the moon having heard the news, while Issa followed her around, like a mother hen waiting for the chicks to hatch not having any children of her own.

It was at this time, Issa broke the news to Corry about her and Rob was to get married in a quite ceremony with just a few friends for like Corry, they never wanted the publicity being a private couple and therefore would organise the wedding so far away from London that it wouldn't at least be headline news.

She also discussed the possibility of help with the modelling agency as the underwear production was expanding at such a rate they couldn't keep up with all the orders. Corry could understand this and therefore was to have a word with Peter to agree that in the near future, Issa would become a full Director and run both the underwear line as well as the modelling agency this giving her the authority to make all the decisions only consulting the board where there was a problem.

She would however, oversee the modelling but would be able to put someone else in to organise the day to day running of it. This would be Corry's way of thanking her for all the hard work she'd put in since the day she started, for she was now like a sister in every sense.

It was getting toward the end of the eighth month of Corry's pregnancy when she decided that enough was enough and would have to take a back seat for a while, feeling so tired by now it seemed the travelling was getting her down although never would admit it to anyone or they would have told Jay and he would have hit the roof being so protective. A couple of weeks in the warm climate of Cyprus would do her the world of good before the baby was due as they had predicted an arrival date of the 24th January.

Now we all know that dates are given for a reason but then again, we all know babies do not come to order, so on the 27th December when Corry was rushed into the hospital, there was no stopping their little girl coming into the world fighting feet first. Oh yes feet first and that's how she would go through life, with her feet firmly on the ground as no one was going to push around this perfectly formed little cookie with the most gorgeous legs.

For when Jay saw her, it was definitely love at first sight, he just couldn't let her go, this beautiful daughter with olive skin and a mass of dark curly hair was all his and she would be named Alexandra but shortened to Alexa as she grew up.

I'm afraid, as time went by, Corry never got a look in with both Jay and Alexa for they were like two peas in a pod, he adored her and she followed him around everywhere he went. It seemed that when Alexa was born, Corry didn't seem to exist in Jay's eyes as this was the time they started to grow apart. She buried herself in the business taking Alexa to London with her when she could, and he drifted off into what she surmised was flings with other women he picked up on the way. Yes, they were intimate, but the times they were, seemed to get further and further apart, which seemed more like a duty that a loving relationship.

Although Corry did her best to keep everything right in front of Alexa, but never the less struggled with it, putting on a brave face when she had to, but children aren't as foolish as we would like to imaging and Alexa started to notice the mood swings of both of her parents. On the other hand, it was different when visiting London on leave for I'm afraid no one had a chance with their child as she was the apple of Agnes's eye.

Agnes had always wished for a daughter and now she had her wish come true in a granddaughter that she could spoil, for Alexa was not only a beautiful child but with good manners and such a pleasant personality you couldn't help but love her.

It was when Alexa was three years old the family got a posting to west Germany, moved around a couple of times before a posting came up in Berlin, for that's how it was in the forces, you seemed to be on the move at the drop of a hat.

Now Berlin was a beautiful city with a lot to offer, they settled in a nice apartment where Alexa started being more independent of her father, this didn't go down too well with Jay for he idolised his daughter. One of the places you would often find them on a regular basis would be the famous Berlin zoo which to be honest was a wonderful place for any child that liked animals, a little different to any other zoo but magical all the same.

In the meantime, Corry was now finding it hard with the travelling back and forth to London; therefore, bringing in a temporary child minder to help with everything was the answer as eventually the relationship starting to improve between them again. Jay did in fact spend a lot of time away and when he wasn't, Corry would organize her trips back to London so that Alexa wasn't without one or the other of her parents, which worked out quite well.

Yes, it was difficult at times but what could she do, she had the business in London that needed her and her family in Berlin, an exhausting problem that many women face when working full time, she thought as she pondered before deciding to hire a permanent nanny to help out, which would also be company for Alexa.

It had come to Corry's attention that if she went through the Army, they would advertise through a forces magazine which would be able to attract the right kind of person for this position, someone who had been brought up to travel at a moment's notice therefore being able to find a suitable girl who understood army life.

The nanny Corry hired was a smart attractive daughter of one of the officers they'd previously met in Cyprus; a clever girl who took to Alexa straight away, maybe a little strict with their daughter but that's what she needed at times. It was understood that this girl didn't get on with her step-mother and was therefore quite unhappy at home, this being the case she jumped at the chance to take the position of nanny/friend to Alexa.

Now upon introduction this young girl broke the ice by saying;

Hello, I'm Dexie, a little unusual name I know but afraid wasn't around early enough to choose my own name so got saddled with something my father thought up and oh by the way I love your apartment"

As they lived in a rather large apartment with five bedrooms, there was no problem for a live in nanny, therefor it became one big happy family for a while as living in Berlin was an experience with plenty of activities, and being such a vibrant city there was always something going on, therefore life was lived to the extreme

Their social life seemed to fit in with both their positions and it wasn't long before their marriage was back on track as Corry never encountered any of the snobbery that she'd experienced in Cyprus, even the love making returned to normal, in fact, it could be described as fast and furious between them not being able to keep their hands off each other.

Travelling to London every other week for meetings together with designing the odd couture garment seemed to fit in to a routine for she had no intention of letting anything slip under her control as a lot of jobs would have been at stake and she'd worked far too hard for that.

In the meantime, Issa had married Rob in a small wedding ceremony, looking stunning in a Victorian lace dress, with Jay and Corry flying over for the wedding which was attended by just a handful of personal friends, for this was her wish, not wanting any fuss at all. Having worked hard, gained a degree in art and design at night school, and poured all her time into the business of luxury lingerie as they now called it, basically it was underwear but with the sheer materials that Issa had used for them, they were luxury at its finest.

Life had settled down for Issa from those days when she was virtually homeless and destitute, knowing she'd never be able to repay Corry for her help and thanked her lucky stars every day for that break that turned her life around. It also appeared, her mother had got in touch and wanted to make amends for what had happened in the past but I'm afraid, Issa stood firm on this account and couldn't forgive, even though she was living by herself in a small house as she had virtually lost everything and was lonely. Some things should always be left in the past as you will never forgive, and yes, this was one of those things for it was unwise to even try and change her mind. She now had a good life with Rob and didn't intend to spoil it for the past would be raked up and the hurt would return together with bitterness, Issa knew in her heart it was the future she had to look forward to now and that's how it would be, for there would be no going back.

It seemed to Corry that everything was changing for the better, work was going from strength to strength, her marriage was great and she was actually starting to take a little of a back seat so to speak with all the others in charge, what more could she ask for.

David Thomas had turned out to be a godsend in many ways, for he had ideas to push the company to outstanding boundary's that no one else would have achieved. Now as far as David's wife was concerned, the rumours were, she wasn't as bad as people made her out to be a few years ago, but as Corry hadn't met her she couldn't judge, therefore the jury was out on that verdict.

Yes, the smooth running of the company had been a godsend but then again she was lucky in the choice of people around her for not only were many of them employee's but they were also friends that had her best interest at heart which made all the difference but that wasn't to last for long as it never does.

For when Jay arrived home one evening from the mess, looking white as a sheet, Instantly Corry knew there was something wrong as not much fazed him whatever happened at work, but this particular evening he was so quiet and withdraw as he changed out of his uniform, sat down for a coffee while gazing into space not speaking a word for some half hour or so before looking straight at Corry and saying in an orderly fashion;

"Get a bag packed were on a plane in the morning, my mother's had a heart attack; she's in a bad way, apparently they rushed her to hospital a few hours ago and notification came through just before I left the barracks"

Corry felt sick to the stomach as she loved Agnes dearly in fact she worshipped her. That night was so strange as they hardly spoke, near to tears Corry could see how much he was hurting but there was nothing she could do to help his pain, and therefore they would leave Alexa with Dexie for it was no place for children at a time like that.

The journey back to London the next morning was agonising to say the least, if words had come out of their mouths, they would have choked and therefore the best thing was to keep their thoughts to themselves as grief hits people in different ways and the anxiety of the unknown was taking its effect as everyone could imagine. It seemed a lifetime before the plane touched down in London, everything had been laid on for someone to collect and take them straight to the hospital, so there wasn't any delay knowing the urgency of the situation.

Arriving at the hospital and being rushed in to the private room, they could see how ill Agnes was for she was tubed up to all the machines, barely breathing or so they thought and with tears in his eyes Jay went forward to kiss his mother as she opened her eyes to what seemed like a smile appearing on her pallor face, Corry then followed but held back the tears as she bent over to kiss her.

Both Corry and Jay looked at each other as much to say, thank god were in time as it doesn't look as though she'll last much longer for she was now ready to leave this world knowing the two people she loved most in it would look after her granddaughter.

And with all the strength Agnes could manage, she held out her hand to both Corry and Jay as they clasped them together, and said;

"Don't be sad, I've had a wonderful life which I wouldn't have changed for the world, now it's your turn to carry on what I'm leaving behind", still smiling, she closed her eyes and passed away to a world beyond.

Chapter 13

Being brought up with the Jewish faith Jay would respect most aspects of his religion and therefore three days after his mother's death she would be buried with her beloved husband while both Corry and him would accept food and best wishes from everyone who visited, which Agnes would have wished in the period of mourning.

Now although being of the faith she had requested a simple ceremony, this wasn't to be due to the friends that wished to attend the remembrance, and so this is where Jay stepped in to accommodate his own feelings of a more lavish farewell letting his mother go in the style of a great lady with all her friends around to see.

The crowds gathered outside the church having come from far and wide to pay their humble respects, for this was a very good woman who was loved by all, she would be remembered for a long time for her warmth, personality, generosity and most of all her talents in the art world.

All this had hit Jay harder than anyone would have thought, consequently resulting in him hardly speaking, not even to Corry since his mother's death; and so leaving him to grieve in his own way as she was left to grieve in hers.

In the meantime, Dexie stayed in Germany with Alexa as both Corry and Jay thought it best, they would break the news to her about her grandmother as they returned home knowing it would be a lot for a child of her age to take in at a time like this loving Agnes as she did for death is hard enough for a grown up never mind a child.

Leaving instructions that she wanted everyone to go out and enjoy themselves after the funeral at a restaurant which she had chosen, sadly again, that wasn't the case for Jay couldn't hold it together any longer, broke down and had to be taken back to Issa's home which was nearby, and although the wake would still go ahead but in a more sombre fashion, than he'd have wanted it to

This was new to Corry, she'd never seen Jay like this before, knowing he adored his mother but never the less not being able to tell her when she was alive, things like that, he would keep to himself. Oh' how he must have suffered as the only one he was openly affectionate with was his daughter Alexa and she would have been far too young to understand.

They were to stay on in London for a further week sorting some of the personal things out while solicitors moved in to activate the will sending it off to probate. Now having come to the will, the solicitors had a meeting with all concerned whereby explaining that it was quite simple and straight forward, therefore a reading would go ahead immediately which was a sigh of relief in many ways for Jay felt his world collapsing with grief.

The meeting with the solicitors was straight forward.

Jay would get all the properties that his mother owned together with her art collection, he would also get his father's watch which had been kept in a bank safety deposit box for him, this was of some sentimental value which had memories attached to both father and son.

Corry would receive all of Agnes's shares in the fashion house which would make her overall majority shareholder, a lump sum which would be for her personal use together with certain bequests of jewellery.

There would be certain bequests to personal friends such as trinkets, paintings and small pieces of jewellery, these items which was listed, were to be given as soon as possible after her death.

The rest would go to Alexa in trust for when she was twenty-one, which consisted of a large trust fund, itemised paintings, jewellery and a couple of properties in Kensington.

Agnes was a very wealthy woman in her own right so that would be a considerable amount including stocks and shares that even her son wasn't aware of, all of these were to go to her granddaughter Alexa being put in trust with the lawyers as trustees.

This didn't please Jay at all, in his opinion he was the one who should have Power of Attorney to manage his daughter's inheritance, also he should have been left a substantial financial gain with maybe all the stocks and shares, yes he could be very selfish when he wanted to and this was just one of those times that it showed through.

Agnes was well aware of this at the time of drawing up the will and therefore appointed Solicitors as trustees knowing how controlling her son could be, therefore alleviating the problem of Alexa having to go cap in hand to her father, yes she was a very shrewd old lady that nothing got passed, that's why she did it this way, knowing he would have to accept her wishes.

Jay had money that had been left to him by his birth parents which he received when he became of age and wasn't short as it was, but like the old saying, much wants more, but in this case Agnes was to have the last word.

After the funeral, it was thought, things would gradually get back to normal in time but I'm afraid that wasn't the case.

Having travelled back to Berlin, Corry tried her best to appease Jay but whatever she did just wasn't good enough in his eyes, yes their personal life was on track and the physical side was getting back to normal, but somehow there was a distance that Corry couldn't explain which had developed between them. In public they were great but in private it seemed as though the relationship was just a matter of course, a show for the outside world.

The death of Jay's mother hit him hard although he never showed the affection towards her when she was alive, it was as though he was a lone lost soul since she'd passed away. Now If only he could have opened up and shared his feeling then maybe that would have helped but no that would have showed a weakness in his eyes for he wasn't capable of showing any kind of emotion. Not even in their love making at that time, it was like making love to a complete stranger even though she tried her hardest to please his wishes but to no avail, for the only comfort he got was in the love he had for Alexa, for by now he was showering her with so much affection it was stifling as she began pulling away from him at times.

Now the properties Agnes left Jay were all sold as he couldn't stand to have anything to do with them, her painting collection was then put into storage for a later date, these again, he didn't want to have anything to do with and so left his attorney to handle.

There was however one request he made to the solicitors, that was; the chain that Agnes wore round her neck with a large fob on the end which had been left to Corry; seemed to be of some sentimental value and with everyone in agreement, this was then handed over to Jay legally.

From that day forward, he never took this chain off his neck, even going so far as arranging that should anything happen to him in the future, then he should be buried with it on, a strange request from him but never the less as he was in morning for his beloved mother who meant so much to him. No one knew the significance of all this until years later when it was found out to be something that Agnes had bought her niece before she died in childbirth and therefore it was the only thing he had that belonged to his birth mother.

By now Corry was beneath herself, not knowing what to do next to help ease his pain, knowing how much he was suffering as she herself was fighting grief over Agnes's death, but suffered her loss in silence as many women do in cases like this.

It was at this time that he not only withdrew within himself but started to drink quite heavily, Corry wasn't too worried at first but as the months went by she started to question his actions knowing what the end result would be if he didn't stop. But whenever the subject was brought up, Jay's answer was, it was a way of getting over his mother's death but unfortunately she knew better for she'd seen too many go down that road and not be able to turn back. Not being able to do too much at that point for she still had to commute to London for the business, therefore feeling her hands were tied, for when the subject of his drinking was brought up, it ended up in a shouting match between them which wasn't needed in front of their daughter.

Alexa was growing up fast by this time both in mind and body and although adored her father she could plainly see the changes in him as he got more and more moody and thinking it was the loss of her grandmother didn't realise, it was a combination of that and the amount that he was now drinking.

Yes, a bright kid that wasn't just intelligent but also quite funny with her little party pieces when she'd the attention of everyone, in fact, people used to comment on how pretty she was with her long flowing blond hair, it was said that she would become a famous actress one day with her talent to entertain a room full of people when she so wished, yes the apple of her daddy's eye they remarked. But that was a long time ago and things change, not always for the better.

It was at this time that Corry had to return to London for an urgent meeting over the expansion plans for one of the new factories up the north of England which Jay wasn't too pleased about her going for some reason, but work was work and off she went. Having pacified him with the trip only being approximately two weeks and would return as soon as possible.

To her surprise he was starting to pull himself round a little by cutting down on the drink and with the acceptance of his mother's death, even to the point of showing feelings when they made love, maybe things were on the turn and they'd be able to get their marriage back on track as they'd done before.

Therefore, it was a possibility she would have something to look forward to as she still loved him deeply, that deep it hurt at times to see her marriage going to pot, but there again relationships never run smooth as they all have their ups and downs somewhere along the line, why should theirs be different to everyone else's.

Saying good byes to everyone, knowing Alexis was in good hands with Dexie as they adored one another, in fact to Alexa, it was like having a big sister around and to Corry it was another pair of hands she could rely upon, for she was like one of the family by now. Not only was Dexie paid very well but Corry bought a new car for her birthday together with the most beautiful designer clothes for when she mixed socially.

As Corry flew out of Berlin, thinking to herself, I only have to get this meeting sorted and maybe bring the rest of the work back to do at my leisure, yes things were getting a lot easier and now maybe they could go in for an extension to their family, a baby boy would be nice she thought, for Jay had always wanted a son to carry on the name.

Back in London she found Peter was already waiting for her, so it would be a quick drive back to Head Office where she'd attend to all the urgent stuff before the meeting. It didn't matter what time she arrived, her friend was always on hand to collect her, this had always been the case, he insisted that it was his way of looking after her and besides, he was always pleased they could have a little time together for she was like a sister in his eyes;

"How's Jay now" Peter enquired knowing that Corry had been troubled over his health and that was a nice way of asking was he was still drinking.

"Well a lot better" she replied as she then went into further detail as to how his drinking had slowed down with the moods getting a lot easier.

Peter just looked at her with a mysterious expression on his face as much to say, I don't believe you, nothing more was said on that subject, he knew Jay a lot better than Corry thought, his opinion of him was he was a spoilt little boy who had been handed everything he wanted in his life and not like her who had to work hard for it;

"First of all I haven't booked you in anywhere as you're coming to stay with us this time, secondly, were all going out for a meal tonight and thirdly, I've found a beautiful apartment that you may just love, right price, right location and just been refurbished in a modern tone" he stated.

"And where may that be", she replied.

"St Johns Wood, overlooking the park".

The excitement on her face was just a picture as they'd been looking for somewhere nice for when they returned to England, a few years now and nothing had ever come up or if it did, then Jay always said it wasn't the right area or big enough, what he really meant was it wasn't grand enough for him.

"Right she stated, let's go and have something quick to eat, look at this apartment and then we'll have plenty of time to get down to business tomorrow"

"Good thinking" he replied, as that put the lovely smile back on her face, the one that had been missing for some time now as everyone had noticed how sad she had become since the death of Agnes and it was obvious to those close to her what was really causing it.

A quick bite to eat in a little pub was all that was needed before they set off to look at this apartment.

Arriving in St Johns Wood, Corry was pleasantly surprised for overlooking the park, there it was, the right position in the right area that stood out with such a pleasant overlook. There was a feeling of warmth that she could sense in the air about this place although it had been empty for a good six months; it still had an air of sophistication whereby you would be able to awake in the morning to the sound of nature. Situated in a block of four large apartments, this being a bottom floor one.

As you walked into the hallway which was spacious, the kitchen to the right then a large lounge/dining room which opened onto a balcony with views overlooking the park. The rest of the apartment consisted of four large bedrooms a walk in shower/bathroom and enough cupboard and wardrobe space for the entire family.

Yes, this was defiantly to her liking, decorated, in a monochrome vision of black, white and grey, throughout;

"You really have excelled yourself in fact you know me better than I know myself at times and it's frightening to say the least" she said in an excited tone.

"Thought you'd love it as soon as you saw it "he replied.

"Yes but can I afford it, that's the big question"?

"You know darn well you can, but the big question is, will Jay like it as much as you or would he want something a lot bigger."

"Sorry, Peter but this is my call this time and if I can afford it then I want you to go ahead and purchase it for me".

There was something new in Corry's tone as she looked over at Peter and he liked what he saw, she was now starting to stand up to Jay instead of letting him walk all over her so to speak.

"You're the boss lady and if that's what you want me to do then your wish is my command" he said with a smile on his face.

"I would also like you to sort this out through the business in my name only, purchasing it from my own personal account and funds".

What was she up to; Peter thought to himself, this wasn't like her as everything had to be above board, yes she had money to cover the purchase of the apartment but this was a new side to Corry that he hadn't seen before.

Jay on the other hand was so greedy, he wanted everything for himself and truth be known; he would have money stashed away that Corry didn't know about, she had worked hard for what she'd achieved and therefore was now seeing the fruits of her determination over the years.

Peter was so pleased that she was now coming to her senses and maybe seeing Jay for what he was, but then again she would tell him in her own time what she'd done.

And as they both walked out of the building, Corry glanced back and said;

"Well I'm so pleased I came home but never expected to end up buying an apartment, a new pair of shoes maybe but definitely not an apartment, I would ask one more favour and that is, you don't mention this to anyone at the moment, for one, they will think I have gone mad and the other reason I will make clear in a couple of months' time ".

Peter smiled again, as he knew she'd made the right decision to buy, it was just the place that she'd been dreaming of for a few years now but had never managed to find. It was a happy face that he was now seeing and not the sadness that he'd seen in her eyes these past couple of years.

"That was a good day's work we accomplished, now time to get back to my place where you can shower before we all go for a meal. It was at Anna's suggestion that we do this as we rarely see you now a days and it's always nice to catch up, and with you staying, we won't take no for an answer.

The night went well and as usual, there was a lot of shop talk to catch up on, Anna was so easy to talk to and with such an amusing personality when she started, Corry thought how well they were both matched, they had a fantastic relationship and he literally worshipped the ground she walked on, she on the other hand understood the hours he had to put in at work sometimes and therefore enjoyed the benefits that it brought to their lives.

The next week was nothing less than hectic for Corry; she had meetings with buyers, this she loved to do as it kept her hand in with them, not letting them get away with anything she didn't know about. She also liked to visit the factories for a flying visit, this was just her way of saying thank you for all the hard work they'd done throughout the year.

Having arranged to travel up north and see the family but on this occasion her brother had decided to take the grandmother abroad for a short stay to Malta having always wanted to go there and see the shipyard where her father had worked when he was at sea, so that put paid to that idea and with that, then left Corry with the thoughts of returning to Berlin earlier than expected which would be a surprise for her husband, giving them a little more time to spend together as a family.

And with accomplishing everything she'd set out to do on this trip and even more if you added purchasing a new apartment as well, she was pretty pleased with herself. Now all she had to do was go to the airport, board a plane arrive back in Berlin to her family, she would then take Jay out for a night to remember, with a nice meal, little dancing before they made mad passionate love, well that's what was planned in the back of her mind.

Booking the first plane back which got her into Berlin just before 9am, she would be walking through her front door by 10am so it would be quite a surprise knowing Jay wasn't working that day. Oh yes, it was definitely, a surprise alright, for fast asleep in their bed was not only her husband but also Dexie, cuddling up like two lovers.

Well you can imagine what happened next; Corry grabbed hold of Dexie by the scruff of the head tearing her long hair out in handfuls, as Jay woke up to his wife screaming and shouting at the top of her voice for all and sundry to hear'.

"And how long has this been going on", she said as Dexie ran to her room without a word just sobbing.

And like all men when they are confronted by such a volatile female, Jay just grabbed his dressing gown fleeing to the bathroom as Corry followed;

"Well I asked you how long has this been going on"she screamed.

"She was just cold and frightened last night when she heard a noise so I suggested getting into bed with me that's all, it was, nothing" he replied.

"Nothing, under our roof, and in our bed, and you say it was nothing" she screamed'.

"I swear I never touched her "was the reply.

"I never even asked you that question so what part of your guilty conscientious, is that coming from" Corry screamed'.

All of a sudden Corry came to her senses and thought about Alexa,

"Where is my daughter while all this has been going on"?

"One there is nothing going on and two Alexa's staying with a friend" Jay called out, from behind the bathroom door.

"Oh that was very convenient for you wasn't it?"

"Well you'd better get that little tramp out of here before I throw her out and if that happens it won't be a pretty sight I can assure you, no wonder her step mother didn't want her, she's nothing but a little slag and your no better sleeping with a bit of a kid like that, you're nearly old enough to be her father".

Jay then tried to turn the whole situation around by blaming Corry for returning early without warning, but she'd seen this happen in the past where everything was someone else's fault and never his, this is what he did to try and make her feel guilty, but no it wasn't going to work this time as she'd had enough of his little games.

Calmly, she walked into the kitchen while Jay not only dressed, but then proceeded to calm Dexie down who by now was crying uncontrollable.

"I've told you and won't tell you again to get that little tramp out of here for good, when I come to think of the things I've given her, just to make her feel part of the family, and this is how she's repaid me, I should have listened to her stepmother when she warned me the girl was nothing but trouble, but no I gave her a chance to prove she was wrong" Corry shouted from the kitchen

"I'd heard rumours what she'd been up to before but choose to ignore them as never thought she would stoop so low as to go with my own husband, but obviously if that's what you want then you will be able to have her in the future but it won't be in this house I can assure you".

Some women may have been able to turn a blind eye to this kind of behaviour in Jay's little world just to keep the family together, but afraid Corry was brought up better than that and wasn't going to stand by and be humiliated in that way for he'd made his bed and now he had to lay on it so to speak.

It wasn't long before Dexie was dressed with a bag packed, as Jay stood by her side telling Corry he would take her to a hotel, and return so they could talk as she'd got it all wrong and was jumping to conclusions about the situation.

But no, she wasn't in any mood for excuses and so informed him, in no uncertain terms, he wasn't going to get back into the house while she was there.

Jay knew better than to argue with Corry in such a rage, as he'd never seen her like this before, so would leave the situation until she'd calmed down by staying at the officer's mess overnight.

With Jay having left the apartment, Corry proceeded to collect her daughter from a friend's house but the astonishment on her friends face when she arrived, said it all,

"Why didn't you tell me this was happening" Corry asked.

The friend just went cold as she replied;

"Because you would never have believed me, it's been going on for a while but my husband told me to keep out of it, the only thing I could do to help, was to bring Alexa out of the house to stay with us, so that she wouldn't see anything".

"Well, at least I should say thank you for that but I'm afraid that will be the end of it as I'm returning to London and divorce proceeding will now be on the agenda for I don't intend to be humiliated like this, if he wants a bit of a kid in his bed then he can have her permanently." She replied with vengeance in her voice.

How on earth could they both betray me in this way, in front of my own daughter she thought, bringing all her emotional feeling out in anger while trying not to shed a tear in front of Alexa.

Going back to the apartment, there was a deathly silence but this time she'd made up her mind once and for all, she couldn't go on suffering in silence with Jay's control over everything, knowing full well he'd blame everything on her as usual for he was never at fault, but that's how it had always been, not any longer for it was now the end.

Having calmed down and thought deeply about the situation, there was only one answer and that was to return to London immediately for the longer she left it the more difficult it would be for Alexa and why should she suffer. Oh how thankful she was that Agnes wasn't alive to see all the hurt that Jay had caused for both her and Alexa as if she had been, he would have been disowned by his own mother.

Although Corry was strong and a survivor, knowing she would get through this; her only worry now was how it would affect Alexa as she idolised her father. But to be fair, her priority now was her daughter, to return to London, move into the new apartment, find a school for Alexa and then start proceeding for divorce, knowing this wouldn't be easy but then again at least she had friends back home who would all rally around to help where possible, but the hard part was to try and explain to Alexa just why they were leaving Berlin

Jay had always been a good father and that was going to be a problem in one way and yet in another he worshipped the ground she walked on so visiting her wouldn't be an issue for he would take his responsibilities very admirably or so Corry assumed for none of this was her fault.

All of this worked out in Corry's head, now the thing was to put it all into action whereby causing the least disruption to all concerned but for now she was to take Alexa back to the apartment, settle her down before breaking the news of, leaving daddy working in Berlin while they moved to a new home in London.

Everything started to go to plan until Jay returned wanting to talk the situation through. It's funny but in the past he would never talk to her or open up with his feeling but now when it was at a critical stage he wanted to talk and although Corry wasn't prepared to listen to the explanation for his behaviour with a young girl who incidentally was nearly young enough to be his daughter, he now had the audacity to open up with his feelings.

Basically he was a control freak and could see straight through him with his lies and on the other hand, maybe some of it was her fault, letting him get away with it in the past, but enough was enough and at that precise moment she was drained and couldn't take any more. For Jay's version of the story was; Dexie had started to come on to him and not wanting to hurt Corry, he kept quiet about it knowing she thought a lot about the girl. Yes, that part was probably true as Dexie always looked up to Jay but that never explained why he should end up in bed with her as far as Corry was concerned.

He continued by saying, when his mother passed away, it was the saddest day of his life and that's the time that Dexie took advantage, coming on to him time and time again until she wore him down with her flaunting in front of him when Corry wasn't there and although he knew it was wrong, she was such a comfort at times, he just couldn't resist.

What made it worse was the fact that when Corry was back in London and he was lonely, he would then succumb to her advances, the fight had gone out of him but every time he tried to stop it, she would threaten him with, telling Corry what had happened. Adding, he just couldn't risk that knowing how much he loved his family and if it got out then it would ruin his reputation.

"I've never heard so many lies in all my life, if you think I believe any of that, well I'm afraid you're wrong, I've stood by you through everything you've wanted to do, working all hours so our future would be a stable one for our daughter and never let you down in anything, and this is how it ends.

Well I'm telling you. this is now the end as I can't possibly take anymore, I now intend to file for a divorce; I'm taking Alexa back to London whereby I've already purchased a place which was initially intended as a surprise for us.

Now she will soon adopt a new stable routine and as for access, you'll be able to see your daughter whenever you like and in the holiday season should you wish to have her for long periods of time, then this will also be arranged for I'll never put any obstacles in your way where she's concerned. You can also arrange for all our personal belongings to be shipped back to England as I don't want anything more to remind me of what we had, I have my daughter and that is sufficient". Corry said with fire in her voice and a temper which he'd never witnessed before.

Now taking a deep breath before adding in a cold and calculated manner;

"Should you wish to contact me further then you already have my solicitor's details. I would also appreciate, if you'd now leave and sleep in the officer's mess until we can arrange for a flight back to England"

As you can image, Jay was in bits by this time as he realised just what he'd thrown away but it had come too late, for Corry was adamant as to what she was going to do and there was no changing her mind at this or any stage in the future. She could see he was a broken man but he'd brought it on all by himself and therefore had to suffer the consequences, yes she wasn't getting away lightly either as the hurt inside of her was like a knife sticking in her heart but that's what love does to you at times like that.

The next few days, she cried uncontrollably as it hurt so much, the only man she'd ever loved but there again Jay suffered too as he loved her just the same. They had meant to be together forever but how long is forever, no one knows and in this case, although it wouldn't be forever in body their love would last a lifetime in their hearts. The pain of packing up and organizing everything to fly back to England was something that no one should have to go through alone but Corry thought it best if she didn't involve anyone at home until she arrived back. Then she'd tell them in person, that being the better option, knowing the support she'd receive from friends and family once she returned where it would be easy to bury her head in the sand as to what her next move would be.

Walking around in what she called a dream, not eating or sleeping but when she had her thoughts to herself, she would just break down and cry, this she tried to hide in front of Alex, fear of bringing more heartache to a child who didn't realise what was happening or how it would change their future.

It was hard trying to explain to Alexa that daddy was staying in Berlin and they were going to live back in London as mummy had found a lovely new apartment where they wouldn't have to travel all the time but these things are always better coming from a woman no matter how hard it breaks their heart whenever they do it.

Children aren't stupid at whatever age and in Alexa's mind she knew there was something wrong but could plainly see her mother was in no fit state to explain the situation properly and therefore left it as she'd seen her mother crying behind closed doors and didn't want to make the matter worse than it was.

Knowing that her Daddy would come and visit whenever he could but it wouldn't be the same as having to move every couple of years uprooting her school and friends was her only consolation she thought. Alexa was now approaching her tenth birthday and a very intelligent child at that, so knew more than she was letting on, for she'd never even mentioned Dexie at any stage and that was unusual as they had grown so close, not putting up any argument as to returning to England she never carried the conversation on any further with her mother

"Oh if only my grandmother was here now she would be able to sort everything out and make all of this go away" she muttered to herself. No, this wasn't going away fast and so would have to get used to it, knowing she had both of her parents who loved her very much and that's all that mattered at that time.

Corry had to be careful as she 'd noticed Alexa had hardly spoken and to top it all, Jay hadn't been in touch with his daughter at all since he left. Corry for her part just told her daughter that daddy was working and couldn't come home, he had to sleep in the officer's mess as he was on standby duties on a 24/7 basis.

It had been a couple of days later that Corry contacted Peter to let him know she'd booked for both her and Alexa to fly home and would it be possible for him to meet them at the airport as usual, adding, could he book them into a hotel for a couple of days, not mentioning that her old apartment held too many memories and on a practical basis was far too small.

Now a week later, they were leaving Berlin to fly back to England with Jay taking a day off to drive them to the airport saying his goodbyes which as you can guess, was a pretty awful situation for all concerned as it was the first time he'd seen his daughter since that dreadful morning he'd returned to the officer's mess. He looked absolutely dreadful but put on a brave face for his farewell parting which was strained to say the least;

"Say goodbye and kiss daddy" Corry said to Alexa.

"No" Alexa replied quite sharply.

Both parents looked at each other with such a vacant look now realizing that their little girl was grown up enough to know what was going on without being told

"What's all this about Alexa" Corry asked in a stern voice.

To this with tears streaming down Alexa's face, she flung her arms around Jay's neck and said;

"I love you daddy, I love you with all of my heart so don't ever forget that as long as you live will you, I will always be your little girl, you won't ever get another one will you"?

This coming from a child as you can imagine, would put anyone in a frantic state and therefore Jay couldn't take any more of the situation, clinging to her like death for he loved her so much and here he was ruining her life for all the mistakes that he'd made and couldn't put right.

"It's alright my baby, it won't be long before I come back to England and we'll be together again I promise, you will always be my little girl, no one could ever replace you sweetheart "and with tears streaming down his face as he let her walk away, his head in bits to what was happening for he had no power to stop it. This was a promise he couldn't keep but all the same he hoped that one day he would be able to change Corry's mind and they would be reunited as a family once again.

The tears flowed for all concerned but afraid there was no turning back for the future was in front and they had to bury the past however hard it may be.

The plane journey although short and sweet, was also uncomfortable as it broke Corry's heart to accept what was finally happening and also the fact that she was on her own from that moment in time with no insight into the future for both her and her daughter. Peter knew instinctively that something was very wrong and suspected the worse so was only too eager to pick them both up knowing there was more to it than he first suspected.

It was all smiles as they met but then the tears came flooding through,

"Don't say anything until we get home" Peter ordered seeing the upset it would have caused if anything had been said there and then but with a look of concern added;

"You are to stay with Issa at her place which is very near to that apartment were purchasing for you, having spoken to her last night; she has arranged to take a few days off to settle you in until your own apartment will be ready".

Corry looked at Peter with tears rolling down her face, "thank you my friend" she replied;

"We've had a word with the solicitors and they say as it was a vacant possession, you will be able to move in this side of two weeks when everything will be finalized, until then you'll have Issa to help furnish the place to your liking or should I say to hers, as you know what she's like when she gets a bee in her bonnet, you're not to worry about a thing at the moment as you have all your friends around to help sort things".

Arriving at Issa's, she knew she'd have some explaining to do straight away so prepared herself for a long talk, with Peter there to just listen as to what had happened for that was his way of handling things.

A meal ready as they reached her friend's house but in her case Corry had lost her appetite a couple of weeks earlier,

"That smells nice" Alexa chirped in, mind you there wasn't much that put her off food as most children her age.

"Well go and get cleaned up and there's plenty for you to eat with jam roly poly and custard to follow, should you be able to fit it down" Issa stated.

It wasn't until the evening when Alexa had gone to bed shattered from all the turmoil of the day's events that they could all talk freely. Issa was heartbroken as to what had happened but Peter just took all the conversation in his stride and said very little for it was always suspected that he never did like Jay but kept quiet for the sake of Corry.

At the end of the night Peter got up to go home saying;

"Look I don't want you to worry as everything will fall into place, you'll return to work as soon as possible to get that rat out of your system once and for all and in the meantime Alexa will be cared for by Anna who'll be thrilled at the chance to help while you move into your new apartment for the solicitors are rushing everything through as a favour to me. Don't forget you have friends and family that love you very much and will bend over backwards in this time of need so don't worry, we're all here for you".

Oh dear she thought, with all this going on and the confusion, she'd not let her own family know back in Yorkshire, and that was going to be the hardest bit of the journey home, to tell them that she had a failed marriage, but just then Peter interrupted her thoughts by saying;

"Does the family know about you and Jay for if they don't I'll send a telegram up north inviting them down for the weekend to see a show and you can break the news to then in the privacy of your own comfort zone"?

"That would be lovely if you could arrange that for me for my head's turning ten to the dozen" Corry replied

"No sooner said than done; now I must be off as Anna will be worrying about where I've got to as you know what she's like, but there again, I'm to blame as forgot to explain the situation before I left this morning".

I don't think anyone slept that night as their thoughts were for Corry but the next day was a different matter as it seemed it was like hell let loose for them as they helped their friend sort everything out.

It had been arranged that the apartment would be ready to move in sooner than expected, a school for Alexa had been found for her to start immediately, and Corry had seen a solicitor to start the ball rolling with the divorce.

Knowing that Jay would agree to everything as he hated bad publicity, therefore they 'd go their own separate ways, keeping their own financial holdings. Alexa would stay with her mother, Jay having open access to whenever he wanted to see her. No it couldn't have gone any smoother if there had been someone up above organizing it.

Issa on the other hand, had gone shopping for all the essentials knowing Corry's taste, the only things that had to be purchased now was all the big furniture, it was going to be a clean sweep and therefore a different style of living what Corry had been used to with the army, for everything would be of an individual taste and not what the army deemed as traditional.

The weekend arrived when Corry's brother and grandmother came down to London to what they thought would be a show followed by a family get together, unfortunately they weren't' fooled, as being suspicious, they instantly knew something was wrong and were expecting bad news of sorts, the only thing was, they never expected Corry had returned to London permanently.

Breaking the news was hard but it had to be done, although they never battered an eyelid when told or had they already guessed what was coming, having suspected for some time there wasn't the closeness that they once shared with Jay being so moody, it was just a matter of time before Corry stood up to him. She couldn't bring herself to tell them the full story about Dexie in bed with him as she herself felt a little ashamed, but would reveal this to her brother at a later date knowing he'd have probably been on the next plane over to see Jay and sort it all out.

Seeing the state that Corry was in was upsetting enough for the family so to make it worse by all the questions, may even tip her over the edge and therefore a lot wasn't revealed at that stage for all they wanted was her happiness as she deserved it.

It was no more than a month since Corry arrived back in London and she'd achieved so much in such a short time, throwing herself into work, moving into the new apartment, settling Alexa down into her new school, it all seemed to fall into place, she wished life was always so simply but having said that, without the family network around her it wouldn't have been at all possible.

The days just flew by but the nights were so lonely, she may be surrounded by people but still felt alone and to be truthful, she missed Jay, it was almost nightly that she cried herself to sleep, with the thoughts of, why did this happen to me, asking the question over and over again but with no answer forthcoming. Was this the way it had to be, was she destined to go through life like this forever or was there a light at the end of the tunnel, if only these question could be answered then maybe she would find sleep would come to her a lot more easily.

The divorce was on its way through without any complications and would be finalized before Alexa's tenth birthday, but still not hearing from Jay on a regular basis only through the lawyers, Corry was worried that he was starting to lose interest in his daughter which wasn't a good sign as Alexa was now starting to play up whereby wanting her father, yes her father, the one who had slept with a girl not much older than his own daughter without a conscience of the consequences that was facing him through life.

Corry could hear Alexa crying at night although this was denied but knowing the child was hurting all the same as she herself was.

Not knowing what to do, she asked the solicitor to contact Jay and see if Alexa could maybe fly over to Berlin for a week and stay with him, the response was, he was far too busy and if he had time then he'd fly to London for a few days to spend with his daughter which never materialised.

As far as the promise's that he made to his daughter at the airport that final day, these didn't amount to anything for he never returned or if he did then he didn't attempt to see Alexa.

Chapter 14

The divorce was finalized with all the loose ends being tied up as far as everyone was concerned with no mention at all to Alexa, but to everyone's surprise she seemed to move on and made a new friend, this being someone who took a big interest in a little girl who he later grew to idolised, this man was no other than Design expert in an extraordinary way Malcomb Chow.

It all came about when Malcomb had turned up at Corry's place to see how she was getting on, when suddenly Alexa came out of her shell chatting away to him like they had been friends for ages, Corry couldn't believe it, as it took her all the time to even speak to anyone who came, except for Anna. Getting on so well with this child Malcomb asked if it would be possible to take Alexa to his factory, show her the new designs he had in mind for young people, then onto an ice-cream parlour for a treat.;

"Oh please, please let me go mummy, I promise I'll behave for the rest of the week if you'll let me go"

Corry was so shocked that Malcomb had such a way with her; for she'd never seen her daughter take to anyone like this since Dexie.

"Well if you promise to behave, then you may go with Malcomb but you must do as he tells you".

This was something new; maybe she was coming around to the idea that although her father wasn't in her life, she was beginning to trust others who would give her the attention she craved for, like all little girls, they need a father figure in their lives.

The day out with Malcomb went well, Alexa never stopped talking about him, it was Malcomb this, Malcomb that and Malcomb the other, oh yes she couldn't get enough of him over the next few weeks following him around whenever she got chance to be around him. Even to the point that she was genuinely interested in all the new things he was producing for his new teenage line.

So fond of Malcomb, Alexa had become, that one day when he'd shown her the new colour range of knitwear for her age, having tried them on, she made a statement that, when she grew up, she would be a model and model his fashions because he was the nicest man in the world. Corry laughed at this statement, putting it down to a young girl's wild dream, when in fact that dream she talked about was to come true in later years.

A few months passed by with Corry throwing herself into work trying to forget Jay, Alexa followed Malcomb around like a little lap dog having never seen her father since they'd come back from Berlin, as far as anyone knew he'd a new girlfriend or was that a few new young girlfriends to satisfy his needs.

Then one day out of the blue, Alexa came home having spent the day with Malcomb, she asked;

"Mummy, do you think that if you married Malcomb, he would be my new daddy"?

Corry had no answer to her daughter just laughing it off as a young girl's dreams but all the same was a little alarmed at what she'd heard, therefore consulting Issa about this comment thinking she was a little paranoid was altogether shocked at her answer;

"We've seen this coming on for a while now, what's up, are you blind, you know that Malcomb has always had a thing about you and yet you let him get too close to your daughter, if that's not asking for trouble, I don't know what is as Alexa listens to him more than she listens to you now a day, just think about it, others have seen it so why haven't you?"

This came as a shock and going home that night with a heavy heart, she tossed and turned in bed with no sign of sleep ever entering her body, Oh My God what on earth can I do, she thought, if I put an end to the relationship between

Alexa and Malcomb, would my daughter hate me, as at present she's getting father like attention from this man, no there had to be a more sensible answer than that knowing Alexa was also falling behind at school.

Morning came with a brand new prospective, take Alexa to Doncaster, enrol her in a school there with grandmother taking charge; she would spoil her to death, and also be company for her, why hadn't she thought of this before, open air, access to the countryside, Alexa would just love it and it would be the perfect solution for if Jay did come round and want to see his daughter then there was nothing stopping him going straight to Doncaster.

Corry decided to break it gently to Alexa that her grandmother wasn't too well and although she seemed fine, it would be a good idea for her to stay and keep her company for a few months;

"What about school" Alexa enquired.

"Oh I'm sure we can come to some arrangements about that"

"What do you think, would you like to go and stay with her as it would be a big worry off my mind if you did" Corry said rather quizzical.

Alexa's face lit up like the rising sun before saying.

"I'd love to, I don't like that school I'm going to, the girls are horrible, if I go to a new school and like it and your lonely I'll come down here and visit you in the holidays if that's alright with you."

"Do you know that's a brilliant suggestion, I wish I'd thought of that idea" was the reply Corry Gave to the relief of the situation

This had been a lot easier than she'd thought, and in all honesty she'd never expected Alexa to go for the idea but on the other hand, knowing how fond of her grandmother she was, maybe she thought she'd get her undivided attention which would be nice. Corry had already had a word and if they all pulled together perhaps they could make it work whereby it would be beneficial for all concerned and should a problem then arise then Paul would be able to step in straight away as he was only a few miles away.

Everything packed and ready, Corry took Alexa back to Doncaster, accompanied by her friend Issa as any excuse to visit Corry's grandmother who she regarded as part of her family now, not having one of her own. Spending a couple of days settling Alexa in, taking her shopping and doing all the girlie things, was a lovely break for them all, just one of many that they enjoyed in the years to come while Alexa was growing up.

While back in London, Corry was now aware it was time to buckle down and get on with some work for if she thought too much about what had happened, knew she'd be heading for a breakdown with everything running through her head at one mad speed. Yes, there were still nights of crying over Jay and that would go on for a long time in the future but she had to be strong and throw herself into work which would alleviate the situation or so she thought.

What she really needed was to keep her mind busy with a new venture, thinking she would restructure some of the working down London and maybe move it up north as it was a lot cheaper to manufacture from there and this would keep her occupied for the time being.

Her thoughts were, if she moved the underwear selection to the Leeds area and concentrated on putting the more expensive pieces in the capital where the tourists visit, then it may create a new market for the buyers, but knowing this would have to be run past Peter first, there would be no doubt at all, he would go for the idea as financially it made perfect sense.

Issa would definitely go for the idea of moving the underwear manufacturing up north as it would give her a great opportunity to spend more time in a place that she loved so much and maybe get an apartment in that area.

As for Peter, well he was looking so tired of late and the strain in his face was starting to tell so it was up to Corry to take some of the weight off his shoulders as when all said and done she was the head of the company and therefore a lot of people relied on her.

Now starting to play the role as a CEO for that's what she was and that's what she would show everyone who worked for her for she'd taken a back seat for too long with her troubles and now It was time she stood at the helm and let Peter stand down taking it easy for a while, not only did he need a rest but he needed to spend a little time with his family.

Alexa was settled up north with her maternal family while Corry had her friends in the city for support should she need them but first and foremost it was a visit to all the factories, where she'd work out what was needed to move forward. Secondly, meet all the staff that was employed, take out all the Directors and their families to a slap up meal, get back into designing and reward all those that had stuck by her these last few years while she travelled back and forth to other countries.

The next day starting her long haul to pull the reins in, calling a meeting with everyone in the office and give insight to some of the intended plans she was going to implement so that the company could move forward. And with the help of Sheila, her right hand man as she now started to call her, was on the ball knowing only too well, what Corry was like when she'd a bee in her bonnet;

"It's alright I saw the note you left and arranged a meeting of all the Directors along with booking a meal at a new restaurant, I've also informed all the factories that you'll be paying them a visit in the next couple of weeks" she said.

Nothing had ever really changed Corry thought; Shelia was still as efficient as ever with military precision, down to the very last detail.

It was when everyone turned up for the meeting and Corry thanked them for putting things aside at short notice, proceeding to make her feelings heard as follows;

"As you will no doubt be aware by now, Jay and I are finally divorced" she then went on to say;

"I've taken a new apartment in St John's Wood, Alexa will be living up in Yorkshire with my family and I am now back at the helm of the company therefore will be pulling my weight with everything, taking a deep breath she went on to say.

A night out with the Directors has already been planned so you will be able to let off a little steam of your own after all the hard work you have put in over this difficult period.

I will also be visiting the entire establishments that we now control, in the next few weeks, this giving me an idea for maybe expansion

Now the last line really gave everyone a surprise for they knew the orders were flooding in but not to that extent.

It's my intention to open shops attached to all the factories and therefore selling our garments which don't actually come up to the high quality (i.e. seconds) we demand; this will generate monies back into the business instead of destroying these items which we have done in the past.

There will also be a slight change of position to one of our trusted and most valuable employees, Shelia as you may know has been my private secretary for a number of years now, she will now become the Company Secretary, which for those of you that don't know is in fact a Director.

Well, you could have knocked Shelia down with a feather as no one was expecting that, not even Peter, although he was thrilled that Corry had recognised all her hard work, Shelia on the other hand was so shocked someone had to get her a chair as they thought she would pass out at what had happened.

I would also like to thank you all for all your hard work in making this company what it is today which is one of the few companies that is expanding and creating a larger workforce than we could ever envisage.

And before the rumour control starts up as to why you won't be seeing Peter for a few weeks, I'm sending him and his family away on a well-deserved holiday as my appreciation for holding the fort together while I've gone through an emotional time and not been able to pull my weight as I should have".

Now after a large pause she finished off on a personal note of gratitude by adding;

"Last but not least which is on a personal note from me, I sincerely can't thank you enough for helping me through these past few months which has been an emotion time on a personal basis.

To me this has been a family business from the start of our small venture and although the family has grown, you are and always will be my family for this is now going to be a new beginning for all of us into the future".

Chapter 15

KAREN

Corry really was on the ball and had a lot of catching up to do, it seemed as though she'd been out of the business for a long time and little things had started to slip in some areas or so she thought, yes it was making money but they had lost the personal touch on a lot of things. What she had to do is start from scratch, building up where she'd left off throwing herself into work; this wasn't only for herself but for everyone.

Knowing she would never get over Jay, it didn't make it any easier with him not keeping in touch with Alexa; she could never understand as he worshiped his daughter from the day she was born, therefore would reconcile herself with the thoughts that, different people have different ways of coping with things but then she'd come down to earth with a bang and think, what the hell, and it's his loss, not wanting bitterness to creep in.

The next few months, not only did she throw herself into work visiting the factories, checking through all the order books with a fine tooth comb to see if the business could be streamline at all. She was so pleased what everyone had achieved in the past ten years or so while the business had taken second hand to her marriage and thanked her lucky stars what a good professional team together with the friends she had around her.

Peter starting to take a back seat to the business for a while now she was back at the helm, mind you that was a bit of an exaggeration for the back seat was; he was only working a five day a week instead of the seven that he usually put in and one person who was thrilled with that decision was Anna for that gave them a little more time together.

That woman was a saint, for Corry had never even heard her complain about the hours he put in, she simply used to accept his position knowing he was doing it for the family, but then again the business was part of his family as he saw it.

Dave Thomas on the other hand was a workaholic, doing so much for the company, that it really was amazing, yes he was of a similar nature to Peter really, relaxed in one way but got on with it in another, outside of work he just worshipped his family and was quite protective towards them, although not much was known about him outside of work for he was a pretty private person that kept everything to himself.

Having still not met his wife but had heard the rumours which were rife about her as it was said, she was extremely attractive, liked her own way, a real demanding bitch who wanted all her own way although the one thing in her favour as far as Corry was concerned, she was also very protective of her boys.

Now for Alexa who was doing extremely well at school; so much so that Corry decided she'd leave her in the north of England, knowing that was the best place for her to grow up as that's where she spent her childhood and it didn't do her any harm, quite the opposite.

Corry had contacted Jay on many occasions, begging him to see Alexa but to no avail and so decided he wasn't worth the energy so left well alone for he would want her one day and she would turn her back on him. Alexa had a loving family support and Corry spent as much time as she possibly could to maintain this.

A couple of years passed when it was decided to purchase an apartment in Leeds, where not only she could stay but also the directors when on official business, so having fallen in love with one on the riverside which had a waiting list, it was her friend David Thomas who stepped in pulling strings to secure this splendid three-bedroom apartment saving the company an awful lot of money, yes he definitely had the Midas touch.

It seemed that work was her only comfort at that time, oh don't get me wrong, she'd had the occasional date that friends fixed her up with but couldn't settle for more than a couple of dates with the same man, no she'd been hurt far too much and therefore put barriers up so that any decent man in their right mind wouldn't even attempt to tackle such a powerful woman not realising the loneliness she felt inside.

Feeling a little low one day, walking down the street when a glass of wine seemed to be such a tempting thought which was unusual for her but with a feeling of what the hell, she found herself at the bar with an order of a large glass of white please when you're ready, and while wandering over to a small table by the window where she could drowned her sorrows, thinking where the hell am I going in life, gazing down into a glass while shedding a few tears as she'd often done before, when all of a sudden she heard a voice from a stranger asking politely;

"Are you alright, is there anything I can do to help".

"No, I'm fine thank you" was her reply as she looked up, smiled and wiped the tears from her eyes.

The stranger, a tall slim very attractive blond, dressed in beautiful clothes which she recognised immediately as her own designs,

"Do you mind if I sit with you for a while as my friends haven't turned up yet and it would be nice to have a little company while I wait" the stranger asked as she knew darn well that Corry was distressed and maybe if she sat and talked, it may help her.

"No not at all, it's not very often I get chance to sit and talk with someone outside of work" was Corry's reply.

"Well that would be nice as I know the feeling, all my husband talks about when he gets home is work. Oh by the way, my name is Karen" she said.

"Pleased to meet you, I'm Corry".

"Not trying to interfere and tell me to mind my own business if you like, but why are you looking so sad? I noticed the tears, so don't tell me it was nothing as don't believe you, knowing full well there must be something wrong when I first saw you sitting alone".

Corry looked up at this stranger who had a wise and caring face, with a reply of;

"Just think everything was getting on top of me, you know how it is at times, it happens to everyone".

But the stranger wasn't going to give up that easily as she said looking down at Corry's hand.

"I noticed, you're not married, do you have a boyfriend then?

"No afraid not, don't seem to have the time for one, far too busy with work and to be honest, I don't trust men as found my ex in bed with our teenage baby sitter which as you can well image, was like a knife in the heart, tried to deny it but then I'm not that stupid enough to believe the story he told me, knowing it would not only be lies but he'd make it all out to be my fault, as he'd done in the past" was Corry's reply.

The stranger looked Corry straight in the eyes before saying;

"Oh you poor thing, it must be a common trend as this happened to one of my husband's colleagues, she feels just the same as you, buries herself in work and tries to hide the upset from everyone but they're not silly as they know she's trying to put on a brave face in front of everyone as most women do at times like that".

Corry smiled knowing she wasn't on her own in that situation before adding;

"Never mind, I'll get over it in time, it's just at the present moment, I don't seem to trust any man that tries to enter my life"

Funny how you can strike up a conversation with a complete stranger, discussing everything from children, fashion to daily life as the conversation flowed over a few more glasses of wine, realizing in the end that you'd been talking for nearly two hours or so and not only enjoyed the conversation but at the end of it felt better for it;

"Do you know I've really enjoyed bumping into you like this" Karen said.

"Me too, it's been wonderful and a complete change of routine for me, we'll have to do this again. Look I'm having a few friends over for drinks on Saturday night, a sort of girly night, would you like to join us, please say yes as I think you'll enjoy yourself".

"That would be lovely, that's if you don't mind, as I've really enjoyed myself talking with you today, in fact I think we will become quite good friends, for we seem to have a lot in common "was her reply.

"Good that's settled, here's the address, come any time after seven as my husband's having a night out with the lads, will you be alright, as better be off now, meeting a couple of friends at their house" Karen added as she got up to leave.

"Yes fine and thanks for a wonderful afternoon, I really have enjoyed talking with you, it's been great, not enjoyed myself like this in a long time".

What a nice woman Corry thought, yes I'll go on Saturday night, if all her friends are as nice, then it will be a good night out, certainly a change from stopping in to do work on the collection. What a difference that afternoon had made, Corry went back to work with such a spring in her step, even the office staff noticed.

The weekend was here before she knew it, having already bought half a dozen bottles of wine as she headed out in a taxi to Karen's house, not knowing what to expect but all the same, it would be different to what she would have been doing and also the chance to meet new people that could maybe share the friendship as this stranger, that had walked into her life that day in the wine bar.

Upon arriving she noticed Karen was already welcoming one or two of her friends, who looked quite a rowdy bunch to say the least but that made it more interesting as that's what she needed to blow all the cobwebs out of her life.

"Oh you made it then, I wasn't sure if you'd come, but pleased you took me up on the offer" Karen said as she threw her arms around Corry in such a warm embrace, it was as though they had been friends for years and not only just met a few days ago

"Look, I've got six more of my friends that's turned up and were in for one hell of a night, especially seen as you've added another six bottles to the list that we've already got", Karen said beaming like a Cheshire cat.

Corry felt so welcome with all these strangers, she couldn't get over how they welcomed her with open arms, they weren't anything like the stuffy army officer's wives that she had to mix with when her and Jay were together but there again that was in the past now

Stepping forward Karen could see Corry was at ease already and that's before any introduction;

"Now let me introduce you to some of my friends",

"Firstly, this is my friend Dianne, Di for short, she owns a small tanning shop in the village, divorced, one son, and hates all men".

"Secondly, my friend Tracy, a single girl who has the hairdressing salon in the village, no children, hates men although she won't admit it, has a boyfriend at the moment or so it is rumoured, but never talks about him for she hides behind her shyness".

"Thirdly, my friend Tammy, 2 fantastic children, on her second marriage to a man that simply adores her, worships the ground she walks on, they live in a big old farmhouse in the highlands, up in Scotland but at present staying with family while the house is renovated".

"Fourthly, this is Elaine, she has an old peoples care home which is out of town, her children are now grown up, she lost her husband some years ago when the children were quite young but with the help of family has worked ever since".

"Then there is my friend Jenny who lives in the city, works at the stock exchange, single, new boyfriend every time we see her, lives life to the full, doesn't care a darn about anything but her family and friends, a real party girl".

"Last but not least this is Carol; she has a small but very expensive boutique in the village, no children and we don't talk about her husband or soon to be, ex-husband, as he is the biggest rat walking at the best of times, isn't that right Carol"?

Karen then turned quickly to Corry to introduce her officially.

"Well girls, this is my new found friend Corry that I was telling you about, she is divorced, one daughter who is being brought up by her grandmother, hates men, has a small shop in the heart of London which I understand sells boutique type clothes. And now you all know one another, I think it's about time we started on the serious side of those bottles of wine before they start to ferment" she said laughing.

"Also for those who are a bit peckish, there is a buffet laid out in the kitchen, so let's start the night as we mean to go on with glasses to the ready and a little music in the background, yes, its party night for the girls don't you all think"

Corry had never enjoyed herself so much for such a long time; and never stopped laughing as she got to know each of Karen's friends on an individual basis, all with stories to tell

It was Carol who approached Corry to start off with stating she'd seen her somewhere before as she recognised her face but couldn't think where it was from, maybe a few more glasses of wine and it would probably come back to her. A few more glasses and she'd probably be on her back Corry thought, but there again there was something about Carol that was amusingly funny in a good way.

"What's this about your husband" Corry enquired;

"Oh we had the perfect marriage, saved up, bought a nice little clothing business, did everything together, decided that there was no room for children as it would interfere with dreams we had for a better life. As the business grew he started to spend time out with the lads, which I didn't mind at all at that stage as it was all harmless fun and he needed male company or so I thought.

Then one day, I came back from a day out with the girls due to not feeling too good, only to find him in bed with one of the staff that worked for us, later found out that it had been going on for months behind my back. There was me working my guts out to make our lives better, while he'd been spending all our money on buying her expensive presents, for that's the only way he could keep her as she was a lot younger than him and I presume that's the only thing that was the attraction, well he wasn't all that good in bed so it had to be".

I instantly packed his bags, threw him out and cried for weeks until the tears just wouldn't come any more, she in the meantime decided to ditch him for a younger model, he tried to return saying it was her that led him on which I never believed for a minute. I just don't know what I'd have done if I'd not got these lot behind me, I can tell you, they were just great, yes it still hurts as he was the love of my life, I'd been with him since leaving school but all the same I couldn't take him back after that as the trust had gone forever, for if a man can do that once then he will do it again.

And if he thinks he's got away with it all he won't get a penny from the business as it was tied up in my father's name due to us having to borrow from him when we first started it".

Carol looked at Corry with such sadness in her eyes, yes she was still hurting and Corry knew just how it felt as she herself still loved Jay but it wasn't to be.;

"What will you do now or don't you know "Corry enquired with a sympathetic gesture?

"I'll go on hating all men for the rest of my life, build my business up, buy a new sports car, never to get married again, and no that's not the wine talking "was the reply.

But, it was the wine that was talking, for Carol met a businessman from France, fell madly in love, went to live there, had two children and ended up very happy in years to come

Tracy, now she was a little different from the rest of the girls, standing taller than most, she was of a slim build, smart but plainly dressed, well spoken, although single, was in fact very shy and found it hard to talk to strangers, she did remind Corry a little of what Issa used to be like when they first met.

Apparently she was an only child who had been bullied by her mother when growing up, her father worshipped her but sadly he wasn't always around to see her mother's jealousy towards her. It didn't matter what she did to please her mother it was never good enough and therefore hid her feelings, resulting in her, finding it hard to make friends She did have one or two close friends but found it hard to confide her thoughts or ambitions in anyone.

It was when she reached the age of twenty-five; both her parents were killed in a car crash leaving her devastated and with no one to turn to, sinking into a deep depression. Although she'd been left quite a considerable amount of money from her parent's death, still couldn't cope in her personal life and so it was at this time when Karen and the family purchased this house, that she eventually became friends with them.

Taking advice from Karen's husband she invested her money wisely and bought a hairdressing business and from that day, not only did she come out of her shell, but the business was such a successful investment, it went from strength to strength, doing so well that she now employs six girls and is seriously thinking of looking for another premises to open yet another hairdresser. Having dated one or two men, she found that relationships didn't come easy for the shyness always got in the way, there were a couple of nice men that came into her life only to leave her disappointed as the communication between them didn't flow sufficiently, and it was a pity really, for she was such an attractive woman.

Rumour now had it, there had been a couple of dates with someone that she'd been at school with but there again it was only rumours. Being such a private person, Corry had to drag information out of her as she found it difficult in the past to confide in anyone until she made friend s with Karen's family.

It came to pass, the rumours that had been circulating were true, she had met up with a really good man that she'd known at school, courted him for three years and eventually married him, sold up and immigrated to Canada.

Now mingling with Karen's friends was nice and comfortable for they were such a good crowd and with the wine flowing as the night went on; it seemed everyone had a story to tell which was fascinating to a stranger such as Corry as the night went on making her way to approached Elaine.

The story behind Elaine was so simple. She married her childhood sweetheart at eighteen, had two children by the time she was twenty-one, with the help of her parents got a deposit for a small terraced house, although things were tight they never went without as everyone pulled together in those days, having a little cleaning job at weekend when her husband would look after the children as he worked away through the week. They were such a devoted couple that whenever you saw them out which was on a rare occasion, they would either be together or with the children for that was their little world.

Apparently, it was a night of celebration for their tenth wedding anniversary as they walked home from the local club in the village, when a car mounted the pavement and killed her husband instantly. The shock sent Elaine into a state of depression whereby her parents had to step in and take charge of the children; this was a very difficult time for all concerned as you can imagine.

A while after, Elaine received a large sum of money from the accident, started to rebuild a new life for both her and the children, rented a large house, turning it into a nursing home for the elderly while her parents helped out with the children. It became such a success that eventually she bought the place out right, extended it, even purchasing the house next door, this doubling not only the house but also the grounds, making them into a beautiful garden area for people to relax in their later years. It was so popular, there was a waiting list for residential care in her home. Now this had been her life ever since, the children now grown up and carrying on the good work that she started by both of them studying hard to give back to their mother what she'd sacrificed for others.

In time to come she would go on to live her dream of looking after those that she really cared for, giving them the best care she possibly could in their senior years. Her children would also carry on her good work, only in a different direction for they both studied to be doctors.

Tammy was a smart and feisty person who'd been married before to a rather strange man who never appreciated her at all, attractive with a great personality but a mystery about her ex-husband although it was thought he was a violent man, nothing was ever mentioned fear of hurting the children and therefore her friends had gathered round to protect the situation as friends always do, It was when she was at her lowest ebb that she met her second husband, having gone up to Scotland with some friends on a girly weekend, out drinking in a bar one night when she noticed a very handsome man kept staring over at her.

It was after a few drinks that she plucked up courage to go over and introduced herself rather cheekily, as this handsome man just turned to her and said;

"My name is Ian and I intend to marry you, all you have to do is set the date".

She couldn't believe her ears, "what did you say" she replied.

"Oh so you're hard of hearing then "was the answer.

"No not at all, but having never met before, how can you be so sure that I want to marry you without knowing anything about you" she replied laughing

"My name is Ian Stewart, I have a farm situated just on the Scottish coast, maybe not to your taste but can be refurbished to your liking after were married".

"I have several men who work for me, am quite well off as you English say therefore you'll never want for anything and before you ask, no I'm not married as I lost my wife to cancer six months after we got married, that was five years ago. Now is there anything else you'd like to know before we set a date for the wedding,"? He went on to say with a straight face.

Flabbergasted wasn't the word for however she tried the words wouldn't materialise as she stood there in shock.

"Oh I think I'd better buy you and your friends a drink now to celebrate our engagement, don't you" Ian asked as he walked over to the rest of the crowd.

Tammy had never been in a situation like this before whereby she was stuck for words, this was definitely a first for her without any doubt, for she had such a bubbly personality, taking everything in her stride finishing with a one-line answer for everything. Slowly coming round to the conversation she started to loosen up, playing along with what she thought was his sense of humour.

The night went on as they all mingled in the bar, Tammy softening to Ian as she'd never done since the break-up of her marriage, even exchanging addresses as the night drew to a close. Having really enjoyed herself if nothing more she thought, he was handsome so what more could be said on the subject knowing full well she'd never see him again after that weekend.

How wrong she was, for that was just the start of a short courtship ending three months later resulting in them walking down the aisle in harmony.

It was now twelve months later and sitting in Karen's home having drinks while her house was being refurbished to her liking as he'd promised on the first night they'd met, Yes, twelve months of total bliss as she had at last found her soul mate in a Scottish farmer

Dianne, on the other hand was a loner, the hurt and loneliness that she'd endured at one time or another sensing the deep and troubled expression in her face, obviously luck had not been on her side when searching for happiness Corry thought.

Tall, slim, long blond hair, great figure and legs to die for, what more could a girl ask for, but no there was definitely sadness in those eyes as you looked into them deeply, what was her story and what's she hiding behind that mask, was it a cry for help that no one could hear in a crowd full of people or was there a deep secret that needed to immerge into the open?

Dianne was one of two girls, born to a couple of hardworking people who adored her. Growing up she was a very clever academic person who got on with everyone around but it seemed when she reached her teens her friends kept their distance for the fear of them losing their boyfriends to Dianne as she was so attractive to men.

Having worked hard in the jobs she attained before meeting her husband and after eight years of unhappy marriage with a son born to her, she divorced, it's not quite clear what happened as it was thought that he was a good man who really cared for her, Dianne on the other hand disagreed with this theory but sometimes when you're standing that close, you can't judge for yourself and maybe this was just one of those times for the loneliness in her face gave no understanding to what had happened.

Having to bring up a son more or less by herself, she worked every hour god sent to manage with the help of her parents, although she did have a couple of relationships but they never seemed to last as for some reason the men she chose all let her down l. The last relationship was also a disaster as like all the others, he spent what little monies she had and slept with a couple of friends behind her back before leaving her in a load of debt, no it seemed she definitely couldn't pick her men for some reason and therefore hated all men which was understandable for what she'd gone through both financially and with great disappointment.

The tanning shop she acquired was what her father helped her buy with his redundancy. Although only a small run down premises, Dianne went to work on re-styling it to her own taste so she could attempt a fresh start and put her life back together after what she called another disastrous relationship, but yet again, the shop wasn't doing as well as expected which was a hard fight to keep it afloat, therefore sold it and joined the NHS as a therapist. Now to the future, Dianne would meet someone who was worthy of her capabilities and live a meaningful life when her son would make her a beloved grandmother.

Now with only Jenny left what could you say about her; she was a very intelligent high class girl with everything she could ever want, a top job in the city working in the stock exchange, smart, attractive and with a personality only you could wish for.

Having wealthy parents that spoilt her rotten, but having said that, she did in fact worship them. It seemed to an outsider, all that really mattered to her was her job, family and friends while keeping men at a distant, those who tried to get near to her failed, this was due to seeing some of her friends being hurt that badly, she didn't want to travel down that road herself.

It was as she walked into a room, her aura made such an impression that everyone was attracted to her not only her statue but also the sensuality, as this was something that didn't fit right Corry thought. Apparently men flocked round her like a bee to honey but that never made any difference for she'd push them away, as though a little shy but no that wasn't it there was something more, something in her past or inside of her that was trying to keep her all to itself. Now it was only when engaging into a full blown conversation that the truth came out.

It wasn't until her mother went into labour that it was found that she was having twins, the first born was found to have died due to the lung not being able to cope and therefore only survived a matter of hours, Jenny on the other hand was not only healthy but thriving with no symptoms at all

The parents being heartbroken were told they couldn't have any more children as nature had taken its toll, damaging the womb and although heartbroken, this was accepted and eventually coming to terms with what they had, for she was so precious to them.

Maybe, Corry thought, it was her twin calling to protect and look after her for there is a special bond between twins that can never be broken.

All the same, Jenny was the kindest, sweetest person you could wish to meet, who made you feel at ease whoever you were; she could also knock her gin and tonics back like no one Corry had ever met.

Now in Jenny's case, she would fight her way to the top of her profession and stay single with an inner haunting inside of her that would be put to peace in later years.

Getting to know everyone was just great for Corry as she thought what a nice set of friends Karen had, together with such a nice house, not far away from her own place; it would be great if they could become friends as that's what had been in short supply for her these last few years.

The conversation flowed together with the drink and snacks, this turning out to be such a relaxed evening with background music which complimented the mood everyone was in. One or two had enquired as to what Corry did for a living but as she never went any further into this, other than she owned a small shop in the heart of London, yes this was true, not the full truth, but didn't want to seem intimidating to these new found friends as she was enjoying herself too much in their company.

These people accepted her for whom she was as a person, not who she was as a high flying business woman and that's how she'd like to keep it. But then it was Carol who still couldn't get it out of her head, as she kept approaching Corry with the same conversation.

"I still know you from somewhere you know, but it will come" luckily the drink was now going to Carol's head and therefore wouldn't remember for the time being.

It was a few hours later when it dawned on her, although she knew a little about everyone present, she didn't know much about her host Karen, having gathered from the on-going conversation that night, her husband was in some kind of business but not to be too inquisitive, she left the subject alone.

The house was beautiful therefore he must be pretty successful at whatever he did, also there were no photos around to give her a clue, only one of the two children as the house was minimalistic, so couldn't put a face to this man. Someone did make a comment about Karen being so talented, but hadn't yet made her mind up as to what path she'd like to follow, also the subject had been brought up about Karen's husband being from the north of England but even that was vague, not wanting to delve too much into this, Corry thought she'd leave well alone, knowing full well that it would eventually come out about him.

The night drawing in, as most of the girls had drifted off home in taxis, even Carol, who by this time seemed a little unsafe on her feet, singing on the way out,

"I wanna go home", well if you could call it singing that is.

It was when a taxi pulled up at the door to take Corry home, that she got quite a shock to say the least, for out stepped her old friend and colleague, David Thomas of all people. The next statement being a shock to all;

"What the hell are you doing here David" Corry asked?

"I live here, more to the point what are you doing here" he replied.

Karen's face was a picture but more of a shock as what run through her mind was just how the hell do they know each other so intimately, was there something more between them that she didn't know about, she loved David but never trusted women around him for he was so good looking.

David just started to laugh uncontrollably, paid the taxi driver, told him to go, turned around to Corry and said;

"I think you'd better come back in the house don't you".

"I think that's a very good idea" she replied laughing.

Karen on the other hand wasn't as amused as those two, with rage in her face she said,

"What the hell is going on, I think somebody ought to explain as I don't think this situation is at all amusing as you two seem to find it".

"Oh but it is, so this is your new found friend then" "he enquired looking straight into Karen's eyes

"Well let me introduce you to my boss, the CEO of the company Corrander Sharp, better known as Corry".

"You must be joking; this is the one you keep telling me about, who hates men with a vengeance"

"Yes that's right my dear, you really have walked into a minefield now haven't you" was the sarcastic answer as he couldn't keep a straight face by now.

"I can't believe it, come on let's have another drink, I think I deserve it after all this", Karen said.

Yes, this was the start of one of the truest friendships of Corry's life and it would go on until the fatal day.

Chapter 16

What a small world it was, you meet a perfect stranger who gives you a shoulder to cry on and not only does it turn out to be one of your colleague's wives whom you've never met before but you also make friends through it, life certainly turns up surprises at times.

From that day, Corry and Karen would become lifetime friends. Maybe though circumstances, who knows but now they'd met, they were there to help each other through thick and thin, this was a true friendship that would go a long way in the future.

Although Karen came from a wealthy family, you would never guess it as she was so down to earth and talented in her own right, all she needed was a little encouragement on what she'd like to do and that's where Corry came in after seeing what she'd done with designing her home, yes her talents were with fabrics for home furnishing.

Her flair for materials was so different and unique but after having her boys she never used these talents which was a shame as far as Corry was concerned, it's as though her confidence had been lost somewhere along the way. And therefore Corry thought long and hard about her friend, until one day asking her for help to put one of the shows together, the answer was a simple;

"Yes, I would love to help",

"That's great, when can you start, how about next week, will that be fine with you" Corry asked;

"That's a yes to everything "was the reply.

"I can see were going to really enjoy doing this project together, I'll take you round a couple of the factories which will give you a better idea what actually happens" Corry stated with a genuine feeling of fulfilment.

"That would be nice as you know what David's like, he keeps everything to himself and never really discusses work at all, I didn't know much about you until we met, all he said was you were an old friend from back home and you'd just come out of a bad relationship but that's all".

"Don't worry we were only friends, that's all so if you have any doubts your wrong, I think things are about to change and change for the better as not only are we going to work together and enjoy ourselves but were about to have the time of our lives starting from now" Corry stated.

"I understand from David that you have a nanny for the children and a mature one at that, so there shouldn't be any problem should you want to travel with me, he also seems to think you'll enjoy the break which will give you a new interest if that's ok with you?".

"Peter has drawn up legal documents whereby you will be established in your own right, making the designs in your name only, although attached to the company to start off with, should you wish to buy out of this agreement then you'll also be able to do this within a time limit. Sorry, but this has to be all above board to safeguard both you and the company, if you agree to all of this, see Peter the financial Director and he'll tie up all the loose ends before you sign the contracts, as I'm sure it will be a happy arrangement for both you and David". Corry stated.

No, there was no fiddling for Corry as she liked everything to be above board and legal to safeguard the business

This was a new venture for Karen, one that would make her an awful lot of money as well as a friendship that would never be broken for there was already a trust between them, with no doubts on either side.

David on the other hand was so delighted; he couldn't believe the offer that had been presented to his wife, not only would It bring a financial achievement that would enable them to live a life of luxury for years to come but would also give Karen a sense of stability outside of the home. He was well aware of his wife's talent and flair for glamour but to gain such an achievement like this only comes once in a lifetime he thought and she would be a fool to turn it down but still it was her choice, knowing she'd make the right decision in the end.

Corry would start by showing Karen the ropes of the business leading up to the fashion shows where the collections they put on would be of the highest achievement, then take her onto Europe where again she had something up her sleeve for the future.

With the knowledge Karen would gain, it would then be up to her to create something new, an asset for the company firstly but then she would have the confidence to work through her own individual ideas as Issa had done with the underwear lines. The more Corry expanded the company, the more the city started to sit up and not only listen but admire her for what she was achieving, it seemed that she was unstoppable at times, but none the less no one knew what it was that was driving her on and that's how she wanted it for the only word she knew was success.

After her divorce most of the people expected her to sit down and go to pieces knowing she loved Jay dearly, but no not her as she was made of stronger stuff and wasn't going to take it lying down therefore with her back to the wall, she was to come out fighting and let people be aware that she wasn't any push-over for a man even though she did still love him with all her heart.

A couple of weeks passed after all the formalities had gone through with Karen joining the company and with Corry back at the helm with such a strong workforce and determination to succeed beyond anyone's imagination, yes she was unstoppable. In the background other fashion companies got together in an attempt to buy her out, but that wasn't to be, for when she got wind of this, a fight was started whereby not only would she terminate plans of a takeover but also put things in motion to take over their business one by one destroying the competition. Yes, there would be attempts, which she never looked forward to but being ready for that, knowing full well what she was up against, the only way to deal with these attempts was to fight them full on as the old saying went, nothing ventured, nothing gained.

Having gained ground in the fashion world, she could command a better timetable for her show and therefore would take pride of place on the first day of the week, this would show all those top names that she meant business and was here to stay, but having thought about this seriously she would stay where she was for the present.

Yes, this mere girl as they referred to, was definitely here to stay without any doubts. With the help of Issa, she could conquer the market with the underwear, with Malcomb, the finery of knitwear and pure silk garments which were the envy of all women, and now with Karen on board, she would make it a hat trick with the fine furnishings, life couldn't be any better she thought.

The couture lines always looked after themselves so there wasn't any need to worry about them, for they were designed for a select group of clients who liked only the best.

The ready to wear was the most ingenious mark on the industry, for they were what brought in the revenue, and with sales that were coming through the Department Stores and going from strength to strength, the company was onto a winner, leaving Corry time to bring in new ideas each season.

Now the department stores although running with the new fashions every season were happy as long as they could keep up with the demand. What the public had not anticipated was, as the company got stronger, she would turn her thoughts to developing another side to it and that's where Karen came in with the fine furnishings, which again would go into the large stores eventually.

Karen, now feeling her feet, as the show was just the start of something big for her knowing the drive and ambition was there, it was now time to show that the ability would follow, taking her to heights that she never could have dreamt of without the break that Corry had given.

Having started at the bottom and worked her way up to design a show with a theme of a winter wonderland, a spectacular that put her in the limelight just as Corry had expected, and so the show would commence;

The first showing was of the most beautiful knitwear that you could ever imagine everything from berets, scarves, long line jumpers, top coats made in cashmere in autumn colours.

The second to follow was that of fitted dresses in pure wool with silk attachments, these ranged from shawls to fitted sleeves set into the dresses and made with fine delicate Japanese silks.

Then came the designs from Issa's exclusive range, these were as expected, lingerie of the finest silk and satin with a luxury sexy tone that all women desire, the main colours being red, black, cream and African violet which stole a large part of the show.

Now it was the turn of the ready to wear for the new season;

Consisting of something a little different as planned; a range of smart little jumpers with pleated skirts which fell mid-calf, dresses the same but with Peter pan collars in various dark shades of blue, grey, brown and navy's.

Last but not least was the bridal section; this consisted of six bridal gowns, all being very plain white silk with attached hoods trimmed with fur and carrying fur muffs instead of the traditional flowers.

The audience went wild as never had this been done before and to add to the scene was a flurry of snowflakes as the models walked down the catwalk making a winter wonderland impression for all to visualize, bells rang in the background accompanied by a chorus of 10 children all dressed in white as they sat at the entrance of the stage singing to their hearts content, some of them a little out of tune but as they were only little children they could at least get away with it.

The audience applauded as they had never seen garments like this at affordable prices, they were so different, very modern and unbelievably outstanding, and with the overhead lighting that flickered, you could just be imaging the reality of stars shining in the sky as the models repeatedly walked the catwalk for a second showing.

Karen really had made her mark in the industry, from now on she would be the talk of the town with everyone who was anyone clambering for her to work her magic in their homes.

"A Designer for the rich and well off" one person commented to her,

"No not at all, just a designer for the working class as well as people who can afford me" she replied in a sarcastic tone.

"Well you certainly made your mark tonight girlie" was the reply to that comment

"Sorry I'm not a girlie at all, I'm a married woman with a degree in fine arts" she replied, for no-one was going to put her down, she had true Yorkshire spirit.

"Like this girl, she has my kind of confidence" Corry spoke out loud, for what Karen had done with the lighting, props and furnishings was unbelievable in anyone's eyes.

From this show came a lot or orders for Karen's designs came flooding in, she was definitely on her road to success, bringing the company to the fore in yet another triumphant field as the papers raved about her work as a newcomer to the world of fashion

Karen's boys, just like Corry's daughter had a strong backing from their parents and therefore was no trouble whenever they were in the limelight with their parents, yes a credit to their upbringing as young people.

It was at this time Corry was starting to relax a little with the business, taking out time to meet up with friends, mostly those six that Karen had introduced her to that night. Things were now starting to look up in her personal life but still jay was at the back of her mind for he'd hurt her beyond belief and then to top it all he refused to see their daughter fear his own person feelings got in the way, telling friends he'd a new life with someone he loved dearly, but knowing Jay as she did, it would all be for show.

Never the less, Corry did get on with her life as she intended to return to Cyprus a couple of times, this was just to put her demons to bed, trying to start afresh by purchasing a property out there but things were still a bit raw for that to happen at that moment in time.

Seeing her friend, a little down one day Karen suggested;

"Why don't you and Carol take off for a week away, I 'm sure we'll be able to manage, now get yourselves a holiday booked and make sure you take plenty of condoms with you" she added with a smirk on her face.

"Now that's the most sensible idea you've come up with this morning, I'll get on to Carol straight away, would be nice to relax and have a laugh catching up with a friend on a girly holiday" was the reply.

"Don't bother, I've already suggested it to her and she's packing as we speak", Karen stated.

As it had already been decided, then it was only a matter of where and when the destination would be, now Majorca sounded great and one week later they were both flying out for a mad hectic time of sun, sand and maybe sex in Carol's way of thinking.

Hotel 33 was a very stylish place but unfortunately the travel agent omitted to tell them it wasn't an English hotel but a Swedish one, but then again it wasn't a problem Carol stated as she remarked she could get by with sign language.

The first four days went well, as they never stopped laughing, the weather was great and most of the Swedish spoke English so there wasn't a language barrier. It was on the fourth evening, when Carol had gone down to the bar early with Corry to follow, only to find that she was surrounded by a few men as usual, they were mainly Swedish but the two that Carol was in deep conversation with, were in fact Dutch that night.

As Corry approached, Carol said in a rather formal accent;

"I would like to introduce you to Han's and his brother Henrick, they're both from Holland, work in the oil industry and enjoying a summer break like ourselves".

It was as though there was an instant attraction for Carol to Hans, this was rare as her reputation was, love them and leave them and don't show any emotion in the meantime.

Henrick was the perfect gentleman that any woman would be proud to say, he was her man but for Corry, there was something missing or was she that hard to please after her divorce. The night went on and the crowd got bigger, with Carol getting more fixated on Hans by the minute but never the less the conversation flowed quite happily with everyone enjoying themselves which was a nice change meeting new friends.

It was just turned midnight when a few more people walked in to join the crowd, one in particular caught Corry's eye, he was tall, dark, and handsome with a smile that could knock the ducks off water, Corry's eyes couldn't leave him as everyone was now starting to notice. But then, Hans stepped forward saying,

"Forget it, he'll break your heart, he's not interested in women, he got badly hurt when his ex-wife left him a few years ago and to this day, has never got over it, and since then he's dedicated his life to his career, had a few one night stands but isn't interested in women at all, some thought he'd turned gay, but that's far from the truth as he's a close friend of ours and we happen to know better,"

Still Corry couldn't keep her eyes off him for the next half hour or so as she could feel his eyes watching her every move and therefore it wasn't just her imagination of a mutual attraction, when all of a sudden he walked over in her direction to speak with the company she was already talking with.

Firstly, approaching Hans, and yet looking directly at Corry, he asked in perfect English;

"Aren't you going to introduce me to your new friends"?

"Sorry about that, this is Carol and her friend Corry who are over here for a week's holiday"

And Looking straight into Corry's eyes, as though there wasn't anyone else in the room he said;

"Hi, I'm Lars and I've been looking for you all my life, where have you been hiding".

This was unbelievable; it was as though cupid had stepped in and shot an arrow into both their hearts, for their eyes seemed to be for each other as though there wasn't anyone else in the room, and for the rest of the night or should I say early morning they never left each other's side, it was as though there wasn't anyone else in the room as far as they were concerned, only parting when they said their formal good night to each other.

Bright and early the next morning Corry woke up to a message that Carol had gone off with Hans for the day and would be back that night for dinner, this was fine as a day sunbathing by the pool was just what the doctor ordered so to speak Corry thought. She had seen this coming for the way Carol looked at

Hans the night before; yes, it was so obvious even a blind man would have seen it.

What she didn't anticipate was, a tall dark stranger coming and whisking her away for a day in Palma, yes Lars had seen her by the pool, took his chance and suggested they go out for the day, making it quite magical as they walked round the port, coffee over a short lunch, window shopping and just enjoying each other's company like flirty teenagers, she speaking about her life, loves and the divorce, but the thing she didn't mention was the fact that she was quite wealthy as knowing this would go no further than a holiday romance therefore he didn't need to know too much about her financial affairs.

Lars on the other hand opened up about his life and how he went to pieces when his childhood sweetheart left him for his best friend causing him to come close to a breakdown. But unlike Corry, he had a privileged upbringing going to the finest of schools, his father very high up in government, with a house situated on the riverbank in Stockholm and a large house in the country, he had three brothers who had done extremely well for themselves and all had families of their own.

Now Corry, felt there was something he wasn't telling her and so decided to delve further into it like all inquisitive females ,and apparently Lars seemed to be the black sheep of the family with his siblings producing children of their own while he on the other hand, was divorced with no children at all, the reason being, his ex-wife wouldn't have a family, she was a career girl, this turned Lar's mother against her as a woman of strong family values and so it seemed he was now cut off from returning home as frequent as he used to.

After his divorce he went to pieces for he thought his marriage would last forever, but sadly as we all know, forever is a long time and things happen to change those thoughts. Pulling himself out of depression, he then went onto apply for a position with a helicopter company stationed in Norway flying back and forth to the oilfields in the ocean thus leaving the commercial airlines that he'd flown for years.

The day coming to a close but not yet over as previously there'd been a party arranged for a crowd of them that evening at Port Andratx which was situated at the other side of the island, and to add another two guests wouldn't be a problem and so;

Dressed in simple but elegant silk dresses, high heeled sandals and clutching a silk shawl a piece fear it got a little chilly as the cool air came in, the girls looked fantastic as they accompanied their new found friends to a special night to remember. Carol having the time of her life being the centre of attention with her flirty ways that the Swedish loved while Lars wouldn't leave Corry's side all evening even escorting her to the powder room. This was a friendship that was developing extremely fast as everyone was now starting to notice, the night would never end for the two of them as they gazed out over the port with little stars shooting down before their eyes, a magical moment that everyone dreams of but not everyone experiences.

No this night wasn't going to end on a sad note for as Carol went back with Hans, Lar's would take Corry back to his room for the feelings were so strong and therefore it was the natural thing to do even though Corry hadn't had an intimate partner since Jay, the entwining of their bodies when they kissed felt that they'd known each other for years.

Lars was such a good lover, he made love to every part of her body, she tingled at his touch as she'd never done before, not even with Jay, it was as though they were meant to be together for he was so gentle, wanting to please her every wish. The kiss on the cheek as he laid her down beside him, turning her over on her stomach, massaging her golden brown back, slightly touching his lips on her spine as he worked his way down to the cheeks of her bottom, guiding the palm of his hand up between her legs to find the mystery that lay in front of him. This was done so passionately it was like velvet running over her skin, with his hand now touching her stomach he slowly turned her over to face him with such a loving look on his face that asked gently;

"Are you alright darling",

"Yep fine I think" she replied, she couldn't even get the words out correctly being in such a trance of her own making.

"I don't want you to do anything, I want to make love to you like no other man has ever done before", as he whispered. jag alskar dig which she found out later translated to I love you in Swedish

Kissing her body all over, he then moved his fingers up gently inside of her with such tenderness that she couldn't hold back the climax that followed with her body shaking This had never happened where she couldn't control the situation, it was as though he had the power to make her body do as he wished, and when he wished.

She was so wet that by now, he could sense that she felt a little uncomfortable, this had never happened before and a with a stranger at that, what on earth was happening she thought, just as he broke the ice putting her at ease by saying;

"Don't worry darling, I promise to make you dry again as I'll drink your juices in an overflowing cup whereby not only will you be ready for me but you will come again to a tune that you have never heard before".

It was sometime later, before his promise came true for he then entered her like a stallion in the making, proving that he was all man and knew what he wanted to achieve. The night was so real that it would stay with Corry for the rest of her life; she would never forget his loving tenderness, they may say that the Swedes are great lovers, I'm afraid that night proved beyond a doubt how true that statement was.

The next two days were spent together, by day they enjoyed being with the crowd and by night they would make the most of being alone should it be a romantic meal, walk along the coast line or even with the crowd that seemed distant to a couple that had only eyes for each other. Making love with Lars was something she'd never experienced before; for he was as thoughtful towards her as she was relaxed when making love with him, it was as though their bodies were meant for each other in such a tender loving sensual way that you could not tear apart what had been pieced together.

But like all fairy tales, they have to end sooner or later and that was the same for this one as Lars had to return to Sweden the day before Corry and Carol returned to England.

This was a painful time for Corry but for Lars, well he showed very little emotion at the parting, maybe because it was just a holiday fling. Although they swopped phone numbers and addresses there was no mention of anything else, as a tear on both sides was visible but that was all, when one of his friends quietly commented,

"I told you, he'd break your heart, he doesn't get close to anyone since the divorce, a man without any emotional feeling which portrays such a cold side".

No, Corry had not seen this side of him at all, the only side she'd seen was a caring, loving and tenderness in this passionate man she'd spent the last few days with, as they said their goodbyes never to see each other again or so the story goes.

When the time came for Corry and Carol to leave the island with a tinge of sadness in their thoughts, it was Carol, who quipped up with a comment,

"Told you I hated men as there all the same didn't I", not wanting to rub it in at all.

"Yes you did Carol and I'm now coming round to your way of thinking as it makes sense" was the reply.

It seemed every time her feelings got in the way, she would suffer the consequences, for deep down she wanted what we all want, which is love and affection. But returning to reality and working through the memories, knowing she'd put this man out of her head due to business commitments while her personal life was a lot to be desired, for it was as though she would never find happiness for herself.

It was now autumn 1999, Alexa was coming up to her sixteenth birthday and with bright ideas that she wanted to join her mother in the company but afraid Corry had a different view to that, she wanted her to study to be either a doctor or lawyer and therefore her education was more important.

Time seemed to be moving on so fast now that after a trip up north and upon her return, Corry was to be given the most unexpected news that would make her dreams come true. For it had been suggested the company take over a few of the factories that were struggling and this would therefore make her company one of the largest fashion outlets in the industry, paving her way to the gateway of the continent as CEO.

Sheila had taken the news of the take over and presented it to Corry upon her return, adding;

"Oh and by the way, you've had a phone call from someone called Lars Lundquist, he's to arrive first thing in the morning and will be with you around 10am at your place, well when I say your place, as he was a friend of yours I gave him the address of the apartment, hope you don't mind", she said in an excited voice.

There were no words to be said at this news, for Corry just couldn't get them out of her mouth even if she tried to the astonishment of her secretary.

"I don't know who on earth he was but he definitely sounded nice, and by the looks on your face, you think the same" said Shelia grinning like a Cheshire cat. No there wasn't any fooling Shelia, she knew Corry too well to even try.

"Can you get me a strong black coffee please as I need it after all that, Oh and by the way, I'm taking the day off tomorrow so put all enquiries on hold"

"Of course, he really must be something special for a reaction like that" was Shelia's lasting words as she disappeared to return with a strong black coffee.

It was shortly after 10am when Corry opened the door to Lars at the apartment, to hear the words of;

"I've tried so hard to get you out of my mind but can't stop thinking about you" was the first words he said as he flung his arms around her so tightly.

"I know how you feel, that's what I've been like these last couple of months, not being able to concentrate on anything much other than work", she replied.

"I know it's going to be hard with me away flying, but at least I've transferred to Aberdeen for a short while, which will be nearer for us to work something out for the time being. I will eventually have to return to Norway but that won't be a problem as I can fly straight into London when that happens", he stated.

It didn't matter how much travelling they had to do, the only thing that was on their mind, was being together at that stage, fate was a good thing and it worked for some but in Corry's case, it never lasted for long, so with that she was willing to take what chance she was given.

The next eighteen months were the greatest times that Corry could imagine, travelling between Aberdeen, Norway and Stockholm on a regular basis to be with Lars, and they were such happy times they spent together. It's as though they were inseparable when he was on shore leave, even when Corry had to fly to Europe on business he would accompany her at times. After meeting Alexa, he couldn't ever imagine being without her as not only did he take to her as if she was his own daughter but loved her beautiful funny ways that she portrayed towards him when they were together as a family.

There wasn't anything he wouldn't do for her, even persuading Corry to let her take modelling lessons in her spare time which to be honest wasn't what her mother approved of, but in the end relented to, listening to both sides of the argument as she put it.

In those eighteen months, Corry had now attained the title of CEO of the group of companies; this had been achieved by buying out a number of very small companies, and bringing them up to date with her own, it was either watch them go bankrupt and people lose their jobs or pour in cash from her resources to help, for she knew what it was like to be unemployed and this wasn't going to happen if she could help.

Initially being a bit tight with finance but in the long run would make her company a lot of money, being less competition, resulting in larger profits.

Issa had gone from strength to strength in the business of designing the underwear lines that would shock the city now and again which she thoroughly enjoyed, but that again was what it was all about, women showing off their feminine side of attraction in the bedroom. And with Rob now completed his army service by her side was so contented in her personal life she couldn't wish for more.

Karen, well she was always in touch with Corry on a weekly or sometimes daily basis, and was so happy Corry had at last found someone who truly loved her. Both David and her would meet when Lars was home and socialize for although he was Swedish, he had the same sense of humour as the English and therefore the four of them got on famously.

Life was so good for both Corry and Lars when they were together but when apart they seemed to be miserable and would talk on the phone for hours together for Lars made her feel she was the most beautiful thing in the world and on her part; she knew he was the most wonderful thing that had ever happened to her for a long time for it seemed that when they were together nothing could ever part them. They made love as though it would never go out of fashion; even to the point of embarrassment for they couldn't keep their hands off each other as the passion raged through their bodies, be it in public or private.

The times she'd met him coming on leave when he'd just flown back from one of the oil rigs, and would be dressed in just a coat with nothing on underneath knowing it would turn him on, silly little things that may have seemed childish to others but then again kept the passion alive for both of them. With Corry by Lars's side his family welcomed her with open arms, she was definitely the perfect partner for him, with his mother saying, she wished they'd met years ago and that Alexa had been his child for she herself idolised her as if she was Lars's own.

It was at this time, Corry decided to go to Cyprus and buy a property where they could be together away from work and the media, a special place they could call their own. What a bad decision that was as it would change everything, for the place she would purchase, was one that had caught her eye on a couple of occasions although it needed a considerable amount of work doing to it.

Having thought this through, she was to go ahead without telling Lars as in her mind it would be a surprise when finished, but not realizing the idea may backfire when eventually taking him to see it. No, she had it all planned, only to consult her friends David and Karen who were very doubtful of this crazy idea for they knew the hurt that she's gone through with the breakup of her marriage, and when all said and done Cyprus was the place Corry and Jay met, therefore there would be a lot of memories lingering in the past which would come back and bite her on the backside they thought in hindsight.

Now having voiced their opinions, she wasn't going to listen as when she'd got something in her head there wasn't anything that would move it which in this case would eventually be her downfall. Lars was strong minded himself and when it came to Corry he was also very protective, they couldn't see him going for the idea at all and although they may be wrong, they could also foresee trouble brewing in the future over her stubbornness in this.

Having looked at quite a few places before finding the property that was right, a three bedroomed bungalow/villa which was surrounded by a few more properties, set back from the sea front, peaceful and yet not too isolated and situated just far enough out of a place called Protaras, which was near the Turkish border line that divided the Greek and Turkish communities on the island, which on a clear day you would be able to look down on the famous ghost town of Famagusta.

Yes, it was a dream of a find she thought so went ahead and purchased it. Everything was straight forward with the purchase of the Villa and even the renovations had gone to plan as expected leaving the place beautiful when finished, and so delighted, she even cried.

But there was something else that made her cry which she couldn't understand, an awkward feeling that made her go cold, never the less she'd brush the feeling off as being a little silly. Returning to England she forgot all about that weird sensation she'd experienced and proceeded to meet Lars who'd just returned for a couple of week's shore leave.

The meeting went well as it usually did; not being able to keep their hands off each other until the next day when Corry broke the news she'd bought a beautiful villa on the shoreline in Cyprus where they could spend quality time together, away from work. To say he was shocked was an understatement as Lars looked at Corry with mixed feelings, he knew the unhappiness she'd suffered there and was a little hesitant to even agree to look the place over, but giving in to her did agree in the end as they would fly out and see it together a couple of days later, although he still had doubts for some reason.

That night as he put his arm around her in bed, feeling the tingling in her body, with a warmth and hunger wanting her so much as his hand drove down her back pulling her close to him, the feel of her warm body excited him to the extent that his penis was so hard with just the feel of her body, so close as his nerves were throbbing at the thought of every tingle and touch that went between them, wanting to love his soul mate by entering her for the fire he was experiencing, whereby she could put it out to both their satisfactions.

"Sorry darling but I have to come inside of you; I can't hold this back any longer, I've missed you so much on this trip", he said.

Corry wasn't going to argue for she felt the same as her body withered with such delight as they would come together in a harmony that most couples never experience in a lifetime.

It was some time later that Corry woke to find Lars had also dropped off to sleep after that short emotional burst of intimacy, as she looked down at him in such a peaceful position with the only thought now running through her mind was, she couldn't leave him like that as a burning inside her body was starting to rise yet again, the wetness between her legs was now quite evident as to what she needed.

Pushing her hand between his legs, she could feel how firm he was even though he was still asleep, not letting this moment go unnoticed, she positioned her head between his legs, taking his penis into her warm luscious mouth gently sucking and rolling her tongue around the tip in such a greedy like way, even an ice-cream wouldn't have lasted long as Lars awoke with a smile knowing what Corry really wanted, his hand reached out to her clitoris which by then was soaking with her own juices.

"It's alright darling, take your time, I have all the time in the world to enjoy your body", he whispered, as his body withered to the rhythm of her suction.

He could feel the heaving of her breasts against his thighs and knew that she was enjoying this as much as he was; for this was the bond they shared together, a rare love that turned them on whenever they were close, something new to most people. It wasn't long before Corry mounted this great Swedish stallion with a firm body that only she could control for that's all he wanted, to satisfy her was always his wish and upmost goal, she on the other hand felt the same as she rode him with such vigour like breaking in a wild stallion to become its master while trying to control to her desires. The smile on his face radiated a room as they both released their tensions together.

"Well satisfied now darling "he asked.

"Of course, you always satisfy me, that's the beauty of it" she replied laughing.

Even so, Lars would still make love to Corry the next morning before they flew off to Cyprus to see the villa, for that's how it was between them all the time, neither of them could say no to each other at any time day or night.

The flight was straight forward, and booking into a nearby hotel for a couple of days when they arrived, where at least they'd be able to enjoy the island together without any interruptions of work commitments on either side The days went quite well, dinner was as you would expect, good wholesome food that was just like mother cooked so to speak, finishing off with a drink in the bar and enjoying the evening ambience.

It wasn't until getting into bed on the first night, that Lars started to notice something different about Corry, maybe she was tired he thought putting his arm around her, no that wasn't it, it was as though she was withdrawing from him with a silence that he'd never experienced in her before.

"Are you alright darling" he asked.

"Yes" was the reply in a quick motionless action.

No he thought there is something wrong here but none the less he'd leave her to get some sleep, maybe she's coming down with something and would be better in the morning when all the cobwebs had blown off, also acknowledging how hard it had been for her these past few months travelling to Europe with the business.

The morning came but I'm afraid there was something strange about Corry for she couldn't settle, maybe after they drove out to the villa she'd be ok. This wasn't to be, although the villa was lovely and knowing Corry had gone to a lot of trouble to find such a gem together with renovating it to her taste, he still sensed, there was something troubling, as she asked;

"What do you think to it darling, do you really like it"

The next words from Lars shocked Corry.

Yes, I do like it in fact, I would go so far as to say I simply love what you've done with the place, so how about we get married out here you know I've always loved you from the moment we first met and I know you feel the same" he said.

To this Corry froze' as the memories of Jay came flooding back to haunt her.

She was terrified of making the same mistake that she'd made with Jay and to be honest wasn't ready to make a commitment, for the thought of that terrified her at that moment. In Lars, she had everything she could ever wish for, not only did he love her dearly but treated her like the woman she was and worshipped not only her but her family and friends, she would be a fool to turn him down as he was everything she could have wished for The only thing wrong was, he'd come along at the wrong time in her life but then again what was the right time for her as she would never find that out.

Corry made light of the situation as she said,

"We'll have to see if it fits in with the work schedule before I can make any commitment".

Lars knew different, he could see in her face, he wanted her so much and it was at that precise moment knew he would never be able to make Corry his wife for the fear of the past would always come between them and haunt her. That night confirmed his beliefs, for Corry was so cold, he'd never seen her like this before and could feel her drifting away from him, powerless to stop it.

From that day forward their relationship was doomed, oh why did they have to go over to Cyprus, it held so many good and bad memories that Corry couldn't wipe out.

Back in England, Lars went on flying while Corry buried herself in work, pushing Lars further and further away, as all her friends and family tried their hardest to get through to her but it was as though she was in a time capsule and couldn't get out of it even if she tried. Alexa was heartbroken to see her mother in this way for she loved Lars and with thoughts that one day both he and her mother would marry as they were meant to be together as soul mates forever.

It was inevitable, that eventually they would part, the best of friends but not as lovers as Lars had wished with the heartbreak on both sides, which took its toll heavily on Corry but it was as though she was on a tread mill and couldn't get off, on a destructive path that didn't know what to do or why she was heading that way.

Even Lars's parents were upset; his mother flew over trying to salvage the mess that had occurred for Corry was now like a daughter to them but to no avail, for it didn't matter how Corry would try to change this destructive cycle in her personal life, there was always going to be something in her past which would come back and haunt her, as it had done so many times before.

Although her heart was aching she knew the only thing to do at a time like that was to bury herself in work as usual which is exactly what she did, like a woman on a mission but not knowing where that mission was taking her.

Alexa, who was soon to reach the age of eighteen and under the strict guidance of Issa was training to be a model herself at that time and although, she tried to talk to her mother about Lars it didn't do any good as I'm afraid even that was falling on deaf ears. Issa on the other hand kept pretty much out of this situation knowing full well that Corry was that stubborn, she wasn't going to listen to anyone and therefore would help Alexa with her modelling career as that was one of Lars's last wishes, to see Alexa fulfil her dream to be a famous model, for he loved her as though she was his own daughter.

Spending most of her time either in London or now commuting, Alexa had started to drift away from her mother as Lars had now returned to Norway, this upset Corry but there wasn't anything that could be done otherwise she may lose her daughter for good. So she just hoped and prayed that time would be a healer and in the meantime Issa would keep an eye on her until that day became a reality.

Lars went on to play a role in Alexa's life for he would contact her on a weekly basis and there was an open invitation for her to visit him in Sweden whenever she wanted or even join him in Norway.

It was as though Corry was all alone yet again even though it was of her own making, yes, friends were there for her but when she went to bed it was all alone with no one to hold and caress by her side, all she had was work together with memories of what might have been should she have excepted that love which was given freely.

This went on for a few months when all of a sudden she received a phone call from Lars saying that he was coming over to Aberdeen for a few days and wanted to talk as a little worried about Alexa, and although it would be painful to see what she'd thrown away, it was in her daughter's interest that was the priority of the situation now.

And having arranged to meet him in Aberdeen, she was curious as to what was going on for it seemed that he spoke to Alexa more than she did, yes she was concerned over this but with time knew that her daughter would come back to her for she put it down to a teenage thing she'd eventually grow out of.

The meeting took place at the Holiday Inn where they'd both arranged to stay for three days and when that day actually arrived, meeting up in the bar, it seemed as though the magic was still alive between them and nothing had ever changed as their body language spoke a thousand words.

It was over dinner they discussed Alexa in detail, Lars being so concerned why Alexa had turned so cold towards her mother and wasn't accepting the fact that he'd returned to live in Norway, he was also worried that Corry was working herself into the ground without taking advice on handing some of the responsibilities over to others as Alexa had informed him in their intimate conversations.

The shock of the evening came when he informed Corry that Alexa had also discussed going alone without the help of her mother which he was extremely worried over at that point, fear she got in with the wrong crowd that would take advantage of her inexperience or maybe go through her to bring Corry down as being such a cut throat industry, and with Alexa being still a child in Lars's eyes and therefore wanted to protect her at all cost

Discussing the subject in detail, you could see how much he loved Alexa and knew the friction was hurting both of them so if there was a solution then he was there for both of them not realizing that Issa had got involved, guiding Alexa through this period of rebelling against the unknown.

Alexa hadn't mentioned any of this before and therefore Corry was at a loss to hear what was coming to the fore, she was prepared to let her daughter take pride of place in the company when she was a little older, but in the meantime if she was so determined to go into modelling professionally, and it not being a teenage fad then she would back her one hundred per cent.

Knowing Alexa could wrap Lars around her little finger she had to put his mind at rest by saying;

"Don't worry Lar's, I know you think the world of her but don't forget she's also very precious to me as well" which ended the conversation as he grasped her hand kissing it gently over the candlelit table before ordering a couple of drinks to be taken into the lounge, where they would feel more comfortable

Well when I say a couple of drinks maybe that was an understatement as the drinks came frequently before he walked Corry to her room, kissing her on the cheek for the night as a good friend would, but the kiss wasn't to stop there for it lingered far too long for that knowing there was a large bed crying out for passion the other side of the door.

The night was made for love and passion as the two of them couldn't keep their hands off each other making love all night long in every position that was invented together with a few that was real to them , the feelings were still there but Corry knew she had to fight them to walk away, yes she was a fool as they'd something very special; but she was on a self-destruct mode with her own feelings and couldn't get off it for some reason, the hurt inside both of them that night was horrendous and it would have been so easy to alter it but for Corry's stubbornness.

That was the last time that Corry was to speak to Lars as he walked out of her life forever, or was it? As forever is a long time and there would be times when that would come back to haunt them over the next few years, maybe only briefly but then again the feelings would never leave.

Alexa on the other hand was in constant touch with him as was Issa but his name was never mentioned from that day onwards in front of Corry.

If only she'd listened to her heart things may have been different but as she'd been hurt once, she couldn't trust any man ever again and would have to walk alone from that day.

Chapter 17

Yes, that night in Aberdeen may have drifted away in memory for the time being but memories are never too far away as consequences of that night may follow in time to come but for now it seemed that Corry was still in a self-destruct mode for her life consisted of work, when she wasn't working she'd often fly out to Cyprus to visit the villa, but even then would only stay for a few days before returning, it's as though she couldn't settle there for long, although there had been a couple of occasions when she did stay for longer but there again that was rare.

It was thought that she'd met someone over there but again no one was saying anything if she had but that was Corry all over for she kept a lot of things close to her chest. It was as though something was driving her to destruction, on a merry go round and couldn't get off for fear of getting hurt, she had power within her own organisation, influence outside of it, also respect in the city, no other woman could wish for more in reality.

Her family, although they loved and cared for her deeply, couldn't seem to reach inside to help, and although Alexa loved her mother, there was still a distance between them since Lars had gone out of Corry's life for she was a different person, a little isolated whereby the trust in anyone had disappeared. Having her personal life turned upside down, she would date men that she met but after a week or so would be tired of them and walk away, it was as though her feelings had frozen in time but this was all of her own making.

Alexa worried over her mother so much at this time, but was there any need to as she thought Corry had realised this situation herself and took herself off to a health club in Scotland where she returned not only slimmer but a little happier in herself. But then again, how long was this to last was the big question as it seemed she made these trips often now.

Alexa was pushing ahead with the career she'd wanted since a little girl visiting the workshops with Malcomb, having learnt from what she called the master of the trade having listened and taken advice from Issa herself.

Being all of 5ft10ins, with the most fabulous long legs to match her sleek body, she had the perfect figure for Issa's Special Limited addition of lingerie and with that in mind, they would launch Alexa as the new face of the season, this idea having been run past Corry as a matter of courtesy, being her mother and also not wanting to offend in any way. The city wouldn't know who this young girl was having been brought up in the north of England with family so it would be kept a secret for as long as possible.

Maybe then, Corry would come out of the depression she seemed to be in, seeing her daughter in all the headlines as that's what they were aiming for, Alexa on the other hand just wanted her mother to be proud of her like any teenage girl would wish, she knew that whatever she did, Lars would stand by her but that wasn't enough as it was Corry's approval she was craving for.

Not hearing from her father for years now, it never crossed her mind, what he'd think of his little girl and how she'd got on in life, it seemed to her, out of sight, out of mind, for she'd put him on a pedestal far too long. This had now gone and her thoughts were towards Lars as he'd been more of a father to her even in the short time he'd been with her mother, and to be honest, she really missed him in her life although made sure she saw him on a regular basis when possible.

Yes, Corry was proud of her daughter but it was as though she couldn't show it for some reason, she herself had been brought up with grandparents and never been shown the affection from her own mother, maybe that was it.

Maybe it was because Jay was always the one that Alexa ran to as a small child while pushing Corry away, or even that work came before everything, but there again she had to provide as so many people depended on her through the years. Material things weren't everything as Corry knew, but sometimes it felt as though she was splitting herself in so many ways to please everyone that she hadn't got time or energy to do the little things that came natural as a mother. Children don't realise what the parents sacrifice for them until they are grown up with a family of their own that they have to provide for and maybe this was the case.

From the day Alexa was born, she'd been given the best of attention from everyone around her but when her father had gone from her life; it was as though there was a big hole that was swallowing her up and knowing full well there must be an answer to that question, it will be a very wise man that was keeping it a secret.

Having family around was great, but she still missed her father and couldn't make any sense as to why she'd been cut out of his life altogether, this would always stay a mystery but then again who can ever fathom men out properly.

She was now on her own to make a success of doing something she'd wanted to do for a long time, thanks to Lars for pushing her mother into their way of thinking, if only her mother could show the affection that Lars showed her, but then again she'd now come to accept the fact this was impossible.

Corry bent over backward to give Alexa her independence, even suggesting to buy a small apartment when she was ready to move out of Issa's place, but that wasn't an option for she loved being with Issa and Rob, they were like family.

It was at the next fashion show that Alexa would make her grand appearance with the launch of a Special Limited Addition of lingerie that Issa had designed herself. This didn't worry Corry in the least as she knew with the guidance of Issa her daughter would be the star of the show as she herself was years before and they weren't disappointed for Alexa then achieved this by becoming the talk of the town as the new face of fashion, flooding all the magazines as it had been anticipated by everyone.

Alexa who was now the age of twenty, with not only her career in front of her but with her mother's looks, talents and head for business together with her father's brains for making money, there was no doubt she would make her mark whatever she decided to do. Having been protected from men in the big city, she'd dated a few handpicked respectable ones, but nothing serious as they were only just flings knowing she was far too young for a serious relationship and not wanting to end up like her mother on a path of destruction in per personal life.

No not her, she wanted the full works, a fairy tale style marriage as young girls dream of with a happy ever after life. Well that was the plan but then plans never work out as we would like them to and this one certainly wasn't going to.

Now visiting her mother at least once a week, having made a promise to Lars that she'd keep an eye on her due to all of them being concerned, she started to confide her inner thoughts at times, not wanting rumours to get out of hand and reach her mother with the wrong stories as you know what people were like living in a rumour control society.

Yes, they were close in that respect but still there was that distance between them, that bridge that couldn't be crossed to meet each other's feelings, probably because they had the same strong will and determination that would drive them through life to attain their own goal, with a fight in their bodies that would see them through the good and bad times in the future.

The business was thriving and should Alexa pull off what they'd planned, then a seat on the board of Directors would be offered to her having worked hard to attain this position. Young maybe, but you could tell in some ways she was Corry's daughter for she worked so hard in the company that everyone was pleased with the input of idea's she supplied, although It did seem she favoured Issa's side of the business.

But as times were changing and with her youthful outlook, would now want to attempt designing garments herself which may adorned women's bodies to delight their partners in the bedroom.

It was thought that if she could excite women in flaunty underwear, this would entice the opposite sex with the end result of desire, producing the sales of the lingerie which would follow, oh yes she definitely had Jay's financial head for making money, but unlike him, she had a caring side to her personality, something that he'd never shown to anyone other than his daughter when she was little.

She would be twenty-one the coming year and would then be a very rich young lady indeed after inheriting her grandmother's legacy. Alexa was no fool, she knew just what she wanted out of life and would make sure she'd get it, for nothing would stand in her way, yes she was willing to fight all the way to achieve this goal as she had her mother's blood running through her veins.

Having approached her mother one day over a discussion as to visiting the Milan fashion show, she noticed some accessories in the office that Corry had been looking over for the forthcoming show. It was a plain black scarf that caught her eye, now that's an idea she thought; if I put a sheer black bra under a black see through blouse it would be fantastic, a little risky but none the less very tempting to the eye, just enough flesh to show but not too much to give away what lay under the bra, that would be left to the imagination no doubt.

Garments like that were considered something quite immoral in those days but, as said before, times were changing as the youth of the day wanted more out of life.

Another idea was to design a bra with wire to fit under the breast, cover it with a sheer fabric over the cup area that showed the pert nipples, it would not only be practical but also very sexual to the eye, all these ideas would just show how talented she was for not only could she model but she could also design the garments she'd want to wear in her own personal relationships.

Not saying anything to Corry, but discussing her idea with Issa, it was then decided they'd put it to the test and with a little tweaking between them, put straight into production. The said bra was such a success it sold out within weeks and had to be produced in a couple of other colours to keep up with demands.

Yes, Alexa's ideas were very modern and when she got something into her head, no one could change her mind, it was her way or no way for she had such a stubborn streak, she'd listen but then ignore it all and carry on with what she wanted, not only intelligent but had that loving streak that everyone came to accept in the end.

You wouldn't think that her mother actually owned the company, for Alexa had no airs and graces, that's how she'd been brought up, for in her eyes she was just one of the girls that worked for a big organisation in fact a lot of people didn't even know she was Corry's daughter unless it was pointed out to them.

Friday nights out after work Alexa was just one of them, it was nothing for her to get hold of a sweeping brush, clean up in the sawing rooms for that's how her grandmother had taught her, should you want a job done to your satisfaction then you must be prepared to do it yourself. Having said that, she was like Corry in so many other ways, always ready to help others that weren't as fortunate, again bringing respect amongst her fellow workers.

Time passed by so quickly and before everyone knew it, Alexa was looking at her coming of age being twenty-one years old with the key of the door; well that's what Corry was arranging, before someone let it slip to her annoyance.

It's not very often Corry lost her temper but on this occasion it was justified, for it was to be big surprise, but after Alexa found out what had been planned, she went mad. All Alexa really wanted was, to spend time with her friends and maybe a small present from her mother would suffice for she didn't want any fuss; no party just a meal out with family and close friends

Yes, the inheritance that Agnes had left would just be reinvested for a day when she wanted to branch out alone in business, but for now she was quite happy with the situation as it was living with Issa and Rob.

Alexa's birthday came but it wasn't what she'd expected as it was tinged with such sadness and a secret that had to be kept away from her until the next day.

As arranged beforehand, a meal had been booked with family and close friends at a local restaurant to celebrate her coming of age; it was only at last minute that she'd been notified her grandmother wouldn't be able to make it as with a chest infection, the journey would be too much for her. Corry had assured Alexa that everything was fine and that her uncle Paul was to stay and keep an eye on the situation, and therefore wasn't any room for them to worry.

Having received a telegram that morning wishing her all the best for this her special day from all her family and friends up in the north, she realised if grandmother wasn't feeling that well it would be selfish to expect her to travel.

The night went well and Alexa looked a picture dressed in a cream long flowing dress with chocolate brown shoes and clutch bag, on her wrist was the most beautiful diamond bangle, sparling in the night which was a gift from Corry thus making her feel the bell of the ball as she sat down with everyone that evening. How lucky am I, she thought, to have such a close family and friends and to be able to share all this, it seemed too good to be true, but then again this is how she'd been brought up, to appreciate what people did for her and never expect too much from anyone.

Having her inheritance from Jay's mother together with shares in the company her mother owned, she was a very rich young lady but to Alexa; this was nothing if she'd not got those she loved around which is all that mattered to her.

Yes, it would have been nice if her father had recognized her coming of age for she'd not seen or heard from him in over ten years but that wasn't to be and although it upset her a little, it was never mentioned for the fear of upsetting her mother.

Some things are best not to be spoken about and this was one of those things, for although time had passed, there was still bitterness in people's hearts as to the way he had treated both Corry and his daughter. But for tonight everything was to be on a happy note as they all gathered together as a family, told their little stories, reminisced and generally had a good time which lasted until the early hours of the morning when returning home, a little worse for wear as Alexa thanked everyone for making her birthday a night to remember.

But then Corry said to her daughter;

"Don't forget whatever happens, we're all so proud of what you've achieved and maybe I don't tell you often enough how much I love you, and for this I want you to remember when you lay your head down on the pillow tonight".

What was all that about Alexa thought in a haze? What a funny thing to say, it was as though there was something wrong but then mother speaks in riddles at times so maybe that was it or was it the fact that she'd had too much champagne which had gone to her head and without another thought it was straight to bed as her head touched the pillow with sleep following immediately.

Awakening the next morning with a little bit of a headache, Alexa went into breakfast to find not only her mother but also Uncle Paul, immediately realising something was drastically wrong;

"Sit down darling, I'm afraid we have some bad news for you "her mother spoke in a voice which was detecting sorrow.

To this Alexa went ice cold for she was now silently aware what was coming;

"I'm sorry to tell you that your grandmother died yesterday, it was decided we should go ahead with your birthday as planned as that's what she'd have wanted" Corry now moving forward, placing her arms round her daughter with hopes of comforting her only child.

Alexa just stood there motionless; it was though a bolt had shot through her heart for that's how she felt, her face drained and pale, while finding it hard to breathe until all of a sudden she couldn't hold it back any longer just breaking down sobbing her heart out. This was a woman that had practically brought her up for the last ten or so years, someone she thought would go on forever being timeless. Gathering her senses Alexa asked only one question and that was;

"Was she in pain when she died"?

The room went silent and it was Paul who stepped forward to comfort his niece as Corry started to crumble, knowing that his sister was choked up for words as she was nursing her own pain over their mother's death.;

"No sweetheart, she passed away very peaceful, she was tired and to be honest, it was her time to go and leave us all" he said putting his arms around Alexa, holding her so tight for he knew how much she needed her family close to her at a time like this.

But as you can imagine, everything seemed to be a blur for the rest of the day as nothing seemed to function right, she loved her mother deeply but it was always Issa, she turned to and on this occasion there would be no exception. Luckily Issa had been informed, for her and Rob had stayed over at a hotel for the night and it wasn't long before she arrived, knowing that Corry would be in pieces, and therefore Alexa would need her more than ever now.

Now the next few days were hard for all of the family but having said that, if it hadn't been for Paul it would have been a lot harder as he was the one that stepped up, making all the arrangements for the funeral.

Through this time Alexa hardly spoke a word to anyone, it was as though she was in a trance whereby, now and again she'd break down and cry but when anyone went near her with a comforting gesture, she'd just push them away; for this was her way of dealing with it. On the other hand, Corry just shut herself away crying in silence until she couldn't cry any more, she may have been hard in business but when it came to family, that was a different matter, providing a financial stability for them was her aim.

Travelling up home to Doncaster a week later for the funeral was so hard, as you can imagine, the crying was over and now they'd to face reality, taking it one day at a time.

"Oh thank god for Paul" Corry had said out loud but afraid those words fell on deaf ears as everyone was still stunned and in no mood for conversation.

The day went off well as could be expected with all keeping their composure to a certain degree knowing that Alexa was near to breaking point but to the surprise of everyone, it was Alexa who stood up in the church making a speech that had everyone in tears, this again was for the woman who had been closer to her than her own mother.

Yes, her grandmother had lived to a ripe old age but still everyone thought she would go on for ever as she was so fit and thinking back, it was at this point Alexa finally accepted she'd passed away, as a smile came on her face which was a look of love.

"She'll be alright Corry, don't worry, people have different ways of coming to terms with death and she's a strong girl who'll go far in this life, having so many people around her who not only love, but also protect her, your mother would have been so proud of her today" Issa declared.

It was a quiet time for all as they returned to London, but now and again they noticed a smile appear on Alexa's face which told them she was going to be fine.

Fine maybe but that was the time that Alexa changed, letting out the wild streak that had been hidden for all those years growing up but now starting to appear and for those who didn't like what they saw, then it was tough because Alexa was now becoming a woman of determination.

She was going to branch out in business for herself and maybe use the assets she was born with which had now developed over the years into a fantastic body, therefore enter into modelling her own designs.

She had the capitol to start on her own and with a little help, would run alongside one of her mother's companies, a plan which would develop immediately. Something had definitely changed in her, it's as though she'd a driving force which was unstoppable, just like her mother's when she first came to London, the difference was, Alexa had not only family and friends looking out for her but she also had a considerable amount of money to achieve this without asking her mother's help.

The coming year was as hectic for Alexa as she turned her hand to designing her own range of sheer lingerie together with swimwear. The swimwear, was then modelled by herself therefore breaking into a new career of which she climbed to the top of the profession, this being one of the highest paid models of her time as there wasn't a week that went by, she wasn't in one or another of the magazines, life really had taken off for her with parties most weekend but keeping the business under strict control through the week.

Life was for living and I'm going to live it to the full was her favourite saying.

Although Corry and Issa were a little worried by this time, as it seemed she was trying to prove something to herself but as time went by there wasn't any need to worry at all for she'd a good brain on her and wasn't stupid, knowing exactly where she was going and there wasn't anything going to stop her until she achieved that goal for she was like her mother in that way.

Although Alexa had more money and power than she could have ever dreamt of, she was a home bird at heart, still living with both Issa and Rob, as they'd now become her second family who kept her grounded when she felt like going off the rails as she often put it politely. T

They on the other hand knew when the time came for her to fly the nest and get her own apartment she would be responsible enough to cope by herself for she'd been like a daughter to them since the day she was born.

Yes, there were men in Alexa's life but they would come and go and they'd never last for more than a few weeks at a time for she'd soon get bored being a bit of a party animal who loved and lived life to the full, that's what she intended to do. Her attitude was, men were ten a penny and would only use you, if you didn't use them first, maybe this was subconsciously going back to her childhood when thinking about the promises her father had made to her as a child.

But things change and so do situations as one night when she'd just finished a shoot for an international magazine, meeting up with a couple of friends who'd decided to go for a drink to a new wine bar which had recently opened in the area, her friends had walked into the bar and ordered the drinks while she visited the ladies room, therefore joining them a few minutes later, calling off at the bar while her friends were already seated in the corner she shouted':

"I'm starving, hardly eaten today and you know what I'm like when I'm hungry I could eat a scabby dog so does anyone else want anything while I'm up here, now speak or forever hold your peace"?

"No" was the reply echoed from the table as she headed to the end of the bar.

Stood in front of her she noticed this tall, handsome, well dressed stranger staring at her, it was like watching an old film when their eyes met;

"Excuse me, would you like a drink my dear" he asked politely.

"Ah yes that would be nice, I'd like a vodka and tonic please if you don't mind" was the reply

"Then a vodka and tonic you will have my dear, for such a beautiful lady as yourself, your wish is my command so to speak".

Her friends looked on in amazement but never said anything for they knew only too well that it would only be Alexa playing with this strangers feeling as she often did. Although men fascinated her, she soon tired of them as though it was just a game, no one could understand why she couldn't commit to any one particular boyfriend and to be honest, she'd the pick of the litter where men were concerned, but all she wanted was friendship and if they wanted anything further then she would get her skates on and leave.

Who was this stranger, was he new in town, he was certainly different to the rest of the men that took her fancy she thought. Over six-foot-tall with the most handsome of faces and a smile that would break a thousand hearts, his deep blue eyes looked into hers as he handed the vodka and said;

"Please let me introduce myself, my name is Tam and am afraid a little new to the area for I've only just moved back to London, been working in Gibraltar for the last couple of years".

Alexa looked into the eyes of this stranger as though she was mesmerized, but finally answered.

"Tam, that's rather an unusual name for a boy, is it foreign by any chance".

"No not at all, it's Jewish and it means, honest ",

"Oh so your Jewish then" she replied.

"Well my father is Jewish but my mother kept her own religion, anyway enough of me, let's talk about you as you haven't told me your name as yet".

"Oh sorry, it's Alexa, look seen as you're new in town and on your own tonight, maybe you'd care to join me and my friends for a drink, it's alright they don't bite, only on rare occasions" she added.

"That would be lovely as being new in town, afraid I don't know anyone and it would be good to meet some of the local people as my family live out in the country".

"Great" Alexa stated, as they both walked over to the table in the corner where all of Alexa's friends were already sitting and waiting in anticipation of an introduction to this new face that they'd never seen before.

"This is my new friend Tam and don't even go there as I'll explain his name later on" well everyone just looked and started laughing as this was a regular thing for Alexa, to pick up new friends or as they all would say, waifs and strays.

"Sit down Tam, and do tell us all about yourself as we've a feeling you're going to be one of us for a short time now" one of them piped up a little sarcastically.

The conversation went from one subject to another but then it was starting to be noticed that Alexa and Tam couldn't keep their eyes off one another, it was as though the electricity was shooting from one side of the table to the other.

Now this wasn't unusual in Alexa's case of flirting with strangers in the past, but there was something different this time and although the conversation flowed it was as though there was a silence between those two, just a mesmerizing look that said I want to rip your clothes off, maybe it was only a look but definitely the thoughts were there, as one of the crowd commented out loud,

"I think you two ought to get a room".

Now in the past Alexa would have made a joke about that comment but this time, the look said it all, for actions definitely spoke louder than words in this case.

A few drinks later and with the crowd splitting up to go their separate ways after saying good night, Alexa turned to walk away but Tam caught her arm asking if he could walk her home;

"That would be nice, I'd love you to" Alexa replied looking all coy.

"Let's go, you show me the way and I'll follow", Tam said rather shyly while grabbing her hand to her astonishment.

Where did the time go as the conversation between them flowed on the way back to Issa's home, it was as though they were old friends that'd just met after not seeing each other for a long period of time, being so relaxed in each other's company. With silly talk about nothing really; just getting to know each other feeling comfortable talking about any subject that came up, mind you it was Tam who did most of the talking for he wanted to know more about this beautiful girl he'd just met, who was she, what did she do and eventually asking if he could see her again, maybe take her out to dinner one evening.

Alexa was in her element as she couldn't get over the fact that he didn't even know who she was, although she was in the magazines ever week plus the talk of the fashion world This really did amused her, but never the less she played along with it as there was something that drew her to him in a most unusual way for he wasn't like any other man she'd ever met before, but still she couldn't explain why and having been kissed goodnight on the cheek, it was finally arranged that Tam would pick her up the next evening for a dinner date.

What a day Alexa thought to herself floating on air for the rest of the evening.

Now the next day was pretty hectic with more shoots for the magazines together with an important meeting with designers. Well the meeting was a waste of time as she seemed to be somewhere else in her mind and couldn't concentrate on anything that anyone proposed, in the end giving up even trying to concentrate for all her thoughts were on the dinner date with this stranger who'd made such an impression on her.

As the evening arrived it was a shower, hair dropping down below the shoulders with the little black dress clinging to her sleek body, just the sheerest of underwear, killer high heels and a light fragrance of perfume she was ready as Tam arrived for their evening date.

"You look absolutely stunning, I've already booked a little restaurant I've found which isn't too far away from my place, not knowing many restaurants in the city as yet, but as I've eaten there before, I think you'll love it for the food is not only to the perfection of your beauty but it's also the perfect place for us to really get to know one another without any interruptions", he said whisking her into an awaiting taxi.

Alexa had never been as quite, as they drove away to this small restaurant on the outskirts of Kensington and true to his word, Tam had arranged everything to her satisfaction. The meal was superb; the conversation flowed as though they'd known each other for a lifetime, an unbelievable match in anyone's eyes.

It was during the conversation that Alexa happen to mention she worked for a small company as a model but this was all news to him and didn't impress in the slightest for he'd only just moved to London, and with no knowledge of any of these people she mentioned which was refreshing for Alexa, knowing he wanted to get to know her for herself and not for what she stood for.

He on the other hand stated, he'd been appointed as a Barrister of Law working mostly at the Old Bailey, this Alexa knew nothing about so the subject ended there as they went on to talk about little things they liked and disliked.

What a success the evening had been from start to finish as Tam wasn't going to let it end there, adding he wanted to see her again, to Alexa's delight.

Oh she felt so relaxed in his company that when he suggested they go back to his apartment for coffee, she naturally accepted without hesitation. This wasn't like Alexa at all, she would never let a man she'd just met take her back to his place alone. But on this occasion felt so relaxed and safe, couldn't see any harm in it and didn't want the night to end anyway for when he held her hand, she experienced such a giddy feeling inside like being a child all over again.

Yes, he was right, a ten-minute walk and they were at Tam's apartment.

The apartment was set in an old building that had been renovated in the heart of London, a two bedroomed luxury modern place which was selectively furnished with high class Italian leather suites along with ultra-modern Swedish furniture.

Oh boy this must have cost a large sum of money she thought; and so tastefully done to her surprise, he must be a rather successful Barrister to be able to afford such luxury. It was when she glanced around the room as only a woman would; she noticed the only photo on show was one of Tam at a passing out ceremony accompanied by his mother. Not being able to resist with a curiosity, that was killing her, she asked where his father was, to which he replied;

"Sorry, sore subject really, but he's never really been in my life until recently when he married my mother".

"You see they were childhood sweethearts, when finding she was pregnant with me they broke up, he thought she'd had an abortion, after that they just lost touch, and mother brought me up by herself not making my father any wiser to the fact that he had a son. It's understood my father went on to marry someone else, that resulted in divorce and it was many years later he and my mother met up again and married, by then there was no feelings between him and me as it had been left far too late for such things"

"What about your grandparents, didn't you have anything to do with them" Alexa enquired.

"No, my fathers, parents lived in the city but no one ever spoke about them at all so never had the chance to get to know them, I understand one of them was some kind of artist but what kind of an artist I wasn't aware of, there again, you never miss what you haven't had so never took that any further.

Mother's parents on the other hand, lived out in the country in a large house with loads of land, so when I was born, my mother lived with them until they both passed away whereby I inherited everything and as I was already studying law, away at university when mother married, my father moved into the house to be with her".

"So have you now got to know your father" Alexa enquired.

"No not at all, it seems as though we don't talk the same language and he's such a dark secretive person, we don't have anything at all in common only my mother's feelings. In fact, the less I see of him the better off I am for there's something about him that doesn't run true as far as I'm concerned, you seem to sense these things don't you?".

"I have to add, he's very good to my mother, worshiping her immensely, so I'm happy where that situation is concerned, but I myself find him cold and calculating, the type you wouldn't trust, but maybe that's because I find it hard to bond with him after all these years and won't even give him the chance to get to know me".

Alexa went, quiet and smiled with an understanding expression on her face as she thought back at her childhood and therefore understood where Tam was coming from, the difference was she knew her father for the first ten years of her life and worshipped him.

"Never mind changing the subject, where is this coffee you were going to make me" Alexa asked with a comforting smile that said she understood.

This broke the heavy conversation with a light hearted grin as Tam strode over to the kitchen to fulfil her request for coffee.

Having spoken in a light hearted conversation over coffee, Alexa stood up and thanked Tam for a wonderful evening stating how much she'd thoroughly enjoyed herself whilst handing her phone number over to him,

"If you ring sometime tomorrow we can make arrangement to go for a drink at the wine bar down the road "she indicated.

"That'll be great as I'm in court all day tomorrow, it's the end of a big trial that I've been working on, therefore I'll be free for the rest of the weekend should you wish to do something special" he replied as he looked down at the number Alexa had given him.

"Oh what's your last name fear there's more than one Alexa", he laughed.

"It's Alexa Hirst" as she kissed him on the cheek to say her good night.

"Now that's handy, as that's my surname, now you won't have to change your name when we get married" he replied laughing out loud.

Having seen the funny side to the remark they examined the spelling and apparently it was a different spelling altogether but such a coincident all the same.

Another hectic day for Alexa but at least she'd the evening to look forward to with her new found handsome friend who she'd not been able to get out of her mind all day, with a slight hope that he had been thinking of her as well.

That night Alexa found the sexiest dress in her wardrobe, well you would wouldn't you, which was a sheer pale coffee coloured silk number that again clung to her delicate body, showing her breasts off to perfection as a bra wasn't needed in that dress.

The delicate thong that engrossed where it touched which was very little having a small diamante tear drop on the front, the kind of thing that would drive a man to the heights of pleasure with just imagination, let alone a woman that he thought he could be intimate with.

As time drew closer, the butterflies in her stomach escalated to a pitch that only a woman can describe, as the doorbell rang killing her train of thoughts, for stood there waiting was this handsome man that had captured her feelings more than she'd ever expected, as he whispered;

"Did I tell you last night that you're the most beautiful creature I've ever seen" while looking lovingly into her eyes, leaning forward to brush her cheek with his lips

"No you didn't, but I think you actually mean every word you're saying".

How is it this man could make me feel as though I'm floating on air in less that forty-eight hours after meeting him she thought, he wasn't even her type let alone know who she was in business, but that didn't matter anyway as with her track record, he would be gone in a week or two at the most she thought.

"Well less of the pleasantries, or we'll be here all night and the day I've had, I really could do with that drink" Alexa added.

"Come on then slow coach" Tam replied as he grabbed her hand guiding her out of the door and heading down the road hand in hand like a pair of lovers, with a feeling they both enjoyed plainly to be seen on their faces.

Now the night went as expected with a few drinks and thoroughly engrossed in each other's company, in fact they couldn't keep their eyes off each other, it's as though there wasn't anyone else in the room but them.

As the night went on and the conversation started to falter, it was at Tam's suggestion that a slow walk back to his apartment for a quick coffee to sober up a little before returning Alexa home, now this was a good idea at the time but as they drew closer to the apartment it seemed they couldn't keep their hand off each other for as soon as the door opened to the apartment, it closed just as quickly

"Forget the coffee", as he pulled Alexa close to him, while sweeping her hair to one side of the face kissing her so passionately the strength left her body immediately.

"I'm going to make love to you like there was no tomorrow and then you'll never go away from what we have at this moment in time, your body will burn with fire that you will never want any other man inside of you but me, this I promise you from the bottom of my heart. I've wanted you from the first moment my eyes saw you and let me tell you, no other man will ever have you but me from this day forth".

All this was coming from a man Alexa had never even set eyes on forty-eight hours ago, so what made him think she would feel the same way as he did, one thing for sure, she wasn't going to fight it as the weakness in her body drained, crying out for whatever he had to offer, and offer he did for this was a man of inner strength who would show her love as never before.

Standing without a stitch of clothing on, he continued by removing her outer jacket slowly glancing down at her body in such a way the lust in his eyes was burning so bright with such fire of wantonness, as she felt the heat penetrating her soft skin. Picking her up, he proceeded to carry her into the bedroom where an extra-large bed was awaiting with sheets already drawn back in an inviting way.

As Alexa looked into his eyes she muttered;

"Shall I take my dress off as don't want to ruin it being such an expensive one"?

"No" came a stern reply, "I'll buy you a new one tomorrow for I'm the one who will disrobe you tonight", as he threw her onto the bed fully dressed in her entirety.

Laying there for a few seconds totally bewildered for no other man had treated her like this before, it was always her that had the upper hand with men and they would do what she wanted but no this was different.

What was he going to do she pondered looking up at him, but soon to find out for as he grabbed hold of the top of her beautiful designer dress, yanking it off with such force making the adrenalin in her body run through it at such a pace, she could have orgasm there and then. The only thing left on was the delicate thong which was nicely placed on her stomach, running down between her legs and over her clitoris.

"Don't worry, that's staying where it is for the time being" he stated as though he could read her thoughts.

"I don't want you to move one inch for I'm going to taste every single part of you tonight, we didn't go for dinner, you will now be my meal as a starter, a main course and even taking in the sweet for afters" he stated.

Oh my god, she thought as her juices were rapidly flowing by now, how on earth am I going to keep this up for any length of time?

But again, Tam could read her thoughts and interrupted with;

"Don't worry darling I'll be patient, you will orgasm many times before the night is over and that I can promise you".

This wasn't like Alexa as she could only reach an orgasm once and sometimes that was with difficulty so what was going to be different this time maybe the heavens would open and an angel would shoot his magic arrow down she thought.

Moving up the bed until he was laid besides her, stroking the long strands of hair, kissing her neck and shoulders in such a tender motion that shivers ran through her body with an excitement that she'd not experienced before, taking his hand and slowly wrapping round her breasts, he tightened his grip on the firmly pert nipples, gently squeezing them to her delight as she moaned with an exotic sound which came from her inner body.

As he moved his generous lips onto the pert nipples teasing them before he strengthened the suction, making them throb with intensity. The suction was so strong that both nipples were aching but was that a satisfaction of her breast or was that an ache for more of what she was experiencing as every time he sucked, her juices flowed more and more in abundance.

Oh yes, he was definitely in charge of her body and was determined, that was the way it was going to stay as he slowly moved down her smooth skin to the small mound facing the opening of her vulvar which was such a beautiful sight for his eyes, parting her long sleek legs with one hand.

His hand now reaching up to her stomach, smoothing the skin as his face moved down taking tender little bites on the way, he could almost taste the oils that covered her body after she'd showered, lowering his hand again from her stomach down to her clitoris, driving his two fingers up to penetrate, knowing her G spot would react to such an action therefore giving an ache that screamed throughout her body parts, causing such an exotic moaning sound that delighted him as he was pleasuring her to such an extent causing the sheets to become totally wet.

Now maybe if she visited the bathroom it would give her a break but no, he wasn't having any of that as he said.

"Don't worry darling you won't be so wet in a minute for I intend to dry you off" as his lips touched her clitoris taking it fully into his open mouth sucking deeply until she was dry, which wasn't very long before she climaxed yet again with the suction they were both enjoying.

But that wasn't the end of it for he kept that action up not giving her room to move until yet another climax shuddered through her weary body as she thought, how much more of this can I take, it was like a lion to its prey as she endured his every move, but the more he satisfied her the more she wanted it yet again.

Her body aching and torn but not with pain but with the desire of everlasting torment. At last, Tam rose up as he straddled her like a stallion, which glancing down at him was a true statement of fact with such an erection that made her eyes water never imagining being able to take such a huge monster.

Hesitating, to look into Alexa's eyes with love and passion before entering her body, he knew there wouldn't be anyone else from that day forward as he'd found his soul mate. Yes, it hurt a little for she'd never taken anything that big before but the excitement of this penis moved her body to such a rhythm that it felt so good as he rode her over and over again to the screams and delight they experienced until a flood of satisfaction reach both their bodies;

"Oh my god she screamed"

"Sorry but I'm afraid he won't help you" as he pushed her knees further up the bed, entering her even deeper than before. I'm going to give you a little extra so that you'll have a good night's sleep" he whispered driving in and out of her like a man possessed until he came to the final furlong where he let go of everything he had to give.

"This is just the start of things as you'll never want another man now we have each other, for we've found a bond that will last forever" Tam whispered as he slowly dismounted her, placing his arms around the body he had so tenderly made his own, knowing sleep would come in the arms where she'd belong forever.

Tam had no doubt in his mind that Alexa was the right one and she was the one he had waited patiently for until this moment.

He like Alexa, had dated many but a few dates and it never worked out as he was looking for the impossible or so he thought at times, for in his mind she would be perfection itself, now in real life he had found her and had no intention of letting her go at any costs. Not only was she intelligent, beautiful with an inner charm but he was drawn like a bee to a honey pot for he couldn't keep his hand off her, these thought stayed in his mind as they both slowly dropped off to sleep that night.

Eventually awaking the next morning while Alexa still peacefully sleeping, he could feel the arousal of his body beneath the sheets while putting his hand down to correct the position between his thighs, but alas there was no correcting what was so obvious to him, the only way to fulfil this desire was to take Alexa from behind.

Bending her forwards slightly with one hand while cupping her vulvar from the front and teasing her clitoris with his fingers, he entered her, to long slow motions in and out until she awakened to the sensual feeling of his fingers playing with her as the sticky sounds of her juices flowed at the top of her legs.

Her stomach muscles by now were all tensed and contracting to a rhythm that Tam was dictating with the firm erection that lay deep inside her; to be woken up by such strength probing her inner depth was mind blowing as her muscles clung onto his penis with such suction.

How could she not enjoy this first thing in a morning her thoughts were as the intensity grew, she begged him for release but he wasn't ready, for having to seek further depths inside of this glorious opening, and with Alexa closing her legs lightly, creating muscle contractions that her body signals were now giving, Tam had no other option than to let nature take its course as they came together with one almighty finish.

Alexa turned over to face Tam and lovingly said;

"Thank you for that, there definitely was feeling in what you did, it wasn't all about you it was as though we were both in it, speaking the same body language".

"Yes and that's how it's going to be from now on, I'm never going to let you go knowing that you feel the same as I do, it showed me a lot last night, brought me back to know exactly what I want and that is you", was the reply.

Alexa had never met anyone as wonderful as this before and knew in her heart it was love at first sight as Tam interrupted her thoughts by saying;

"I think you should sort all your things out over the weekend and I'll arrange to get them picked up sometime next week, but all you really need for the time being is toiletries which can be purchased locally".

"What did you say," Alexa enquired as though she hadn't heard him properly.

"You heard me, so don't say you didn't, you'll be moving in and I'll not take no for an answer, so don't make it any harder than it is for were meant to be together and you know it, if there's something you don't like in the place then we'll change it to your liking but never the less you are moving in and that's final."

Alexa looked Tam straight in the eyes and without any denial she knew he was right, she wanted the same as he did and that was to be together;

"But you don't know anything about me whatsoever and I definitely don't know anything about you other than what you told me the other night, I may be a girl without any future, even someone after your money that's if you have any" she answered with emotion in her voice, adding;

"I live with a close friend of my mothers and don't even have my own place let alone enough money to rent one".

"Look, I don't care what you have or where you live, nothing really matters to me, the only thing I do know for sure is that I have fallen in love and nothing's going to stand in my way and if you were to be honest, I think you will feel the same, if you don't then I'm sure you will when you realise it" was his reply

Oh she knew alright, she'd never felt like this before and definitely never let a man take her body and dominate it as he'd done. but having the last word she added;

"I'll think it over and let you know when I've decided".

It was two weeks later that Alexa was moving out from Issa's and moving in with Tam, although she'd been staying with him since that eventful night.

All relationships are difficult to begin with as you have to get to know each other and this relationship was no different to any other for they were both so strong willed and argued quite a bit, but there again it was the making up that counted and the more time they spent together, the better it became for it truly was a love match made in heaven.

Altering the apartment was something of an achievement for although it was just perfect as it was, there was the general lack of femininity about it and so she went about putting her stamp of approval into action and making it more desirable to the eye where they could invite friends and family around for small intimate gatherings, which would also have to include her mother at some stage she thought to her horror.

Now the last bit was going to be difficult as Alexa knew when that time came, her mother would no doubt dislike something about Tam for like all mothers that scrutinise their children's partners, there is always some fault they'd find. either not good enough not educated enough or could do better, so no change there she thought and to this end, Alexa organised a small cocktail party which would suffice all close friends and relations.

The cocktail party came and went by with such a success that really Alexa had no need to worry, for Corry fell in love with Tam from the moment they met and as for Issa, well she adored him, there was something special that reminded her of someone in the past but couldn't put a finger on it although she couldn't get it out of her head, it wasn't his looks but it was something about his mannerisms. Never the less eventually, it would come back to her and as long as Tam made Alexa happy, that's all that mattered as far as she was concerned.

It was a couple of months later that Alexa suggested that either they should visit Tam's parents or invite them up to London to stay as she'd not had the pleasure of getting to know any of his family, but to her surprise, the answer to that was a definite no from Tam who was quite adamant to that decision.

"Why are you, so against your parents meeting me, is it because you think they'll say I'm not good enough", Alexa asked feeling quite uneasy at that point.

"No it's not that at all so you can get that out of your silly little head, but since my father returned, all he does is manipulate mother in such a controlling way, she can't see what he's doing as her world is built around him which is quite embarrassing.".

"Yes she's my mother and I love her deeply but having said that, I don't trust him for he's so devious and mother can't see it, now don't get me wrong, she doesn't want for anything but she has no life without him even to the point of cutting off her friends who have also tried to make her see sense but to no avail". It's not about money for he's a very shrewd business man with many a large business interests both here and abroad, but from the first day he came back into mother's life, she changed and not for the better, it broke my heart to see what he was doing to her, turning her from a happy go lucky personality into someone that no one could recognize due to his controlling attitude.

For this I will never forgive him, as long as I live, no I don't trust the man and never will, it's as though he's got something to hide, some dark secret, if you met him, you wouldn't get on with him at all and your mother definitely wouldn't. Now that's final, end of the conversation as far as I'm concerned, I don't wish ever to discuss this matter again with anyone so we'll let the matter drop now" Tam stated quite firmly with such a frosty look that Alexa knew instantly he wasn't about to change his mind.

And from that day onwards the matter of Tams family was never brought into any conversation between them, although Alexa did tell her mother and Issa about this conversation, whereby both agreed, they should let sleeping dogs lay as it may cause an awful amount of trouble should any of them try to make a peaceful gesture in bringing the family back together.

Things moved forward with Alexa getting closer to her mother at this time, maybe it was the influence of Tam but whatever it was, Corry enjoyed this closeness.

And with Alexa watching as she saw her mother go from one venture to another, wishing she'd slow down, but to no avail as the company was her mother's life and therefore it wasn't any use at all in talking to her.

If only she'd settle down, let Lars back into her life, she'd be so happy, Alexa thought, for he was the person that could bring happiness into her life once again, but knowing how stubborn her mother was, she couldn't slow down no matter what anyone said for she was on a self-destruct mode.

Alexa knew all about her mother's new friend Marcus in Cyprus but felt sure, although she was close to him, he wasn't the one she really wanted at the end of the day, although she had nothing against this man having met him on several occasions and thought he was the right man for her mother at that moment in time, but then time moves on and she knew her mother could never settle down with him no matter what happened.

Even though Alexa had even heard rumours about an engagement ring but as far as she was concerned, if that was true then it wasn't a lasting thing for when it came to marriage, then her mother would walk away as she'd done in the past breaking hearts on the way.

No the only man that Alexa would accept for her mother would be Lars as she loved him from the first day they were introduced.

Having discussed all this with Tam as he'd also fallen in love with Alexa's mother, to him she was nothing short of wonderful, but even he had to admit Corry worked far too hard and after meeting Lars, he would have to agree with Alexa's decision, that he was definitely the right man for Corry and knowing women, she' could change her mind and Lars would still be waiting.

It was the same with Marcus, Tam could understand why Corry was fascinated with him being such an upright decent typical Greek god who was a business man like Jay, he could give her all the love she desired as he would treat her like a queen but at the end of the day on judgement alone, he felt, there was something missing from the relationship that Corry couldn't commit to.

It would never be like that between him and Alexa for their relationship was for life as there would never be anyone else for either of them, their bond was so strong it could never be broken whatever happened. Their lives were hectic both in work and pleasure, Alexa a top model who could command any fee she wanted; she also had her own range of lingerie and swimwear together with shares in her mother's company.

Money wasn't a problem, but having said that she never abused the fact that her position in life was anything else but a normal way of living, her only luxury that she afforded herself was a little sports car and that was two years old when she bought it. Tam was a barrister who defended cases in the high court, these were mainly on charges of murder and although the work was tense it was also very financially rewarding which provided a stable future for them both.

The love that was between both of them was undeniable for everyone to see as you couldn't imagine a better couple together, to the relief of Corry for she didn't want her daughter to go through the same heartache as she'd suffered in her search for happiness.

Yes, it had left her scarred but she loved her daughter so much she wanted only the best for her and that's what was going to happen. While the business was running on course everything seemed to go with the flow but the only problem was Alexa was now starting to look a little tired for she'd been working such long hours lately and it was starting to take its toll which was understandable.

Tam had seen this coming on and suggested she went to the doctors for a check-up, but Alexa wasn't having any of it, she knew her body and eventually she'd get over it with some extra sleep which was her way of thinking, being just as stubborn as her mother. Tam on the other hand thought different and therefore arranged he would take her into the country over the weekend to a little cottage that he'd heard about, down the road from a large hotel that one of his clients owned.

Arriving home that night and seeing Alexa looking so tired but not admitting, he suggested in a polite way of telling her:

"To pack an overnight bag, get your most ravishing dress out with underwear to match, put them all in the car as I'm taking you out for a meal in the countryside, now I'm not going to tell you where it is, but you will be away for a few days as I'm going to spoil you rotten, yes were having a break as work is getting both of us down especially you my darling".

This was Tam all over as he loved to surprise and spoil her; she in return always played to his commands which gave her the satisfaction of pleasing him.

"That sounds fantastic, I have a gorgeous new dress and shoes with the most divine underwear that you haven't seen as yet, so will be perfect for this romantic escapade that you've in mind" she said laughing.

"Well that's sorted, were leaving Friday morning and returning sometime on Sunday so you can inform everyone that you don't need to be disturbed".

"But of course my master" she replied sarcastically.

That's the kind of relationship they had, each of them thought how they could please the other, which is why it worked so well between them with an ambiance of unsuspecting breath-taking love and excitement.

Friday came and before they knew it, they were off on the road to who knows where so Alexa thought, but to her surprise, it was when a taxi came to pick them up she enquired;

"What on earths happening, I thought we were going to drive in to the country".

"Well we are sort of, were getting the train as it's going to be a lot easier" looking rather sheepish as he glanced over at her.

"I'm afraid I told you a little white lie, were going up to York for the weekend, knowing you love it so much and never have the time to visit there, thought it may be a surprise but didn't want you to know or you may have informed the rest of the family, when all I want, is this weekend to be just the two of us, I've never been to York so you'll be able to show me around all your old haunts" Tam said smiling at her, knowing she'd be thrilled at whatever he'd arranged.

Thrilled wasn't the word, she was totally ecstatic, loving York as she did and if truth be known, would move up there to live, if ever given the chance and therefore throwing her arms around his neck whispered;

"And that's why I love you so much darling, you never stop caring about me, everything you do is for me, never putting yourself first, it's always me".

"Well I won't love you if you don't hurry up as the taxi's already waiting patiently and if we don't hurry we'll miss the train." he said with a mischievous look on his face.

Being a main line from Kings Cross station, it wasn't long before they arrived in York and sat in the hotel bar having a nice coffee to start the evening off.

"Well as you're in charge and full of mysterious surprises I'd better ask if I'm to wear the new dress tonight or is it a casual do whereby we do a pub crawl round the city" Alexa enquired.

"No, just put a pair of trousers and a nice top on, were going out on the town where you can show off your talents to the locals who will no doubt recognise your body outside of a magazine, tomorrow you can wear the dress, looking your sensual best, for I've already booked a special meal in the hotel so that you won't have far to walk in those killer heels you've brought." he replied.

"Fine then, its shower time and then, I'll show how the northerners live it up in style,

To this, Tam headed to the shower room knowing it would be ages before Alexa got herself focused enough to get ready and in practice being a man it would only take a matter of ten minutes before he was ready and waiting for her to even get dressed. Stood in the shower with the warmth of the water dripping down his body when to his amazement, in walked Alexa stark naked.

"Now that's a nice surprise, have you come to dry me off" he asked with an expression of mischief on his face.

"No sweetheart I've come to do quite the opposite and get you all wet again" she said as her soft hands drifted over his body and down to his penis which was so erect now with just the thought of her naked body brushing up against him.

"Arm mm I don't think you're going to have any objection from me, so I suggest you carry on, as no way am I going to put up much a fight tonight I can assure you "was his reply.

Her hand cupping his scrotum, playing with his testicles, the excitement was rising rather rapidly and so was his penis which was at full length by now, yes she could always bring the best out in him knowing where his weakness lay.

And with the water now slowly falling to more of a dribbling pace as she lowered her face down between his legs while he obliged by moving them apart to accommodate her actions.

Moving her tongue towards the tip of his erection, him obliging while moving forward slightly, her lips reaching out to take him fully into her awaiting mouth with a suction and speed that drove him wild, his whole body shaking with excitement as her teeth tantalised the end of his manhood with such an exotic movement he was almost coming down her throat but enjoying this as he may, his mind was on other positions.

And so grabbing those golden locks of hair, lifting her to a position whereby her legs parted wide enough so he could enter with a forceful mount, ramming this giant tool inside with such passion that they immediately came together.

"Now that's my girl", he said as he carried her out of the shower and carefully placed her on the bed, their bodies still wet as he laid down beside her

"Now you can ride me as I need to feel you're satisfied and with the erection I have at the moment, you will definitely have the power to do so.

Alexa couldn't wait for her body was throbbing for more; she had to climax at least a couple of times more for that was the intention when she entered the shower. It wasn't always like this at the start but now it seemed that she needed the fulfilment of what he gave her almost daily. She rode him in every position imaginable, until the last almighty scream that brought her juices to an end, a smile appearing on his face at the same time.

"Now that you're satisfied my darling, shower and were going out on the town so you can show me a little of what this wonderful place is really like and why it's so special to you" he said.

Up, shower, dressed, make up done and on their way out for a bite to eat and a pub crawl as they put it. The meal was what was to be expected with Yorkshire cooking, all good fresh food and then a night of drinking, laugh's and entertainment as many of the bars had either local singers or groups on with 60's music, what more could they ask for as they sang and danced the night away with no thought of what the next day would bring.

This was just the tonic Alexa needed to let herself go and let all the energy take over bringing her back to life, oh how she missed this as London was so high brow when it came to enjoying themselves in this manner, it seemed that some of the upper class needed to get out and enjoy a few nights in the north, then maybe they'd come down to a level whereby they would enjoy life.

The night drawing to a close as they headed back to the hotel, Alexa flinging her arms around Tam, while he holding on to her a little worse for wear which she'd never in a million years admit to;

"Have you enjoyed tonight as much as I have, Oh I'm so glad we came to York instead of a boring weekend in the country with all those horsey type people that really don't know how to enjoy themselves she muttered in a slurring tone.

Holding her tightly while kissing her forehead, he whispered;

"To see you enjoy yourself as you have has given me more pleasure than you could ever imagine, you don't realise how much I love and worship you, if this makes you so happy I'll look into buying a house up here, then we can spend a little more time away from the city".

"You would do that for me" she asked in a slightly inebriated voice.

"I would buy you the world if you asked, for you've made my life what it is today, a complete human being with feelings that I never thought I'd have".

It was at this moment they arrived back at the hotel, having had, such a great time in the true northern spirit, as both were too shattered to do anything else but sleep.

Saturday morning and breakfast was over, as the hotel was quite near to the railway station, it was a short walk over the bridge into the centre of York which would blow the cobwebs out of the air so to speak after the night's drinking session.

Now York was such a vibrant place where tourists flocked all the year around and with cobbled streets leading up to the Minster it was such a pretty site for all, most of the building being of ancient times with even an old fashioned pub which claimed to have spirits visit in the night and they weren't the kind of spirits you could drink either.

But for Alexa and Tam it would be a show of adventure where she would take him to visit the railway museum then down to the river for a spot of light lunch. Yes, the river, where the pubs became flooded when the river broke its embankment to rise up and fill the pubs which was situated close by.

Now that sounded unbelievable but afraid not as every year when it happened, the owners marked the walls to let everyone know just how far the tides had risen. Although in the nice weather, that was a different case as you sat outside watching the boats sail by and people watch.

The rest of the day was spent doing a little site seeing before returning to the hotel where Tam had already booked a meal in the hotel restaurant.

Yes, everything was going to plan or so Alexa surmised but afraid that wasn't the plan really as it had been slightly altered and there again this was a city that anything could happen at short notice which didn't bother Alexa at all for she was having the time of her life with her true soul mate.

Arriving back at the hotel she headed for the shower as the night was going to be so romantic for both of them, after the meal she thought they would have an early night where she could show her appreciation to the man she loved in more ways than one.

"I want you ready for seven o clock on the dot" Tam shouted to Alexa who was now getting out of the shower';

"That's fine, don't worry I'll be ready, I only have to slip into a dress, put a little make up on as my hair's already done" she declared.

What on earth is up with him she thought, they were only going for a meal in the hotel so why was time of the essence when all they had to do was walk down the stairs to the restaurant she thought, men they don't half fuss when they've made arrangement but it's a different matter when you've made them.

The new pale grey silk dress with little shoe string straps clung to her smooth body, a darker shade of grey high heeled shoes with matching bag, the diamond bracelet mother had bought for her birthday which adorned her wrist, yes she looked utterly stunning but then she always did.

"Do you know darling, I've never seen you look as beautiful as you do tonight, it's as though there is an inner radiance within you", was a statement more than a compliment.

"Oh come on Tam, I think we've been together too long for you to get all soppy on me tonight" she replied although he often got like this, usually after a few glasses of wine in his case.

Walking down the stairs to the dining room, one of the waiters approached and stated that they would be dining in one of the private rooms tonight due to overbooking.

"Now if you will accompany me Sir, I will direct you to your room where everything should be to your satisfaction", he said graciously.

What the hell's going on Alexa thought as she looked at Tam rather quizzically, but his only response was a shrug of the shoulders; therefore, she never gave it a second thought until they entered the private room where low and behold and to her utter amazement, there waiting for them was a few family and personal friends.

Now this really is going over the top she thought and with that asked Tam;

"What on earth is going on"?

"Sorry darling, but I thought it would be nice for you to have all those that are dear to you on this special occasion", he answered quite boldly.

"For god sake stop talking in riddles and tell me what special occasion, what on earth are your talking about", Alexa enquired thinking she'd missed something at work.

"I think you ought to ask and put us all out of our misery" Corry said as she walked over in the direction of both her daughter and Tam.

To this, Tam turned to Alexa as he pulled out a box from his jacket pocket, where a three carat diamond solitaire ring sat shinning like a huge star in the sky and said;

"Alexa, I have loved you from the first moment I saw you, would you please do me the honour of becoming my wife", as he reached for her hand to put the ring on the engagement finger.

Alexa stood there a good few minutes trying to get composure as all the wind had been knocked out of her sails, not realizing anything like this was going to happen for the thought hadn't even entered her head.

Coming to her senses, she flung her arms around Tam and screamed

"Of course I will, as for my mother, I thought she may have at least warned me of this."

"No darling if I had done that, it wouldn't be a surprise, and the other surprise is, I have already bought you both a house just outside of York on the Tadcaster Road, and that surprise neither of you knew about", they both looked at Corry with such a look that spelt out a million words of love and gratitude.

And with two surprises, there would have to be a third as things run in three's but that was to come later which was the biggest surprise of all.

With about twenty friends and relatives the night went splendidly for everyone, not only did they all catch up on their busy lives but it was an evening of happiness that went on till early hours of the morning. Corry was so proud of her family and now that her daughter was engaged to be married to a wonderful man like Tam, she couldn't have wished for more.

One thing that Alexa had to thank her mother for was the fact that she'd invited Lars and not brought Marcus over from Cyprus to the party.

Yes, she was very fond of Marcus but to her Lars was the one she'd always wished her mother would marry and she'd do anything to get them back together for he was the one that held her affections.

Morning came when everyone had left, thus leaving just Alexa and Tam, therefore it was decided a quite lunch before returning back to London where the engagement would officially be announced. Bags packed in the room but still not being able to keep their hands off one another, for that would be the last time they would make love in York for a while so making the most of the opportunity he asked was he going to take her clothes off or just take her as she was fully clothed

There was no answer to that question only a hesitation, for before she knew it, he'd grabbed hold of her, pushing his hand up her skirt while yanking off her knickers, as he did, he could feel the soft warm drizzle of her juices coming to light which turned him on immensely making his own body thirsty for this astonishing beauty before him.

This time he hadn't got time to play or fondle her as he needed to be inside of her warm virgin body as that's how he always felt, knowing she was his and his alone.

Pushing her legs wide open as he dropped his own trouser, she could see how instantly erect he was pushing his penis straight into her while grabbing hold of her bottom tightly, the heat of her body made his penis swell with such excitement once inside as the contractions of her muscled grabbed hold of it.

" Sorry darling but I have to come now so you'd better put your best effort into coming with me for I'm going to dig deep down as far as I can, and fill you with everything I've got for this monster can't wait to show you fulfilment any longer".

To this they both let out one almighty moan as they came together.

"I am really sorry about that darling, I don't know what came over me, just had to take you there and then, the urge and feeling was so strong I just couldn't help myself, for that's what you do to me at times, you bring out the animal instinct".

"Don't worry, I really enjoyed that, we should do that more often "Alexa replied laughing with a silly little giggle as she did at times.

It wasn't long after, they were making their way back to London with memories they would never forget, a weekend that was about to change their lives forever in an unknowing cruel way.

Getting back to normal after such a great time is always hard for everyone but for both Alexa and Tam it was a lot harder as they'd to settle into a routine which suited both their professional lives. They were the perfect couple as everyone used to say and it wasn't long before the news was leaked to the press;

TOP MODEL TO MARRY PROMINENT BARRISTER IN THE CITY

Yes, this was the headlines in all the society pages.

Corry could now settle to the fact, that she would soon be gaining a new son in law which she fully approved of, and with this, a well-deserved holiday to Cyprus would be booked before arrangements would be in progress for her daughter's wedding. The one conciliation to all this was, with both Alexa and Tam's work schedules, they would be looking at another eighteen months to get it organised.

No there was no time to rush the wedding as they had lived together for nearly two years now and therefore as the fashion industry worked to a seasonal calendar, work would have to be their priority, picking a date that would fit in with all concerned, this would give Corry plenty of time to design something outstanding for her only child.

Alexa would be over the moon with this, as the dress would be designed by none other than her mother personally something so special it would be a family heirloom to be showcased for the company that she herself would own one day in the future.

But again that was the future, for the love they had between them, no one could ever destroy, they'd been happy for the last couple of years and when all said and done marriage was only a piece of paper at the end of the day and paper can't hold you together only love can and with an afterthought from Alexa herself.

The feelings were good and everything was going so well, what a perfect life we will have she thought, but that wasn't meant to be was it?

Chapter 18

BACK TO THE PRESENT

In a deep sleep, it seemed that Corry's head slipped from side to side in a restless motion as though there was something on her mind subconsciously, when out of the blue a voice in what seemed the distance, together with a slight awareness that someone was talking to her;

"Miss Sharp, Miss Sharp. We're about to descend within the next ten minutes, so if you'd like to freshen up before we land, now's the time to do it".

"Oh thank you, I'm afraid it's been such a hectic time just lately, what with the shows and then my daughter's engagement, afraid it's all caught up on me" Corry replied coming to her senses.

To be honest, she'd not realised just how worn out she was and it was only when she started to relax that it all started to creep up, never mind, the thought of a week or so at the villa would do me the world of good she thought as the plane touch down to a perfect landing. Having sailed through customs, her taxi would be waiting as she walked out of the airport, oh what a wonderful feeling to be back on firm ground in a place that had so many memories, yes there were some bad ones but with the turning of the tide, there were some very special ones as well she thought.

The exhaustion was now starting to leave her body as she approached the awaiting car, her driver kindly passed the time of day as to her flight and health as he usually did when coming to pick her up.

"Just get in the car and I'll sort everything else out, you'll find an ice cold bottle of water on the back seat" he said.

"I honestly don't know what I'd do without you being there to meet me; in fact, I would say you go beyond that at times "was her reply.

"Well you are a very special lady, so we have to look after you as you've always looked after us on the island" he stated.

Yes, Corry was well aware of that, as it was now a couple of years past since she'd heard rumours of his wife who'd been rushed into hospital and as it was the talk of the village that an operation was needed to save her, but being poor people they couldn't afford the medical bills, the villagers had clubbed together the best they could but fell short in the total amount which was needed for the operation.

These were very proud people and if there had been an offer to help from a stranger, it would have been turned down and so giving it some thought, she came up with an idea on how to help without anyone finding out, well, that's not exactly true, what she did was ask around about the medical facilities on the island to find the best possible surgeon for the operation due to it being a rather complicated procedure.

She immediately contacted the Chief of Staff at the hospital in Nicosia arranging to cover all the expenses with the conditions that it would be registered that an anonymous gift from a person unknown, who was to cover all the medical bills, consequently the operation went ahead and was successful. As there were two children of this family, she also made sure that everything was taken care of whereby they would be looked after financially.

Nothing was ever mentioned about what had been done in this case, but having said that, this was a small village the family lived in and like all small community's secrets were never divulged although word got around and people put two and two together, knowing exactly who had financially stepped in to pay for the treatment. You see in Cyprus everyone is related, therefore there are no real secrets so to speak, only the ones that are silent and never mentioned but everyone knows just what they are and that's what makes the magic of the place.

As Corry sat in the back of the car taking the ice cold water to her dry lips, she asked with genuine concern;

"How's the wife Alekos, and how's the children getting on now" yes this was the name everyone knew the driver by although his full name was Alexandros but then no one used it.

"Fine, she's now attending college, training to be a teacher, having never looked back since her operation, I thank God every day for what that person did to save her life, to come forward and pay for everything, even to helping financially with the children.

"My son has left college and is now studying to be a Doctor and the daughter in her last year of college also going in to be a Doctor, so as you can see I am very fortunate", he replied.

"Good, it's a worthy cause; we need all the medical staff we can get as I understand that a new hospital is opening soon".

In her heart, Corry knew it was the right decision she'd made when donating the monies to help this family, but there again, this is how life had been, she never wanted the praise or recognition, it was just enough to know that she'd been able to help someone in need as she'd been helped on the path to success all those years ago.

It wasn't long before the car pulled up outside the villa as the heat of the day was now just starting to take its toll on her weary body. Hot and sticky by now and yearning for a shower to rinse all those troubles of the past weeks away, she stepped out of the car with a huge sense of relief, for this is how she felt when coming home as this is where she called home, everywhere else was just a place to put down her head and sleep.

Maybe when she retired it would be a different matter but for now too many people relied on her and she couldn't let them down, in other words her life wasn't her own so to speak but for now the enjoyment of the privileges she had rightly earned was appreciated.

Looking round at the garden as she walked up the drive, a few shrubs lay on the soil, the aroma of sweet flowers that drifted through the warm air was just pure perfume, the patio all set out with a small table to one side of the villa and a couple of sunbeds which lay around a small pool, a large table with six accompanying chairs positioned round the other side of the villa which served as a dining table for breakfast and the villa itself which was painted all white with black surrounds making it a monochrome look, as that had always been her trade mark since she started the business, yes, she was proud of her achievement, and why shouldn't she be.

As you would enter the villa, you were instantly aware of how large it was from the inside, being open plan and with a certain degree of a warm and homeliness.

Four large bedrooms now with en-suites, due to her having the bathroom demolished, with French doors which opened onto the large patio's overlooking the sea, a large lounge with an American fitted kitchen that spelt luxury dining for small cocktail parties, yes she'd tweaked it over the years bringing it into the modern villa but then again it was still home.

"Home at last" she said out loud as she sauntered up the white marble steps leading to the large solid wooden door which was now slightly open with a welcoming presence and a softly spoken voice in the background. Yes, this was her friend of many years who looked after the place when Corry was on her travels;

"Ah it's lovely to see you again", Maria said as she flung her arms around Corry so tightly;

"I prepared a light meal for us both on the dining table, and then you can tell me all about Alexa's engagement and discuss all the news that's been happening at home, it will be lovely to catch up as I've missed you, my friend".

"Don't bother too much about the bags as we'll sort them out later, Alekos will put them all down in the bedroom for the time being, as I want to hear all the news as to what's been happening since we last met and put the world to right".

Yes, Maria had been a good friend and confidant over the years and to be truthful Corry didn't know what she'd have done without her.

"Look, you go and have a nice shower, wash all those cobwebs off while I get you something to eat and then with a nice glass of wine we'll be able to catch up. Maria said as she noticed an expression on her friend's face that spelt trouble

Well there was no arguing with that, as Corry walked towards her bedroom before suddenly stopping dead in her tracks.

"Look on second thoughts, is there any chance we can have a catch up tomorrow as I can't seem to get rid of this tired feeling, perhaps if I have a little nap, I'll feel better Corry shouted".

"No problem, you have a lay down and sleep it off and I'll be round in the morning to make your breakfast. was the reply.

Maria was a saint as far as Corry was concerned as she couldn't ask for a better friend and maybe if she did have a sleep as suggested, it would make her feel a lot better in the morning she thought as she slipped into something a little more comfortable before laying down on her bed and drifting off, into a deep sleep of time.

HER MIND WONDERED BACK TO THE DAY THAT SHE FIRST MET HER FRIEND MARIA.

It was a hot steamy day just after she'd moved into the villa, the workmen were busy doing renovations while dust flying all over the place which left her with no option but to sit outside away from all the noise they were generating. Sitting on the Marble steps at the front of the villa a woman walked past and shouted;

"I'm having a walk down to the village for a cold coffee and brandy, would you care to join me, as you look as though you need one".

"Thank you, that would be nice, that's if I'm not putting you out too much" Corry replied.

"Not at all, you look as though you need to get away from all that renovation works, and the company would be much appreciated I can assure you" Maria said.

Maria was all alone since losing her aunt, although born in England of British parents she was brought up in Cyprus by her aunt when her parents died in a car crash. The crash killed both parents outright but as Maria was asleep in the back of the car she was saved upon impact. And with no living parent to bring a child of ten-year-old up it was decided by Social Services that they would put her up for adoption.

This was the case until her mother's sister heard about it and came forward, not having any children of her own as she was a career woman owning a large property company in England therefore approached the courts to adopt her niece, moving out to Cyprus lock stock and barrel to make a new life for both of them due to the fact there were to many memories of the accident.

Bringing in private tutors to educate Maria, she relished all the love and affection she could on the child, and together with losing her only sister. This resulting as the sacrifice was made, to stay a spinster. It was only when she died that Maria got the shock of her life, inheriting all the wealth that her aunt had built up over the years which was quite a sizable sum.

Yes, Maria had a long standing male friend but like Corry she didn't wish to get married and therefore he lived in a large villa at one side of the village while she lived in a large villa at the other side of the village and this had been the case for over twenty years now. She keeping the property business going and therefore running this from Cyprus as her aunt had done before she died; plus, doing a lot of charity work for the children on the island, also being the

President on the board of the local hospital, but there again not mentioning that to anyone, another close secret that never came out although everyone was aware of this.

Meeting Corry was like a breath of fresh air, both having the same mentality therefore getting on like a house on fire having come from similar backgrounds, it was when Corry came to the island, Maria became a different person for they seemed to be like two peas in a pod laughing from morning to night having the same sense of humour. And it was from that day on a friendship was born between these two women for when Corry was away, Maria would look after the villa and when she came back, it seemed as though they were inseparable most of the time, well that's how it started out until one day when both shopping in Larnaca, this being the port on the island.

Maria had taken Corry into a large fashion shop called Joseph's, but I'm afraid as they were leaving the shop, Corry slipped and took a fall down the steep pavement onto the road, shaken and with her leg bleeding, Maria took her friend into a nearby restaurant, which was owned by a close friend who immediately practiced his first aid skills, whereby cleaning the leg, administering the appropriate plasters before giving her a Brandy for the shock.

Consequently, Maria introduced her friend whose name was Marcus and not only was he the owner of the restaurant but he also owned a considerable amount of properties on the island. Yes, Marcus was a gentleman, not only in wealth, beauty, values and loyalty but also of generosity, a rare man indeed with a body that women would give their high teeth to get hold of in any position.

The tender loving care that he showed Corry was unmistakably overwhelming to everyone who witnessed this attention; it was as though cupid had shot an arrow into his heart that day, but were talking about Corry here, and to many, she was a woman with a heart of ice where men were concerned although on this occasion the ice seemed to be melting a little as she looked into his dark eyes for there was something very soulful, that she couldn't quite put her finger on. Never the less he had been so kind in helping, in her hour of need; she must thank him in some way, maybe take him for a meal, was the suggestion;

"Not at all", Marcus replied being quite offended at this suggestion.

"Look I know a little restaurant down on the coast road and as you're the one who is the invalid, I would suggest that I pick you up at seven tonight and take you for a meal instead, for I think you'll enjoy the food immensely, and there again we do have to keep your strength up, you being a visitor to the island, so be ready by seven for I'm not taking No, for an answer".

To this. Corry smiled with a reply of;

"Well seven it is", if there's one thing she'd learnt about the people on the island, and that was they were a very proud race and therefore you could quite easily offend when refusing an invitation.

Maria couldn't believe her eyes as to what had happened for Marcus was a man who was not only a private person but wouldn't be as bold as to make a play for a stranger, there were many women who would give their right arm to get so close to him but he would never let his defences down since the death of his beloved wife some years ago, but that's another story.

Yes, the story goes whereby Marcus met a girl when he was in his early twenties, courted her for some two years or so, eventually marrying her in such a lavish and grand affair. They'd only been married for approximately six months when she was killed in a boating accident and since then, he'd never really looked at another woman, yes he'd had the odd dates but they never amounted to anything as he never got over the death of his wife.

"Be careful my friend for you may get hurt as everyone knows he has no feelings" Maria warned Corry, but then no surprise there for neither had Corry so they were well matched in that department.

Chapter 19

At precisely seven on the dot, up rolled Marcus in his very smart white Mercedes sports car and to his astonishment already waiting was his perfect date for out walked Corry dressed in white linen trousers topped off with an ivory camisole that highlighted her pert nipples which showed though the silk material, white leather sandals tinged with gold and a neat little clutch bag which finished the outfit off perfectly;

"You look stunning" Marcus said as he went to open the car door for Corry, any man would be proud to have you on their arm tonight, but then I'm not any man and tonight I am the proudest man alive to have your company, so here is to the first night of many I hope".

They drove for a while before coming to a little restaurant on the sea front; the music softly playing as they entered the tree lined path to the main entrance;

"Your usual table Marcus "the waiter asked,

"Yes, that will be fine" was the reply.

The food was beautiful, Marcus was right what he'd said about this place for they were treated like VIP's, nothing being too much trouble but then the Cypriot people were always that courteous and with the wine flowing and conversation between them, the night silently slipped by to the early hours of the morning before they noticed, being so wrapped up in each other's company. It had been a long time since Corry had enjoyed herself in this way she thought and to be honest she had enjoyed herself a little too much for the wine was starting to go to her head in a big way making it feel a little more than tipsy to say the least, when Marcus looked into her soft green eyes and suggested it was time they started back.

Stumbling out of the restaurant and into the car Corry hadn't a care in the world for at that precise moment; it was a moment of pure magic not only for her but also for him as they drove along the coast with the warm breeze for company;

"I think you'd better have a coffee before you retire tonight young lady, now will that be your place or mine"? was the question.

"Oh I think mine as its closer than yours" she replied still feeling quite light headed for not only was the breeze blowing through her hair it was having an effect on her body as the nipples stood to attention with an ache between her loins, was it the wine or was it the man that was sat beside her that was having that effect she pondered. It wasn't long before they arrived at the villa and still Corry in a giddy mood singing her heart out as she got out of the car to open the large wooden door, missing a couple of steps on the way, obviously,

"Come on my dear let me, as you're going to fall" Marcus suggested.

"I'll tell you what, you go and get changed out of those pretty clothes, make yourself more comfortable, while I make you a black coffee" he said in a concerning voice as she toggled off to the bedroom.

More comfortable, who does he think he is she thought, I'll show him what comfortable is as she stumbled around the bedroom dropping her clothes on the floor as she disrobed. Standing in the light of the full moon she grabbed a silk robe draping it around her body but forgetting to tie the belt, returning to the lounge where Marcus had obviously made himself at home with a drink in his hand.

It was when Marcus looked over at Corry in astonishment before saying;

"Don't you think you'll get cold in that gown your half wearing; you've obviously forgot to fasten it".

Looking down at the robe, then across at Marcus, she replied in a defiant manner,

"No if you want it fastened then you'll have to do it yourself or aren't you big enough"?

Corry wasn't used to men standing up to her, for after all she was the CEO of one of the largest fashion companies in Europe and men did what they were told, but this was something different or was it the drink talking, for she was rebelling at the thought of him taking charge of the situation in her home;

"All I can say is, should I walk over there to you, young lady, I can assure you it won't be fastened as you requested "was his commanding tone.

"And what will it be then" she asked sarcastically?

"It'll be taken off altogether young lady".

"I don't think so as you're not big enough to take it off".

Although the drink was now wearing off, it was as though something was pushing her on with this seductive conversation which wasn't like her at all.

"Well we'll see wont we" Marcus said as he started to walk towards her with a powerful stride in his step

Corry now half naked as the robe had slid apart showing her body from a frontal view, assuming Marcus would eventually stop, but no this conversation had gone too far and before she knew it, his hands were on her shoulder with such a firm grip that she couldn't move even if she wanted to.

This was a challenge as far as Marcus was concerned as he picked her up in his arms continuing towards the bedroom without a word.

"Where do you think your taking me" she sighed, still defiant as ever but with a weakening in her body which she couldn't explain;

"Just stay quiet and I'll show you" he replied quite harshly'.

And to her astonishment, that's exactly what happened, for it was as they reached the bedroom, and he gently laid her on the soft white cotton sheets that were pulled back in an inviting position as his eyes caught sight of this wonderful creature before him with her soft, smooth, tan skin which had now started to work on his imagination sending tingles throughout his body. There was no time like the present as he now proceeded to disrobe his own clothing attire which automatically dropped on the floor where he was standing thus becoming totally naked showing his manhood like a huge stallion ready to mount his conquest.

Although the moon was full that night giving a sensual light as it shone down in the room, a warm breeze drifted through the open patio doors with a lightly perfumed aroma that arose from the scented flowers outside, a perfect setting to the end of an evening he thought although the perfection was going to be, in how he would satisfy this raving beauty.

Moving slowly towards Corry he gave what was left of her robe a sharp tug adding;

"You won't need that now, will you"?

"And why not" she replied still with a defiant attitude, even though the alcohol was now starting to wear off, but still calling his bluff and yet not flinching at all.

"Because where I'm going, it would only get in the way" was the reply as he then disrobed her entirely.

Then bending over her body, touching her soft tender lips with his finger, noticing the fire that was still in her eyes as he moved towards her face, his hands caressing her golden hair as his lips slightly touched hers with an excitement raging through both their bodies which was quite electrifying, slowly moving from her lips to the ears, down the neck, working his way down past her shoulders while holding her tightly against the bed sheets.

And with the movement of one hand he stroked her firm suckle breasts in a way that sent an ache through her body for more, it was now that her enormous nipples was starting to stand to attention and it was attention that they needed at this moment in time But Marcus wanted to kiss Corry all over and as he leapt back to her awaiting lips in a teasing manner, he could feel the blood flowing inside of the huge erection that had started to take place between his thighs, the throbbing that he'd not experienced for a long time. Yes, he'd had his moments with other women but not like this.

What was it about this woman as no other woman had aroused him so quickly in this way before, as soon as he touched her he knew she was something quite different, someone he wanted to please in every way unlike in the past whereby he only wanted to please himself and not the partner he was with. Was he getting into deep waters he thought to himself, maybe so but he just couldn't fight the ache he felt in his body and the fire in his loins which was the driving force that wouldn't go away.

Corry just lay there hardly moving due to the enjoyment she herself was experiencing for if she had moved, he may just stop and then she'd be devastated for that wasn't what she wanted to happen, she wanted to go all the way, over the top of ecstasy.

And to that Marcus reached out while grabbing her hand, his mouth darting towards her nipples, slowly kissing them in turn then taking them one by one further into his warm luscious mouth as his sliver dribbled down on her breasts, sucking with such action, that the it became quite intense to the limit of pain that shot throughout her body, this he knew as her finger nails tore into his back drawing blood which intensified the sexual urge throughout his body.

By then Corry's body was all of a burning sensation from her toes to her brain, the weakness had always been her nipples and Marcus in all his wisdom had sensed this from the start as her flaunting awareness began in the restaurant which teased him all night giving him an erection in which he couldn't satisfy.

Not only was he enjoying this but to see Corry who by now was withering from side to side with tension, driving her not only crazy with an aching delight but wanting the release that would give her a will to fight yet another day.

Moving his head down her body, taking his time to explore every little inch which would give her pleasure, having let her hand go as he started to move down her smooth body which was reacting to his every touch by now, down to her thighs when suddenly parting her legs in the middle with such a jerked movement that her whole body quivered.

Trying to pay no attention to this as she attempted to move from his grip but finding she was frozen in a time warp whereby it was impossible to even think straight let alone object, moving his head between her legs, kissing her softly before moving his tongue round her clitoris to a soothing suction which was driving her wild, her juices now flowing like a tap which had been left on to slowly drip.

Oh yes, although fully sober by now and realizing what was happening she wasn't fool enough to start objecting for she'd not experienced enjoyment like this for a long time and on the other hand didn't know how long she'd be able to survive without exploding for he'd literally been working his magic for what seemed hours now When suddenly she blurted out;

"And what do you expect to achieve getting me in this state".

"I'm going to suck you dry over and over again until we soak together, and now you will pay for interrupting me" as his tongue reached inside of her, clamping his teeth tenderly on her clitoris on the way in, knowing he was driving her insane as her body tossed all over the place.

"I don't think I can take much more of this she whimpered".

"Oh yes you can".

You still have the best bits to come yet" he replied, slowing down to a speed whereby she would be able to gain control or her emotions.

This was a woman who enjoyed every move he made, kissing her from the toes back up to those nipples which were now standing to attention for that pleasurable kiss as her heaving body moved to the delights of his every touch. Her skin so soft as he worked his way back down to the peach of fruit he was now seeking to manipulate before enticing into that warm sensual grip which would intensify the orgasm he would give her;

"Told you, I can't take any more please for God sake just fuck me".

Now that was definitely an invitation if ever you heard one for at that precise moment, Marcus who was fully erect and with such a throbbing that had been the driving force behind him, eagerly moved on to mount her like a large stallion for that's how it felt when he entered her with such vigour.

The mounting was an easy target, finding she was ready and waiting for such an erection to take its course, the breathing became more and more intense as he started to tease, drawing in and out like a cat wanting the cream but not taking it, yes she was tight as she accepted this throbbing invasion into her body, how could she not be when she'd suffered two hours of foreplay.

But he was no amateur at this and it definitely showed in the performance he was delivering, somehow the Gods had been kind to him, blessing him with such attributes together with the knowledge of how to use them, not only to his advantage but also to the one he was pursuing as his prey.

Her body tired with exhaustion, she controlled her stomach muscles to a steady pace whereby knowing just how to draw all the juice from him, as he had done from her, but it seemed that now the tables had fully turned as he screamed out with a painful wanting;

"Take me into that wonderful cave of magical explosive eruption"

As he pushed deeper and deeper inside of her which made her eyes water with giddy excitement. knowing her body was almost ready for the fulfilment that was ready to follow.

Was this the woman of his dreams he thought, wanting to give her all the pleasures that he himself was experiencing at that moment in time, or was she someone he wanted and couldn't have and maybe the chase was going to be his final fulfilment as he walked away.

But Alas, No for all of a sudden the tables turned as she was controlling him with a suction of her own muscles drawing on his throbbing penis, his body now wrecked with such throbbing desire that he could no longer hold on as his tormented screams of please, please, give in and let it go, pushing in so deep inside of her and with two final almighty attempts to release the pleasures that would finally be theirs that night, the accompanying screams of delight which could be heard throughout the room finally followed.

Alas, sleep was on its way as the exhaustion of the last few hours had taken over both of their bodies.

The morning came as the heat of the sun burst into the room, half asleep, Corry turned over not focusing clearly but to find that she was all alone.

No Marcus beside her, did she dream what had happened that night, had this man really got under her skin to that extent. Glancing round the room observing the state it was in, with bedding all over the floor, that definitely wasn't a dream she thought coming to her senses a little quicker than expected, for as she lay there in a world of her own with the sun streaming through the open patio doors, the sound of the waves gushing on the shore, all alone with her thoughts as the smell of fresh coffee filled the air, when all of a sudden there he was;

"Black coffee and toast for my lady, after last night you deserve a treat, you worked your little arse off to my delight", he stated as he disrobed and climbed into bed beside her.

The toast went down a treat, the coffee was quite refreshing but what came next was a fulfilment of his insatiable appetite for he couldn't keep his hands off her, he needed to make her understand that she was his and his alone.

And so straggled legged he mounted, with such a huge erection that she was now seeing it for the very first time, in true delight;

"As your coffee was a little too strong, I think this will sooth your taste buds far better" as his penis drove towards her mouth.

"Accepting that you had the main course last night I'm about to give you a taste of your desert young lady" and before she knew it, there it was a huge throbbing sensation in the back of her throat, giving off a sticky salty taste that filled her mouth as her tongue leapt around for only a few minutes before it was pulled away sharply.

"Now my darling you are going to get the main course inside of you yet again" he reiterated, moving down the smooth body to enter her awaiting slender channel of excitement, so sharp and satisfying was this tool of domination as he pumped every last bit of juices into her, thus screaming with a pain of exotic intoxication.

"That's my girl, and that's what will keep you happy, whenever you need it which I hope will be forever" he stated leaving the bed and heading towards the shower, leaving Corry smiling to herself with a sense of relief.

That was the start of a beautiful intimate friendship for whenever Corry came to the island it was with Marcus she would be seen with, as a couple of lovers.

On Corry's side, it was a relationship that grew, someone she could confide, enjoy and be herself with, yes she loved him in a pleasant sort of way but not in the true sense of love for she couldn't commit to him in body and soul, not being able to fault him as a man in any way, for he was kind, reliable, good company, trustworthy and would give her the earth but that wasn't enough for Corry she wanted something else but didn't know what it was.

For Marcus it was a second chance in life, for he really worshipped Corry, to be near, want and adore her wasn't enough for he loved her so much he wanted her as his wife to spend the rest of his days with, but knowing that wouldn't be of his decision.

Although he had his young love tragically taken away from him, this was different as it was a more mature feeling from the first time his eyes looked into hers, and he just knew his feelings for this woman was so sincere.

He was no fool, for he was an astute businessman who was self-made and a workaholic, never mixing business with pleasure as he'd willingly tell everyone, but it was when Corry wanted his time and attention, then I'm afraid everything would be dropped for in his eyes she came first and foremost, as far as he was concerned.

They experienced a good relationship really for a few years, for Corry returned to the island at least six times a year for a break to be with Marcus and even arranged some business meetings over there, feeling that this was her second home. In the meantime, he would fly to London to be with her, but for some reason he always felt as though he didn't fit in with city life and so on those occasions they would either spend time together in Leeds, York or even Harrogate for it felt more comfortable in those surroundings rather than under the preying eyes of family and friends.

With work coming in so fast, Corry was now starting to feel the pressure and therefore decided a quick break was what she needed to refuel her batteries so to speak and therefore getting Marcus to pick her up from the airport the next morning as she would catch the early flight out to Cyprus for a lazy week in the sun.

But what was to happen on that trip, she didn't anticipate at all

Meeting her at the airport, he confirmed, he'd already booked a table at the little restaurant they'd spent their first date and would therefore pick her up at seven, Corry pondered for a while thinking it must be some event that she'd forgotten but not to disillusion him, kept quiet with agreement, for she'd rather have spent an evening on the veranda with a bottle of wine and a meal for two of them.

As good as his word, seven o clock on the dot as usual and Marcus rolled up to the front door dressed in black linen slacks with an open neck black silk shirt, his toned body said it all to those who would look at him in admiration. Yes, he definitely was a man of sensual style, for when he walked in a place woman couldn't help but notice his toned body, swaggering in front of them, just like the James Bond character, his presence didn't go unnoticed.

Corry on the other hand wore a delicate pink soft silk chiffon dress which was edged with black lace around the shoe string neckline, little pink and black high heeled sandals finishing off with a clutch bag to match the outfit, a very smart couple indeed.

Passing the air conditioning at the side of the villa you could see at a glance, not only had she very little underwear on but her pert nipples stood to attention as the cool air reached the top of the dress.

"You smell fabulous tonight, is that a new perfume you're wearing, not smelt that one on you before "he asked with a compliment he always gave.

"No not really, it's one I often wear when I'm going somewhere that people don't know me, it's called Shalimar and it's one of those perfumes that put you in a sensual mood" she replied smiling.

"Good, now that's my girl, that's the mood I need you in tonight as I have a surprise coming your way later". She really was beautiful in more ways than one, which never ceased to amaze and with such an excitement that she commanded, whenever she glance in a certain way which caused an ache in his loins, being a Greek Adonis you couldn't expect anything else.

"Well, come on what's the surprise, you know you're dying to tell me, you never could hold a secret for long" she said laughing.

"No, you're going to have to wait for this one" he said adamantly, as they drove up the coast road with the soft breeze in their hair, the sound of Ricky Martin blurring out over the sound system in the car, both in a mood for dancing, with Corry now relaxed but also wondering what this great surprise was going to be, for in the past he would just give her presents with never any mention of secrets or surprises, but tonight he seemed as he wanted to tease her for some reason. But having racked her brains for a while as to what this big secret was, knowing he wasn't going to tell her, she decided to give up thinking about it, for whatever it was she'd be thrilled as Marcus knew her only too well, never to disappoint.

The night was young, the mood was high and nothing could spoil the moment so what will be, will be she thought, knowing he only had her interests at heart and therefore with music coming from a couple of the roadside bars as they called in for a drink before reaching their final destination, as hunger was now starting to set in big style.

The meal was fantastic, wine flowed just at the right pace throughout the night for the mood they were in and even the music had softened from the exotic Latin American to a slower smooth seductive sound of Lionel Richie, whereby she'd now totally forgotten about the surprise that had been mentioned earlier, now lost in her own little world, oblivious to the outside one, that had started her hectic week off.

Yes, this was the life she wanted but then again we can't always have what we want and therefore we have to settle for what's been given, which Corry well appreciated, for she'd been blessed with a talent that had earned a lot of wealth and respect for not only herself but also for others around her, it's just a pity that the only thing she yearned for was taken away many years ago by a man that was selfish in thinking he could have everything.

And as the night was now drawing to a close they would return to the villa along the coast road where the moonlight shone brightly onto the waves lashing against the shore, and with an echoing sound of a romantic serenade, of thoughts to end a perfect evening. But then the evening wasn't yet over for the surprise was yet to come as Marcus stopped in his tracks when opening the front door saying as he turned to Corry;

"I think I'll have one last drink to celebrate your return to the island darling, you go and shower and I'll follow in a few minute with a glass of champagne for both of us as I put a bottle on ice, earlier on today," he said walking into the kitchen leaving Corry to make her way to the bedroom for a shower.

"What happened to the drinks you were getting?" she shouted as she walked from the shower to the side of the bed aborning her body with her slip, not wanting to admit that a glass of champagne would go down well now

"Don't worry darling coming right now" was the reply, as he walked in carrying a tray, placing it on a bedside table with two glasses of champagne perfectly placed on it, thus taking one glass himself and handing the other to Corry before telling her to be careful otherwise she'd spill it, adding only to take small sips at a time

Here we go again telling me what to do as though I'm some little child she thought, ignoring him as usual, but then he was used to that, only this time it was different as he sternly repeated himself, looking at her as though there was something wrong.

"Oh for goodness sake, you'd better watch if you don't trust me, I'll only take little sips as your master commands" she answered sarcastically, looking down in the glass before drawing it up to her lips, but just as the glass got closer to her mouth she could see something sparkling and it wasn't the champagne bubbles for attached to the rim was a fine silver threat that when she pulled, her eyes flashed opened wide to the sight of a beautiful platinum five carat diamond solitaire ring.

"Oh My God, that is beautiful" she screamed.

"Just like you, I know you've always maintained you won't marry again but I want to show how much you really mean and would be the proudest man on earth should you wear my ring" Marcus said with tears rolling down his cheeks.

Corry was so taken back as she'd never expected this coming and to be honest was actually stuck for words, for once in her life.

True she'd always made it quite clear to everyone that she'd never re-marry, for couldn't trust a man enough to give her heart again. No she was definitely lost for words but wearing his ring, she couldn't see any harm in what Marcus had suggested, an engagement for all who knew them as a couple but that's where it would stay, as marriage was definitely out of the question.

"I would be proud to wear your ring darling but I'm afraid will never change my mind on the subject of marriage for if I did, it would only end up spoiling what we already have and I don't intend to sacrifice that".

To that, Marcus took the ring out of her hand and placed it on her engagement finger for he understood and accepted Corry's decision saying;

"As long as I have you, that's all I want out of life for I could never love anyone as much as I love you, now drink your champagne and get into bed".

Well, what could a girl do but obey an order like that, as she longingly looked down at her finger sparkling in the moonlight.

It wasn't long before she felt Marcus's warm naked body move next to hers, his hand reaching out as she lay flatly on her back, turning her slowly towards him as his lips reach out and brushed her cheek, winding his tongue down to her sultry lips with a kiss that was more than an invitation for them both, the warmth of his mouth as his tongue enticed her mouth open wider feeling her passion rising within her body.

Now this was the Marcus she had come to love, caring, soft, and gentle and with compassion that she would never find in anyone else, his was a love that wanted her for herself with no ulterior motive. His hand now moving down the small of her back, pulling her that little bit closer, he could now feel the outline of her small tight bottom as his hands rounded up to her thighs, gently pushing her back against the sheets as to make her more comfortable.

"Put your hands up in the air" he whispered softly as he removed the sheer night slip Corry was half wearing by now, she looking up at him grinning like a Cheshire cat.

"Sorry darling you shouldn't have put it on, and then I wouldn't have disturbed your concentration, you've always got me to cover your body should you feel a little cold."

Again Marcus seductively pressed his lips, entwining his tongue in and out of her warm sweet mouth until the suckle sensation of his kiss made waves down his spine. Waves that had come to excite him on many occasion before, it never ceased to amaze what this woman could do to him even just thinking about her, the power she had over him was amazing, he'd never let her out of his sight if he had his way.

Moving his hand over her breast, cupping them one by one, slowly moving his head down to rest on the breast bone like a new born baby ready to suckle on her prominent nipples, which were now screaming for the attention of suction that only he could provide.

Moving from side to side as not to show any favouritism, a teasing suck with his tongue, knowing how much this excited, now and again he would take each nipple fully in his mouth with one long hard tweak from his teeth as she screeched with a painful delight that run through her now excited body which was demanding more of the agony she was experiencing.

Oh how he loved her body, it didn't matter how he approached it, she was always willing to accept the delights that would follow, her breast now hard and heaving as Marcus moved his hands tightly to grip her thighs, his mouth gently kissing down towards the small mound of pubic hair which he could see in the moonlight.

Oh how her skin tasted so sweet, lavishing kisses on her stomach, his hands now eager to push her legs wide apart as his tongue darted forward to her awaiting clitoris, entwining it at such a rapid speed that her juices flowed constantly. This enough to make him think she was climaxing but no fear of that for the enjoyment she was experiencing at that moment was too good to let go, her breathing was quite heavy by now, moaning with every little touch until he took his two fore fingers and shot them up inside of her making her scream with a painful pleasuring climax which her body shouted out for more of this insatiable feeling knowing she couldn't get enough of it.

No, she wasn't quite ready for him yet, he was well aware she'd only climaxed twice and really wanted her to dry out before entering that smooth channel of excitement, giving him the tight pain that made it all worth the wait, when the tip of his penis would anticipate the oncoming flow of juice that would spill towards it.

Pulling his fingers out of her sharply, Marcus moved forward rolling his teeth on her tantalizing clitoris, sending tingles throughout her body knowing full well that she was ready for him yet again. Only this time, turning her over face downwards as he would take her from behind, sinking his swollen penis straight into her for his pleasure as she climaxed again.

No if this was a game of who could last the longest I'm afraid Corry was now going to give him a run for his money, having a few tricks up her sleeve for there was no clouded vision in her eyes and with no trace of alcohol in her system by now, it was time to put on a show that he never anticipated and therefore she demanded Marcus lay down on the bed beside her so they could take it a lot easier, and then resume action when their bodies had calmed down, to which he was quite amenable wanting to saviour the work he'd already put in.

Big mistake, for giving into a woman in those circumstances spelt disaster, for now it was her turn to take charge of the situation and see if he liked it when the tables turned on him.

Taking the situation in hand as she started to kiss his lips with such a tender touch of velvet while glancing down to see the effect that was happening to this huge penis that was so erect and squirming. Now she thought, you're going to get a little of your own medicine. I maybe a lucky woman to have that inside me but you're now going to learn what a Greek God feels like when his powers have been taken away from him as I now intend to do, leaving you at my mercy, she thought.

Positioning herself by his side, while slowly working her way to his lips as she tenderly brushed her taunt nipples against his mouth, then drawing back before he could catch hold of them in a teasing way that was driving him mad.

"Don't move" she said harshly proceeding to position one leg over his waist in a straggled leg position, kneeling against the softness of the cotton sheets which made her feel quite comfortable, she moved towards his lips with a slight kiss as her nipples brushed over his chest, giving him an exciting rush of adrenalin which would fill both of their bodies'

I'll teach you that two can play at this game she thought to herself, firstly biting and then sucking his lips in a sensual movement which she knew would drive him crazy and keeping that erection firm and strong for when she decided to use it

His body and nerves on end to such an extent, he thought he was ready to explode as he grabbed Corry's face intending to control the situation, but then found she was a little too quick for him as her body had already started to move downwards to that awaiting swollen manhood which by now was dribbling with the wet delights of intrigue.

Trying to stop her was impossible at this stage as she'd made her mind up, she was in charge and the power was all hers for the taking, steadily moving to such a position that all she had to do was lift her body to an angle whereby she could mount this almighty Greek manhood.

Looking into his eyes she laughingly said;

"Keep still as I'm in charge now or you'll suffer the consequences dearly".

The poor man had no idea what was coming next and to be honest he wasn't bothered for all the nerves in his body was on such an edge he just wanted to come inside of her. No the night wasn't over and the stage was all hers to play, as her finger nails gripped his thighs, tearing into the fresh which meant that her control was just as strong as his that night, sliding her body down his legs and approaching this huge throbbing article in her midst, as she thought, now this is all mine for the taking to do what I want to do.

And like a fighter jet on a combat mission she proceeded to close in as her tongue glided up and down the great shaft in front, sending shivers throughout Marcus's body like it was doomsday. If only she could see the expression on his face now as it twisted in a painful rhythm of wantonness, while her teeth grating on the tip of his now aching penis, her mouth taking a little in at a time as she began to suck in a pausing rhythm.

This was the time when Marcus's was to suffer as she had done earlier, his body on fire as she pulled her mouth away from time to time, before moving further up his body as she again straggled her wide open legs with just enough distance to tease with an oncoming destiny as her own juices flowed in abundance onto his quivering bare skin sending exotic waves throughout his body before his final fulfilment as she lowered herself onto his stiff erection like a woman possessed but still in control.

Now gathering speed, Corry moved up and down over this huge shaft, grinding her inner muscles around the tip of it knowing full well that the nerve ends were so raw by now, tensing her muscles so tightly, together with a jerking movement that he'd experienced her doing on other occasions. How this woman could be so good with her body and yet look so sweet and innocently ladylike, he would never realise how far she would go to satisfy both their desires.

Like the Greek God he was, Marcus took everything that Corry had to offer, but having said that his throbbing penis inside of her was at such a pitch, he didn't know how much longer he could last and so there was only one way to make her stop this madness, that was to go for her weakest point as he reached out to grab those luscious nipples, taking them one by one in his mouth with such a strong suction. First one then the other, sensing the intensity in her body knowing she couldn't resist the infant coming out in him, grabbing her bottom so tightly as he pushed deeper and deeper inside her until the fulfilment of the night came satisfying both together with an almighty sigh of content.

Both exhausted, but wanting to get the last word in, he remarked;

"If that's what I get for buying you a diamond ring darling, think I'll get you one every day from now on."

Corry ignored that remark but the smile that came on her face said it all, before they both dropped off to sleep in each other's arms like young lovers.

The relationship between them stayed on course for a few years from then, but there was always something missing as far as Corry was concerned, for she still had flashbacks of Lars at times, but then again she knew he came along at the wrong time in her life and therefore it was impossible to go back.

And with time, it seemed as though she was working her socks off and yet when she returned to Cyprus to be with Marcus, the fire that they once had seemed to have dwindled on her part, yes he was everything a woman could ask for and she did love him but it was getting more of a convenient love than a passionate one, for all the excitement had dwindled over the years.

Was she looking for something that didn't exist or had she now missed her chance of happiness for she felt so alone at times.

Yes, she had her daughter and close friends but she needed more, a meaning to cling on to, something to look forward to and not look backward.

Chapter 20

BACK TO THE PRESENT

The sun shining through the window as Corry woke from a deep sleep to her friend Maria's voice in what seemed a distant future;

"Really, you must have been exhausted as you seemed to have been travelling back in time, talking in your sleep about things that happened years ago, when you first met Marcus that day".

Corry looked up at Maria in bewilderment when slowly coming to her senses asking for a strong coffee to bring her round.

"Not a problem, it's just that I was a little worried, you seemed to be out like a light when your head hit the pillow, so thought it best to let you sleep it off whatever it was that was bothering you", Maria replied.

"Thanks, don't know what came over me, just how long was I asleep by the way".

"Since you arrived yesterday, thought you went for a shower but when I looked in to check, you were dead to the world, so thought I'd leave you and come in early this morning to get you some breakfast" was the reply.

"Sorry, got a lot on my mind at the moment and also fear there's trouble brewing but don't know exactly what it is" Corry said in a weary tone.

"Look, go and have a shower, breakfast is already on and then we'll talk, as whatever it is, we'll be able to sort it out one way or another, two heads are better than one my aunt used to say, oh and by the way Marcus dropped round last night, saw you sleeping and decided not to disturb you as he'll be here shorty for a little breakfast with us".

Whatever would she do without her friend she thought as the water tricked down her body before catching a towel to dry off, now with the sun beaming down outside it would be a nice cool linen dress and a bite to eat before Marcus would make an appearance which wouldn't be too early she hoped, as needed a girly talk to her friend whereby they'd catch up on all the gossip. Maria informing her all about what had been going on since the last time she was on the island, also about her love life, adding a bit of sex in to spice the conversation up, as two friends usually do.

Although Corry had all the advice she needed from those she worked with, there wasn't anything better than discussing with a close friend, things she'd got on her mind about the business as that's what friends are for, to off-load their trouble, and then moving forward onto Maria's love life and what was happening with the new hospital etc.

"Now stop, there's something missing here, your only daughter gets engaged to the man of her dreams, you come out here for a rest looking not only shattered but worried out of your mind, and never mention a thing about any of this, do you think I'm stupid, what the hell is going on and don't tell me nothing because I don't believe a word of it, so you may as well tell me before Marcus arrives.

Corry looked at her friend before bursting out crying for if there was anyone she could confide in; it definitely was Maria;

"Well I'd better start from the beginning then, for as you know, I arranged a surprise engagement party for the couple up in York with just close friends and family, which by the way you declined to attend as you'd already made prior arrangement which I understood.

 The party went off really well and with the news that I had bought them a house on the outskirts of York they were thrilled to bits. Alexa's engagement ring was a beautiful diamond solitaire which was just to her taste; yes, we had a fabulous weekend. The problems started a few days upon our return to

London when the press got hold of the story and printed it for all to see, Top Model Marries Prominent Barrister".

To this, Maria looked somewhat mystified as she asked; what was wrong with that story, as for the life of her couldn't see any harm in something that was true.

Looking down with sadness, Corry continued;

"Well just before I came away, I received a phone message that my secretary had taken which stated Jay wanted to speak to me as a matter of urgency, obviously he'd seen the headlines and wanted to know why he'd not been informed that his daughter had got engaged".

"Sorry but I still can't see the problem, he's not had anything to do with Alexa since she was ten, so why the urgency all of a sudden or has he got a guilty conscience, now wanting to play the ideal father of the bride" Maria stated.

"Don't know, the answer to that, but all I do know is, I can sense trouble brewing for all of us and that's what the worrying part is, for him to phone instead of going through the solicitors, there's definitely another agenda I would say".

And that's what's wrong with you, look your over here for a week and you're going to have a great time, so forget what's going on back home, you've done your bit with Alexa and I'm sure this will be nothing you can't handle, you're just worrying for nothing and if you think about it, you would have contacted him before leaving, wouldn't you"? She asked trying to pacify her friend.

"No not really, I don't want anything to do with him unless it's through our lawyers as to be truthful; we haven't anything to say to each other in my opinion".

As an afterthought Maria asked:

"Thinking about it, why didn't he contact Alexa if it was so important"?

"Now there's the thing, when he phoned up and asked to speak to me, Shelia said I wasn't there and would he like to speak to Alexa, to which he replied no, it was urgent and needed to speak to me, so I thought well he can go to hell and wait my time as I'd already got a flight booked to come out here and no way was he going to spoil my week away as I needed a break",

Maria could see Corry was hurting and therefore decided not to take the conversation on any longer as they both heard a car pulling up, knowing it was Marcus and as he walked in the first words were;

"I'll bet you've had a right catch up on all the gossip, well now it's my turn because I'm going to take you both out for the day starting with a shopping trip to Nicosia, then were meeting friends for cocktails and finishing off with a meal, so it's up to both of you to get your glad rags on and after my coffee I'll expect you to be ready in an hour" was his parting words as he left the villa temporarily.

Things are easily said than done for still Corry couldn't get that phone message out of her mind however she tried for it kept on going round and round in her head. Why after all this time did Jay need to speak to her urgently she thought, never had he tried to contact her before not even to enquire how his daughter was getting on, which in her opinion was more of an urgency than anything so why now, the only thing she could think was, he would be seriously ill, but then again that thought went out of her mind as he was a proud person and wouldn't have told her anyway, no whatever it was she sensed it was, a can of worms that was about to be opened.

The best thing would be, to block it out of her mind altogether for now was the time to have a little fun and relaxation with friends that she enjoyed spending time with, but all the same, there was no fooling Maria, she could see the torment in her face.

"We're all going to have the time of our lives today so get all dolled up while I go and change into something a little more suitable, I would suggest something rather bright and sexy, while I've got a nice little pale blue number I've been keeping for just the right occasion as knowing Marcus, he'll have pushed the boat out on entertaining us both today", Maria said leaving the villa for her friend to get ready.

Yes, Maria was right, she had to snap out of it otherwise she'd spoil the day for everyone.

Returning and with two heavenly dressed ladies waiting on the steps for him, Marcus felt so proud to be seen in such company as they drove off along the road heading to Nicosia.

Shopping first, which he didn't mind at all, coffee on the sidewalk with a couple of cream cakes to wet their appetite before meeting some old friends and acquaintances for cocktails, exchanging pleasantries while the drinks flowed at a steady pace.

By this time Corry was starting to forget her troubles and seemed to be enjoying herself that much even Maria wasn't worrying about her, and as dust started to fall they all headed off to a restaurant that had been pre-booked for the merriment to carry on, yes it was good to have friends like this that you could let your hair down with and so the night went on with her favourite dish being served which was Lamb cooked to perfection in cream sauce.

And with a little singing to the music in the background after the meal, it was with this, that everyone moved the tables back to have a bit of a rave with the throwing of the plates which was a Greek tradition, god only knows why as it made such a mess whereby they would be picking splinters of pot up for days but there you have it, some traditions never fade away, and this went on till early hours of the morning and therefore booking into a hotel seemed the only solution to any sleep at all before the drive back.

Now with Maria spending the night in the hotel with her long time gentleman friend, that left Corry in the position to be with Marcus on a night that was just made for love after such a wonderful day they'd all spent together.

But the night wasn't to be as fulfilled as expected, for as they reached the hotel room, Marcus started to be violently sick which was thought to be food poisoning as they rushed to the hospital to confirm this, but no it wasn't that at all it was in fact a poisoning from eating the paella that night which contained prawns, as a few others had been rushed in with the same symptoms. Never mind there would be many other nights where their relationship could celebrate their feelings for each other.

Up bright and early the next morning and with a drive back to the villa. Corry driving due to Marcus still feeling a little under the weather, it would be a day of relaxation to get his strength back, but by this time he had noticed there was something different about Corry, as now and again she would be so snappy with everyone which wasn't like her at all, but rather than question this action, he'd leave it alone, knowing she'd tell him when she was ready.

Arriving back at the villa, Maria went onto to her friend's place, while Marcus and Corry would enjoy a day relaxing by themselves taking in a light lunch and a walk along the beach to wash away the cobwebs before going into the village for a quite bite to eat that evening thus showing signs of togetherness as a couple which is what they'd been for quite a while now.

A few days past and still Corry was agitated, but had no intentions of giving in to her feelings as that would show a sign of weakness where Jay had won the battle, whatever the battle was, and she wasn't having any that, after all the pain he'd caused. Having worked so hard to build up an empire whose respect she'd definitely earned through hard work. she wasn't ready to lose it just on a whim to satisfy his urgent pleas. No he would have to wait her time she thought on this occasion, he'd had too much of his own way in the past.

To everyone else, it was quite clear, she'd never stopped loving Jay and for all his faults never would, but then again if the truth be known, he'd never stopped loving her, yes it was called male pride and he definitely had an abundance of that.

Well the week went by as Corry spent all her time either with Marcus or Maria as for some reason it seemed she didn't want to be on her own which in some ways was understandable. The problem was, she wouldn't let Marcus near enough to give any comfort to her let alone the intimacy of a loving relationship and under those circumstances, he sensed this immediately, therefore kept his distance knowing she was hurting for some reason, but couldn't ask for help as her pride would get in the way.

With all this on her mind she was determined not to do any work while out there for this was purely going to be a relaxing time although she'd attend a few meetings with the project management which she'd already set up in London before flying out. The project in question was an idea she'd had some years ago brought on by an incident she'd witnessed one day when walking down a road into Larnaca.

It was a brief meeting with a young boy, she'd found crying and distressed, that urged Corry to initiate this project, and one that was very close to her heart. All alone, this child sat by the roadside sobbing his little heart out and when stopped to enquire what the matter was, thinking to herself he'd probably lost something, looking up he replied;

"Dad's been made redundant due to the British Army pulling some of the troops out of Cyprus and now we won't have enough money for food as there's no more jobs on the island".

Now that sounded strange coming from a child no older than ten or eleven but as curiosity caught her attention, thought she'd look into it and see what could be done to help the situation if anything;

"Look don't worry sweetheart, I'll see what I can do to help your family, I'm sure you won't starve" she said smiling down with deep concern as she handed him some change and a large chocolate bar from her bag.

No Corry couldn't leave it at that for these people had been good to her, treating her like one of their own and therefore would look into what the child had told her. It didn't take long before she'd gathered all the information about the workforce being laid off from some of the camps nearby, whereby the child had been right in what he'd told her in a childlike fashion thus meaning. It would hit the local villages that relied on the work and with very little employment in sight, they'd be in for a hard time which bothered her immensely, now if only there was a way she could come up with an idea to help she thought.

It was a couple of days later when thinking quite seriously about this matter, there it was right in front of her, a brain wave of enthusiasm, a meeting in the town hall to discuss ways in which she could perhaps help was quickly arranged. The idea was, one of her companies would open a sawing factory on the island whereby it would be run by a management team, made up of both Cypriot and British staff for a period of time. Cyprus would manufacture the garments, London would organize the sales side, shipping them globally from Cyprus and yes it would work as over a five-year period the employees would then be able to take shares through their wage packets resulting in them taking over as a co-operative and therefore owning the company themselves after the said period of time had expired.

There would be agreements made whereby after the five-year period, the factory would only produce designs made for Corry's companies and therefore an exclusive clause would have to be added to safeguard all concerned.

Now this would give employment to the local people and should it take off to meet her expectations then it would not only benefit sales overseas whereby she'd go into the Middle East with new designs but maybe open other factories to help with the employment on the island. Determined to help these people in their time of need as they had helped her, she put into action the said proposals, carried them through, resulting in achieving her goal with the opening of five factories in as many years.

Corry had not only brought fashion to the island with the London designs but also made a large financial contribution to her own company before handing them over to the co-operatives, giving them financial achievement but also recognition as employers.

The project meetings were lengthy but that was mainly due to the fact she'd suggested, they start thinking about fashion shows on the island which would boost their sales and should that happen, they would come to an agreement whereby there would be a relaxation of the exclusive clauses, meaning they would be able to design with their own people under licence, this took time but like all matters, the end results had come in sight whereby their goodbyes were inevitable.

Back at the villa, still she couldn't relax although trying her hardest knowing there was something wrong back home and in the end this feeling would get the better of her until she couldn't take anymore and booked an early flight back to England. Braking the news to Marcus that she was to return to London early was upsetting for both of them, but at least he understood when she told him what had happened, realising it wasn't anything that he'd done to upset although he did have reservation as to what Jay was playing at with all this so called secrecy, for what he'd now come to know of this man, he wasn't a fan to say the least.

As they would spend the last night together before Corry departed, it was a romantic night out with a nice meal, few drinks to lighten the mood of her leaving the next afternoon and then a return to the villa where they shared a couple of glasses of champagne which was to celebrate a belated engagement of Alexa and Tam.

Retiring to bed that night, it was with a heavy heart that Marcus made love to Corry, knowing in the back of his mind that something dreadful was about to happen and no matter what he did, he was powerless to prevent it and so when sleep called upon them, it was Marcus that had a turbulent night.

As the light appeared through the morning dew, Corry awakened to Marcus caressing her tender body not knowing if this would be the last time he would have the love he so wanted in his arms before asking;

"Is this forever or will I never see you again for I have a feeling I'm losing you"?

"What on earth are you on about, I explained why I've got to return, it's because this situation is driving me mad and I've got to find out just what Jay's playing at and sort it out once and for all before he wrecks all of our lives as he's done in the past".

"Look, I'll be back when its sorted, then maybe we'll go away for a good holiday but first this has to be put to bed before it escalates, now shut up with such talk and make love to me".

Well what can a man do, with such a request from a beautiful woman as he obliged her wishes taking her to the upmost of erotic desire, making their bodies combine in one whole gratification, but with a lasting thought in his mind that he was about to lose her.

A light breakfast with her goodbyes to Maria as she'd popped round to see her before her and Marcus left for the airport, which again seemed to be painful for both of them knowing there was trouble brewing back in London with the situation that was outstanding with Jay.

It was the same at the airport when they said their goodbyes in each other's arms with a few tears that was to follow but it had to be done and therefore as she boarded the plane, it was with a heavy heart that she returned to London where Peter was waiting to pick her up from the airport.

 Not hardly talking but with hindsight Peter knew as well as Corry did, this man was only here to bring back painful memories and therefore the least said the best mended for it wouldn't be long now before the truth was out, having notified Shelia of her early return whereby a meeting with Jay had been set up immediately upon this.

Not being able to keep quiet for long Peter interrupted Corry's thoughts by saying;

"It's alright, Shelia's brought me up to speed with what's been happening between you and Jay, you should have told me about it, bet you've been out of your mind with worry as to what he's up to".

"Don't worry, whatever he wants, I can handle it, he can't hurt me anymore than he's hurt me in the past, so whatever he has to say that's so urgent then let it be" Corry remarked, with a smile on her face which told a different story, for she knew in her heart there was about to be trouble on the horizon.

"Well if you need help, you know we're all here for you, apparently he's to meet with you at eleven in the morning at your office, and now I'm going to take you for a bite to eat as you look exhausted", Peter added.

It was nice to be back on solid ground with all your friends around but they couldn't help what was going on inside your stomach as you seemed to choke on every little mouthful but none the less it won't be long before tomorrow and we can all settle down to a routine yet again Corry thought, knowing Peter was feeling the anxiety but trying not to show it.

That night Corry tossed and turned but couldn't get Jay out of her mind however she tried, if only things had been different between them, why did he have to spoil the dream that they both had, a perfect family for their love was solid, just because of a fling with a bit of a girl who was young enough to be his daughter, but there again that is the weakness in men.

Early to rise was the tonic of the day after a restless night, Corry now ready to take on anything that Jay had to throw at her she thought heading into the office that morning with intentions of a right showdown with him. And with the tension that had built up inside, she was ready to take on an army so to speak when Jay arrived for the meeting on time as he always was, no nothing had changed in that department.

The pleasantries were false as both Corry and Jay felt uneasy in the same room but whatever was coming had to be civil and knowing it would be hard as the love inside of him had never died, but in her case had turned to hate.

"Good morning, you haven't changed a bit; take a seat as coffee is already on the way". she said in a soft sensual voice. Yes, a little formal but then Corry had to keep her composure whatever the urgency was.

"Thank you its appreciated, as I think you'll need the coffee by what I've come to say, and may I add, not only have you done very well for yourself but you are more beautifully radiant than ever", Jay replied.

Coffee came but there was a hesitance in the air as Jay couldn't take his eyes off Corry, it was like going back to the first night they met in that bar in Cyprus, the bond that tied them together was still there on his part although they had both moved on.

Taking a mouthful of Coffee Jay looked across the desk at Corry and started to unfold the mystery that had wrecked her short break in Cyprus;

"There isn't any easy way to say what I'm about to tell you and with all my heart I wish it were different, but the truth is, I'm afraid Alexa can't be allowed to marry Tam, the wedding has to be called off".

"What on earth, are you talking about, who do you think you are, you've not seen our daughter for years and yet you have the audacity to walk into my office, yes my office and tell me she can't marry the man she loves" Corry screeched.

"Calm down and we'll talk about it" Jay said in a quiet voice.

"Calm down, who do you think you're talking to, telling me to calm down when I've brought our daughter up single handed with no help from you, listening to her crying for her father at nights when you've never even had the decency to keep in touch with he. No Jay you can go to hell whatever your reasons are" she said as her temper was now raging out of control.

"Shut up and listen for once in your life Corry, Alexa can't marry Tam as Tam is Alexa's blood brother" Jay said rather sharply.

"What the hell are you talking about, Tam is Alexa's brother, have you gone mad" Corry replied looking rather bewildered by the last comment from Jay.

"Right, I'll explain if you can shut up until I've finished, for I was as shocked as you are now. "

Although raging with temper Corry knew she had to listen to what he had to say as her head was now spinning, therefore started to calm down in an attempt to listen to some feeble excuse as she thought.

"It all started at university, I met this girl who was from a good family just like mine, we palled around in a crowd as everyone did in those days, but on her side she formed a bit of a crush on me. And to be honest I never thought she was anything special although my friends warned me she was a bit of a loner, in fact if I was honest I used her for sex when I wanted, knowing I could as she'd always be there to do what I wanted and when I wanted. Well you know the score; it's a man thing that you don't turn down when it's given as freely when you want it.

No she wasn't easy and never looked at anyone else in all that time, so it was easy game for me as she'd do anything I wanted her to, and before you but in, I'm not proud of that now, but all the same I have to admit, the sex was good, and as I said before, she would let me have it whenever I wanted, over the two years we were together in university, which is all that mattered at the time, well you know what university was like in those days", he stated.

"No, I don't know I had to work for a living, not being born with privileges and a silver spoon in my mouth" Corry replied in a defiant manner still raging inside.

Jay ignored that remark and carried on with the conversation for it wasn't going to be easy to explain when Corry was in this mood.

"It was after I left University and went out into the big wide world, eventually joining the Army, she on the other hand went back home and therefore we lost touch, she wasn't really my type, For I was ambitious and wanted to go out into the wide world and make something of myself, never knowing or even bothered about what ever happened to her, she was just a fling that I had in my youth as far as I was concerned. But it was when you and I split up that I started to drink heavily for a period of time, I just couldn't let you go and yet I couldn't get you back as my stupid pride wouldn't allow me to.

This had gone on for a while, when one night, I attended a friend's birthday party, bumping into some old school friends who couldn't wait to have a go at me for leaving her holding the baby so to speak. That was the very first I'd heard of it and so felt it my duty to go and find out for myself if this was in fact true knowing what rumours were in those days. For her part, she'd never stopped loving me, had my son and with the help of her parents brought him up, a fine boy, well-educated but never the less I couldn't really take to him as too much water had passed under the bridge by then".

Taking a deep breath before carrying on;

"She was still a sweet mild mannered girl, just like she was all those years ago, a little mouse maybe but still on her own, I suppose I felt a little guilty at that time, maybe a moment of weakness, I can't answer that truthfully for I still couldn't get over you and maybe thought I would settle for what seemed second best, what I did think at that time was, she'd sacrificed her life in bringing up our son, then it was now my turn to bring a little happiness and a duty to stay with her.

Don't get me wrong, yes we were happy in a way, spending time together but it was more of a brother/sister relationship in many ways as I did my own thing and had affairs on the side, making sure that she never found out for I wouldn't want to hurt her as she'd been hurt enough through me. But in all that time, I can honestly say, I thought about you and Alexa every day, for ours was a love you just don't put to bed and walk away, it was a love that goes on till the end of time which had been broken by my stupid adultery.

And, I know what you're going to say, but I'm afraid your wrong this time for the women I went with was out of lust and nothing else, just to get you out of my system, although even that didn't work, for after I'd used them it was her bed that I returned to knowing she was a comfort that I relied upon whenever I pleased whereby there was no feelings involved, it was just company and sex. So you see that's why they can never get married or be together."

Corry was just speechless for this in her eyes was another act of betrayal.

"I'm sorry but I honestly didn't know about Tam and when I found out, it never even entered my head that he would one day meet Alexa "

"And how much of your past does your son know or haven't you told the story of our marriage to him?"

The simple reply to that question was:

"No for it was none of his business".

Corry was numb as words wouldn't appear from the silence, how on earth was she going to break the news to her daughter and what could she say for it was such a mess that had been created, and for once it wasn't Jay's fault entirely.

Looking over at Jay, the silence was deafening for neither of them could speak, it was only when Sheila knocked and walked in the office that the silence broke as she said;

"Alexa has been on the phone and said can you call her back soon as possible, she needs to speak with you urgently over the wedding plans, I told her you were with an important client and couldn't be disturbed at the moment".

Corry smiled with a hurtful look on her face asking;

"Would you do me a favour Shelia, just ring Alexa back and ask her to come into my office straight away as need to see her urgently".

Although Sheila was worried at this request, she could see the pain in Corry's face and just replied.

"Will do that straight away, is there anything else I can do to help".

"No thanks, just get us another couple of strong coffee's will you please".

There wasn't any need in prolonging the truth of this matter so the sooner it was all out, the better for everyone concerned Corry thought but how the hell was she was going to explain all of this to her daughter, god only knows. By now, Jay was just sat there staring into space not knowing what was coming next when to his surprise Corry said out loud'.

"Look this is all of your making and therefore you're the one that's got to tell your daughter the mess you've created as I honestly don't know where to start".

It was then that Sheila rang to say that Alexa would meet her mother in the little restaurant down the road in about an hour's time, to which Corry's reaction was;

"You're not getting out of this, you're coming with me to sort all this mess out and tell her yourself so you'd better get used to the idea as she's your daughter as well as mine and it's about time you stood up to your responsibilities and sorted this out as you should have done when you found out that you had another child".

Jay looked over at Corry in such admiration that she felt the love from him as she'd done when they were together those first years, love that had never really died between them in many ways.

They didn't have long to wait at the restaurant before Alexa entered singing her head off in such a happy mood not noticing her mother and father at all as she shouted out to the owner;

"Roberto have you seen my mother today".

"Yes, they're both at the table in the corner", he replied.

Both in the corner what on earth is he on about she thought, walking over to the small secluded table situated at the back of the restaurant, this was until she heard a voice which stopped her, in her tracks, yes a voice that was embedded in her brain since she was a small child, no this can't be she thought as she froze then suddenly coming to her senses shrieked.

"Daddy is that really you, oh my god it really is you, where have you been, why haven't you been in touch, when did you get back, I've missed you so much," all these words were coming out of her mouth but none of them making sense as she clung to Jay with all the strength she had not, daring to let him go.

Corry just sat there staring at them both, not daring to move an inch as she was heartbroken at what she was seeing, until all of a sudden Jay grabbed Alexa's arm pushing her away gently and said;

"Sit down darling and I'll explain everything to you rationally".

"Oh daddy you've come back for my wedding, I just knew you would when you heard about it, I've loads to tell you, I'm getting married to the most wonderful man in the world and I know you will learn to love him just as much as we all love him" Alexa blurted out.

"All in good time darling, but first of all I have to tell you, that I've never stopped loving both you and your mother in all this time and I'm so proud of what you have both achieved in your careers. I don't think there is a father in the world who could be any prouder than I am of you, but what I have to tell you now breaks my heart as much as it will break yours" Jay said with a sadness in his face;

"Whatever it is, it can't be as bad as the day we all parted at the airport in Berlin for that I will never forget" Alexa said quite sternly.

Corry was mysteriously quite in all of this as Alexa observed, but as she was in her own little world, this was her moment when father and daughter got back together so she was going to just sit it out and then attempt to pick up the pieces when these two worlds collided.

"I understand that you've got engaged to a prominent Barrister and have now set a date for the wedding darling" Jay asked quite sympathetically.

"Yes, and you Daddy will give me away" Alexa said with a beaming smile all over her face.

"Sorry darling, but I'm afraid you can't marry him" Jay stated quite adamantly.

"What do you mean I can't marry him, of course I can marry him, were engaged, what's to stop us, were old enough to know our own minds having lived together for a couple of years, and know all we need to know about one another, I don't see the problem Alexa replied quite sharply.

"As I've said, you can't get married as you don't know enough about one another, and that's final" jay said quite harshly.

Alexa looked over at her mother for some kind of explanation but nothing was forthcoming as Corry's face was drained by now,

"Mother, tell him, please tell him, he can't just walk back into our lives and tell me what to do after all this time" she screeched. But all the same she'd not finished yet as she turned to her father and cried out.

"Well, seen as you're the expert in all matters and know him better than I do, tell me why we can't get married in your opinion"

With such sadness in his face Jay looked straight at his daughter before answering that question in short but shocked words;

"Tam is your brother".

"What on earth are you on about" Alexa asked.

"I'm Tams father by blood, his mother was my girlfriend when we were at university and when I left to join the army she was pregnant with Tam and I didn't find this out until some years later after your mother and I divorced.

And although we're now together, it's a relationship of convenience and not love as your mother is the only woman that I have ever truly loved".

All of a sudden Alexa thought back to what Tam had told her a couple of years previously about his father, and all of a sudden it started to make sense. Oh my god what a mess she thought to herself, and what will happen when Tam finds out as there was still a lot more to come.

The room went quite when all of a sudden Jay broke the ice by suggesting that Alexa go to Cyprus for a while, where he'd explain everything to Tam as not to cause any more distress to his daughter.

"So you think that's the best way forward, do you daddy?" Alexa asked in such a sarcastic tone, not realising how headstrong his daughter was at times.

"Yes, darling I do, your mother and I will explain everything to Tam and if he loves you as much as I think he does then he'll see that's the best way of helping you get over this dreadful mess".

Calculating but calmly and with a defiance that Corry was aware of in her daughter's attitude, Alexa stood up looking at both her parents for a short while before choosing her words wisely;

"And are you also going to tell Tam that he is about to father the child I'm now carrying in approximately four months or is that something else you can just sweep under the carpet and pretend isn't going to happen ".

Well the shock that run through the air was electrifying for both Corry and Jay, for this isn't what they expected at all, not even Tam was aware of the news that he was shorty to become a father.

"And before anyone can suggest any other, I'm definitely going to keep our baby so with all the suggestions in the world, someone had better come up with another idea as I've no intentions of listening to either of you, for as I see it, between the two of you my life has been ruined" Alexa said calmly walking out of the restaurant.

Corry who had been silent through the last hour was still speechless until Jay said;

"Look I'm staying at the Grosvenor House hotel for a few days till all this mess can be sorted out and Alexa can get her head round things, I think it best, I pick you up tonight and we have dinner, maybe we can talk this over and come to some compromise that will see them through the situation, even if it's only temporarily until the baby's born".

"That's fine, Corry replied, "pick me up around seven", not thinking clearly about what she'd agreed to, as at that moment in time nothing made sense, she seemed to be in a world of her own knowing her daughter wasn't going to take the news laying down and would fight to get her own way r whatever Jay suggested.

What a day and it wasn't over yet, for Corry couldn't settle, she tried to do a little work in the office, keeping out of the way of everyone except for Shelia, but still couldn't concentrate, not knowing how to handle the situation, she turned to Issa who had already heard Alexa's side of the story, knowing if anyone could help it would be her.

Issa thought the best thing to do was leave everything alone for a couple of days letting things calm down so that Alexa and Tam could talk, she on the other hand would keep an eye on her, but by all accounts there would be no change of mind as she was determined that her and Tam was not going to split up whatever the consequences were.

At least that was one less worry for Corry; if Issa was to keep an eye on Alexa for now it would be wise to take into consideration Alexa's health being pregnant.

Approaching seven and dressed in a little black dress with court shoes to match, Corry looked stunning to say the least as Jay arrived to collect her for a meal that evening. She wasn't in the mood to go out at all but thought a few drinks would make her relax whereby things may look clearer in the morning, although it never even dawned on her, she'd forgot to contact Marcus and let him know what had happened.

Knowing he would be worried but that was the last thing on her mind at present for her head was now spinning ten to the dozen and therefore, she'd contact him the next morning with all the news of what had gone off;

"Where are we going" Corry asked as she got into the taxi.

"Oh I thought we'd eat at the Grosvenor, well you always liked the food there and it's so convenient" jay replied.

"Yes, that will be great, not been there for a while as never seem to get the time lately" Corry answered.

"May I say you look absolutely stunning tonight, mind you always did", Jay remarked as they got out of the taxi.

Corry just let that remark go as she wasn't really in any mood for compliments.

"Look, if you'd rather eat somewhere else you only have to name it as I'm totally at your disposal and after today's events, only want to have a relaxing evening in good company" Jay said grinning like a Cheshire cat, knowing that remark would bring a smile on Corry's face even in this situation.

"No honestly the Grosvenor is fine as you know darn well I love it here, so stop making a fuss about nothing; I'm not in the mood for your wise cracks tonight"

Fine it was, as the meal was excellent, the conversation was flawless as it flowed between them both and the champagne well I'm sure that was good the way that Corry was knocking it back, which to be truthful was understandable in the situation. Jay knew very well what he was doing, knowing full well Corry's one weakness was good champagne, it only took a couple of glasses and she'd be on a high, in a mood of devilment throwing all her trouble to the wind.

To an outsider, they just looked as though they were a couple of middle aged love birds out for a romantic evening but inside they were both hurting for different reasons, his was the thought of what he'd lost in the love of this woman, while her thoughts were, of what her daughter was suffering at this moment in time.

The night went on as the relaxing mood was highlighted by Corry getting tipsier and when that happened there would only be one outcome, she would either get very romantically sensual or stroppy, wanting to argue with everyone and tonight was no different for the look on her face was a look of sadness and love for her daughter which no one could mistake.

"I think you've had enough to drink young lady, it's about time we called it a night, as you're not in any fit state to go home, you'd better stay here with me" Jay suggested helping her up as they walked towards the lift, knowing that when she was like this, there wouldn't be a care in the world on her part.

The intentions were to put Corry to bed and let her sleep it off while he slept on the chair and therefore as they reached the room, he swept her up in his arms gently laying her on the bed before adding;

"Come on you've not got anything I haven't seen before so let's have your clothes off before you spoil them" as she glanced up to see no emotional expression on his face at all but there again that was Jay not showing his feelings as usual, no nothing had changed.

"Take them off then, and see if I care" she said in a mimicking voice

Now there was no reasoning with Corry when she was in this mood, so he disrobed her as requested, leaving her naked on the sheets in front of him and what a naked site it was, for she had not changed at all since the last time he'd set eyes on that body he thought.

Looking down at her tantalizing sleek naked body in front of him, he could feel the old sensation that was erupting down below, the sense that his body was now on fire for what he'd missed all these past years, a sensation of lust, passion and need all rolled into one which was getting harder to fight being transfixed into a frenzy of growing lust.

This wasn't just a woman scorned but a woman who was revengeful and, knew her own mind as to what she wanted and how she was going to make him pay for what he'd done to her over the years that she'd suffered through his stupid actions back in Berlin. Corry was in all her glory for she could now get her own back for all the pain and suffering he'd caused the day she found him in bed with that young girl.

"Come on then, take it, as you know you won't be able to keep your hands off me for much longer, but then again I'm going to show you what you've been missing all this time without me" she said being quite sober and knowing he couldn't resist as he disrobed.

Now was maybe her chance to get her own back, for the suffering and humiliation she'd endured and when it was all said and done, it was only sex with vengeance in her eyes, even though it may be enjoyable for the time being. No, she definitely knew what she was doing, seeing Jay who was stood over her quite naked with such a strong erection, starting to caress her tingling body as he moved her onto her stomach, mounting her from the back violently as he came with such a powerful force inside. Their bodies soaking together as Jay turned Corry over to face him with the intention of recharging his energy to make love in a more passionate way this time as she asked rather sarcastically;

"No one has ever been able to take my place then?"

"You know darn well the answer to that without even asking, no one can turn me on and satisfy me like you can" was the reply.

She had waited a long time for that answer, they say that time is a healer but revenge is far sweeter where a woman scorned is concerned.

Jay never liked admitting he was wrong but in this case knew that Corry was the only woman he'd truly loved and if there was the slightest chance of starting afresh, he'd take it with open arms whatever the cost, even accounting for the humiliation that he'd have to endure and therefore willing to accept at any cost.

Knowing she had the upper hand, she instructed him to lay flat on his back, then positioned her wet open legs on his luscious mouth ordering him to suck her clitoris until the warm sticky juice flowed down the back his throat adding;

"You may then take me slowly whichever way you want, but you will make a night of it as you have a lot of making up to do".

Although Jay never liked taking orders from anyone at least not from a woman as he thought it was humiliating, but in this case he did exactly what she said, wanting to please her in every way he could, if there was the slightest hope of winning her back. Not only did his tongue tease her opening canal but with the suction being so strong it wasn't long before she came to his delight.

"Now how would you like me to make real love to you as I should have done all those wasted years, for all I want to do is pleasure you to the heights of eternity" he stated.

It didn't matter what Jay said, it mattered what he was doing right now for Corry felt as though she was in a time capsule that had travelled back to the night in Cyprus when they first met, to imagine that period in her life was one thing but to experience it all over again was another, this was the real Jay she'd met that night and fell in love with.

Oh what a fool he'd been, a strong willed male who for a flight of fancy, had ruined not only his life but all those around, could he perhaps put all this heartache right and walk away knowing he'd hurt so many people yet again or should he be so selfish as to stay and try and put his feelings to the fore he thought.

Whatever the answer to that, would have to come later, as tonight was a night like no other and the chance he had been given, was going to be taken for the love of the only woman that he'd ever cared for, and with this in mind he would attempt to show his feeling by reaching out his hands onto her smooth body and working their way to those pert nipples he'd dreamt of so many times in the past, the succulent taste of the tips as they entered his mouth wanting to be controlled by him alone, yes this is where he felt comfort, as the quiver's shot through his loins like a bullet looking for its target. He'd had women that would satisfy his needs but none of them could turn him on with little teasing habits like she could, for he wanted to be deep inside with that throbbing erection but not to be selfish, knowing it was her appetite he had to fulfil before he could ask for satisfaction himself.

Taking her in his arms he held her tightly as he whispered;

"Just look at the time we've wasted, I noticed you've got a diamond ring on your finger but he can't give you the love that I can, and if he did try, it wouldn't be precipitated for I know you too well, you wouldn't be here with me if you loved him, as you love me".

Corry wasn't in any kind of mood to answer those questions and why should she, for she was the one who was betrayed, therefore that conversation would be left for another day.

Not one to show her feeling even though it made sense what he'd just said, as her hand slowly slithered down to the tip of his penis while it started to leak all over her hand knowing he was under her spell for the time being. Lowering herself on top of this huge manhood she started to grind her inner body round it until she could feel the throbbing of this large member inside of her, the swelling that was giving her so much enjoyment. Yes, Marcus was good the way he made love to her and she did love him but with Jay it was a different kind of love for she was in love with him or was it revenge that she was experiencing that night as forgiveness wasn't in her vocabulary.

And with the feeling that he was almost ready for exploding, but knowing from experience that he would hold back as long as he could before he filled her body with his hot juices, therefore taking advantage of this knowledge, she moved her body in every angle to get her pleasures but all the same Jay was no fool as he swung her round to fall flat onto her back while pushing her legs up around his shoulders as he mounted her with such force.

"Come on Corry, I know you too well and know that you like it deep inside, that deep that you can feel my sperm shoot up inside your body, for there's plenty of that coming your way I can assure you" Jay whispered, as he pushed up that deep inside, she could feel her stomach explode with both pain and pleasure screaming out in exoteric bliss.

Falling asleep in each other's arms seemed so natural but waking up the next morning was to be quite a shock for reality was to set in and that's where the real trouble was to start, for Alexa and Tam would never accept Corry and Jay getting back together. there had been too much heartache caused and she wasn't prepared to lose her daughter with such an action.

Still, Jay wasn't going to give up without a fight, that wasn't in his nature and as he looked over at Corry lying flat, he couldn't resist one last look, that look became so possessed, his manhood rose to the attention of her body, wanting to be inside of that wondrous cave it knew so well, a perfect fit to bring them both the satisfaction they were craving for by now as the eruption of fluids came in abundance, while looking lovingly at Corry, he whispered,

"Well darling, I think it's about time we made a move and faced the music".

Tears rolling down her face Corry blurted out.

"Look Jay none of what happened last night can come out, well not at the moment for the situation's so explosive I don't know which way to turn, and if any of this reached Alexa I'm afraid I'd lose her for good, we also have to consider she is carrying our grandchild".

Jay looked so bewildered at that remark; even he didn't know what to do next but not wanting to antagonise the situation, totally agreed with her, thinking to himself, what else could he do but just go along with her suggestion, knowing she was right as far as the baby was concerned.

"We can't let her down again, she's the most important person in all of this, but you do realise I want you back and I'm willing to do everything in my power to achieve this" he said in a meaningful voice.

Corry didn't have to be told this as she knew in her heart that's what they both wanted but life isn't that simple as they were to find out, for too much water had passed under the bridge for both of them, perhaps if his pride and stubbornness had not got in the way years ago, things may have been different. But with the situation as it stood at the moment, they had to be careful and take other people's feelings into consideration.

Therefore, with such an explosive situation at hand, it was decided they would have to both face the day in different directions whereby;

Jay was to return to the country and break the news that he was moving back to London to sort his life out, for he could no longer live a lie, being with someone that he only loved in a sisterly way, and being considerate, he would further explain, that although there were complications in London with his daughter, he had decided moving there for all his business interests which would be the most sensible idea. Knowing this would cause a lot of heartache he then went on to say that he wanted to be on his own, for things weren't working out as a family man.

He knew Tam would be pleased at this decision as he'd never accepted Jay as a father figure and always had an inkling; there was a dark side to him. Corry on the other hand, had to talk to Alexa but that wasn't going to be easy either for she had the same stubborn streak in her as Corry herself and knowing the only person who would be able to get through to her daughter would be Issa. Therefore, it may be a better to approach the situation through her, but again, that was another thing, for Issa herself would be on Alexa's side and would probably go against any idea where Jay was concerned.

And so it was going to be total bedlam, and that's before anyone knew the whole truth about Jay, what a mess all this was Corry thought.

In the meantime, Alexa had broken the news about their father to Tam who had taken it with his casual self-control although seething inside, yes it was heart-breaking news for him for he adored Alexa and couldn't ever imagine life without her, but with news about the baby, well this situation wasn't going to be easy although he was an ecstatically proud father to be who couldn't help but show his emotions as he broke down crying.

It was decided that a meeting would be arranged between Corry, Alexa, Tam, Issa and Rob to sort this mess out although there wasn't any mention of Jay at this point for that would definitely antagonized the situation and they didn't want to risk upsetting Alexa any more than could be helped, with her being pregnant, they had to think of her health which was paramount at this stage.

With both Issa and Rob present, it was thought that they would be impartial and therefore see the situation in a clear light with maybe one or two solutions in view and therefore a couple of days later when they all met up at Corry's place, the atmosphere was frosty to say the least but knowing this mess had to be sorted out one way or the other, it had to be done even though it was strained for everyone.

Issa was there as the peacekeeper as well as trusted friend to all but whatever was suggested, it would be Alexa who had the last word for she wasn't going to budge on anything that was suggested, it was her way or no way she stated adamantly;

"I will stay engaged, won't get married, have my baby, carry on with my career, run the business myself with my staff and should you all want to be in my child's life then you will have to abide by this decision", Alexa proclaimed all in one breath.

Looking at Tam who had not said a word at all but in deep thought, Alexa went on to say;

"And if you don't agree with my proposal, then I'm afraid it's over between us and you'll never see my child ever".

Everyone just sat staring at Alexa who was not only stubborn but when she'd set her mind on something she'd fight through hell and high water to achieve her goal, for It wasn't any good trying to talk to her, knowing she was on her high horse and nobody was going to topple her off it.

She definitely had Yorkshire blood in her veins, showing everyone how she could do this on her own, should the need be just like her Mother had done many years ago when she returned to carry on the business after the split with her father. Only in Alexa's case she also had her father's blood, and that would be to destroy anyone who stood in her way.

Meeting over and everything agreed, that was going to be the way as Alexa wasn't going to budge, now it was time for Tam to break the news to his mother before anyone else could tell her for she'd been hurt so many times in her life and he wasn't going to add to them if it could be helped.

The problem was, how was he going to start and explain how Alexa and him couldn't bring up their own baby as man and wife but little did he know, that his own father had broken the news that he was returning to London beforehand. What a mess, no one could ever imagine what the future would hold, for not only the unborn child but also everyone around who was trying to protect the situation. Still someone had to be sensible enough to sort it out for the good of all and that someone happened to be Tam who was the most level headed man you could ever wish to meet.

Taking the bull by the horns he piped up and stated quite categorically what was to happen in the future and there would be no argument as Alexa would carry on living with him at his apartment until the baby arrived, after that they would buy a new place in the city for the three of them and commute to York, so they could at least live as a family in private.

This would be his baby as much as it was Alexa's and therefore he had to plan for the future as a family unit, there would be no more talk of them splitting up and would deal with each and every problem together should it arise.

A few weeks later where everything had been sorted in accordance to Alexa's demands things quietened down to a certain degree, although it was at this time that a big showdown between Tam and Jay happened whereby they never spoke after that as Tam naturally took the side of his mother who was devastated at Jay's leaving, but luckily she never knew the real reason why he'd left and never would as not a word was spoken over the relationship.

Now Alexa thought it only fair she should meet Tams' mother with compassion for the trouble her own father had caused, awkward as it may be, she was going to be a grandmother and therefore putting it into prospective, it was the most decent decision.

But after meeting with his mother for the first time when all the trouble had come to the fore, Alexa's impression of her was, one weak woman who had been spoilt all her life and didn't live in the real world although she never voiced this opinion in front of Tam.

What Alexa couldn't get her head round was the fact; she couldn't understand what her father had seen in this plain and weak woman, yes she was what you would expect so far as being well bred and a really lovely lady that made them all welcome but definitely wasn't her father's type at all, but then again she didn't know the full story about her father using her for his own pleasures.

Corry had gone quite, over this period, having returned to Cyprus a few times on business whereby meeting up with Marcus, it wasn't the same as he'd picked up on this straight away, thinking it was all to do with Alexa's pregnancy, not realising Jay was now back on the scene in the city and had in fact purchased a large property in Kensington, where he and Corry would meet a couple of nights a week without anyone being any the wiser.

Funny really, but as Lar's was never far out of Corry's mind at that time, if only they'd got married then perhaps none of this would have been so bad, for Lar's was such a strong character and where Alexa was concerned, he would have made sure Jay wouldn't have been able to return to upset the apple cart. Yes, we all think about the what if's and this could have been a far better outcome for all, as Jay wouldn't have stayed in the country with Tam hating his father so much.

Issa and Rob stayed in the background awaiting the fallout of the situation when it finally came to a head for there wasn't any more they could do but wait to pick up the pieces of those they loved so much, especially Alexa as she was like a daughter to them. It must be said at this stage; the business didn't suffer at all, in fact, it become stronger with everyone running on adrenalin trying to ward off outside influences.

To the outside world, there was no change both in business and also personal lives of all concerned, but then again they were all professional people and never showed their feelings to anyone outside of their own little group.

By now Corry was playing a dangerous game for when she was in Cyprus she would be with Marcus and when back in London it would be with Jay. Perhaps she was torn by the past and the present for she never really got over Jay although she'd never forgive him, but with Marcus, well she loved him in so many ways as he helped her sanity when at a low ebb, it is also said, the respect Corry had for this fine standing Greek God was beyond reproach as he'd always been there for her through thick and thin.

But combining all of this, it was Lars that would have given her everything as he was the selfless soul that loved not only her but also her daughter whom he regarded as his own. All he asked was Corry's love and for that he would have been satisfied and would have gone to the ends of the earth to look after her.

The only person who knew about this situation was Maria in Cyprus and Karen in London, knowing full well that neither of them would breath a word to anyone although both of them individually had tried to tell Corry she was playing a dangerous game and Jay would only end up hurting her again in some way, or was it that she wanted revenge? Marcus loved the bones off her and if he found out, would have accepted the situation just to have her with him when possible, so in her eyes she wasn't doing any harm knowing that, but if it came out about her and Jay then Alexa would probably never speak to her again and therefore couldn't risk that ever happening so to the outside world things were just progressing slowly.

Alexa sailed through the pregnancy although she wouldn't slow down where work was concerned; she had to be at the helm of everything just like her mother with Tam keeping an eye on every move fear she would overdo it. Although having the house in York, it was only at weekends they managed to break free and spend time up there in what they called their little Love Nest, due to the fact they lived together as though nothing had ever happened, which to them, nothing had happened for love is a healer when the heart is in trouble.

Now it was at this time that Alexa started to soften with her feelings towards her mother as she never blamed her for the ongoing trouble her father had caused. Therefore, once a week they would get together for lunch whereby they could discuss not only work but also her pregnancy.

Now it was on one of these day's when out to lunch, Corry noticed Alexa didn't seem her usual self, drawn, pale and lethargic with no sparkle in her eyes, there was definitely something wrong but rather than say anything, she'd wait till Alexa mentioned it, but with a mother's instinct, couldn't keep quiet for too long before asking her daughter that vital question;

"What's the matter darling, are you feeling alright as you really do look a little pale, is there something troubling you, is it the baby,"?

"I honestly don't know but since yesterday, just can't stop crying, don't know why I'm crying but it seems as though my heart's braking for some reason, my chest is so tight that I keep getting spasms and can't breathe, and you won't like this, but I can't stop thinking about my father" Alexa said with tears rolling down her face. I know you still hate him and I don't like him at this moment in time but I do still love him you know; he is still my daddy whatever happens"

Corry looked at her daughter with such pain and admiration before saying;

"Listen darling, that's natural at this stage of your pregnancy as your hormones are all mixed up, your body is fighting what you're going through, but don't worry it will sort itself out when its ready and everything will be ok you watch, so don't worry your silly little head as its going to be alright", which was to be Corry's famous last words looking at her daughter. As a relaxed look came across Alexa's face so did an acute expression of pain and fear as she doubled up in agony;

"What's the matter Alexa" Corry screeched.

"I think I've wet my nickers" she answered looking down on the floor to the start of a dribble and then a gush of water falling down her legs into a pool of uncontrollable water breakage.

It was at that precise moment a waiter rushed over to the table having realised what had happened;

"Don't worry, someone is already calling for an ambulance as we speak so they won't be long, is there anything I can get you" he added handing a clean towel to Alexa to help save her embarrassment.

"No that will be fine" Corry muttered as she comforted her daughter with an expression of concern.

In true fashion for a lady in such circumstances, the ambulance arrived in record time whisking both mother and daughter to hospital.

Corry tried her upmost to contact Tam but as he was in court, had to leave a message with the usher who promised to tell him at the earliest of opportunities, which would be a surprise as Alexa was a couple of weeks early and there'd not been any signs of discomfort in the previous days. Well as usual, babies don't come to order they arrive when it's convenient to them and not to anyone else, as in this case.

It was some two hours later that Tam arrived at the hospital, just in time to be told that he had a beautiful baby boy which had been delivered a matter of minutes before. Alexa had gone through a really rough time, and in the end had to be put to sleep as the baby was born in the breach position which meant he'd come into the world feet first with the help of doctors who had assisted the birth. Yes, she had a bad time but afraid there was more bad news to follow as with the complications at birth they had to operate and give her a full hysterectomy, meaning she couldn't have any more children.

Corry. knew this would come as a shock to her daughter as Alexa had talked about having a second baby so that the two could grow up close together and not be an only child as she'd been, but never the less it seems that things only happen for a reason, however heart-breaking it seems at the time, and obviously this was one of those unfortunate times.

Tam on the other hand was elated at the fact he had a son, also Alexa had come though it safely, for now he had the two loves in his life and therefore nothing else mattered to him. It was now getting to be the trend that you could adopt children as the snobbery had been put to rest in this matter, so in the future should they wish a daughter then they would look at proceedings whereby they could do this through the authorities.

As Corry had been with her daughter all through the labour, seeing the traumatic birth, her thoughts were, as long as they were both alright, that's all that mattered. Now Alexa, that was a different matter for when she came round from the anaesthetics they sensed there was something wrong for she didn't want to see the baby, all she wanted was Tam and her mother.

It's all right the hospital staff assured everyone, sometimes this happens if they've had a bad time and their body was still adjusting, a couple of days and she'll be alright loving her son so much she won't be able to put him down.

No, this wasn't going to happen in this case for Alexa wasn't going to take to the child at all and I would go as far as to say, she rejected him totally, telling her mother to take him.

The final day arrived when Alexa was to be discharged from the hospital, and I'm afraid she still hadn't changed her mind about the baby, therefore it was suggested by Tam, that Corry should take him back to her place for a while until Alexa was well enough to take charge, for his priority was his beautiful wife who needed him the most and knowing the baby would be well cared for by Corry for the time being, he wouldn't be worried in the least.

Now although Corry managed to see her daughter on a daily basis, nothing was mentioned about the child as she thought Alexa would ask when she was ready, knowing the pain her daughter had gone through, maybe it was her way of letting the body heal as nature intended, for if we ourselves haven't gone through these things then how can we criticize others that have.

A couple of weeks passed by, when one day Corry asked Alexa cautiously about the registration of the child, as time was passing by so quickly and therefore he had to be named and registered by law, for up to that moment the baby was always referred to as tiddly winks and the poor little mite had to have a name.

But quite unexpected and out of the blue an outburst came from Alexa to her Mother;

"Oh you can name him whatever you like as far as I'm concerned for I've no feelings for him what so ever, so just change the subject".

Corry was heartbroken at that statement but still tried to keep her composure as not to show real feelings towards the situation, Alexa still in a state of shock and trauma and therefore it was rather a sensitive question, yet one that had to be answered for the sake of all concerned as Tam had enough on his plate with handling the everyday things without the worry of what seemed a trivial matter like a name.

"Look you just choose a name or have you already got one in mind and I'll go to the Registry Office and sort everything out with Tam, Corry said softly as not to upset her daughter who was still in what you would call a fragile state of depression.

"How about Lars as a name, for that sounds alright to me", she said with a mocking attitude, knowing that it would upset her mother.

"No I don't think that's appropriate in the circumstances, do you." was Corry's reply.

"Just name him what you want, you choose a name, anything but James as I definitely don't want him named after my father" Alexa 'stated quite sharply.

It was only when Corry arrived at the register office with a letter of intention from her daughter stating permission to register the child's name, that a name came to her, a name that had been going round in her head since the child was born, so that would be the boy's name, Jilles Hirst, and he would be called Jay for short.

That was a beautiful name but no one knew where it had come from, some people speculated that it was the child's grandfather 's Christian name as everyone called him Jay but that couldn't be any further from the truth for the only person that really knew, was Corry herself and maybe her friend Karen. Tam quite liked this name as it was unusual but then again he was more concerned about what was happening to Alexa than the baby being so worried about her sinking deeper into a depression whereby nothing seemed to get through to her.

Jay on the other hand took every opportunity to see the baby as he'd always wanted a son with Corry but afraid that was never to be.

Time was now starting to pass so quickly and coming up to the three months after the birth of Jilles when Corry took an unexpected phone call from her daughter stating that she was to visit the apartment in order to discuss a new line which was running through her head.

Now Corry was quite taken back by this call as Alexa rarely discussed her ideas with her, if she needed to discuss anything to do with the business; it was usually Issa she went to. And so this seemed a little strange, wanting to visit the apartment knowing the baby would be there, but on the other hand only too pleased that at least she was coming out of her shell having been back at work for a couple of weeks by now, and therefore agreed to the request.

The one thing that Corry wasn't going to do was hide the baby away even though Alexa had never seen him since he was born; in fact she'd never even held him as he'd been with Corry all the time. Now a couple of days later, Alexa came to see Corry with a large bouquet of yellow roses.

"Just thought I'd bring these around as a thank you for all you've done for us and also run an idea pass you about a new line I'm thinking of starting" Alexa said, with no mention of the baby what so ever.

"Thank you darling, that was very thoughtful of you" Corry said as she took the flowers, walked into the kitchen, adding,

"Maybe you'd like a coffee and a nice piece of your favourite cake while you're here".

"Yes that would be nice, as thought I'd go into work for a couple of hours later on so as to finish a little paperwork off before getting down to a few designs to keep me busy" she shouted to her mother.

This was a real surprise to hear Alexa in such good spirits as it seemed she was quite enthusiastic about the new line she was working on; maybe it was a sign of her getting better at last Corry thought.

Now the next move was going to be interesting, as Jilles was in his crib in the corner of the room gurgling his little heart away with Corry having no intentions of moving him, so taking her time in making the coffee, she left her daughter and grandson in the same room for some ten minutes or so, and with no sound in the air other than the baby gurgling. When eventually entering the lounge to see Alexa sat on the settee with Jilles in her arms, loving him with so much love and affection as you'd do naturally, being a mother of a small child. But not wishing to disturb the moment, put the coffee tray down and just looked in admiration at her daughter knowing the time had come when she'd finally returned to her old self, leaving the depression behind her;

"Oh isn't he the most beautiful baby you've ever seen mother, and just look at him smiling, do you think he will ever be able to forgive me for not wanting him when he was born" she asked as tears rolled down her face.

"Of course he will, you weren't yourself, you were very ill at the time and we all knew when you came out of this depression you'd love him as we all do" Corry replied with a smile of satisfaction on her face while adding;

"It's now time you took your son home to be with you and Tam and whatever arrangements you may come to, for its now time to build bridges for everyone and especially for your son because he is the most precious thing you will ever have, you don't realise just how proud we are of you, and especially me".

"Yes Mother, I think your right but I'm afraid I'm going to need your help to do that for I can't do it on my own, as I don't really know anything about babies so if you wouldn't mind? I honestly don't know what I'd have done without you these last few months, and can't thank you enough for standing by us all, oh by the way, where have you got the name Jilles from as I absolutely love it having never heard it before".

Corry just smiled with the intention of changing the subject as she replied

"Oh it's just a name of someone I once knew".

This answer never got a question after it, as Alexa was so taken up with the baby she wouldn't have taken any notice of what her mother had said anyway.

Now this was a first for Alexa to actually ask her mother's help, for she was a proud person who looked up to Corry but never asked anything of her, maybe things were starting to change and change for the better and eventually lead onto building bridges, you all need to take little steps and Corry knew this only too well so wouldn't pursue the conversation any further.

Tam was over the moon at what had happened, his little family back together although he knew only too well that things had to change sooner or later due to the situation, but for the time being he just wanted to cherish the time they all had together, knowing there had to be a way to reunite the family for his son's sake, but what it would be, he couldn't even imagine at this stage. Corry on the other hand was only too pleased that Alexa was now getting on with the baby and making such a good Mother, she'd pulled herself together leaving the depression to diminish as fast as it came but also to realise that her daughter was still fragile deep down.

A couple of weeks passed by whereby the subject of Jilles being christened was being talked about, Corry now a lot closer to her daughter thought she may suggest Jay coming to the christening for when it was all said and done, he was the child's grandfather. Although Tam was totally against this idea, Alexa was softening her feelings towards her father with memories of the good time when she was a little girl, totally blocking out how he'd turned his back on both her and her mother so brutally.

Now It was Corry's intention to work on this as she wanted Jay to be back in her daughter's life as well as the baby's, but knowing it wouldn't be that easy to persuade Tam to come round to her way of thinking, the only way to do it was, to work on the fact that family meant everything to Alexa.

In the meantime, relations between her and Marcus had become strained, she wasn't going over to Cyprus as much and to be honest he had an idea that Jay was back, fighting to win her back at all costs.

Corry was no fool therefore as much as she still had feelings for Jay, she wasn't going to let him back into her life to the extent that he could hurt her all over again, as he had in the past, yes, he'd made promises and maybe in his mind he had regrets but once you've been hurt to the extent that she had, you think very carefully before making the same mistake again.

Her heart had been broken by this man once and she'd be a fool to let it happen a second time for in her heart, all she really wanted to achieve was, Jilles to have a loving stable family around him which was her main priority. As the situation stood, her loving grandchild had been born into an unforgiving world of family and circumstances beyond control and so it was up to Corry as the matriarch, to try and put things right before things escalated beyond reason.

The business interests still going from strength to strength for all the companies so all there was left to do was get Alexa and Tam sorted to some kind of arrangement where they could live together as a family, for the only people who knew they were half brother and sister was Jay and very close friends who was sworn to secret. She was aware that Jay wouldn't say anything to jeopardise losing his daughter so the secret was safe and as for the close friends, they were too close and involved with Alexa to let the cat out of the bag, yes this had to be kept a close secret just as they had done so many years ago when only families were united by secrets that were never mentioned.

Tam, now aware of this factor suspected just what Corry was doing and so to keep his family unit together, was prepared to go to any lengths in his power to make it all work. Having agreed that Jay could visit Jilles and also attend the christening which was against all his principals, things would now start to move forward for everyone or so it would seem.

I must admit, Jay was now a changed man with a more considerable attitude towards everyone, Alexa was secretly over the moon that her father was back in her life, while Tam, on the other hand was very wary of Jay and would never trust him, Corry too, was happy, but just like Tam, she didn't trust Jay either.

Now the big question was going to be how they could have Jilles christened with Jay at the christening along with Tam's mother for there was bound to be something mentioned about the baby and why there was no talk of a wedding between the couple.

Unfortunately, this problem was solved two weeks before the big day, for Tam was to receive news that his mother suffered a massive heart attack and sadly died. Her friends placed the blame on Jay, for when he left, she not only went to pieces, she never came to terms with the fact he'd left and wouldn't return and therefore went into isolation, not wanting to see anyone even to the point that she'd make excuses so as not wanting Tam to visit.

It was only a matter of days before the christening that Tam buried his mother in the village where she'd lived most of her life, yes he was upset but he he'd never been that close to his mother, it had always been his grandparents that had cared for him and so didn't take the death as badly as one would expect. Jay on the other hand went to the service out of respect but at Tam's wishes, stayed in the background knowing the village folk had no time for what they called a high flying coward and to be honest, wasn't welcomed amongst them anyway.

Apparently, it came to light that the will she'd left was to go into a trust for Jilles when he attained the age of twenty-one, these monies were left to her by her grandfather in a trust that she'd hardly touched and with no property of her own the will was executed without any problems.

Now came the day of the christening, and the gods must have definitely been looking down that day for the sun shone down brightly which they all thought was an omen for Jilles to lead a happy and prosperous life.

Dressed in a traditional christening gown of cream lace with studded pearls and created for this very special baby by no other than his grandmother herself, this was Alexa's personal request to her mother, for the child looked so angelic, it was also at Alexa's choice for the Godparents as Tam couldn't agree more, with her decision. No there was no surprise there, the choice was simple, it was to be Issa and Rob for as it was a unanimous decision, so too was the third godparent which was to be Lars.

Alexa's reckoning was, if she couldn't have Lars as a step-father then she certainly wanted him as godfather to her only child, so for those that didn't agree, then it would be tough as this was how it was going to be with no arguments raised. Corry knew she couldn't even try to persuade her daughter against this idea as when Alexa's mind was made up, there wasn't any way it would be changed for she was stubborn to the core and wouldn't budge no matter how hard you tried.

Having requested that everyone should be dressed in coffee and cream as it was a bright and becoming colour for such a great occasion, this again was a good choice and went down well, to see all the outfits in the sunlight was simply stunning as in her mind this was a new beginning for the family whereby a chance to build on relationships.

The service was held at the same little church that Corry herself got married and therefore brought a meaning of solidarity to the family as well as a tinge of sadness to both her and Jay with memories of the past and thoughts of, if only Agnes could have been there to see her great grandchild on this special occasion.

Again the Christening party was held at the same local restaurant that had been Corry's wedding reception due to it being near to the church and also with the same memories of happier times. The food was a simple buffet which Alexa chose although Corry did suggest that The Grosvenor Hotel would have been far grander for such a celebration, which Alexa just laughed off as a sign of her father's influence in wanting to interfere. No nothing was going to spoil the day, well so it was thought until it was time for all to depart, as Corry and Jay left together overlooked by Lars, who seeing the tears rolling down his face with hurt in his heart;

"Oh how could my mother be so insensitive", Alexa remarked as Issa was stood by.

"Look this has been a beautiful day darling and your mother probably didn't give it a thought about Lars, so don't upset yourself and move on or it'll only destroy you in the end as it's destroyed your mother, although she won't admit it" Issa wisely stated.

Yes, Issa was right as usual so I'll leave it this time Alexa thought.

It had been such a trying time over the last few months, what with the unfortunate news of Tam's mother, her mother and father seeing quite a lot of each other, coupled with work commitments and so Alexa suggested that both her and Tam should go up to York, spend a spell of quality time with the baby, living as just a normal family away from the hectic life of the city but with an open invitation for Lars to visit them whenever.

With Alexa and the family up in York, this gave Jay a clear run to take Corry out without having to hide the fact he was becoming a permanent fixture in her life. His intentions were, he would try and persuade Corry to marry him again and therefore booked a meal at the little restaurant they had celebrated their engagement many years ago, hoping it would bring memories back to both of them.

They say you should never go back in time but on special occasions then maybe that's a good thing as that was the night they were so happy together with a lifetime to look forward to or so it seemed at the time. Looking radiant, yes a little older but still as beautiful as she did the day they got engaged Jay thought, oh what a fool he'd been, if only he could put the clock back there and then but then fate doesn't work like that;

"So this was my surprise you promised me, well it was one of the best surprises I've had in a long time and I honestly think you've surpassed yourself in thought and feelings" Corry laughed as she looked over the candlelit table which was conveniently situated in a corner near to an open fire flickering away in the silence of the night.

"No, this isn't the surprise at all", and taking a small box from him jacket pocket reached out for her hand saying;

"This is the surprise, and I would like you to take that ring off your finger and replace it with this one, for you know full well where this ring came from" Jay said with tears in his eyes.

Corry couldn't get her breath for there it was in the original box, the most beautiful diamond and Amethyst ring which she recognized immediately, yes, this was the ring that was designed and made in Germany for one special lady in Jay's life, it was Agnes's engagement ring.

This was the only piece of jewellery that Agnes had officially left Jay when she died and yet no one had seen it since that time as it had been kept in a bank safety deposit box in London for what was thought to be his daughter's coming of age, and for some reason had been forgotten about completely.

The silence was deafening between them both as Jay glanced across the table and into Corry's sad eyes which was now starting to fill up with tears as she thought of the woman that had given her so much, yes Agnes, maybe she had gone but she would never be forgotten for she gave her the opportunity to achieve the status and acclamation she now enjoyed in life.

"You know how much this ring means to me, well that's only a fraction of what you mean to me, because I could never express in a thousand years how I feel about you". Jay said.

Corry was totally dumbfounded at what had come out of Jay's mouth, yes he could be romantic but this was another side to him that she'd never seen before, and gathering her emotions she replied.;

"I love you for many reasons but not in the way I did when we got married, for there's been a lot of water passed under the bridge since then, yes that ring means a lot to me as it was your mothers and should have been passed down to our daughter".

With sadness in his face he went on to add;

"All I'm asking is that you think about marrying me and in the meantime I'd like you to wear my mother's ring for it would mean so much to me".

Now that was the biggest sacrifice Jay could ever make, his Mother's ring, for she knew the ring was worth more to him than all his worldly belongings and glancing down at it, had a ting of sadness in her face knowing in that ring was the woman that Jay worshipped above everyone, until his daughter was born when all his attention was diverted to her.

Corry was so confused at this gesture and still not being able to trust, wasn't going to be taken in by emotions alone and so after a few minutes answered with honesty.

"I'll think about wearing the ring, only because I know that you've given it from the heart but if anything goes wrong then it must go to Alexa, as for the suggestion of marriage, that's one thing you can put out of your mind altogether as I've no intention of getting married to you or anyone else, she answered with a heavy heart.

Oh why does things have to be so complicated, just when they were starting to run so smooth Corry thought as she reached her hand over the table to clasp Jay's with such a loving gesture.

From then on, the night felt so tranquil on the surface but inside of Corry stomach, well that was a different matter for she'd so many questions to ask herself, not knowing the answers at that moment or if she ever would to be honest for her head would be spinning for days trying to put her life on course again and then there was Marcus to think about.

How on earth was she going to tell him about what had happened or did she want to, was this just a way of making up with her, was it because Jay had realised how much he needed to be part of his family again, there wasn't an answer in sight as far as she was concerned but as usual it had to be her decision as the final word she thought.

The day had gone so well from start to finish therefore it wasn't worth worrying about at that moment, tonight was a celebration of their grandson's christening and therefore nothing was going to spoil the day and to this, a celebration would carry on in style as the champagne flowed.

"I think a nightcap would just finish the perfect day off" Jay whispered as he leant across the table in Corry's direction.

"Yea I think your right" was the answer from a slightly inebriated Corry.

Jay was no fool; he knew Corry's weakness for champagne as he suggested the nearest place for a nightcap would be his place, in which a taxi was duly heading some ten minutes later.

Large, minimalistic and decorated so tasteful all in black and white, Corry just loved the apartment and felt quite at home in the surroundings, the only ornaments were the German light fittings, the walls plain but revealing a large photo of Alexa modelling on the shores in Cyprus being Jay's pride of place for his daughter over the large modern fireplace. Again, the bedroom plain with fitted wardrobes subdued lighting with a spotlight on a portrait of Corry that took pride of place on the wall opposite the queen size bed.

"I think I'll have coffee before going to sleep" Corry stated as she entered the kitchen.

"I think you'll have a lot more than coffee my dear, you'll have a perfect ending to a perfect day for that's just what it's been, a perfect day" was Jays reply, grinning all over his face.

"Oh we'll have to see about that, wont we "Corry answered.

"I don't think so, by the look on your face I can hear a pussy purring for its owner so to speak" he said laughing with a mischievous light-hearted tone.

Yes, he knew her so well, when she'd been on the champagne, her sex drive was at its highest peak, therefore wouldn't be able to keep her hands off him, wanting him as much as he wanted her in the bedroom. Stripping off, Corry walked or should I say swayed into the shower room, it wasn't long before he followed,

"Thought I'd scrub your back" he remarked solemnly.

This wasn't an urge of passion; this was a true feeling of lust that both of them felt as his arm entwined her waist pulling her to him in a gentle way as he asked;

"Have I told you lately how much I love you" while looking straight into her eyes as the water trickled down both of their bodies, with results of his manly arousal, being so close to her, for that's what she did to him without even trying.

"Come on darling let's go to bed and make love for tonight I want to prove to you just how much I need and want you back in my life" he said with a wanting eagerness glancing down at her sleek wet toned body.

The sheets pulled back in readiness as Jay laid Corry down with an eagerness that had arisen between his thighs, kissing her with such passion, her body responding at his every movement, wanting him to take her with a forceful outcome, but no that wasn't what he intended for this was a suckle tenderness, wanting to show that holding her in his arms for a while where a safe and warm feeling would suffice.

It was when they were together, no one could come between them as the bond was so strong, it couldn't be broken, he knew he'd hurt her but would do everything in his power to take back that hurt, it may take a lifetime of trying but was willing to sacrifice that for his one and only true love. Kissing her passionately he suckled her breasts with an ease that made them both comfortable but all the same brought to the fore her longing of togetherness as he worked his way down her body to her most pleasurable bit which to his amazement was a little different from what he'd experienced a week earlier.

Yes, in modern times, Corry had now followed the fashion and done what many others had, and that was, shaved herself completely smooth not only for herself but for the excitement of her lover. This was such a turn on for Jay; it took him all his time to control the pleasure he was to give Corry as he opened the gateway to his oncoming fulfilment, kissing every little inch while working his tongue to create the excitement that ran through her body.

Her juices sweet and sticky as his tongue entwined that small clitoris that had a beckoning need to be salvaged before a shipwreck, as not only was he giving her pleasure but with the feelings he was experiencing, was also to give him pleasure the same, for that was love when two bodies meet.

"Tonight I want to enter your valley with an explosion that will fill all your desires", he whispered as his huge erection entered her inner loins with such force that made exotic music touching the highest of notes to fill the silence of the night like a cannon ball hitting its target with full explosion shattering everything inside as it came to rest at the target.

"Does that prove how much you mean to me", he asked.

Glancing deeply into her eyes was a satisfaction that she needn't answer for the truth was staring him straight in the face, for tomorrow was another day but the night was theirs and theirs alone.

Chapter 21

From that day forward, things started to look up for everyone.

The business was spread across quite a few small countries by now with an opening of others to follow, having started in Cyprus which was now fully independent but as such a success over there, Corry had done the same in Greece where there were small communities that had little work and so after seeking advice, started the same co-operatives that had worked so well in Cyprus, turning out ready to wear garments for export. Designs were done mainly in London but the bulk of the work was carried out locally in each country she set up so it would help bring work to the community.

Issa and Rob both working every hour they could to create new projects as well as running one side of the business, having now moved out into the country, bought a farmhouse with horses and chickens, still had a place in York which was a peaceful retreat as they put it, also adopted two little girls that had lost their mother to cancer. But unfortunately, their happiness had come at a price for Rob had also lost his mother to cancer which made them appreciate their little family all the more, still making time to spend with Alexa and Tam as Jilles would be brought up as cousins with their own girls.

Peter and Anna, well what more could you say about two people who were so dedicated to each other, their only son that was studying in France to be a pianist and who had achieved such honours in the music world, was to go far in his art. Yes, Peter never let go of the rains in the company, for he always thought he owed Corry a debt of gratitude which he would never be able to repay for all she'd done for him, but in fact Corry thought the other way round as she couldn't ask for a better man to be her eyes and ears in the company, he wasn't only a trusted friend but also a very valued asset to her empire and that she would appreciate till the day she died.

Malcomb was another valued and trusted friend although in his case he never trusted Jay and if the truth be known he disliked him immensely but being the soul of discretion never went as far as to mention any of this to anyone for his work was everything to him having never to meet the right woman, as the one he did meet was too far beyond his reach.

So many people and so many lives she'd helped over the years and yet she couldn't help thinking, it was her life that she couldn't get synchronized, for whichever way she'd turn, it would only hurt someone in the end. Yes, there had been two others she'd loved over the years but they were at different times, for when they came along it was the wrong time as Corry had other responsibilities whereby her personal feelings always had to take a back seat to her professional ones and so sacrifices had to be made to accommodate the situations as they presentenced themselves.

In her heart, she knew eventually there would come a time when Marcus would have to know about Jay, but not wanting to hurt him, put it off for as long as she could, eventually going over to Cyprus for a couple of days whereby taking Jilles with her, knowing everyone wanted to see the baby.

Marcus was overjoyed at this visit for there was nothing more than the thoughts that he would one day become part of the family, as family life was everything to the Greek people and a boy that would eventually inherit all of his wealth was a heartfelt dream. Nothing was mentioned about the business or anyone else other than family but then again, Marcus wasn't really interested and Corry wasn't going to spoil the atmosphere bringing up ghosts of the past for this visit was all about the baby, as he was the full focus of attention being the apple of his grandmother's eye.

Maria on the other hand had gathered from some of the things Corry mentioned when they were alone, that Jay was now permanently fixture back in her life, and if that's what made her friend happy, then she was happy too for its happiness that Corry needed although she would reserve her judgement on that situation till a later date.

On that occasion, Marcus was so attentive you couldn't fault his love for Corry and she knew this, but in her mind thought, could she settle for second best even knowing he would never do anything to hurt her and would always stay faithful.

It was one evening when Marcus and Corry were walking along the beach he noticed she kept putting a hand up to her head as though the pressure of work was getting too much or did she have some worries that he wasn't aware of;

"What's the matter darling, have you got headache", he asked.

"No, it's just all the pressure of work and having the baby from time to time, think I must be getting too old for it all", she replied with a weary smile.

"You do far too much, it's about time you started to slow down and let the young ones take over the responsibilities, take a little time out for yourself as the businesses can run themselves now" he stated with concern.

"Oh it'll be alright when I get back to London, think I may go to the apartment in Leeds and spend time with my brother and his family as haven't seen them for a while, she answered.

Marcus hadn't any need to question Corry's distance with him as he just put it all down to her being overworked and tired for on her finger, she still wore his ring and if there had been any other reason, she would have told him, but for the time being although the relationship was a little strained on her part, everything else was pretty normal he thought. Alas this break was over as when they returned to the villa, Maria was waiting with Jilles, having taken a message that Corry must get in touch with the office straight away. Yes, Corry had to get back to London it seemed there was something of a crisis, with special orders of pure silk that was coming in from Japan for the new show?

All of these little things could be handled with those left in London but instead, it was always Corry who felt it her obligation to sort out as head of the organisation.

Waving good bye to everyone at the airport was a little sad this time as something was bothering Corry and she didn't know what it was, maybe on the next visit to Cyprus she'd put her cards on the table with Marcus, stating she could no longer wear his ring but for the time being she'd make her mind up on a positive decision, and in the meantime she'd wear the ring and Jay would have to accept it, for the one that he'd given her was always passed off as the ring that belonged to Agnes, which was in fact true.

It would be hard when the time finally came, very hard but she had to make her mind up one way or another as it would only be fair on two men who loved her.

Luckily the flight back to London seemed to be over in such a short time or was that because entraining a baby, time seemed to pass quite quickly, never the less it wasn't long before they arrived back at Gatwick airport where her dear friend Peter was waiting to pick her up as usual;

"How did the visit go and what did everyone think about our little Jilles" he enquired with his usual smiling face.

"It was fine and everyone loved him, not a murmur out of him, he slept all through the flight going but wanted to be entertained on the return flight, he was so good it really was a pleasure to take him," Corry replied with a beaming smile portraying just how proud she was of her only grandchild.

"Well, don't worry about those silks coming for the show as it's now been sorted with the help of Malcomb who literally went to town on the suppliers, therefore you can go home, get some sleep and we'll see you in the morning as Alexa is coming round to pick young Jilles up later on from our place", Peter said.

"Good, that's just what the doctor ordered so to speak as I seemed to have one of my headaches coming on again, so a couple of tablets, a hot drink and a good night's sleep is just what's needed" she said with a sense of relief on her face.

"Headaches, I think it's about time you slowed down, no wonder you get headaches, you take on everyone else's problems instead of sorting your own out, should you sort your love tangle, then maybe you wouldn't get any headaches" Peter stated quite harshly.

"Yes, maybe your right but life is so complicated at the moment, and I just don't know if I'm coming or going" she replied with a big weary smile on her face knowing Peter was never that keen on Jay and only put up with him for her sake.

A warm soak in such an inviting bath when she arrived home, creaming her body with sensual oils before a hot drink, a few pain killers and retiring to bed alone was what only a woman would appreciate before falling into a sound sleep which would relax her body for the start of a busy schedule.

The next day was quite hectic for Corry, having meetings all morning, check on the design teams early afternoon and keeping her hand in as she usually did with the big shows, together with a little designing of her own in the late afternoon. For it was decided that this year, they would pull all the stops out and go with a pure white seersucker fabric which was young,

fresh and rather flouncy, although the silks she'd ordered from Japan had more of a flamboyant look to them, which would team up with the bomber jackets she had in mind. The more expensive look would be made up in pure pastel shades of silk which would be all hand sawn, by Macomb's team of girls, keeping his eye on those last minute touches of elegance as he often used to say, was his special trade mark.

As Corry had secured a range of footwear s from a manufacturer in Italy, made to her designs in metallic leathers that would no doubt wow the public, it was bound to be a winner yet again as they could all be adapted to the ready to wear ranges that hit the department stores. No she'd not lost her touch when it came to designing something different and even now she enjoyed her work so it wasn't a chore, for the buzz came when the girls hit the catwalk with a theme that impressed the general public and not just the elite of the country.

Still making time to see her grandson nearly every day which was her priority and having him on the occasional weekend to give both Alexa and Tam a break, although now Jay was trying to make up for lost time wanting to be with the baby which was an excuse to spend the weekends as part of a family. Although life was hectic her mind was never too far away from her dream of fashion and therefore the thoughts were to be for the coming show.

Now the autumn showing which she named the winter white season, crossed over from white fabrics teamed with metallic leathers to the winter white leather boots finished off with fur attachments, even the wedding gowns were trimmed with fur as brides wanted to get married in something that little bit different other than all lace and satin.

Bridesmaid and flower girls wore bright red with little posy baskets and some even went as far as gowns in dark navy, grey and even black but that's fashion and who are we to argue if there is a market for it.

Corry was at her best when in the thick of it, leading up to a show, it wasn't just for financial gain but the satisfaction of what she'd achieved coming from a small village in the north of England to such a powerful position she now held with no airs and graces so to speak. Her friends who'd stood by her through thick and thin with a friendship that could never be broken, and therefore finding time to spend one night a week with the girls to keep her sanity, was her idea of heaven.

Karen had really been an asset to the company for not only did she do well in the UK she went on to branch out into Europe with eyes set on conquering Berlin, being a place that she'd fallen in love with, yes, Berlin, this was the place to be as the fashion seemed to have really taken off over there in her line of interior designs. The weather seemed to go to the extremes with winter being unbelievably cold and yet the summer months was a lot warmer than in England, but to her the place was just magical, nothing out of the ordinary except for the fact that the British trends were now starting to catch on with the younger Germans.

It was also noted that since the Berlin wall had come down there was a predominant move toward gay men moving into the city which again brought a lot of money to the fashion industry, due to the fact they always seemed to be dressed so smart, making sure they spent money on designer clothing. oh yes, this was a very up and coming market for fashion and therefore very lucrative to Corry's business.

The irony was, both Corry and Karen just loved this city with its vibrant night life and warmth of the people, who in fact were much like the British in many ways. Although the city had changed tremendously since the days that Corry and Jay lived there, the memories never faded but having said that, a lot of new memories came to the fore as Corry and Karen often visited for short breaks with the intentions of going there to start new ventures in the eastern side of the city where time had stood still for many a year.

But as time was now moving on at rather a faster pace with very little unemployment. This again would work to their advantage thus creating more capital investment into the city. Should this have taken off then it would give her a foot hold into something of great magnitude due to the re-building of the eastern side of Berlin

Having thought all of this over, a planned visit to Berlin was now on the cards for them both to have a few days there meeting with some business associates that had shown keen interest in Corry's ideas, but then again that was arranged for after the fashion week which understandably took precedent over everything at that moment in time.

It's funny really, as it didn't matter what everyone was doing all the year round, fashion week in the city was something of a special event where you all pulled together making it a family tradition, a bit like Christmas without the presents and trimmings.

The week of the show now here, with all the celebrities arriving into the city, parties flowing with the hype that went with such gatherings, only this year it was a little different, for Jay was never far away from Corry's side, as in his opinion she was overdoing it working every hour she could manage only stopping for the little things like the odd meal and of course her precious grandchild, with a few coffee's and tablets to keep her going through the pressures.

There was no need for her to work as hard as she did, as money wasn't a problem, they could even retire quite comfortably, go to the place in Cyprus or even go further afield to buy a place and settle down, but no Corry wanted to be near at hand for Jilles growing up as she'd missed so much of Alexa's childhood.

The headaches seemed to be getting worse but knowing she had deadlines to meet, therefore it was easier just to take a few pain killers to drowned the slight thudding in her head that came at regular intervals and so kept quiet about them not to worry Alexa.

It was when Jay put his foot down one morning demanding she had a full check up at the doctors fearing the headaches were something to worry about, that she finally had to admit and therefore promised to do exactly as he suggested., Yes, he had definitely changed. being more attentive than she could have ever have imagined, for this wouldn't have happened when they were married as he was far too selfish. All of this was kept away from Alexa as she had enough to worry about with both work and a small child to cope with for if she'd have known, she would have dragged her mother to the clinic for a full check-up.

The week of the show was rather hectic for the family, with Alexa putting an appearance on the catwalk having got her slim figure back to what she called normal after the birth of Jilles, she didn't need to carry on modelling having a good set of girls working for her by now but really, still enjoyed the buzz that it gave her, the raves about the designs were what they'd all come to expect for perfection was what they strived to achieve.

Issa would also make what she called a guest appearance on the catwalk, but again that was a personal thing that promoted her lingerie line as she also liked to be hands on with everything just to show the workforce of her commitment to the new lines of sexy and sensual underwear that had been designed in bright red with gold trimmings.

Oh the bedroom was definitely going to have some very thrilling and exciting love making with that line she thought as women were now becoming more adventurous. Maybe the public would see another side to Issa, other than the shy, cool calculated person that everyone thought she was, well if her thinking was right and it turned men on. Then the next thing she had in mind would really arouse them, for the idea was to delve into the sexual fantasy of both male and female a little deeper by introducing sex toys that would not only enhance the lovemaking but would also give great satisfaction to both partners.

The completion of yet another major showing as the week drew to a close, a total success in every aspect for an ever changing world of fashion with quite a few surprises that wowed the public, which again would result in large orders from the buyers both at home and overseas.

Although they had to admit, the press played a pretty big part in it for they never let Corry down, as that favour was reciprocated giving them personal information when it was necessary for the magazines. She had always shown such compassion to them in the past and that was held in high esteem as far as they were concerned, a real lady in their eyes, going as far as putting on Christmas gatherings for their families every year. This was financed through her lawyers so as not to divulge any knowledge of favouritism, although they did have an idea it was her.

The week had gone to plan and now time for the families to go their separate ways after a well-deserved break which would mean a big night out in York to celebrate taking it easy for the rest of the weekend, as It had now become part of a ritual that after fashion week was over they would go up to York for a small celebration and enjoy the weekend doing their own thing before getting to grips with starting all over again on designs for the next season.

It was at this time Issa and Rob decided to buy another place in York as a base to work from, this would leave them time to be alone as a family but also close enough to travel to the city at a moment's notice, being only just over an hour on the train. And with Alexa and Tam living up there it was thought to be an ideal situation so they could escape from the city whenever they thought fit, although the place in the country they had was lovely, there was something about York that attracted them.

Corry had to admit, York was just the place to take a break for not only was it historical with its cobbled streets, wonderful restaurants and heritage, it was also pretty central for getting out into the countryside and up into the dales for a few relaxing hours, and with Jay by her side most of the time, everyone was now starting to warm towards him. Knowing that his only concerns were for the wellbeing of his family, maybe a few years too late but for Corry's sake, they were prepared to give him the benefit of the doubt.

Leaving London by mid-day on the Friday, they would be booked in by early evening whereby a gathering would be in the restaurant that night as their own little celebration for all the hard work that had been put in to achieve the outstanding shows of the past week.

Even little Jilles who was now walking and getting most of the attention, had travelled up to York with his parents although by now, Alexa had hired a full time nanny for him with having to put all the hours of work into the business

No, she never made the same mistake as her mother did when she hired Dexie, Alexa had more about her than that, she hired someone many years older than herself for she wasn't going to tempt fate and let history repeat itself, she was far too shrewd for that one, no, that wasn't going to happen to Alexa, what was hers was going to stay that way and god help any woman that tried to take her man away from her. The idea was that Alexa and Tam would stay on a couple of weeks more in York while they looked for a larger property with a considerable amount of land, maybe an old place that could be done up from scratch to their own liking, somewhere that would be away from the deafening crowds of the city perhaps. Well this was the intention, for not only would it be big enough as a residence but maybe with private buildings, Alexa could organise a workshop to do her designs away from the city, it would also have the advantage of prying eyes into their personal lives as most people thought that they were now married, having sneaked off abroad without anyone knowing.

Yes, this was going to be the weekend of all weekends, for happiness was definitely in the air and what could spoil it now or was that being a little too presumptuous.

Having discussed the weekend's itinerary to suit everyone concerned, the obvious solution would be the females would do a little shopping and lunch locally while the men would play golf on the Saturday.

An early dinner and maybe a pub-crawl round the city as York was one of those places that night life was definitely on the cards with a mixture of old and new style pubs that had the music blaring out as you tried to talk and yet never heard the full conversation the others were talking about.

Itineraries are great when you make them but when it comes to the crunch they always fall fowl of someone not wanting to follow, and in this case it was Alexa as after the day shopping, it was thought a quite meal in a nice restaurant for the Saturday night was a far better idea to finish the night off, to the enjoyment of all, and with the conversation flowing admirably.

It seemed the relaxation of the night or was it the wine that flowed, put them in such high spirits with laughter and tales of the past, the tensed up feeling of the last week seemed to disappear, if only the atmosphere could be like this all the time between them Corry thought, but nothing lasts forever.

It was a perfect ending to a perfect day as everyone departed from the restaurant that evening, each going their own way with Corry and jay being the last to leave for their hotel;

"Well my dear, I think that went rather well don't you all considering" Jay said in a soft voice seemingly thinking that he'd won everyone over.

"You may be right but I still think you have a long way to go before Tam accepts you, he may be pleasant to you in company but I suspect it's a lot to do with Alexa for he doesn't want any animosity where she's concerned" was Corry's reply thinking to herself that Jay had miss-read the signs of everyone that evening and therefore didn't want him to assume his role as the loving family man.

But the night was young and she didn't intend to spoil it with her observations at that moment in time for what will be, will be, for the future will work it out without her having to worry about it. Arriving back at the hotel was a quick nightcap in the bar before retiring to their room.

Now leaving the bathroom in a cream satin nightdress, her hair flowing down like silk with the fragrance of perfume that filled the room as she sat on the side of the bed, reaching over for the glass of water from the side table while taking a couple of tablets before getting into bed beside him;

"You got headache again darling" he asked sympathetically

"Afraid so, think it's been a bit too much for me with the shows, board meetings and now the excitement of this weekend, I just haven't had much time to myself lately, it'll be ok when we get back home, I've already booked a few days off, so can go to the country if you like", was Corry's reply, as her head touched the pillow.

"Could you ever forgive me for what I did to you, what a fool we've both been wasting our lives when all we wanted was in front of our very own noses" he whispered as he lay down next to her.

Corry looked up at him and smiled but no words came out of her mouth for however much she loved him, she would never be able to forgive, as for all the success she'd achieved, it had been done the hard way with a loneliness that no one would ever be able to understand unless they had been in that position.

To give a man your whole being, trust and devotion and have him break your heart like Jay did was something no woman could ever forgive and forget as long as she lived and that's something they'd take to the end of time as the heartache may ease in some cases, it would never ever go away, it's just locked away in time, forever.

With fuzziness in her head due to the tablets and maybe the vodka, she pulled Jay towards her kissing him gently but holding him so tight at the same time while saying softly,

"Make love to me like there would be no tomorrow".

"But there is no tomorrow without you, I know that for a fact" was his reply as his hands started to circle her heaving breasts.

Reaching out onto the bedside table, Jay grabbed the bottle of bailey's he'd brought up from the bar earlier, opened, and poured it all over Corry's body.

"Thought you may need another nightcap" he sniggered as he started to lick the alcohol inch by inch from her skin, taking extra suction over those pert sticky nipples which by now were increasing the delight that was running throughout her body.

"A little more down below I think" he murmured, proceeding to pour the rest of the bottle into her smooth loins which by now was starting to sting with the alcohol burning, as gasps came traveling down to his face which was resting between her open legs.

"Yes this is the part I really enjoy for it seems when I eat you and my tongue slides up inside, your excitement increases which makes me want to please you more and more".

No he wasn't wrong for he knew every little part of her body ached for his touch as she laid there withering from side to side, her breath increasing to moans and sighs that filled the air, the extracts of alcohol that had actually slid into her canal was now starting to smart as she asked him to suck harder to relieve the pleasurable pain, and being the perfect gentleman, who was he to argue with a lady in this position, bringing her to a delightful orgasm as she withered and panted for more.

"Look I'm so sticky I'm going to wash all this Bailey's off while you stay where you are until I return" Corry ordered as she marched off to the shower leaving Jay sat on the side of the bed just as sticky as she'd been.

Not a couple of minutes passed before she returned with a sponge and small towel demanding Jay washed his face while she took care of his lower body. Oh yes, and did she take care of it, lowering herself onto her knees, she took hold of his generous sized penis and placed it carefully in her mouth after stating;

"Now I'll get my shot of Bailey's like you did, only in this case it will be served in a bigger glass" as she sucked it with such strength that he came without hesitation trickling down the back of her throat.

"No my girl, there's plenty more for you where that came from and it won't be watered down by ice" he said picking her up, swinging her body round while placing on her back with legs held high in the air and over his shoulders.

Entering her with such vigour, and throbbing from the tip of his penis due to trickles of Bailey's which was now starting to smart on it, but that didn't matter for the enjoyment it was bringing both of them which was sensational to say the least as he shot in and out at such a steady pace together with the withering and grinding of her body that was slowly bringing them to an almighty climax as he shot all his juices as far as they'd reach.

Now that's what I call a new headache cure, perhaps we should put it on the market, knowing it would be a sell out in any sex shop he thought, for after a good shower sleep would call them to the land of dreams. The bed would look like world war three the next morning but never mind for the cleaners were handsomely tipped;

Waking up with such a hard on which was pushing into Corry's back as she opened her eyes; "It's a little dry this morning" she laughed.

"It won't be in a minute when I've played around, you see how quickly you'll welcome it with open arms so to speak, I can assure you".

Turning her on one side while playing with her clitoris he pushed that huge throbbing hunk of fillet steak inside of her from behind.;

"Sorry baby I can't drink your wine this morning I need to get rid of this stiff before it bursts and the only way I know how, is for you to clench your inside and make it come".

This Corry did as she was enjoying it just as much as Jay but like all morning sessions, they were over as quickly as they started for they had become necessities without the erotic feelings of love making.

As everyone strolled down to breakfast looking starry eyed and knackered so to speak, there was very little talk of the night before, only of the day in front of them where they all decided that a good walk and Sunday lunch would do the trick before getting ready to travel back to the city, for the weekend had been such a success, it was suggested they should do it more often in the future which was a unanimous decision.

As arranged Alexa and Tam stayed behind at their house as the rest travelled back to London, this was Alexa's suggestion for she was determined she was going to look around for an old property on the outskirt of York which could be done up to her liking knowing that if she found the right place then Karen would only be too pleased to help out with the interior, this being her field of design.

Now back in London, it was business as usual where Corry seemed to be doing the rounds of meetings for the company while Jay on the other hand was complaining that she didn't have to work that hard as the business run itself without her running herself into the ground health wise, knowing the headaches were still bothering her.

But as usual, Corry wouldn't listen, she had said many times in the past, about keeping her finger on the button for so many people depended for their livelihood for things to run smoothly, no she'd never altered and was still as stubborn as ever in that respect.

It was a couple of weeks later that Alexa, Tam and little Jilles returned to London with the happy news they'd found a large eight bedroomed house just outside of York which was set in a couple of acres of grounds. Although very beautiful there was a lot of work to be done as it was quite derelict and although this didn't seem to faze them in the least, knowing they'd set their heart on it. Now with the intentions of Alexa being able to adapt some of the outbuildings into an office whereby she could run her part of the company from there rather than living in London all the time, it would be all systems go for them.

Corry was thrilled at that idea for then she could go up to York, spend time with her daughter and the baby whenever she wanted a break, it would also take the pressure off the relationship between Alexa and Tam not being so near to Jay.

What Corry didn't realise was the fact that Karen and David had also got the same idea for they'd always loved Yorkshire and the chance to move back near to York itself would work out right for her to open an office close to their roots. This again, was thought to be a good idea as it seemed now their children were grown up and with Karen travelling so much, they hardly had time together which was starting to emotionally drift them apart from each other so a change of lifestyle had to be worked out before it was too late.

Jay however had different ideas for he wanted Corry to take a back seat for a while, letting Peter take the helm at the company, he was well aware that she wouldn't leave this to Peter altogether and so with a suggestion that three days a week would keep her hand in until the shows came around, hoping to see her in a healthier position.

Yes, this maybe a selfish suggestion on his part as he wanted to spend more time with her but looking at it seriously, it was her health that was paramount to all of this and to his surprise that was what she gracefully accepted.

This situation went on for six months or so when it seemed that Corry was now starting to pick up and feel a lot better, having more time to spend with Jilles while Alexa and Tam tried to get organized with the new property they'd successfully purchased in York. Life really was looking good for everyone but as usual when everything looks good there's always a downfall and that was to come, for while Tam was busy working in the courts in London, Alexa was overseeing the renovations to the house in York

When one week Alexa arrived down in London to collect little Jilles from her mother's, that's when tragedy stepped in.

Arriving at Corry's apartment all excited about what was happening to the house and how well it was coming on she went on to say;

"Another couple of months and everything should be completed with the house, together with the office/workshop, and to prove how pleased we are with the project, I've bought you a nice marzipan cake from Betty's Patisserie in York so go and put the kettle on while I sort Jilles out".

Ten minutes now passed and no coffee, and so Alexa walked over to the kitchen only to find her mother on the floor unconscious, and without hesitation she bent over to check for a pulse, found that although Corry was breathing, she couldn't seem to wake her as she was out cold. Her face drained and lifeless, while keeping calm and not panicking, she grabbed the phone with a 999 call then proceeded to call her father and Tam knowing Jilles was safely playing in his playpen by this time.

It seemed as though it was hours before the ambulance arrived and yet it was only a matter of minutes, the paramedics were brilliant as they worked to bring Corry around, getting her stable before taking her off to the hospital under the blue light. emergency

Tam arriving just after the ambulance had left, taking Jilles with him while Alexa left for the hospital with Jay following shortly behind. Arriving at the Hospital simultaneously which was a matter of twenty minutes behind the ambulance and just as Corry was coming round with the doctors asking a multitude of question to check responses, before examining her any further. It was at this time Jay suggested they transfer Corry to a private hospital where she'd get looked after far better, but no, Corry wasn't having any of that, she was a big believer in the National Health Service and that's where she was staying as she was rushed down for further tests and scans before a diagnosis could be established.

It was some hours later before the Doctors received tests back and therefore stated that Corry would be kept in overnight as they weren't satisfied and would therefore have to do more investigation as to one or two problems, Corry would therefore be put in a private room and kept quiet as the headaches had now returned, that being the main factor of the problem which was to be investigated further.

In the meantime, everyone was assured that Corry was fine for the time being and rest was the best thing for her while Doctors looked further into the cause of her passing out. Alexa was to return home while Jay wanted to stay with Corry but in the end was persuaded the best thing was come back in the morning when things would be far clearer. Oh Yes, it was to be a long night with everyone so worried and not getting much sleep at all but eventually morning came and after a quick breakfast Alexa and Jay went to the hospital leaving Tam to sort things out after they'd left.

Arriving at the hospital a little more assured than the day before, they were greeted with Corry looking a lot better which was put down to the medication and sleep she'd managed to get, now looking bright, breezy and full of life as though nothing had happened the day before.

She was ready to go home alright but that wasn't the end of it for the doctors hadn't finished with her and decided to send for another scan, which wasn't necessary in her eyes as she'd put all of this down to being tired and overworked but they were to have the final say as down for another scan she was sent.

There seemed to be a lot of toing and froing after the scan with different people in white coats having their say until a man appeared stating that he was a Neurologist, in fact he was a surgeon who was head of the neurology department, a very pleasant man who stated, that after viewing all the scans he was quite satisfied, to now put forward his diagnosis.

Speaking very softly, he introduced himself as Mr Khan and proceeded to say;

"Unfortunately, I'm afraid Corry has a tumour on the brain which was growing rather rapidly, that rapid, it is now inoperable";

"What do you mean you can't operate" was the words that came out of Jay's mouth.

The look from Mr Khan said it all without much more explanation as the room went silent.

"I'm afraid it is inoperable due to the position and size of it. I would suggest that you take Corry home where I'll give you some pain relief for the headaches, take her on holiday and have a good time with the family" Mr Khan stated in a sharp but softly spoken tone.

There were a million questions that Jay wanted to ask but nothing came out of his mouth as shock had set in with sudden explosion, Alexa just sat there crying while Corry just looked into space words not materialising.

"I know this is all hard to take in at this moment in time but I'll send my nurse in to help you through this period, she will also make you an appointment to come back in a couple of days where I'll be able to explain in more detail for you", Mr Khan said as he left the room at the same time the nurse entered.

The feelings in the room was so tense that whatever the nurse said went over Corry's head as nothing registered, it was just a blur of silence and although sympathetically the nurse advised on just a few things, she knew the patient would be in shock and wouldn't be able to take anything in and so with a card she handed to Alexa for the appointment leaving the room forthwith

Having composed themselves the best way they could in the situation while Corry dressed with the help of her daughter, they started to leave when another nurse called them back saying there was another number on the card they could ring should they need to talk to anyone in the meantime for help or advice.

The journey back to Corry's apartment seemed to take ages as time seemed to be standing still with them all in shock, and with Jay driving, knew he had to be level headed so thought it wise that after dropping them off, he should return to his home as Alexa and Tam would want family time with their mother to support her through the night knowing it would be a sleepless one for all.

Yes, it was a long night alright, and it would be a long week before they could all get their heads around the news returning to see the specialist as requested, but in the meantime Corry stated that only family and close friends should be told fear of upsetting everyone unduly, until all the facts were presented, whereby she wanted to tell them herself.

How on earth they kept it together, no one knows but a brave face was put on by all as they had a company to run. Jay now visited Corry for short intervals as Alexa seemed to take over and to be honest he didn't want to cause any animosity so decided to stay in the background until needed, this went down well with everyone as even they realised he was hurting although the emotions didn't seem to portray his real feeling.

A week later as they all returned to see the specialist, fearing the worst but more composed than before, it was Corry who asked the surgeon in a strong but none the less trembling voice;

"Firstly, I'd like you to tell me straight, not pulling any punches, how bad is it, what will happen from now on and also how long have I got to live", as the room went silent.

This may have sounded all matter of fact but having always faced life front on, there wasn't any time, to be any different in her eyes, she needed the truth however bad, she could then attempt to handle it, making arrangement for whatever was in the future;

"Having looked at all the evidence and discussed this matter in depth with my colleagues who are of the same opinion, I'm afraid it's exactly as I suspected in the first instance and therefore it would be futile to attempt to operate as the tumour is growing at such a rapid speed", Mr Khan replied in an understanding way as he paused before adding:

"We will do everything in our power to make things comfortable as possible for you when the time comes and fear complications may set in and the pain may increase, but on the other hand you may not even get pain at all should your organs just start to shut down, there again all this will be monitored".

Corry wasn't taking that as an answer for what she really wanted to know was just how long she'd got left which was her main concern, so that she could put everything in order, not about her, but about the ones she was to leave behind.

"All I need to know is how long I've got before it becomes impossible to really carry on in life", Corry asked quite sternly having got her strength back.

"That, I'm afraid, I can't answer, it may be the tumour will slow down, but in all honesty, I would say approximately six months or so, we'll probably have a better idea in a month as we monitor the growth. As you haven't had time to fully take everything in which is understandable, one of my nurses will make contact arrangements to visit you at a mutual time for all concerned, should there be any questions you need the answers to, then write them down and I'm sure the nurse will be able to facilitate you with the answers". Mr Khan replied in a sophisticated manner, knowing this was a difficult situation for the family to take in

Standing up to shake everyone hand he added;

"I'll see you in one months' time after you've had another scan and therefore we should know a little better what were up against".

Jay wasn't going to take this lightly as he asked;

"What if we get a second opinion, maybe go to America or even Switzerland?"

"I'm sorry but one of our team who has just joined us from America, has looked at your wife's condition and agrees with what I've just told you, it's your prerogative to do as you wish but I would advise that you will be wasting precious time which I'm sure you don't want Mr Khan replied.

To that, Corry then stood up, shook Mr Khan's hand, thanked him for all his time and patients and said to everyone's astonishment;

"I think it's about time I got on with sorting my life out, what's left of it".as she turned to leave the hospital walking in the direction of Jay's car which was parked outside. Now heading to Corry's apartment where decisions were to be made for the future, but then again Corry was now in full control and wasn't going to have any of it, for she was going to live life to the full as the surgeon had wisely suggested.

Starting with an urgent meeting that was to be called for the next morning with all senior management whereby she would explain about her future intentions and the reasons for the decisions, this meeting would be held in the boardroom to start with.

Secondly a group meeting for those who were close to her and had been the backbone of the company from day one, they would be told exactly the same intentions and reasons leaving nothing out for there was nothing worse than to hear something second hand as she used to put it.

This was all set out in Corry's mind as a step forward to taking control of what little time she had left but the hardest thing of all was, she had to break the bad news to Paul and the only way around that at such short notice was to phone, she intended to tell him the week before but knew he was away on business and so had to leave it till he returned. That night Corry rang Paul and explained that she'd been rushed to hospital and they'd found a tumour on her brain that was inoperable, as usual Corry was calm when explaining to Paul but afraid it didn't last for long as they both broke down crying;

"Look sis, I'll get the next train down to be with you looking at all the alternatives and see what we can find out about sending you away for another opinion" he said in a devastating voice as though he was choking on every word.

"No Paul, come down to see me by all means as I've a lot to sort out and may need your help but I'm afraid nothing more can be done as it's far too big and situated in such a place they can't remove it without complication" was Corry's reply.

"I don't care what you say it's worth a try and we never know if we don't at least try as these doctors aren't always right, so I'm coming down tonight even if it's on the last train I'll be with you before midnight, you are my big sister and I'll do everything in my power to get you help".

Corry wasn't going to argue as she needed all the moral support she could at that moment, she felt totally drained as the news of the day was starting to sink in and therefore was also starting to get very tired by now.

"Sorry everyone but I can't seem to keep my eyes open. I just need my bed now, so if you'll sort something to eat yourselves before you retire then I'll see you in the morning, I've a long and hard day ahead of me tomorrow therefore must be up bright and early, and I don't want any fuss" to which she turned and headed for the bedroom

It was getting on for midnight when Paul finally arrived at the apartment, having travelled down from Yorkshire. Crying, Alexa welcomed him with open arms for she knew if Corry was going to listen to anyone it would be Paul, adding that she'd made him a little supper and would fill him in with the situation after he'd eaten.

But Paul was far too upset to be patient as his first words were;

"Where's your mother and how is she, when we spoke on the phone it sounded as though she'd not taken the news in properly".

"Yes, that's right, she hasn't taken anything in at all as far as we're concerned, she just thinks it's another problem and she'll sort it as she usually does but it's far more serious than that" Alexa replied.

"Well, I've decided that I'm staying down here to be with her for as long as she needs me, if I can't stay here then I'm sure you can put me up Alexa".

"Look, there is always room for you with us, no problem" was the reply.

And with a hot cup of tea and sandwich it was to bed they all headed although it would be with a restless night ahead of them.

As the dawn was breaking so was the noise coming from the kitchen as they all woke to the sound of pots and pans being shuffled around, oh my god, don't tell me my mother is up already Alexa thought, but then again that was Corry, not letting anything phase her as the smell of freshly ground coffee drifted through the apartment.

"Come on you sleepy heads, time for breakfast, as we need to make an early start with everything, and as you're all Directors, you have to put on a brave face to help me through the day knowing this isn't going to be easy" Corry stated.

The bad news was now starting to sink in and as she'd always worked these things out in her head, this time wasn't any different for when you've walked alone all your life you then become accustomed to it, she may have had friends around her but inside she'd always walked alone to get through life making all the decision by herself. A good hearty breakfast to start the day but, afraid most of it was forced down as no one had much of an appetite for food.

Arriving at the office to find the boardroom was full of concerned members of staff looking sullen faced, those that were already seated now fearing the worse, thinking the company was in deep financial trouble and worried their jobs would be at risk, but none the less if that was the case they were all prepared to stand by Corry as the CEO for she had stood by them through thick and thin in the past.

Realizing there was something gravely wrong with the expression on all their faces as Corry, Alexa, Issa and Paul entered the room accompanied by Peter who had held the board together since Corry had been rushed into hospital, however the other Directors who had arrived earlier in anticipation of the news all stood up in respect.

"Sit down everyone, we'll, all those who have seats that is", Corry declared, having taken a seat at the head of the boardroom table while glancing round to validate the mental support she needed for the oncoming speech she was about to make, and without hesitation started by saying;

"I'm afraid I have some bad news that I must share with you all and couldn't think of any other way to tell you, therefore would like to thank you for coming in early this morning for I realise this would have been difficult for many of you".

The room quite in anticipation of what was about to happen with many of them thinking how strangely pallor Corry looked, not herself at all, it looked as though she was finding it difficult in getting the words together for what she was about to say, but whatever it was they would all support her.

Now standing up tall in front of everyone Corry started to make a stand eventually speaking to what was silence in progress;

"As one or two of you know, I have been getting headaches quite frequently, well it now transpires that I have been diagnosed with an inoperable brain tumour which will rapidly get worse and therefore I've only a limited time left on this earth with you all".

The shock that went round the room was amazing for every single person couldn.t even make a sound, you could have heard a pin drop, it was so quite as Corry smiled and carried on by saying;

"You will see me in work as much as possible for not only have I to organise everything for when that uneventful day arrives, I have also got to secure the company into the future for all concerned. The company is strong and therefore there will be no need to worry over your jobs as they will stay the same under the direction of Peter who will be standing in for me when and where possible in the next few months.

There will be no need for any fuss as this situation deteriorates although I may call on you for your support and help. I would appreciate if you wouldn't discuss this meeting outside of these four walls to any other member of staff as I intend to tell each and every one myself.

Having made this companies a family business and with the respect that you have shown me over the years, I would like to thank you all personally for your loyalty in this matter."

The room was deadly silent for no one expected this kind of news; it was after a few minutes that Alexa stood up and said her little piece, reassuring everyone that their jobs would be safe in the foreseeable future knowing there would have been an automatic worry for their livelihood.

"I would now like to thank you all for your co-operation and understanding in this matter on my mother's behalf and will keep you informed on the steps we will take looking after her. but as you are aware how ridiculously stubborn she is in wanting to carry on to the end, I'm sure you'll all help her in every way you can as you have in the past. If there is anything, we as a family can do to soften this blow to any member of the staff, you know where to find us, for one of us will be at your disposal whenever needed. I would also like to add that should anyone be in fear of their position with the company due to the fact they have family commitments, there will be no need to worry for I'll be stepping in to take charge whenever possible.

As my mother has already stated, this is a family company so to speak and will pull together at this sad time".

The heartbreak that showed in Alexa's face was something that no one in that room would forget for a very long time, she'd not been that close to her mother when growing up but all the same she put her on a pedestal for no one could have worked harder than Corry and the industry knew and respected her for that same reason.

The meeting over as everyone proceeded to walk out the boardroom with tears flowing down their faces although trying to keep it together for not to make the situation any worse than it was.

Now as the second group of employees were to be told the sad news, repeating the same procedure as before only this time it was Issa that stepped in and did her speech as Alexa was so devastated, she couldn't have gone through with it for she was hurting beyond belief.

It now conspired; the next few days were hell on earth as each of the Directors took their turn travelling round the factories to break the news personally as that's how Corry had requested it being a family run concern.

Corry on the other hand spent that time with lawyers, and with the help of Tam to make sure all the assets were tied up, not allowing anyone to take advantage when they got wind of Corry's situation or even attempt a takeover for this was done so Alexa could take over with the help of the present board of Directors to run the companies when the time came.

A Will had been made long ago so there wasn't any worry about that for Corry knew in her heart that Jay would step forward should she need advice and be the father he'd never been when Alexa was growing up.

She felt assured that the mistake he had made that time in Berlin some years ago wouldn't be repeated and as far as he was concerned his daughter would come first in everything for he was a businessman at heart and a very good one at that.

As for little Jilles, he would be taken care of to the maximum as Corry would now spend as much time with him as she possibly could.

Now for one of the hardest parts of this cruel situation and that was what Corry had to do by herself, she had to go over to Cyprus telling both Marcus and her faithful friend Maria the full story.

It was when she asked Shelia, to book her flight to Cyprus on an open ticket wanting to spend three or four days there, that Jay wasn't too impressed at the idea as she would be travelling alone, but knew only too well Corry would object at him interfering. So as a last minute phone call he made unbeknown to her, it was arranged with Shelia there would be two tickets, the second ticket being in the name of Mrs Karen Thomas.

Jay knew Corry would agree to Karen accompanying her as they were with each other quite a lot when travelling abroad so knew only too well he was on safe ground when Karen stepped in at his request.

It was a week later when both the girls were heading off to the island of love, yes, this was Cyprus at its best but afraid it wasn't going to be the best as far as the news they were about to break to a lot of friends which they'd made over the years.

The journey was a little tiring but then again the last few weeks had been somewhat hectic and therefore it was now catching up on everyone which was understandable in the circumstances and again was just thankful that both Marcus and Maria were there to meet them this time, it was as though they had sensed something wasn't as it should be, with a call to say they were visiting as something urgent had crept up.

Oh she was so happy to be back on the island she loved so much and although a little weary was determined not to spoil the homecoming as it had been arranged that after a shower and a couple of hours nap they would head for her favourite restaurant along the coast road where a table had already been booked in advance for the four of them.

Oh what a perfect night that was with clear blue skies and brightness of the full moon only to be spoilt later with the news that they had to deliver in such a beautiful setting which was to be Corry's favourite restaurant on the coast road.

Now arriving with an appetite for lamb done in cream sauce together with vegetables and strawberries for afters, was definitely something to look forward to and being in such excellent company was something that Corry would cherish but that was only the beginning of the evening for unfortunately the sad news had to be broken before rumours reached the island and her friends heard them from an outside source. Having said that, both Maria and Marcus had been close for a long time and wasn't stupid for they knew something was wrong but could never have imagined just how wrong it was.

Now, although Marcus could sense some kind of fear in Corry's voice when she spoke, he decided to leave it until later when they were alone and the subject could be approached in private for he intended that the evening would be a pleasant one where four friends would just get together spending time to relax. But as the night went on this wasn't to be the case for Marcus seemed to be on edge for there was a dark silence which he could detect surrounding Corry.

And as his feelings became more and more uneasy, felt he couldn't just sit back and say nothing any longer, so taking the bull by the horns so to speak, looked at Corry and asked in a roundabout way;

"You look tired and grey around the eyes, what' on earth's happened, if its money troubles or problems with the business then you only have to ask ".

At this Karen looked straight over at Marcus before saying;

"I think it's about time you told them, don't you"?

Maria went very quiet as though there was a cold air sweeping through the restaurant, while Marcus just froze knowing something bad was going to happen.

Corry looked from one side of the table to the other with a cold stare before saying;

"I don't want any fuss made for what I'm about to tell you has been confirmed and nothing more can be done, I have a brain tumour which is inoperable, it's growing at a rapid speed and they're looking at approximately six months left to live, I'm under one of the best specialists in London who assures me that I'll be able to carry on for as long as I feel alright, and will know when it's time to stop, I'm not in any pain and am assured that they'll do all they can, so I won't suffer".

Taking a deep breath, she carried on to say;

"With this information at hand, I therefore intend to be with you as much as I possibly can, for it's at times like this you need friends and I couldn't have asked for any better friends than I have on this island".

They were expecting bad news but nothing as devastating as this, for when the silence hit the air Maria was in floods of uncontrollable tears.

"Oh why, oh why did this have to happen to you" she asked.

Marcus on the other hand took a stance of composure whereby he was trying to keep everything together although inside was crying with heartbreak that no one could imaging for the love he had for Corry was everlasting.

There wasn't any more to say that night, as if there had have been, it wouldn't have made any sense for nothing was registering, a good night's sleep would have to be the call of the day as to be honest the wind had been blown out of all of their sails, maybe a fresh day would bring light to the situation but even that was just a vague assumption with such a dark cloud hanging over them all.

The Sky was blue with not a cloud in sight the next morning but with the news that had been delivered to Maria and Marcus the night before; the only thing on the horizon for all concerned was very black.

A meeting with the hospital the next day where Corry was to break the news of her illness due to her being on the Board of Governors as it was only right that she would tell them on a personal basis. Again this was a sad day, for she would step down from the position although wouldn't give up supporting them in every way she could at fund raising, feeling so strongly about the good work they did with the newly built children's block.

Not wanting to let anyone down, she even found time to fit in a short visit to the factories she'd initially opened all those years ago, this again was such a sad time for they knew without Corry they wouldn't have been in the position they were today all owning a piece of the company.

The next couple of days were taken up whereby both Corry and Karen visited personal friends on the island to give them the news. The nights were then filled with friends gathering around to visit, giving their well wishes personally as the respect for a lady that had cared for them in times of crisis, in fact at times it seemed as though it was an open party at the villa with everyone bringing food and wine, making themselves at home relaxing like a long lost family.

It was decided that both Corry and Karen would perhaps stay a few more days than originally arranged, this would give them a little time to themselves for Karen wanted to spend a couple of days in Nicosia with friends and therefore giving Corry a break to spend time with Marcus alone, knowing that it may be the last time they would ever be able to spend with each other as lover's, and as Corry had declared at the onset of the illness, she was going to live life to the full for whatever time there was left. it was going to be enjoyable whereby she'd go down fighting for her life to the very end.

For the next two days Corry lived as man and wife with Marcus, he taking her to all the places on the island they'd shared together over the years, she wanting to turn the clock back to those happy memories where they acted like teenagers in love as love is what they had together for such a long time and that couldn't be taken away from them. At first Marcus was a bit wary of getting too close to Corry but that didn't last for love took over the situation and the feelings they had for one another came flooding back, Corry didn't care as in her eyes she wasn't betraying Jay as he had done to her, she was just living for the time she had right up to the last moment.

A nice meal out in the Harbour restaurant the night before Karen was due to return, Marcus knowing it would be the very end to the relationship they had enjoyed over the years and therefore was determined for it to go out with a memory of his everlasting love for Corry, a woman that would remain in his heart forever.

Tender and caring as usual he took Corry to bed for the very last time; sensing the night would make a memory that would never fade in his heart, to express his feelings for this wonderful woman who had given so much of herself to others and yet still walked alone through the unknown to meet her destiny.

No, life wasn't fair at all, it gave you hope knowing that it could snatch it away from you at any time, the same as love which was being taken away from two people who obviously adored each other in the past and in Marcus's case was going to repeat its self for the second time only this time was a love he would treasure till eternity.

Lying next to Corry, with his arm around her, not wanting any more than to just hold her close, until the silence was broken as she spoke those haunting words;

"I want you to make love to me like you did on the first night we met, to feel safe for the oncoming journey that I have to travel alone for then I'll know the journey won't be wasted and I'll have my memories of the time we spent together".

His heart breaking inside as his lips touched hers with such sadness and passion knowing the excitement and arousal which was starting to run through both of their bodies by now, to an extent that he could never deny her wishes for his body had been hers from the first day they'd met.

"Don't be afraid darling, just love me and remember all the good times we've enjoyed, for I'll always be with you in spirit as you've always been my rock from the start, I want you to remember, whenever your lonely I'll be right by your side to help you through" Corry whispered as she kissed the side of his neck tenderly.

To this, he wanted to pick her up, carry her away to safety where no one could harm her until a cure came forward to heal this devil illness, but knowing in reality this wasn't possible he had to be strong at this moment in time and love her for all she was worth.

Kissing her body softly he worked his way down to the warmth of her breasts knowing that she would react instantly to the soothing of his lips upon her firm nipples, the blood rising inside of him as he sucked like a baby wanting its first feed of the day, until her body quivered with a sensation that he'd got used to over the years, a wanting for satisfaction that only he could fulfil the needs of that moment. Knowing the harder he sucked, the more she yearned for his tongue to wander unto parts that were crying out for the same attention and not to deny this request he obliged by trailing his kisses to the wonderful silky smooth mound down her body where her waiting eagerness was crying out for more.

Still his mind wandered back to when this was normal as they were a couple in every sense of the word enjoying each other at every opportunity that rose, oh how cruel fate was at times to give with one hand and yet take back with another, if only they had met in their teenage years, to have a life together would have been a dream come true, spending every minute of the day like lovers on an island so famous for love its self.

Parting her legs as he went down between them, her juices flowing so quickly by now, shooting his tongue up inside as far as it would go while clasping his teeth around her clitoris at timely intervals knowing the spasms that would run through her body until she climaxed with her sweet juices down his throat. Now sitting up Marcus pulled Corry towards him saying;

"Listen darling, you have created such a monster down below, he's requested the only way to calm him down would be to sit on top of him, putting him in his place where he would be happy to shower you with affection to your delights as he knows his place having enjoyed those surrounding for a long time.

To this request Corry instantly obeyed knowing what a thrill she got when she rode this monster being in control not only of her body but also Marcus's at the same time teasing him with movements that drove him wild as she proceeded to kiss him passionately.

This went back to old times when they made love for hours but times had changed and Marcus knew time wasn't on their side so he took hold of the situation by darting his mouth to catch her nipples sucking them rather vigorously while pulling her into him so close that he was now in charge.

"Ride me baby, ride me to the finishing line, we will then have a photo finish as I shoot everything I possess inside of you for all eternity" he said, knowing this would probably be the last time he would make love to this adorable and gentle woman that he loved with all his heart.

Corry was so far gone that even she couldn't argue on this, she wanted him so much at that moment, the hot liquid which would fulfil her with the desires that she'd experienced in the past so many times before but alas this would have to be an unhappy ending to a wonderful love story that they had enjoyed for many years now.

"Just drive it up inside of me and give me the release that I will never forget forever or even beyond" Corry screamed as they came together in one final spurt of passion.

And that memory would stay with Marcus until the day he would die for that was a release of the woman that he loved more than life itself.

The morning broke to the birds singing with the sadness at hand drifting away in a mist of memories for a relationship that had lasted for many years but unfortunately due to circumstances had now run out of time.

Maria arrived shortly before Karen had returned from Nicosia, this being their last day together before they flew back to England the next day.

All packed for the flight, this was going to be a relaxing day whereby they would do a little shopping, say goodbye to the local people they'd made friends with over the years, lunch, a couple of drinks sat out by the pool putting the world to right and then a meal at the fish restaurant on the front in Larnaca.

It was a happy day for all of them or so it seemed for it was a united front they put on for Corry's last day and at the end of it was a tearful drink to all the good times they'd enjoyed before an early night.

Lunchtime, and Marcus picked both of the girls up for the airport as he always liked to take them personally, this time was different for Maria insisted she was accompanying them not knowing if she'd see her friend again and therefore would be able to say goodbye to her faithful friend properly.

Having reached the airport and checked in, they all said their farewell which in itself was soul breaking with poor Maria breaking down in floods of tears while Corry took Marcus on one side and handed him the box with her diamond ring in saying;

"I think this belongs to you and should you ever give it to anyone else then give your heart alongside of it for she will be a very lucky woman, I want you to always remember that I wore your ring with pride and love" as tears in her eyes spoke a thousand words.

Marcus looked mesmerised as the tears rolled down his face, his heart breaking as he threw his arms around her and said,

"That ring was for you and you alone, no one else could have brought me the happiness that you have, and therefore it must stay with you whereby it should then be handed down to Alexa to bring her the happiness that it has brought us whatever the circumstances".

Corry's look said everything as she whispered

"Thank you and never forget I did love you and wished that circumstances had been different".

Boarding the plane, Corry looked back only to see Marcus for one last time and that time was heartbreak for both of them as the times they had spent together was times that only two lovers could experience.

It had been more or less love at first sight for Marcus and the love that Corry felt was something special as the time passed, a bonding of two mutual minds, something that memories are made of which can't break, a love affair in which two people met and shared love together but unfortunately it was the wrong time for them to find happiness and now their souls would part with only the memories of time that would never heal.

Chapter 22

The flight seemed longer than usual or was it because of feelings that had been left behind, maybe so but then she intended to return in a couple of months' health permitting, but maybe that wouldn't be possible as everything had to be organised and she'd want to spend as much time as possible with her grandson who was now becoming such a lovable little character.

Walking through the airport to see Jay waiting with little Jilles, brought her down to earth literally for seeing the baby in Jay's arms giggling his little head off, all she wanted to do was love and cuddle him for he was the apple of her eye, now having to put everything into prospective with the time she'd got left. Approaching, as Jay handed the baby over to Corry while he sorted her cases out, asking if they'd both had a nice time and was everything ok to which Karen replied instantly that the weather was great and time was relaxing as they'd had chance to catch up with friends having not seen them for a while, not mentioning Marcus by name at all.

"Home at last and we have Jilles for a couple of days as Alexa has gone up to Yorkshire to sort new contracts out for the business" Jay said, changing the subject knowing they weren't about to give any more information out to him while adding.

"Look if you like, we can maybe go up to Scotland with the baby and spend a few days relaxing, it won't be as warm as Cyprus but I'm sure the baby will love it ".

"No that's alright; I want to get into work and sort a couple of things out with Shelia over the new collection, for It seems that since the Chinese have been importing things into the country, we have stopped being individuals with individual designs so should Issa or Alexa wish to visit Italy then I'm sure we can between the two countries have our own production of an elegant shoe line as the Italians are renowned for their quality of leathers", Corry stated. As for some unknown reason Corry would never allow Jay to accompany her when she visited Scotland.

You could sense the irritation in Jay's voice as he replied to this;

"Do you ever stop working, you should have realised by now that you have to slow down and take it easy".

"Listen to me, the day I slow down I'll be dead" Corry said not realizing just what words came out of her mouth.

But she was right for she'd worked all her life and taking it easy wasn't in her vocabulary so if Jay stopped to think he would have realised that to Corry's annoyance, but there again men don't always think before opening their mouths and this was one of those occasions.

A week passed with Corry going into work every day as though nothing was wrong, and in that time she'd had meeting after meeting, plus managed to organize talks with the Italians to get a deal with a top manufacturer whereby she'd get Alexa to set up an outlet in York for top sophisticated lady's shoes.

Things were going so well that even she was amazed that her headaches didn't seem too bad, since her return from Cyprus all she'd suffered was a few fuzzy heads so to speak which again was understandable due to the hours she put in working on a limited addition for the next fashion show.

Jay on the other hand knew it was no good moaning about the hours she spent at the office as she wouldn't take an ounce of notice and it would only end up with angry words passed between them which he didn't want, knowing how fragile her condition was, and therefore got the surprise of his life when she came home one day and announced that he pack a bag as they were flying off for a couple of days to be all by ourselves.

"And where will that be may I pray, although I'm not arguing, for where ever, as long as it'll slow you down a bit ", he sneered.

"That you will have to wait and see, it's a place we can make a memory of past and present where love took a break but eventually came back online" was the answer in a sarcastic tone.

"What are you on about, oh never mind as I know you're not going to tell me, so I may as well accept the fact that you're in charge and I'll find out when I get to the airport" he said with a sigh.

It was when they arrived at the airport Jay had a feeling there was something more going on than he knew, just a feeling but knowing how unpredictable Corry could be at times, thought he'd leave it. But when approaching the booking in desk, the penny all of a sudden dropped, to what she'd said about past and present, memories, with the gateway stating passengers for Berlin.

Walking over for a coffee Jay was still uneasy about something but was too proud to ask until he glanced out of the corner of his eye only to notice two familiar faces, and there in front of him stood Issa and Rob.

Now things were starting to fall into place as going back in time it was that night they all met in a bar in Cyprus and this is what Corry had arranged, she wanted to spend a break with her close friends that had made up the memories in life for her.

Corry knew that when Jay had time to think, he would realise that it was a good idea spending time with friends and yet, they would be able to spend as much time as they wanted to be alone with each other, taking in sights and sounds they never had the chance to when they actually lived there, thus making good memories for Jay when the time came for them to depart.

Although they'd lived in Berlin many years ago, things had changed and it was a new Berlin with a new modern outlook, a very different one to the one they knew and so after the initial shock he was rather looking forward to this wonderful break, and realising what Corry had in mind when she arranged all of this; knew it was time to spend with those she loved in happy circumstances where they would remember after she'd gone

The days were filled with laughter, shopping and sightseeing, it was as though they were all teenagers doing whatever they liked, for in England they had a certain status to live up to but in Berlin they were free to eat German sausages in buns while drinking beer out of plastic cups in Alexanderplatz Square, where the TV tower now stands, and knickerbocker glories in a street café on Kurfurstendamm were a must, for people watching as they passed by.

Visiting the brand new stadium which that had replaced the old one was a sight that astounded them knowing the history of the original although the original Olympics swimming pool had never been touched since the day it was built before the war. And you could never visit Berlin without visiting the famous Berlin Zoo, which had an oriental feel to it; in fact, it looked very much as though it had been transported from China with lanterns that greeted you as you approached the large ornate Chinese gates that stood proudly in a traditional colour of red.

Reaching another part of the city where stood the Reichstag building where parliament gathers together, the castle where Jay's mother lived opposite as a little girl and to top it all was Brandenburg Gate that they could walk through, not like years ago when the city was divided.

Checkpoint Charlie was another must for them to see as they wandered over to the eastern side of Berlin, the difference they could clearly see with the inadequate accommodation, poor roads and very little social activity although it had to be said, the building works that was in progress was to the highest quality and in years to come would be an architect's proud accomplishment for all to see.

But the highlight of everything stood in Charlottenburg, yes it was a church situated on an island in the middle of the carriageway, not just any church but a part replica minus the roof of the original abbey used by the German royal families, the original being bombed nearly to the ground in the war, next to it was the chapel that had been fully erected in large panels of minute pieces of royal blue glass stuck together, inside was a marvel to be seen for your eyes only as one architect would describe, this being when darkness fell, it would light up the skies with a tower of blue reflected shining light.

Having taken as many pictures as possible on this visit for not only others to view upon their return home, but also making memory albums for later when things were finally drawing to a close and maybe memories fading into the twilight as years go by. Yes, this was such a happy time with the present in mind, and with no thoughts to the bad times that caused the divorce, you could even say it was like a second honeymoon only for four people on this occasion having the time of their lives with no thoughts for others.

At night they would go for a meal then on for a quite drink together, why on earth hadn't this happened in the past instead of putting work first, maybe if they had done a little more socialising together then things may have worked out different instead of putting others first it was thought, but then that was another case of WHAT IF'S.

That night Jay made love to Corry in such a passionate way, it was like a new lover had come out of the woodwork, tenderly caressing her like a porcelain doll which she enjoyed as it was very different for him to be so loving and attentive

It didn't make any difference to Corry that a few weeks before, she was being made love to by Marcus in Cyprus, for that wasn't a betrayal in her eyes, it was life through circumstances for when all said and done, it was Jay who'd betrayed her years before, which she would never forgive or forget and therefore what goes around comes around she thought, having loved two men in two different ways and yet a third man that came along at the wrong time to change her life.

"Don't worry darling I intend to make up for all those years we were parted, knowing how badly I treated both you and Alexa, for it really was inexplicable what I put you through he whispered in which he meant every word, for not only had he hurt Corry but had suffered himself through pride and vanity.

"I realise you regret that now, but that time of weakness not only ruined our lives together but it also ruined other lives as well as your own daughter's so for that I'll never forgive, although I may still love you, but not in the way that you want" was the answer that was put in front of him in a serious tone which was expected.

"Look were here now and have to move forward with life not knowing what's around the corner, therefore I'm willing to drop the subject forever as we don't need it to get in the way of what future's left for us" Corry said wisely.

Although the words stuck in Jay's throat, he knew she was right and they had to make the most of the time they had left together.

After a continental breakfast the next morning, this being the last day before they were due to fly home, so a little shopping for presents which mainly consisted of baby clothes for little Jilles, it was decided a last look of all the places they'd missed with another visit to that wonderful church made with blue glass which they'd all fallen in love with before returning to the hotel for a shower and dressing in their finery for their last night out on the town where they'd eat at their favourite Italian restaurant which was opposite the famous Ka Di We department store.

The meal of pork loin in cream sauce, vegetables and sauté potatoes, with tiramisu to follow washed down with champagne, together with romantic sounds in the night, what more could they ask for on this special evening.

And to this, as the night drew to a close, there lay a passionate feeling which was in abundance as they headed back to the hotel for Corry never could take her champagne and as she'd knocked nearly a bottle of it back, was well on her way to being quite amorous by the time they reached the room.

Stripping off, flinging her clothes to the floor as she usually did when she'd been on the champagne, Jay knew only too well what she wanted by now and knowing full well she wouldn't stop until she got it, for the mood that champagne dictated was, she wanted to rule and have it all her way, but the problem was, getting her to bed which was half the battle, as when in that mood she couldn't wait and therefore it could be anywhere.

I know this may have sounded strange for a man to turn this suggestion down but he still had to consider the fact, she could have one of her turns at any time;

"I wanted to make love in the lift" she said.

"Look Corry, you're not in any fit state to make love in any lift, now come to bed" was the reply.

"Well how about the shower, we can make love in the shower and then if I slip you can carry me onto the bed" was her suggestion.

"I've told you that's not an option, now if you don't come to bed there will be no nooky for you tonight" he said laughing.

Corry looked Jay straight in the eyes and said "you do realise that's blackmail and you know darn well I can't fight you on that score".

So giving in to his command she walked over to the bed where he lay fully naked and said;

"Right you're Gonne pay for that statement" draping herself on top him while kissing his body all over.

Oh yes, she was in that mood alright, mind you, it was always the same when she hit the champagne bottle, so was fully aware what was coming next as he waited to enjoy in anticipation the fruits of her endeavour while the blood rushed through his body at a passionable speed of delight making an awareness of senses that was erupting to a sensual appetite. For after all this time, this woman only had to touch him, whereby the thought of her body turned him on instantly like no other woman could do as far as he was concerned; she had mystical powers that could never be explained in his opinion.

Laying quite still as Corry moved down the body with her perfume lingering on his skin, pushing his legs apart to the sight of that enormous erect penis, knowing her way without the help of a satellite navigation to guide, opening her lips before reaching the final destination, while taking it fully into her mouth, sucking the glistening tip as she slowly moved up that huge shaft taking in as much as she possibly could to Jay's whimpering, as she drove him mad with every nerve in his body tense by now, when he asked in a heated voice;

"Corry please don't do this to me as my balls are aching and I don't want to let go this quickly, I need this to be a memory that I'll never forget".

"Oh shame" she replied rather sarcastically. "Perhaps I should massage them better if they're as bad as you say they are".

"Don't you dare', you know darn well I don't want to come yet.

Jay knew what he was up against with Corry in this mood, there wasn't any reasoning with her at all and therefore had to take the situation in hand knowing she was so wet with juices of her own trickling at a steady pace and nor turning her onto her knees while sinking his tool inside of her from behind, one hand playing with her clitoris while pushing in deeper and deeper as she screamed in delight for more.

"Be quite or I'll pull out and you won't get what you're craving for", he said.

"You bastard, you do that and I'll never speak to you again" she screeched in desperation.

No, she wasn't having of that as her muscles tightened around his throbbing shaft knowing he wouldn't be able to control himself and therefor shot everything up inside of her as they both came together in unity, while adding;

"Now that was a result, just proves I've still got what it takes to control you whenever I want, doesn't it", she said before turning over to where a good night's sleep was calling her, due to the champagne taking its course.

Early the next morning, it was breakfast before making their way back to the airport and the flight back home; yes, the flight, as the plane took off from Schonefeld airport, they were all to look back on the wonderful time they would always cherish till the end of time for that was the reason of the trip, to make an everlasting memory.

The next week was spent with little Jilles as Corry had missed him so much and with him growing at such a pace, she couldn't keep up with therefore wanted to spend as much time as possible, which was quite understandable. Both Alexa and Tam recognised this but wasn't worried at all knowing that should anything happen, Jay was always around to take over.

But alas, having worked all her life, it wasn't long before Corry decided on going back into the office and design rooms, and with the new show coming up wanted to have an input as this may be the last chance she may get.

Her ideas were to create a show where colours were so vibrant that it would knock the socks off the fashion scene, which is exactly what she did, some even saying that you needed sun glasses to look at the colours. But then again she wasn't bothered for she'd always gone her own way and hadn't any intentions of changing it now, even roping Alexa and Issa into the idea of taking swimwear and lingerie into the same vibrant look, which would make any one wear sun glasses to protect from the glare of the fabric, let alone the sun rays.

In the meantime, Alexa got in touch with Lars, informing him that she wanted to see him urgently and could they meet up in Aberdeen. Yes, it was a long way from Sweden but upon a request such as that he knew there was something amiss, but as he was due to visit Scotland in the near future, he would arrange to do this much earlier rather than expected.

It was the week before the fashion week commenced that Alexa had stated she was taking her mother to Scotland over some important business and to back the story up, she'd roped Corry's best friend Karen into the plot, with a suggestion that she was to take over a small company in Aberdeen and wanted her mother's approval.

Corry was only too happy to assist although it would have to be a short visit due to the shows being so close and therefore with the help of Karen, booking arrangements were made for them to fly up to Scotland a few days later not knowing the real reasons for this said visit.

A small overnight case packed for each and they were on their way for that short flight which was far better than driving up all that way it was thought. Now arriving in Aberdeen, where a taxi took them straight to the Holiday Inn Hotel which had been pre-booked.

Making excuses that nothing could be done that day and after a couple of drinks in the bar with a light lunch, Alexa went to check if Lars had booked in while Karen entertained Corry so not as to give rise to any suspicion, the news was Lars had already arrived and was in his room and to that, Alexa rang not only with her welcome, but also to arrange a meeting in her private suite that evening where she'd explain everything.

This wasn't exactly true as the suite was where her mother was booked into. Furthermore, Alexa had arranged that she and Karen would go down into the bar as soon as Lars arrived at the suite, thus leaving Corry and Lars alone to say their good byes as Lars wasn't aware of Corry's illness at all. Everything seemed to be going to plan as they all dressed for the evening looking elegant.

But when the knock on the door came at eight o clock on the dot as Lars arrived thinking he was coming to collect Alexa for drinks, opening the door she greeted him with;

"Good evening, I have a surprise for you".

Walking straight into the room his face was a picture for what was in front of his eyes was the woman he loved from the first time he set eyes on, and to this day, he had never got over her, still as beautiful as ever even though it had been years since they'd parted;

"What's going on" he asked Alexa.

"You may as well ask for I don't know either" Corry replied looking rather bewildered.

Alexa just looked at each of them in turn before saying;

"Mother, I think you have something to tell Lars as he deserves to know from you and not hear from anyone else, he also needs an explanation as to why you pushed him away when you plainly still had feelings for him".

"And you Lars need to listen and not to be so stubborn when you've wasted all this time not knowing the truth, so I'm leaving you both to put this to bed before it's too late as my mother will explain fully".

Closing the door behind her Alexa proceeded to join Karen, leaving her mother and Lars alone to put the final touches to their lives before something was to happen, whereby they would have missed their chance to say goodbye, instead of leaving everything up to Alexa to break the news when her mother passed away which would be a cruel way to break Lar's heart yet again, even after all that time, for although Alexa had been in constant touch with him, she thought it only right that her mother should break the news personally;

"What's all this about" Lars asked Corry as they were alone at last.

"Sit down, have a drink and we'll talk, it's a long story and we have a lot to catch up on" was the reply.

"Well I'm listening as promised Alexa I would. So you'd better start at the beginning, by explaining why you walked away, when you knew how I felt, you never even tried to explain, for what we had together was real and to this I deserve an explanation even at such a late date," he said in a harsh tone.

"Sorry, but it was hard for me as well, for I did really love you and we could have had such a good life together but due to circumstances, that's the way it had to be for you know how Jay had killed all the trust I ever had in men and was frightened it may happen yet again with you and wasn't prepared to take that chance".

If it's any consolation, Alexa adored you, and your family made it so hard for me to give you up but I was so mixed up at that time, that's the reason I buried myself in work and the longer we were together, the harder it became to walk away knowing I may get hurt at any time as complications set in which I'd rather not go in to". Corry said.

"Oh Corry, why have you left it till now to put me out of my misery, why didn't you tell me all this before, we could have worked it out together, you know full well how much I worshipped Alexa, even to the point of keeping in constant weekly touch with both her and Tam".

"No, I didn't, Alexa kept that pretty quiet, she's never mentioned anything about any of it" Corry said with concern written all over her face.

"Well that's up to those two to tell you, but what I can't understand though, is why they haven't got married as they're made for one another which you can visibly see when there together" Lars said as he noticed the concern in Corry's face, thinking something was wrong with Alexa and that's why she'd invited him over, so that her mother would be able to break the news in a far better way than she could.

This puzzled Corry a little for how would he come to this conclusion unless they'd seen Lars on a regular basis or had they been to Sweden to stay with him, which sounded more like the truth which obviously Alexa had omitted to mention to her mother.

Yes, Lars was the Godfather to little Jilles and was in fact at the christening but as Alexa made sure their paths never crossed at the celebration, not even introducing Jay as her father, he wasn't aware of any connection other than it was a friend of the family she was with, which again was where pride kicked in. All this was backed up with the help of Tam who didn't even want Jay at the christening and only agreed to appease Alexa by inviting him.

"So you don't know about Jay then", Corry asked.

"No what about him, why bring him up after all these years as he wasn't any father to Alexa as I recollect", Lars replied harshly.

"This is where it all gets complicated for Jay is not only Alexa's father but he's also Tam's father, now you see what I mean about complicated", she replied.

"Oh my God what on earth is going on, why didn't you contact me?"

"I would have thought Alexa would have told you or maybe she kept it from you so as not to hurt" was Corry's reply as she put her head down knowing the next bit of the story was going to shock him even worse.

"What's happening now then is everything sorted Lars asked as he saw the sadness and stresses automatically appear in Corry's face.

Looking at Lars, she knew, she'd made a mistake all those years ago but would never admit it, for she was just as stubborn as he was, in fact looking at it quite realistically all the men that had been in her life had all been of the same characteristics which was, loving, gentle and strong but on the other hand, were also very stubborn to say the least not giving to show their feelings.

And with tears welling up in her eyes as she looked at him, still so handsome with an air of dignity that had attracted her the first time their eyes met, knowing he would never have cheated and would have bent over backwards to make her life so happy, they could have been soul mates forever, as his love for her was real but she being so stubborn, was blinded to the fact. Now being rather hesitant before she continued, seeing the hurt in his face for what they had both lost between them.

He blurted out "Come on then, tell me it can't be any worse than what's happened to Alexa" sensing that wasn't the entire story and there was a lot more to come by now.

Oh my God, this is going to be harder than I thought, but obviously I have to tell him or Alexa will never forgive me having brought him all this way to break the news, and so with a deep breath she started;

"I have an inoperable brain tumour with only limited time left to live".

"Time, how much time and what is being done about it" Lars cried out in anger.

"A week, a month they can't say, I just have to take it as it comes, there is nothing they can do, so I'm just living on borrowed time so they say".

Lars stood up with such anger and hurt in his face before saying,

"Oh Corry what a waste, what have we done, what ruined lives we have created, when we could have been together to get through all this".

"Who is looking after you, is there anything I can do or is that such a stupid question".

As usual, Corry had to get on her high horse before saying "I don't need looking after I can manage myself".

"Oh for God's sake get off your high horse Corry, and let people show how much you mean to them without putting up a fight and pushing them away as you usually do" was the reply.

Taking a deep breath Corry decided to get the next sentence out before, he would assume the right to take the situation in hand to be with her.

"There is also something else I'd better tell you", and so;

Telling the story of Jay contacting her when reading about the engagement of Alexa and Tam, and with the news that they couldn't get married due to the fact, Jay had found out Tam was his illegitimate son to an old girlfriend, then having to break the news to both the children who was not only devastated but Alexa being five months pregnant. So as things moved on and a split in the family became inevitable causing tremendous problems all around, it was then, as she hesitated looking rather sheepish at that point.

"Come on Corry spit it out for goodness sake; I can see your hiding something.

"I took Jay back, due to a lot of pressure but don't worry I'm no fool, it was more circumstances than anything else, yes I still love him but not in the same way, I loved you, I love him as he is the biological father of my daughter, he has changed and has turned out to be a good strong man, which will help Alexa when I've gone, but he knows I'll never trust him for what he did and definitely can't forgive. He wanted to get married again and put everything behind us but you know that wasn't possible, I would never forget the hurt he put me through when he took a young girl to our bed, this was unforgivable in my eyes which killed me inside, never to trust again "she said.

"Oh Corry what have you done, Alexa would have been ok, she has a perfectly good family in Sweden who care for her, there was no need to have taken him back, but yes I can see where you were coming from for Alexa's sake, what does Tam think to all of this" he asked;

"The only words I can describe that answer, he hates him with vengeance and would never trust him, although he suffers him only for the sake of Alexa".

"I can't understand why Alexa didn't get in touch with me before now; she knows I'd have come straight away" he said with a hurtful look on his face.

"All I ask of you now is that you stay in Alexa's life as I've a feeling she's going to need you more than ever in the future, as you will no doubt need her. I think when the time comes, she'll turn to you rather than her father for some reason, and he may not like it but then again Alexa and Tam have their own lives with a strong moralistic value" Corry stated.

"There is nothing I could ever deny you and to this, there will be no question as I've always looked on Alexa, Tam and the baby as my family" Lars replied with tears streaming down his face as he walked over to Corry, putting his arms around and holding her so tightly with a mutual love and respect that you would imagine from two people who had shared so much love and who still had strong feelings for each other in their time of need which was paramount at that time.

"Thank you and always remember, I have loved you from the first days we met all those years ago, now let's go down in the bar and join the others as this is a happy night and I don't intend to be miserable" Corry stated with a lump in her throat.

But it was as they were going down in the lift to the bar Corry turned to Lars and said;

"We have loved and we have created something that I could never give anyone else but you and with time you will realise the sacrifice I made in the name of love for you to hold so dear to your heart, still keeping part of me which you will cherish for the rest of your life", so remember when the time comes it was always you and you alone that I gave it to"

Lars looked at Corry and with a strange feeling knew there was more to that saying than he could possibly understand but that was in the future and he was too upset to go into that conversation any further.

For there the mystery would stay, for death may bring sorrow but to some it would bring joy.

Joining both Alexa and Karen in the bar, it was clear to see the heartbreak in both Corry and Lars's face; as Karen said;

"I think we all need a drink to finish the night off as you two deserve it by the looks of you" knowing it wouldn't have been an easy meeting for either of them.

Enough said as for the next hour this is what they all did, drink but not to the future knowing how bleak it looked on the horizon. Having enjoyed a nice meal, and drink after in the bar, sleep didn't come easily for any of them that night and so with heavy hearts the next morning, they all said their farewell's with both Corry and Lars in such a state. For it had become quite obvious the hurt they were experiencing between them as the air of love showed for all to see and with compassion, Alexa taking Lars on one side, promised to keep him posted on the situation knowing how distressed he looked.;

"I'm sorry you had to learn about mother's illness this way but you know how stubborn she is when she sets her mind to something as it's her way of handling things alone".

"You know I'll always be here for you when the time comes, for you're my daughter in every way other than being biological, so don't ever forget if there's anything you need call me as I'm only at the other end of a phone".

Those were the final words Lars spoke as he walked towards Corry for one long and lasting kiss before walking away into the distance, tears streaming down both of their faces as the goodbyes were to be the last parting words between them.

Nothing was said on the journey back to London for words couldn't describe the feeling that all three people were going through in their own ways.

Back in London, it was quite hectic with the fashion week commencing in a few days' time, and as usual, Corry had to be there to put the finishing touches to everything as in her mind, she started the business and therefore she was going to see it through till the end, stubborn all the way but that's what got her through life.

Tired and weary, she was now finding it hard to get through the busy days and maybe a few early nights would help although to be fair, Jay tendered to wait on her hand and foot making sure that a lifetime of missing meals wasn't going to be the problem. It may have been early to bed but somehow she couldn't sleep for her mind was elsewhere, yes, it was in Sweden, she couldn't get Lars out of her mind, what a fool she'd been.

All her life she seemed to have been walking through a wilderness, helping others instead of grabbing a little happiness that was right in front of her, a man that not only adored but also loved her daughter unconditionally. Try as she may to get it him out of mind but without any success until sleep overtook its course eventually through exhaustion.

The start of the fashion week was horrendous with all the foreign buyers arriving, parties, press meeting and of course the celebrities who wanted to be seen at all the top shows but as usual with Corry's insistence that the end of the week was her priority showcase this year, then at least there would be a few days' grace before the mad rush. Nothing had ever changed in so far as the press, for they would look after her in turn for when it came to the final showing of the week she would be presented on stage as the CEO of one of the largest fashion houses in Europe, although in her eyes this accolade wasn't for her, but for her loyal staff which was a national scoop, for them due to the fact she was up for a big award within the industry.

It was on this last day that everything went to plan but unfortunately there was something wrong for she not only had a blinding headache but her eyes weren't focusing very well that day for some reason.

Brushing the symptoms aside while taking the medication that had been prescribe for such occasions; she seemed a little better when taking the stage and so carried on as planned for fear of letting anyone down, this was Corry all over, she would always go that extra mile to help out and make sure everyone else was o.k. regardless of her own feelings.

Knowing in her heart this would be the last time she would ever take to the stage for the presentation and therefore accepted this with pride at the gratitude and respect that was shown to her. This was felt by all the staff as they also suspected it would be Corry's last show, therefore wanted to show their admiration and love for this great lady.

The show went as expected with a flamboyant theme of colour that wowed everyone, the dresses were modern flighty and with a general touch of youth which always pleased the modern woman, the shoes again were of the same vibrant colours and designs that had been especially ordered from Italy and when it came to the lingerie well what more can I say other than sensual sleek and extremely sexy which left very little to the imagination, which again was what everyone was delighted to see.

To end the show was always a highlight and again Karen had pulled a surprise out of the hat by a mock church alter where two brides appeared in designs which were identical, soft heavy peach satin, cap sleeves, sweetheart neck, fitted down to the floor and accompanied by a long train which was attached at the shoulders. The train was carried by two small eight-year-old girls dressed in satin peach blouses, short check trousers, held up by braces, little check flat caps on their short bobbed hair and to top it all off, they wore hob nail boots to which the audience was in hysterics at this wonderful originality, although they had now come to expect something totally different to end these kind of shows.

Yet another success was had by all, as they celebrated after the show, yes it was a small but meaningful celebration to show their gratitude for a boss who had kept them in the limelight for all these years earning them a good living and in doing so brought profitability to the company beyond belief. But as the night slowed down so did Corry as it seemed to have taken it out of her more than she realised.

So it was now home to bed after calling off to see her beautiful grandson Jilles, such a rewarding day it had been, a memory that would never fade she thought as her head touched the pillow that night, still with thoughts of Lars going round in a wondrous daze.

As the morning came, so did the newspapers, again hailing Corry as the wonder of the week, showing the brightest of shades the industry had ever dared produce and to this they would hit the magazines within the next few days, whereby, no doubt the orders from the buyers would exceed the production. Again, she had taken a gamble with these vibrant colours and it certainly paid off, just as the small girls dressed in what people would call little boys outfits.

Yes, another show that came to a successful end.

Chapter 23

The next day was to be a relaxing one as Shelia had made all the arrangement for the Directors and their partners to have a knee's up at a local restaurant that had been booked for the night, Corry would therefore be able to spend the day with her pride and joy, Jilles, she would probably take him to the park and then on to McDonalds as that's what he loved to do more than anything, this giving him the excuse to eat with his fingers as he wasn't allowed to do things like that when at home.

The day started off fine but there was something wrong and Corry couldn't figure it out, it was as though there was a cloud looming over and trying to tell her something, but whatever it was she'd no idea until eventually it disappeared.

Spending the day with the baby was the greatest joy she could foresee and having taken the opportunity to enjoy it to the maximum with little treats all day long, they were both in their element, but time flies when you're enjoying yourself and this day wasn't any different to any other when spent in the company of your grandchild.

As the day rounded off and they walked leisurely back home, it so happened they were to pass a pet shop to which thrilled Jilles so much, a closer look was a positive move where he could take a look at the pets, obviously the wrong decision but never the less we all make these from time to time.

The only problem was, she couldn't get him away from one in particular and that was this little cute six-month old dark brown Labrador that apparently had been purchased as a present and unfortunately returned the following week as not wanted. The thing is, there was definitely one person who wanted it and of course he wasn't going to leave that shop until his grandmother had bought it for him, bad decision, yes we know as we've all been there and done that, but never the less we still go there and do these things yet again, never learning the lesson the first time round.

Arriving back home with this extra guest was a sight to be seen on Alexa's face and with Tam in the background who just couldn't keep a straight face looking at Alexa's expression, knew only too well what had happened, Corry could never deny Jilles requests, but a puppy, now that was a new one even for her as she was never really an animal lover, and to be honest thinking about it seriously, knowing it was a good move as a companion for their young son, maybe it would keep him out of trouble as he was a little scoundrel into everything now. And knowing she'd lost the battle even before it started, Alexa just smiled, looked up at the ceiling with a remark of;

"I can't get my breath" and left it at that, well what more could they say as Corry attempted to scurry out of the door adding;

"Right see you all at eight on the dot tonight, this is going to be one of the best celebrations we've had in a long time as feel it in my bones" she said leaving.

That night Corry wore a plain silk vibrant blue dress with matching Italian leather shoes and bag, a simple diamond bracelet together with the ring that Jay had given her which belonged to Agnes on one hand while the diamond which Marcus gave her on the other, looking utterly stunning as she walked into the restaurant on the arm of Jay, for this was to be her night as everyone commented how well she looked, and with no sign of the illness that blighted the horizon, looking strong as though she could go on forever.

Of course she thanked everyone for all their hard work in making the seasonal shows such a success with profits rising at a steady pace and therefore everyone to benefit by this. The restaurant had pulled out all the stops to accommodate such nice people and therefore a credit to them in every way, from the atmosphere, service, to the food, with Corry suggesting that they should in the future use the place for all their private functions to the delight of the management.

The night went really well but having said that, Corry got that strange feeling yet again. It was as though she was walking a tightrope but couldn't get to the end of it, still the feeling only lasted for a short time as she put it out of her mind, not understanding what it was all about for the night was going so well, and therefore not wanting to spoilt it for everyone, as they'd worked so hard to get the collections for the show and this was a way of letting their hair down after so much pressure they'd endured along the way.

Having thanked everyone again, it was time for home due to the night starting to take its course, getting a little tired; saying goodnight to everyone, it was now home to bed after a big kiss from Alexa and Tam. Strange as it seemed, a feeling that she wanted to go back for one last time into the restaurant and kiss her daughter, tell her how proud, and how much she loved her, funny but she'd never felt this way before but on this occasion the feeling was so strong that Jay took her back just to appease the mood, to Alexa's surprise.

"Well now that's over and such a success it's to bed for you young lady" Jay stated with a commanding authority as they stepped into the awaiting taxi to head back home.

Home at last after one hell of a night and having undressed, she lay her clothes on a chair beside the bed which was strange for her as she was obsessed with putting them away as she took them off, laying down next to Jay, as he turned to cuddle up to and with the suggestion that she ought to go straight to sleep having had such a hectic day".

"No" came a firm reply "I have no intentions of going to sleep" she said in a defiant manner as Jay had come to realise there would be no room for negotiation when she was in that mood. "I need you to love me tonight" she demanded quit firmly.

"But I love you every night so what's special about tonight" was the reply;

"I don't know, but I'll think of something before the morning comes, so you'd better make it good" she stated in a high pitched voice.

Jay knew Corry was getting weaker by the day but wouldn't admit and definitely wouldn't slow down so there wouldn't be any argument from him he thought;

"What more can I say, I can't refuse a lady in distress when she makes such a request as that" was the reply as he pulled her tighter to him brushing his lips against hers with such passion that the blood was already starting to rush through both of their bodies.

It wasn't long before he started running his fingers through her hair, tenderly caressing the neck, moving slowly down to those wonderful large nipples, which was so succulent that no man could ever resist the temptation to feed upon. Knowing she wanted this just as much as he did and her wish was to be his command tonight, for there was a strange feeling in the air that they both felt.

As he moved further down her body, kissing it lightly as though there were no tomorrow, her sweet luscious lips beckoning his attention for what he thought was a matter of urgency, taking the petite clitoris onto his tongue before sucking the flowing juices from her beautiful opening river of excitement. Now he'd done this on many occasion but for some reason tonight was different, when all of a sudden she cried out;

"Stop!"

"What's the matter darling, am I hurting you "

"No, I just want you to come inside of me and make love with your body, I want to feel you pushing up that deep inside that I will be able to feel every cell in my body explode to your desire and passion, making a wild, unstoppable, explosive combustion like never before "was the answer.

This wasn't like Corry at all but then if she was tired and wouldn't admit, then probably this may have been the answer Jay thought as he followed her instructions, for the results would still be satisfactory to both when she screamed with ecstasy as he shot everything he possessed up inside of her

"Now I'll go to sleep" she said turning over with a strange smile on her face and the thoughts of Lars on her mind.

Having slept soundly that night although a troubled look on her face when she awoke, to what ends, she wasn't aware but as usual she brushed it off and decided to call and see Jilles on her way into work for a kiss and cuddle off the little man as she now called him. This wasn't unusual, but what was unusual was the fact that she drifted into work late, for Corry was always a stickler for time, if not, one of the first to arrive.

A morning meeting with a few of the press and then back to her office for a coffee with a remark of it being the best coffee that she's ever had, again this was a strange comment for her to make, as she kicked her shoes off and sat back in the chair.

"Look can you get Karen on the phone and ask if she'd like to meet for a little light lunch around one o'clock as I fancy trying that new Bistro down the road" she asked Shelia, while staring into the coffee cup which was still in her hand.

It was roughly ten minutes later that Shelia popped her head into Corry's office to inform her of the meeting, but as she did, holy hell broke loose, for Corry was slumped over the desk and looked to be out cold.

Shouting for help as everyone rushed in to assist, it was a mad panic, the ambulance crew arrived within what seemed like minutes and to say they were marvellous wasn't an exaggeration for she was unconscious and after the attempt to bring her round failed it was a mad dash to the hospital where she'd to be put on life support straight away, for it seemed her body was now starting to shut down.

The machines working their wonders as Alexa and Jay arrived only to be told the seriousness of the situation and that Doctors were doing everything they possible could, but again it was now in Corry's hands as to how she reacted to the drugs they'd administered.

By now the only thing they could do was hope and pray as she started to respond or was that just an imagination that caused her eyes to flicker they thought. It was at this time the specialist arrived and ordered a scan which would no doubt tell a little more what was going on as he informed them that an operation may be required to help with the swelling but that wouldn't prolong the inevitable, it would only give a little more time, but then he'd know more after the results of the scan, he did however assure them that she wasn't in pain which was Alexa's upmost concern.

Having received the results of the scan a little while later, the Specialist stated, if Corry lasted the night then she may have a little longer as the tumour was so large it was now taking control of the brain therefore controlling other organs.

Having been assured that she wasn't in any pain yet again, which to them was a relief, for she'd never brought pain to others so why should it happen to such a good person wasn't right, there wasn't any justice in the world that you should suffer in this way.

It was decided between Alexa and Jay, they would take it in turns to stay by her bedside talking to her all night, maybe she couldn't hear them but knowing she wasn't alone being the main thing, and that one of them would be present for when and if she came out of what Alexa called a deep sleep, for that's what it seemed to them as she lay motionless with all the tubes fixed to her body.

With only black coffee to keep them awake their exhausted bodies tired and weary but still fighting to talk their way through the night with strength and hope that their love would pull her through, even if it was only for a short time so as not to cheat them of a last chance to say goodbye. As morning broke, a sign of light came with a flicker appearing to her eyelids, slowly the movement of her hands followed by the slowly awaking of the eyes opening, looking around the room in a bewilderment, before asking;

"I really enjoyed that coffee, is there any chance of another one".

Alexa looked at Jay as much to say what's happening while replying;

"It's ok, Shelia's just gone to get you another cup" while Jay walked out of the room to get hold of medical staff, with the news that Corry had now regained consciousness.

As the doctors came rushing in to check Corry over, stating she was well as could be expected suffering no pain at all, Corry in the meantime was in a world of her own being drugged up to the eyes so to speak.

It seemed ages before Corry started to regain her senses thus realizing just what had happened and therefore putting into perspective just what was going to happen in the very near future. Alexa and Jay by her side looking weary and bewildered but not enough to hear the next sentence that came out of Corry's mouth;

"Look I'm no fool, I know I haven't got long now, I'd like you to bring Tam, Issa, Peter, Karen, David, Malcolm, Shelia and last but not least Jilles in to see me, one at a time but I insist that they come today"

Jay looked at the doctor and acknowledged the nod that passed between them as much to say, do exactly what she's asked for time was running out fast.

That afternoon it was decided by all, it would be a happy event for time was of the essence and they realised this, so when she asked for a small get together with even tea and cream cakes provided adding that a couple of marzipan flanges for herself would go down nicely, that's exactly what they would do, organizing everything from her bedside as usual Corry being in charge, determined to hold on to the reins for as long as possible for when they all arrived, as requested.

Having stated, she would see everyone individually and then hoped they would stay for a small get together and with her being in a large private room, there was no problems with this request for when all said and done she was a large donator to the hospital having purchased equipment for the children's ward on many occasion.

Some two hours later as they all paraded into a private room just down the corridor, Corry discussed with her daughter just how she would play this out, meeting each and every one in turn for a final goodbye.

First of all, she would see her faithful secretary Shelia, who had stood by her from the beginning not only as a trusted employee but also as a loyal friend who watched Corry's back through thick and thin over the years.;

"I would like to thank you for all that you have given the company, your time, your skills, your loyalty and most of all yourself for not only have you been a trusted employee but also a very good friend in time of need" was her words to Shelia. As a mark of respect for your loyalty to myself, I thank you with all my heart and know that you will look after Alexa in time of need, being by her side to guide as you have done with me through the years", Corry said smiling as Shelia bent over to kiss her with tears streaming down her face before leaving the room.

Secondly, Macomb entered the room for a quite word with Corry, holding her hand so tightly while gazing into her eyes as she smiled with a genuine token of respect for this man who was not only a good friend but a fine artist in his own right, with fabrics that was specially designed by him, since Corry brought him into the company giving him an opportunity to enter her exciting world of fashion.

"Malcomb, the only words I can describe you would be, you are a pure genius, to architect a show of pure silks and wool, making the finest of knitwear Europe has ever seen. No one else could manage that magnificent art of design that you've achieved over the years. And without you, we would never have been able to achieve the reputation and success that we have today on the open market. As a loyal friend I would like to thank you for everything that you've done to make our little family a success, I would now ask you one more favour, and that would be, you carry on looking after my daughter as you have for many a year now" and to this end, Malcomb kissed Corry before walking out of the room as he couldn't keep it together for much longer.

From the first day that he met Corry he had loved her but dare not mention it for the fear of losing her friendship and trust and it was now that she would soon lose her life to an unknown illness that was beyond their control, a woman of such great power and beauty was so rare in this life, nothing seemed fair, for she'd put so much into other people's lives and done so much for the good of others with the only consolation that her talented daughter would carry on where her mother had left off.

As Peter entered the room Corry's face lit up like a ray of sunshine for that's just how she felt when he was around, she knew he had her back through thick and thin, not letting anything get to her in any way that could hurt or do her harm, from the day he joined the company, he had been her rock, fighting in her corner to make the business successful in every way possible, being there when she needed him, arranging that she was always financially secure to go forward both in business and her person life.

A friend in need was her friend indeed and for that she thanked him with no words passing between them just the hug and kisses before he left the room his heart visibly breaking for everyone to see as he closed the door behind him. No, like the others before him, he couldn't keep it together for Corry had been his soul mate in so many ways, she knew just how to handle and get round him should there be any need to, therefore when she was in a happy mood so was he, when her troubles came to the fore it really cut deeply until she was on the road to recovery, all of this Anna knew and accepted as it was a sisterly love like no other and should Alexa turn out like her mother then he would be there to guide her as a debt he owed Corry.

Issa, well what more can I say about the friendship they had from the beginning; She worshipped Corry from the first day they met, they were like true sisters whereby neither of them ever had one. Corry owed Issa a debt of gratitude that only family could understand for she'd taken Alexa under her wing and not only taught her the tricks of the trade but also acted as a second mother to her in times of need, she and Rob had always been there to help back her up in all decisions, not only with her daughter but also taking the company into a position of expansion through her lingerie lines, so when Issa entered the room with growing concern, her heart breaking to see Corry with life draining out of her, saying;

"I would like to thank you for all that you've done to make life easier for me. You are my sister in every way possible and to that, I couldn't have wished for a better one if I'd chosen her myself, there is no words to describe what we have been through together and what you mean to me so all I can say is thank you from the bottom of my heart for everything, as I truly love you and pleased you finally ended up the richer in life with a man that worships the ground you walk on, and has done since the first time you met.

Take care of our family as I leave it in your hands from now on", Corry said. There were no other words to be spoken; as Issa kissed her friend with tears flooding down her face only to whisper;

"And I love you with all my heart" as she ran out of the room heartbroken.

David's turn was so short and sweet for he was a man of silence and mystery who had always been the same since he joined the company, a company that he'd worked very hard to promote all over Europe getting the results that everyone desired and benefited from financially;

"David I would like to thank you for all your hard work over the years and what you have achieved for all our little family, I trust you will carry on with the good work for they all need and respect you in your decisions. I would also like to wish you well with your family as you have a very strong moral background that will carry you to the upmost of heights, you have a wife in a million that many men would give their right hand for, I pray that you will never forget that and look after her as she needs the love and attention that only you can provide for she feels so alone as though you're pushing her away with ambition that she can't match up to at times. She is not only beautiful on the outside as well as an enormous asset to both you and the company, being my close friend for many a year now I don't know what I would have done without her" Corry said smiling to herself.

"Thank you, I've taken on board everything you've said and thank you from the bottom of my heart for what you've done for both me and my family as a friend, for I couldn't have done it without you" David said kissing Corry on the cheek before leaving her bedside.

David knew only too well what Corry was trying to say, in not so many words for he did have a tendency to put everything in front of his wife at times and as for business, well, that always seemed to come first which wasn't intentional by any means, yes Corry was definitely right on that point, as some people would put that down to neglecting their partner but in his defence it was taking care of his family. Making a solemn promise for the future to himself, he would stand back, take things a little easier and give Karen the attention that she craved for at times for he loved her deeply and it would break his heart if anything like this should happen to her he thought.

As everyone sat outside of Corry's room in a dull silence, it was Tam who now entered with an air of authority that he brought out when he entered the Old Bailey court. Looking straight up at this fine figure of a man Corry smiled as she softly spoke with concern in her shallow voice;

"Look after my daughter and grandson, never mind what obstacles may be put in your way for you was meant to be together as a united family, don't ever destroy what you have together, listen to your heart and you will never go wrong, marriage isn't as important as love and you both have plenty of that to give so carry on giving it and nothing will stand in your way. Should you wish to marry Alexa at a later date then find a country which will accept that as it is your right and love which will prevail to the end of your days"

Taking a deep breath Corry carried on although you could see she struggled at times;

"Alexa is going to find it very hard for the next twelve months and will need you by her side to help physically and emotionally, I know you'll never forgive your father or even like him for many reasons and I for one would never give him the trust that he yearns for, so to this I trust you will be there and manage the situation for both Alexa and Jilles to carry them through, as I know in my heart you are soul mates to be together forever. Lastly, I want to thank you from the bottom of my heart for bringing my daughter the happiness and secure foundation to her life, as she loves you not only with feelings but also with trust, which to her is very important.

"Now for the baby, I would ask one favour of you and that is; he should be brought up knowing his grandfather even though I realise that Lars is to be in his life in a big way, don't let hate create a situation whereby you have to pick one over the other or you'll have regrets as your own father has at this moment in time. Alexa will always love her father but it will be Lars that she has the respect for".

Tam had such a strong personality, but the words that Corry spoke, came from the heart and therefore brought him to tears as he left the room in his bold quite manner.

Outside of the room Tan had time to reflect on Corry's words, knowing he could never forgive his father, but also aware of the hate which would eat him away, should he let it, and that wouldn't help either him or those around him, and so decided to put his feelings for Jay aside and get on with bringing harmony to the close knit relationship although in truth the forgiveness would never subside on his part.

It was at this time Alexa strode into the room knowing her mother would be getting weaker and also knowing how she would fight to her last breath to see everyone, yes, her mother who had not only brought her into the world but had been her role model through life, the life that would see her through to the end. Crying as she bent down with a kiss while snuggling up like a baby;

"Don't say anything as it's breaking my heart, I can't bear to see you go through all of this alone, if only I could take your pain, I would willingly do so", she said;

"Listen darling, I'm not in any pain as the drugs they've given me are taking that away so dry your eyes, your son needs you to be strong and channel your love through him for he is your life now and with Tam by your side, you will never be alone for he's your soul mate who will be by your side forever, trust me in what I say. You have all these people around who will help and protect you in everything you do, achieving all your wishes, listen to them carefully and take their advice for you may need it, don't be too proud to ask, they have valuable experience and won't put you wrong, watching your back as they have done for me, so treat them well with respect".

"But the only wish I have at this moment is that you could stay with us and be here for a little time longer", Alexa said sobbing.

"Look darling, none of us have a choice in this matter, I've lived a good life and met a lot of good people who've helped me on the road to success. Yes, I've walked alone for a long time but that was due to circumstances and meeting the right people at the wrong time in life, but that's what the cards have dealt me so I can't really grumble, for on the other hand it also gave me the most beautiful daughter and grandson I could have wished for.

Now dry your eyes and think of all the good things that life will bring, don't be too hard on your father for he hasn't had it that easy, he knows I can't forgive and forget what he did to us but let him make it up by being in Jilles' life for they both need each other. I would also ask a favour of you, but then again you will know about this when the time comes as Karen will tell you, now give me a big hug" Corry said.

Alexa stood beside her mother's bed for a moment before asking;

"Why haven't you seen Karen, she's been with us all the time while everyone else has come in to say their goodbyes?".

"I know, that's for a reason which you'll find out later but in the meantime, go into the safe at work, give the envelope that's marked Private and Confidential underlined with the words, "from me XXXXXX to you", to Karen and she'll know what to do with it, under no circumstances should anyone else know about this envelope, only the two of you, so don't breathe a word to anyone".

"Karen will then ask you accompany her on a journey after my funeral whereby you hand this letter over to the person in question privately; I really need you to do this without anyone else knowing", Corry muttered as her voice now being a little strained.

Alexa was so confused what her mother had said, for none of it made any sense at all but then it was Karen's turn to see Corry so maybe she'd be able to explain what it was all about, as her head was so mixed up with the tears flowing uncontrollably as she walked out of the door.

Although Karen had waited for a while now to say goodbye to her friend, never the less she wasn't prepared for that final moment as her face, drained with emotional anger of the situation they were all having to experience, a woman who had been a mother, friend, lover, companion to all that had entered her life was now being taken away from them.

"My dear friend Karen, over the years we have shared the upmost secrets, having laughed and cried over that time but yet having the time of our lives in each other's company, someone I could not only talk to, but talk with as often we'd see the funny side of all the misgivings that entered our lives.

We met in a bar under sad circumstances that day, but will part all the wiser at the end, for you have been a true friend in every aspect, having given you the chance to make something of yourself, you took it and never looked back for now you're a very creative successful woman who the company is very proud of, making a name for yourself throughout Europe. So it is now that I ask a very special favour from you" Corry said in a faint voice.

"Anything, you know whatever you want it's yours for the asking" was the reply.

"In the safe at work, there is an envelope which I've already told Alexa about, she is therefore to collect this, hand it over to you whereby the two of you will deliver it to Lars personally as I don't want it to get into the wrong hands, if you know what I mean, under no circumstance should this envelope be left with Alexa as I wouldn't trust her, not to open it," Corry stated.

"Say no more, it will be done as requested with no questions asked, I know just how much that man meant to you even if you were a fool in not grabbing him with both hands at that time", Karen replied.

"Thank you and God bless you my friend as that's what you have always been", as Karen gave her friend the biggest hug she could in the circumstances.

Walking out of the room crying Karen asked Alexa to take Jilles in to see his grandmother as she could see Corry was now getting very tired and knew she wanted to see the baby;

"Nana tired, Nana tired," his little voice screamed out as he could see Corry's eyes fully closed.

"No darling, Nana is just resting, I think we shall go and maybe come back later to see her" Alexa said as she tried in vain to keep Jilles quite.

"NO" his little voice screamed out, to which brought Corry out of her faltering sleep.

"Oh my little darling come and give Nana a big kiss, that's my little man" Corry said with smiles breaking out all over her face.

No there was no fear in his face, he wasn't frightened at all to see his Nana hooked up to all those machines, for they maybe babies in the flesh but all the same they always sense when something is wrong and in this case the child knew.

Corry was so proud of her grandson for he was a fighter which would eventually stand him in good stead for the life in front of him she thought, he wouldn't ever have to fight for the love of his father like Alexa did, he was blessed and would have a wonderful life with two loving parents around at all times, together with an incredible extended family circle to take him through life in his chosen path.

Hugging and kissing him the best she could due to the situation was a wish come true but then Corry was now beginning to get tired and seemed to be losing focus so would have to give him back to his mother, who in turn took him out of the room where Tam was waiting to take him home.

In all of this time Corry's brother Paul had stood by knowing he would be by his sister's side until the end as she was fighting like hell not to leave them all. Having stated, he would be the last to have a quite private word with her, it was agreed, that would be the case for here was her only brother who had shared so many memories together growing up, it would be hard to define which one would be the best memory for this certainly wouldn't;

"Corrander Sharp you are an inspiration to us all", he said walking into the room and sitting by her bedside while grasping her frail hand;

"You've not only looked after us in every possible way, making all our ambitions come true, standing by everyone through thick and thin, being there whenever we've needed you, provided for us in ways we could never repay, but have also been the most wonderful sister that anyone could have wished for. Now the one promise I will make you is, whatever happens we will stay together as a family for that's what you've created a long lasting family that can't and will not be broken, for I know in my heart that everyone loves you, but most of all I am proud to say that you're my sister.

We came from such a humble background and through you, we've risen beyond belief due to your hard work and determination, if there is a god up there then you will have a special place by his side I'm sure, if not then you will be running the place in no time" he said lightening the tone.

"What more can I say but thank you for everything you've done, I will always love and respect you sweetheart", he said putting his arms around his loving sister for the last time, while leaving the room to join the others where he could compose himself.

By now everyone was aware just how weak Corry was, therefore as she'd wished, they all filed in one by one in short procession to kiss her before leaving the hospital where it would leave just Alexa, Paul and Jay to spend the night by her bedside.

The day had been long but facing the oncoming night would be even longer for they would stay by her side until the very end as the doctors had warned, she couldn't last much longer and to be honest they were amazed that she'd lasted the time she had, fighting it to the end in true spirit but that was her all over, yes it was going to be a long night.

Having said her goodbyes to everyone, there was still one person shed not had a private word with and to be truthful, she'd nothing really to thank him for as he entered the room to see how she was doing. Then all of a sudden Corry seemed to brighten up for a few minutes only to take a long look at him before saying;

"You may have a second chance of righting a wrong with your daughter and I would advise you to take it with arms wide open asking her forgiveness, although I could never forgive what you did to us, I would say thank you for giving me the most precious thing in life and that was Alexa".

No not even with death looking down on her could she forgive him, as his eyes filled up with tears of emotion only to say;

"Yes darling I know, and I'll never forgive myself for what I put you all through, I have now to live with a conscience that is literally tearing me apart, but I'll make a solemn promise that from now on I'll dedicate my life to making up the wrong I did".

Oh yes, he was hurt alright by those last words but then he knew they were true being his own stupidity, he had ruined their lives and was now paying for that pleasure.

Sat in a chair by Corry's bedside Jay was totally exhausted with what had been said knowing every word was true and with dusk falling quite fast now eventually dropped off to sleep. Alexa on the other hand was positioned opposite holding her mother's hand, resting her head on the bed with her Uncle Paul's hand over her shoulder as she dropped off to sleep.

It was just gone midnight when the nurse appeared to do her rounds that the machine went off, indicating that Corry had peacefully passed away in her sleep not being able to fight anymore. It was a painless end to her suffering in this world the doctors told them when both Alexa and Jay woke up, but for Paul the pain of seeing his sister take her last breath wasn't what he wanted to share with the others for the time being and therefore kept it to himself.

Appearing in the doorway a new nurse came forward with three cups of sweet tea asking them to drink it whereby she would leave them alone, for them to say their goodbyes in private before they left for home.

Both Alexa and Jay said their goodbyes to Corry in private as that's what they wanted for a mother's love is forever and Alexa's heart was breaking to see her mother for the very last time, it was something that you couldn't describe unless it had happened to you, this was a woman that had given birth to you, given life itself in every possible way and now was leaving this earth, never to be seen again.

The words were private between them but the meaning would last forever as Alexa kissed her mother, her wonderful mother goodbye for the very last time, leaving the room crying. Jay was a different matter for he kissed his one and only true love for the very last time asking her forgiveness before leaving the room, knowing that she couldn't forgive him in life so definitely wouldn't forgive in death.

Paul stayed a while longer only to say a prayer that his sister be looked after in whatever life she may go to.

Chapter 24

The next few days were manic in one way or another but at least they didn't have to sort any funeral arrangements out, for they'd already been taken care of by Corry herself when she found out about the illness and the only thing left outstanding was, informing everyone, which there again Sheila came forward to carry out that painful task being the obvious choice having been Corry's secretary for all that time.

As the sadness hit the workforce, it was therefore evident that a solemn cloud would rest over the horizon for everyone, but in true spirit to Corry's memory they all played their part in helping sort things out for the funeral.

Corry had requested that her will be read out before the funeral for some reason that no one could fathom out, but there again it was a request to the lawyers and therefore had to be executed in this way, for they knew she had done this for a particular reason.

Being straight forward; the will was read as follows;

"All my shares in the company to go to my daughter Alexa, which everyone agreed was only right.

My jewellery and personal belongings to go to my daughter including her grandmother's ring together with the diamond ring that Marcus game me, which was at his personal request.

I would also state that personal requests to certain members of staff and close friends, be given on my behalf, but these, are to be private in sealed envelopes.

The apartment in Leeds is to be given to my faithful secretary Shelia who has served me in my hour of need which she alone will understand.

The properties I own in Britain are to be split between Alexa and Paul on an amicable basis.

The Villa in Cyprus was to be a gift from her to Marcus with All her affection, the deeds to be handed over by either Alexa or Karen."

Short but sweet Corry had tied all the loose ends up so there wouldn't be any problem and therefore Jay wouldn't get involved whereby causing trouble with Tam who was in fact an executor together with Karen and Issa.

She had also requested that personal friends together with any member of staff that wished to attend the funeral, which would be held in London, would be allowed to attend whereby the company would close for one day only.

Although having already made prior arrangements to be buried in her home town of Doncaster, with a blessing done at the big white church that was situated on the outskirts of the town.

Everything was carried out to her wishes and for once, Jay took a back seat letting Alexa be the main focus with the help of Tam.

He may not have liked it but what the hell; he couldn't do anything about it.

The eventful day arrived where the funeral possession came to a halt as it passed the small premises that Corry had started her career, with everyone turning out to say their fond farewells out of respect for all that she'd done for them.

The procession now reaching the church, when it was noticed two men stood in the background which had also been part of Corry's life, yes those two men were Lars and Marcus who had flown over with Maria for just this occasion, to pay their respects to a great lady, a lady that they would never forget.

It was when Alexa saw Lars, Marcus and Maria, that she duly approached, stating, it would be more appropriate for them to accompany the family at the front of the procession as they had played such a large part in her mother's life.

Jay looked at Alexa with a mystified expression of who on earth are these people not realising they had loved Corry at a time that was unspoken about and maybe he'd not seen them before, but there stood two men that loved her and yet never betrayed her as he had.

To this Alexa stared back at her father as she softly said;

"They are very close personal friends that have been part of my family as I grew up".

To which Jay shrugged his shoulders and just smiled as he knew when Alexa dug her heels in there wasn't any point in arguing as she was as stubborn as her mother had been and really it was what Corry would have wanted.

Although this was a sad time, there was a sense of relief in one way as they never wanted Corry to suffer, so for all intent and purpose they had to put on a brave face as that's just what she would have wished. The amount of people that attended was quite remarkable with the church so full it was standing room outside for they couldn't all be accommodated within; she was not only a well-loved person but also respected by many.

The service went to plan just as Corry had pre-arranged down to the finest of details which left Alexa with little to do thank goodness for otherwise she would have gone to pieces, this was also, what Corry had stated for she didn't want Jay interfering in any way what's so ever, for this would have caused ill feeling amongst the family and friends that still had memories of what had happened in the past as it was obvious that they still didn't trust him.

One thing that didn't go unnoticed was at the back of the church stood a stranger that no one knew, tall dark and quite handsome for his age, there was something about this man who had such a sad look on his face but with such a strong likeness to Lars and that's why only few people noticed thinking it may have been a relative

The funeral over, as family and close friends went back to a nearby hotel where food and drinks had been laid on with a celebration memory book of this wonderful woman's life which was to be shown on a large screen, the memory book had been organised by Alexa and Issa with the help of Shelia to the surprise of everyone. And while the coffin was to be kept at the church till the morning before leaving for Doncaster, the close family and friends that were to travel up with it had said their fond farewells and therefore far more relaxed while initial emotions had died down, for the time being.

Although it was when the movie of Corry's life came to the screen that all of a sudden Jay fathomed out how close these two men had been to Corry and at that, wasn't too thrilled at the idea they were in attendance as part of the family, but Alexa realised this and wasn't going to let it spoil the day.

She could see the expressions on her father's face and walking over to him said;

"Well you did walk out of our lives for all that time, what did you think, my mother was just going to wait for a day when you realised your mistake, don't think so," she said in a harsh but controlled voice.

Yes, Alexa could be sharp at times and this was just one of those times that the memories of her father not contacting her all those years came flooding back and he wasn't going to get away with it so easily.

The rest of the day lightened up after that little speech until everyone had departed going their separate ways with a heavy heart after such an exhausting day.

Sleep didn't come easily that night for many of them losing a dear one as you can image, but with the morning in sight and the long trip back to Doncaster to lay Corry to her final rest, it was inevitable peace would settle their minds for the long journey ahead.

As the bright sunshine broke through the clouds, the tearful thoughts of the day before arose, bringing an awakening sadness of reality, of the loss they'd all suffered but knowing they would have to pull themselves together and think of the day which was in front of them, it would be a brave face they had to put on.

Again, all this had been pre-arranged and therefore, there was hardly anything to do only drive up for the service which was enough time for Alexa to compose herself before arriving at the White Church for the ceremony.

The White Church stood on a main road that was approximately three miles outside of the town centre, why it was called the white church no one really knows only that it was painted white and stood quite prominent in the eyes of the local people.

This was a more relaxed service, a service that normal people could relate to with a few hymns together with kind words being spoken, not only by the family but also those that made a special journey to pay their respects.

People that had become close to Corry over the years and regarded her as one of their own, and therefore a lot more of them had turned out so say their goodbyes making the church a celebration that would give a wonderful send off to a wonderful woman, which Alexa had not anticipated at all, just how well respected her mother was both in her profession but also amongst local people.

The service over as Alexa accompanied by Tam and Karen, stood thanking everyone for making time to pay their respects before leaving for a buffet at the Danum hotel, it was then that they happen to notice the same stranger they'd seen in London at Corry's funeral only this time he approached Alexa as she walked out of the church with Karen and said in a slightly foreign accent;

"I would like to give you my condolences Karen, also thank you for being such a good friend to Corry" he added as he turned towards Alexa.

"I'm sorry, but do we know you, was you a friend of my mother's" Alexa asked.

"Yes sweetheart, a very close personal friend I'm proud to say, my name is Jilles", and with tears in his eyes as he turned and walked out of the church leaving the two women staring in amazement.

"Who on earth was that, oh dear, I don't expect we'll ever find out now as he's disappeared" Alexa stated rather bewildered.

Karen stood for a few moments pondering as to whom this stranger could have been that no one knew, before a smile appeared on her face, a smile of satisfaction for she alone had now guessed just who this man was, yes he was like the other men that had passed through Corry's life, a life that had many secrets, some they would never know about but then again there was another man in Corry's life that helped her though a difficult situation that she'd told Karen about, but his name was never mentioned although it was suspected that Jilles had been named after him.

The day over with sadness and relief but not yet finished as there was still one more thing that was outstanding, and that was to deliver the letter that Corry had entrusted to Karen, this would be with the help of Alexa by her side, as the last wish she'd promised her dear friend she'd deliver in person.

Yes, her forever friend from the day that they'd met in that bar.

How things had changed over the years for Corry, but today was a day of celebration where time stood still to reflect for everyone's memories, a day that they would all remember for the rest of their lives knowing SHE WALKED ALONE.

Chapter 25

The next few weeks were quite sombre for all, as Alexa and Tam retreated back to their home in York with Jilles and the nanny, while Peter, yes wonderful Peter, he went back down to London to keep everything under control in Head Office.

Corry's death had hit Alexa a lot harder that she though, but Tam was to stay by her side to help her through the next few weeks knowing the difficulties she was to face when returning to London. The main concern, was she didn't crack up with all the responsibility of running the group of companies, knowing there were plenty of close friends around to help with this, but seeing her face through these difficult times, Tam wasn't too sure and thought he should keep an eye on her for it was now starting to tell like never before.

Now in the meantime Jay kept a low profile not wanting to rock the boat so to speak, he knew by now that Alexa had inherited her Mother's will power and therefore would be on dodgy ground should he make any suggestions or challenge his daughter's wishes. Oh yes, this was definitely the right thing to do as knowing his daughter and the situation as it stood, she would have lashed out and then maybe he would have lost all rights to see Jilles and that would have broken his heart for he had come to love this child so much. And with a reflection of the past when he wanted a son with Corry all those years ago, knew if he interfered in any way, it would bounce back to hurt him.

A few days passed and the strain of Corry's death was still taking its toll on Alexa and so a night out at their local would maybe lighten the situation and therefore with a little push from Tam it was suggested a meal with a couple of drinks was the order of the evening, although Alexa didn't totally agree to the idea, she would perhaps go along with it knowing it would please him to see her make an effort as depression had understandably started to take hold.

Walking into the local with so many people paying their condolences gave Alexa the lift she needed knowing her mother was so well thought of and then the smell of homemade cottage pie and chips brought her appetite back yet once again with a few drinks to finish off, well I say a few drinks but that was an understatement to say the least, for by the end of the evening she'd let herself go to the stage of being quite tipsy.

"Time to go home darling, I think we've had quite a good evening, so say good night to everyone while I call a taxi".

Alexa wasn't having any of that as her answer was;

"Why do we want a taxi, it's only a few minutes up the road, and we can walk" she blurted out in an intoxicated manner.

"Spitting with rain, I thought it better you don't get wet" was the excuse knowing she wouldn't be able to make it in those high heels, also the fact she was unsteady on her feet although wouldn't really admit with pride, which again was a woman thing.

"Home at last" he said getting out of the taxi, opening the front door and carefully helping Alexa up the stairs, knowing she'd be fast asleep by the time her head hit the pillow, waking up the next morning with a bad head, but that was his thoughts for he hadn't considered her thoughts for one moment.

Kicking off her shoes as she entered the bedroom, Tam knew only too well he was seeing the old Alexa returning as there was only one thing she needed and that was to be in abundance that night, which he wasn't about to complain or even deny her pleasures, as she now turned to face him with that glint in her eyes, while sliding out of the little black lace number that had adorned her body that night.

Carefully removing the bra and then panties to show her perfect body before laying down on the pure white silk sheets which she adorned with pride, looking up at Tam who was still fully dressed, but even so, taking in all that was before him before saying;

"Don't just stand there, make yourself useful, and take everything off because tonight I'm going to fuck your brains out" Well there's no answer to that and what kind of man would argue with a lady at this point as it would be futile for when a woman's made up her mind, there is definitely no stopping her even if you wanted to, which again, was debatable, well only for a few seconds at least Not wanting to disappoint his lady, he did exactly what he'd been told and climbed into bed as a good little boy would do without any question.

"Oh I've missed you darling but had to wait until you were ready" he whispered snuggling up tightly while kissing the side of her neck slowly and gently, rolling his tongue around her ear, not wanting to hurry things, fear it was the alcohol talking.

"Well if you want to change your mind, there are other ways I can satisfy myself as you're well aware" she answered mockingly.

"Don't worry I have no intentions of that "he muttered as he felt the throbbing in his loins with the erection firing up to a point of direct action that he'd been waiting for these past few weeks, but having to take care of, his situation personally, knowing Alexa wasn't quite ready to fulfil his needs.

His mouth on fire with the passion of eagerness, kissing her neck gently, moving down to those nipples he'd missed, which he was now going to show just how much he'd missed them by the twirling of his tongue to a vibrant suction that drove her crazy with passion and a wetness that was now starting to trickle down her bare legs, turning him on with such a passion.

Oh how he loved those nipples, pert, powerful and with such a turn on for any man to play with, like a baby suckling for its first bottle of the day, knowing the goodness was reaching the parts that was to give satisfaction;

"Oh baby, that is so good, just suck them as long as you like for you're my breast fed baby who may be teething but then I like it as the suckle feel of your teeth is sending me up the wall with delight" she said as she squirmed with a sensation that was attacking her inner body.

"Yes, I know you like that, the question is, are you ready for me to move to that waterfall that's gushing onto the bed sheets "he asked knowing that whatever he did would be alright for both of them;

"Just get on with it and stop talking" she replied in eagerness.

"So you're demanding now, well let me tell you, you'll have to wait my time as a punishment for those demands" was the answer to her little tantrum, moving down with his tongue over her smooth skin to the mouth-watering opening that was screaming out for action as the small ripe peachy clitoris just lay there awaiting to be found and smothered by his soft lips.

Now this was going to be easy he though taking the tiny bud into his mouth to sooth with heated tongue's movement, knowing her G spot would erupt in floods, her body withered from side to side, his teeth again grating with a sensation to bring her pleasure that she'd come to expect by now, from him. The results were just what he'd expected when turning her over to enter with such a thrust that she begged for more as it had been a long time before she'd felt like this and as she begged, that's exactly what she, received with an explosion from, him filling her totally.

Her back flatly on the sheet as he looked down with a cheeky smile on his face, asking in a weary voice;

"Was that to madam's satisfaction?"

"No, I want more so if you think you're going to sleep, you've another thought coming as what I want, is what I get tonight, I told you I was going to fuck your brains out and that's exactly what I'm going to do, my inside is so tight and screaming for you inside of me, the feeling won't go away, so you'd better get used to it".

Tam knew what was coming next, for when Alexa was like this, it didn't matter how tired he was, there wouldn't be any sleep insight for him soon, so he'd better go with the flow so to speak and enter her from a side position where the thrusting would penetrate more violently and therefore settle her down for the night in a moment of peace for the time being.

Throwing all cares to the wind he did exactly that but no chance as the more he buried himself inside of her wet canal the more excited she became with the tightening of her muscles gripping the end of his penis so tight that a suction formed to a point whereby he couldn't fight it any longer as they both came together.

Now that was a signal of sleep which was on its way for both of them as the fulfilment was starting to kick in with a smirk on their faces as they cuddled up in each other's arms to a loving position.

Waking up after such a night for both of them wasn't that easy as Tam was so stiff in more ways than one, while Alexa was still frustrated wanting more of him with that certain feeling in her stomach that women get when they're craving for their partner to enter with a release of all their anxieties that had built up in the body. And it only took a certain look for Alexa to give Tam before he knew the only way to settle both of their feelings were to enter that forbidden fruit and pluck it from the tree of desire making the juice seep as it fell to the ground;

"Open your legs wide and suck my toe sweetheart" Alexa demanded as she moved on top of him, grabbing hold of his leg while moving on top of this huge stiff peak that was standing to attention waiting for orders that she was about to give with her body.

"And what if I say no" was his reply.

"Well, I will have to punish you like a naughty little boy" was the answer as she mounted him in a position that he enjoyed immensely, knowing that he couldn't argue as he could sink deep inside of her to give both of them a mutual pleasure that would start their day on the right note.

Yes, she was definitely back to her normal self he thought and that was a good thing for both of them with a bond that would go on forever as they climaxed with one hell of a cry.

Like all good things, they have to come to an end, and this was no exception, for the next thing would be, out of bed, shower, dressed and an appearance at the table for breakfast with a satisfaction that would make their day.

Life had to go on and it was now time that Alexa had to put an appearance in at the office back down in London where she'd present herself as head of the company being the one who had inherited all her mother's shares and therefore becoming CEO of the company Knowing this wasn't going to be easy.

Now having new ideas for change to an established way the company was run, but hoped the board would at least take her suggestions up, as times were changing and they had to move with these times to survive in what was now becoming a cut throat industry as the Japanese were starting to really get a hold in the markets with the Chinese that would then follow.

And with hindsight, she remembered her mother saying;

"Suggest Changes instead of demanding them and then if things go wrong there will always be someone to help you out and therefore with the new ideas she had for the company, she'd decided to do exactly that for she needed the workforce behind her all the way if she was to accomplish her goals".

CHAPTER 26

All packed and ready for the return to London was the plan for it was now time for Alexa's introduction to the board as the official CEO of the company but with a thought in the back of her mind about the letter that had been entrusted to Karen by her mother which was to be delivered to Lars, unfortunately this had to wait until a later date.

God only knows what that contained, she hadn't a clue but all the same it had been Karen that had to deliver this with her help but why on earth couldn't her mother trust her to give it over to Lars as it would have been far simpler instead of all the messing around, but thinking about it seriously she knew deep down she wouldn't have been able to resist opening that envelope, and yes Corry was right not to trust Alexa knowing full well her daughter's curiosity would have got the better of her before long.

Corry had many secrets and perhaps this was going to be yet another one that hadn't yet come to light she thought, still it had to be a matter of priority and the board meeting was too high up on the agenda so with this in mind she instructed Shelia to call a board meeting with a difference. This would consist of all the Directors, senior managers and personal friends that had over the years invested in the company.

She would also require a couple of employees from all branches of the shops, designers, personnel, factories and HR to attend the meeting, this request was a little strange as never before had so many people from varies parts of the company attended such meetings but there again Alexa was the new CEO and as the saying goes, a new broom sweeps clean with many a new change and maybe this would bring new life into the company.

With all of this on her mind, she knew that things had to be put in place sooner rather than later, for time was of the essence if her plans for the future of the company was to be adhered to before the new shows were to be organised, it was hoped that everyone would back these ideas on how she intended to run as a modern day venture bringing the companies into what looked like a digital future.

The meeting alone would take a few days to arrange and therefore, had adequate time to prepare the speech before going into action, this would also leave time for a meeting with Peter, taking his advice just as her Mother would have done not only as a Director but also a trusted friend for he knew the company better than anyone else.

Yes, oh yes, Alexa was definitely Corry's daughter alright, like a bull in a china shop when she wanted her own way with no stopping her, only thing was, she was right, they had to move with the times and who better to do this would be the daughter of the person who created such a successful company for there was no getting away from it, Alexa's ideas were not only modern but good for the company.

Now to the big day whereby Alexa would show the company just who she was and what she stood for, dressed in a beautiful tailored dark grey suit, white pure silk blouse, matching grey and white shoes as she walked into the boardroom to take her rightful place as CEO of the company. There was a moment of silence, before she nodded in Peter's direction, whereby he asked everyone to be seated.

Standing at the head of the table she began to make her speech as follows;

"My name is Alexandra Sharp (Alexa for short) and for those of you who don'

t know, I am the new CEO of Sharp industries".

"First of all I would like to thank each and every one of you who showed loyalty to my mother in her days of need, she would have been so proud having so many loyal and trusted friends, I don't think you realised but she made a point of reading up on everyone's personnel files to make sure she knew just who worked within the company even though you may never have met her, she knew all about you and her door was always open should you have needed her in bad times as that was the policy she brought to this company.

For those who didn't know my mother, she started this company from scratch walking the streets trying to get someone to listen to her ideas giving her a break for working in a man's world such as this industry was then, it wasn't easy, but it was one day that a lady came along and acknowledging her talent, gave her that long awaited break that she'd always dreamed of, which a few of you here will no doubt remember.

There were no fancy department stores in those days and her first premises were filled with items that had been kindly donated by well-wishers that could see the talent she possessed and therefore backed her financially.

Having such high aspiration, she then decided a showing at the London fashion week would surmount to popularity achieving something bigger for the small little shop she started in; designing all the outfits personally at that time with such a creative mind she then became a small success.

Small was never in my mother's vocabulary, therefore having a bigger vision for her small band of angels as she called them ending with the results of what we have before us today, one of the largest fashion houses in Europe.

As CEO I now intend to take my mother's dream that bit further by making changes that some of you may not understand but in the end will hope to bring fruition to you all, in one way or another.

You may notice there seems to be quite a few strangers at this meeting, this is because I have changed the way we intend to work at all levels of the company starting with the board and working its way down, different yes, but the reason to me is quite clear.

All departments know how they run but having said that they don't realise how others conduct their side of the company so therefore all meetings from now on will consist of a couple of staff from each section of the company coming to the meeting.

The reason for this is; any employee who may have a suggestion that will enhance their department's running will be able to have their say, i.e. the customers that purchase in the shopping outlets know more about what they need than those who maybe sit behind a desk, therefore the design teams will be able to get a better idea of the market instead of just going with ideas they think will suit the general public.

Pink may be the colour for the season but if blue is the colour that takes their fancy, they won't bother at all, resulting in a waste whereby those garment become sale items leaving a financial loss to the company, I am aware this is a new way of looking at this but should you sit back and think, it's quite logical.

I would also state, for all the ideas that we capitalise on, there will be rewards for those who have made the suggestions, giving each and every one the chance to be rewarded in their pay packets, therefore an incentive to work as a team.

We have already tied up a contract with the Italians to help produce our own line of fine leather shoes after opening two successful shops in York, these have taken off at such a rapid speed, that we had to move pretty fast to organise these contracts.

I will therefore reiterate this to all, ideas are important so don't stand back and think it may be right, we want to hear these ideas and work on them with you and your colleagues in mind.

Should anyone have personal problems then I would appreciate that you will come to a senior member of staff whereby you'll be able to talk it over, now should this be a more sensitive issue, then mine or any of the Directors doors will always be open to help in any way we can, for as from today all senior managers will operate an open door policy for their staff to discuss a problem with.

Last but not least, I intend to add three more days on to everyone holiday entitlement due to all the hard work that everyone has put into making the company a success, this may take a couple of months before it goes through but due to all the intended changes this will take a little longer to organise than I anticipated.

Well ladies and gentlemen, I think that will be all for now as I feel my financial Director will be shortly having a heart attack at the thought of all these changes" Alexa said with a smile looking straight at Peter.

To Alexa's astonishment, Peter just sat there laughing as it was like watching a younger version of Corry doing her hell raising act to get the best out of people with them not realising it.

Yes, this was something different and obviously it worked, for the entire board room let out a screech that filled the air with approval as a chorus of thank you went round the room like a world wind.

As there was no time like the present, an email of the minutes was dispatched to all employees, this was done mainly due to the fact that there was an international showing coming up shortly and with Corry's sudden death, they all had to pull their fingers out if they wanted to take it by storm in her name.

Six weeks now passed by with everyone working flat out to achieve the show which was a tribute to Corry and as that final day became a reality;

The showing of the new seasonal garments would be a tribute to her mother and the collections would be named The Corrander Dream, taking in everything from couture to the new children's line as It was decided that everything had to be designed with Alexa overseeing this collection, the colours she chose would be a theme of black, white pale grey and purple, these being her mother's favourite colours. She knew, after the proposals that were in the boardroom, the staff would honour her requests to make this possible in memory of Corry and what she'd achieved, being not only their boss but to many of them a good friend that had stood by them through thick and thin.

The only couture lines for the show were two pure white organza empire line wedding dresses, one beaded with black pearls on the top and the other purple crystals and accessories to match, to say they were outstanding was an understatement. that would go on to steal the show which was already anticipated.

The knitwear that Malcomb had achieved with great satisfaction, turned out to be perfection as expected, starting with, a pale grey and a black theme with the odd purple long line coat style cardigan that came just above the knee showing a flair for extravagance not only in the fabric but also the style.

Now coming to the swimwear which again was a mixture of black, white and pale grey, this was superbly designed personally by Issa as a tribute to her dear friend, showing off all the curves a woman possessed with minute bikinis and backless swimsuits with high legs.

The same efforts of Alexa, when she threw her hand in at doing a collection of the most sexy underwear in purple and grey silks and satins, draped over the shoulders was to be long dressing gowns in black and grey fine velvets.

But this year was to be a little different; they had a new range of Italian ladies kid leather high heel shoes which was delivered just in time to put their steps into the new venture that was going to take them on another route to success which Corry would have approved of immensely

The press was marvellous as usual with the headlines stating;

A woman that not only inspired all but reached her goal in life before an untimely death.

No it wasn't on a sad note for Corry wouldn't have had that, she was the life and soul of the party when letting her hair down, that's how everyone wanted to remember her and with that in mind her daughter together with friends made that possible as one person kindly put it, a chip off the old block as they referred to Alexa.

The strain was now starting to show in Alexa for she'd never really had time to grieve since her mother's death; therefore Tam had taken it on himself to make sure she spent some time with family and friends away from the hustle and bustle of the city where she could never find time to relax. It was marvellous how he protected Alexa but then again he loved her so much it hurt to see what she was going through, not being able to take the pain away for her grief. Not only that, he also sensed, something was starting to trouble her but it wasn't any good asking, as the answer would always be the same, If she'd wanted him to know, then she'd no doubt tell him when she was ready to so, it was a matter of a waiting game for him.

Little did he know, this was one secret even she couldn't tell, not having any idea what was in that letter for Lars, the only thing she could be sure of, was the fact that whatever it was, it was definitely going to be explosive knowing her mother.

Yes, getting away to the house in York was a great idea, for it would be just the opportunity to bring Lars over for a few days and then at least they would be able to plan just how this brown envelope was to be handed over without too much upset as the thought kept running through her mind.

On the other hand Tam would be in his glory getting them all together under one roof, method in his madness, for then he'd be able to get a few rounds of golf in without feeling guilty about leaving Alexa to her own devices knowing she wouldn't be able to leave work alone but would have to entertain friends.

Arrangement were made that they'd go to York with Dave and Karen after sending an invitation to Lars who would spend a weekend with them having not seen him since the funeral which was under more sensitive conditions, and knowing the pressures he was put under in those last few days, couldn't begin to imagine how his feelings were now.

Putting the plan into action between Alexa and Karen was easy as the men wouldn't suspect a thing, carrying it out was going to be far more difficult as they had to pick the right moment to hand over the letter for only the two of them knew about it, never the less it had to be done so no matter what was in that letter they would all be there to soften the blow for that's what it surmounted to be they thought.

All arrangements made as they travelled to York, but the only thing on both Alexa and Karen's mind, was how they were to do the dirty deed as they put it, handing over that letter, but sometimes in life we all have to sacrifice our emotions to help someone out and this had been a promise made on the deathbed of a great lady.

Arriving at the house, as usual, there was a hot meal laid on for them all with little Jilles being the centre of attention, this easing the situation as far as Alexa was concerned, for awaiting on the coffee table was a telegram from Lars thanking them for the kind invitation and stating that he would be arriving at the weekend, looking forward to seeing them all.

Well that's one obstacle crossed, all we have to do now is relax the mood and pick a good time to hand over the letter Karen thought. It wasn't so easy for Alexa though as she was suspicious as to the contents of the letter, she had a feeling that there was a bombshell about to be dropped where someone was to get badly hurt and the feeling just wouldn't go away for some unknown reason.

Settling down for a quite drink and an early night before the men would be up for their round of golf the next morning, Alexa and Karen would have a browse around York to hunt out all the little designer shops which would further their ideas to open yet another shop in the famous Shambles, an area where it was old fashioned shops and cobbled streets, then onto a light pub lunch, few beers was also on the cards before embarking on a fool proof plan whereby they would hand the letter over to Lars.

Friday night would be taken care of with a good night out on the town with maybe a meal or even the fish and chip shop as eating in the city, maybe a little upmarket but good old fish and chips always tasted far better after a few drinks up in the north. Saturday they would all go down to the local pub which was popular for the locals with karaoke, where everyone could join in, again this would relax the mood or so it was hoped. Sunday would be a traditional lunch of Yorkshire pudding and Roast Beef at home which would give them the opportunity to give the letter to Lars.

This had all been worked out over the few beers, so on that note it was definitely going to be a success as the conversation flowed from one subject to another before getting a taxi back to the house.

The only thing was, Tam and Dave wasn't stupid and knew there was something amiss but couldn't put their finger on it so whatever was suggested, they just agreed, if only to keep the peace, knowing two strong women would only get their way should they disagree with any of the arrangement that had been planned. Funny really, but if they hadn't agreed, then both women together would have thought up something else to make it look as though a new idea, was only the original one in the first place.

Believe it or not, the week went quite quickly, although it was designed to be a relaxed time but that idea went out the window with people to see and things to do, therefore it was found that none of them seemed to have a minute to themselves.

As time went by it was no good, for Alexa couldn't relax and so with the help of Karen decided to move into the workshop and start organising the changes which was intended when they all returned to London, this was so that it wouldn't be as hectic with the things they had in mind.

Even though it was supposed to be a relaxing time for Alexa, she was so much like her mother that relaxation wouldn't come easily, she now held a position that not only was high powered but also commanded respect, and to gain that respect, she would have to earn it by living up to the standards her mother had adopted all through the years, putting the company and staff first and foremost.

Her ideas to expand the company in a different direction had to be thoroughly thought through but again having such faith in Malcolm, who would travel to

Japan with an aim of opening the markets with some of the western designs, maybe a little out of their comfort zone, but what the hell, with his knowledge hoped to pull it off.

Before they knew it, Thursday had arrived whereby Lars was to arrive in the morning and so after a few drinks that evening it was decided to retire a little earlier for the tension between the two girls became so obvious knowing they weren't in for a goodnight's sleep. It was when Alexa got into bed first just laying quite that Tam couldn't take the silence anymore before asking;

"What's troubling you darling and don't tell me nothing, as I happen to know you far better than you think, so you may as well spit it out and if it's something that I've done then we can rectify it".

"Sweetheart I'm sorry I just can't tell you, please be a little more patient and things will be back to normal after the weekend I promise", was the reply.

"Well if it isn't, you better sort it out quickly as I hate to see you like this when I'm here to help, come closer let me hold you, this distance between us, it's driving me crazy" he said pulling her body closer knowing she would respond to that growing desire that was erupting between his legs as her skin touched his body, her breast heaving, wanting the love of a man she could never say no to in any situation, for just his touch had her wet with juices seeping down her legs.

Yes this man could create a fire within, a fire of lust and passion which raged through both their bodies as he cradled his arms around her, caressing her shoulders to a sensational feeling that swept throughout both of their bodies.

She could forget all her troubles and doubts when he did this and couldn't resist his growing passion as he moved down her body, slowly with the tip of his tongue barely touching her smooth delicate skin knowing he had the power to make her forget whatever was troubling for the time being but then, what he didn't realise, it was only a temporary release as the problem would still be there in the morning to an accelerant pace before the weekend was at an end.

Her body so clean and smooth as he parted her legs to that little bit of heaven that his tongue so liked to tease as the wet sticky fluid trickled from her canal of wanting him inside, it seemed that all her troubles were fading for the present moment and not only her body had come alive but her mind too. Reaching down, it was obvious how hard Tam had become and therefore demanded that he came further up the bed to meet her, well what was a man to do when he was under orders like that, but do as he was instructed in which he was only too eager to please her demand;

"Seen as you want to play then, I can play as well so you better lay there" she instructed.

Taking her hand round his strong firm penis, she brought it up to her mouth with her tongue teasing his body on the way taking one mighty suck on the end causing such a mind blowing sensation that ran through his body like an electrical current;

"Oh My God", he screeched with the pleasurable pain that hit his brain'

"Sorry darling I'm afraid, god can't help you on the journey that I intend to take you" she said laughingly.

She knew what she was doing alright as she proceeded to suck violently taking the whole of him into her warm mouth as though sucking an ice-cream, enjoying the nerves holding their own, knowing that he was about to explode into the back of her throat.

"Oh no you don't, the only place you're going to put that will be inside of me as I need all of you and therefore it would be a waste if it went anywhere else"

"Please Alexa, let me come, you're driving me mad and you know it"

"What part of NO can't you spell is it the N or is it the O, which ever it is, the answer is still the same" was her reply as she slid to one side of him, therefore pulling into an advantaged position where she could place one of her legs over part of his thigh, her other leg between his legs whereby he could enter her with a deep throbbing ache that would thrust up her wet juicy canal to a suction that she enjoyed so deeply. This would give them equal control, knowing that his demanding body was so hot, and if she paused, it would then slow down leaving her to master her plan of domination.

But tonight I'm afraid, she was out of luck as he wasn't going to let her have her own way and having thrust up inside of her with such powerful force her body became a tower of strength craving for more and more of this demanding delight as eventually the fulfilment of hot bodily fluids would only suffice.

"Deeper, deeper", Alexa cried as Tam thrust that mighty throbbing manhood of his into her controlling inner muscles that hung on to the tip of it, for living death, until both of them couldn't stand it any longer approaching the final explosion of ecstasy.

Yes they were so compatible, both in ambitions and sexually and that's why he sensed her trouble over the past few weeks. Maybe tonight Alexa would finally sleep tight instead of tossing and turning all night as she'd done since her mother's passing away, he thought

Well he was right in one thing and that was after that little session, she slept like a baby for the only thing on her mind was Tam.

The next morning was showered, dressed, breakfast and then on to the airport to collect Lars from that early morning flight from Sweden and it was so good to see him under much happier times, the only problem was Alexa had a feeling that those happier times wouldn't last for long.

As usual Lars had brought loads of toys for Jilles, mostly ones that grownups play with like remote control aircraft but then again that's a man thing that time never changes.

You could visually see the love in his eyes as he glanced at the baby, it's a shame really he'd have made a really good father, if only he'd have been blessed with a son of his own, then things may have been different, but then life was cruel at times and it wasn't obviously meant to be so they all thought.

That night was to be a meal in York giving them chance to catch up since the funeral, a pub crawl, sing song with the karaoke crowd as Lars never had the chance when he was in Sweden for the drinking laws were so very different to the British ones, and a great night it turned out to be for all, which wasn't surprising. Saturday the men went for a game of golf while Alexa and Karen went into York for lunch, a trip round the shops, home with a new dress each and already to gather down at the local pub where they'd been invited to a birthday party of the landlord's daughter.

With such a nice gesture that had been given to them being newcomers to the area, Alexa had sent a large bouquet of flowers to the pub with a cheque for one hundred pounds in a card for this girl, although never having met her, she thought being a young girl it would be more appropriate to receive the monies, where she'd spend it on clothing or toiletries rather than choose some sort of present whereby it wasn't her taste. Having arrived at the pub that evening whereby the landlord greeted them, they were surprised to find that the landlord's daughter Christine, legs were in fact deformed

Such a beautiful girl with a great personality, what a pity they thought as Christine smiled and thanked them for the kind generosity adding; it will go in my fund;

"And what fund may that be", Tam enquired with a puzzled expression.

"It's a fund that's been set up by local people to send me to America for an operation which will enable me to walk like everyone else" was the reply with such a radiant smile.

We grumble at the least little ache and here is this brave girl who has difficulties and perhaps pain that we could never imagine and she's so happy to manage her disabilities until they raise enough monies to have an operation in another country, somehow the system just isn't right Tam thought. Listening to the conversation but keeping quiet, Alexa had other intentions as if this girl needed an operation, then an operation she would have, for she would pay for it herself, arranged through her solicitor as an anonymous well-wisher through a bank draft that wouldn't be traceable as far as the local people were concerned.

Now this was the kind of thing her mother would have done and would have been immensely proud of Alexa's compassion in this matter. Alexa was so much like her Mother in many ways, caring for others that weren't as fortunate as herself, the things she'd taken for granted in her childhood and so, it was a way of giving back some of the opportunities to other in her eyes.

The party was to have been a small one for Christine's birthday but being in the north of England these things tend to get out of hand thus ending up with quite a large amount of the locals enjoying themselves as the night went on. This again included Alexa, Tam, Karen, Dave and Lars, the only thing was, someone forgot that when Alexa started on the champagne, (just like Corry) there wouldn't be any stopping her having the time of her life, for singing was in her blood and when it was all said and done this was a party to sing her heart out and sing she did.

It was approaching the early hours of the morning before a taxi was called to take them home, yes Alexa was a little worse for wear which was expected when you knew how much she'd drank but at least she'd had a good time and that's all that mattered for the next day was going to be a difficult time for all of them as no one knew what that dammed letter contained.

Sunday was a relaxed day, pottering around the large garden and the enjoyment of a beautiful lunch with real Yorkshire puddings as Lars always called them, a run out into the country, back in time for a late tea and good night kisses for Jilles who was shattered by now with all the attention that he'd enjoyed since Lar's arrival.

It was then that Tam suggested a drink at home in the lounge taking into consideration that it had been a long time since they'd all sat down for a relaxing evening whereby they'd be able to catch up on all the gossip without talking shop about the company but unbeknown to the men, this would also be just the opportunity to approach the subject of Corry's letter which the girls were to hand over to Lars.

Such an enjoyable weekend one of them commented as the conversation flowed around the room with such suggestions of having to repeat this again, before Alexa blurted out;

"Look I'm sorry to interrupt this fascinating evening but when my mother died, she left an envelope in the possession of her dear friend Karen with the instructions that upon her death this letter had to be hand delivered to Lars, therefore we had to pick a moment we were all together to accomplice this request.

The silence in the room was deafening as Karen opened her briefcase and handed a large brown envelope to Lars.

As the astonishment set into the room, Tam' now started to realise why Alexa hadn't been herself these last few weeks, she must have found it hard that her mother had entrusted such a letter to Karen and not herself, but thinking about it again, he knew what Alexa was like and knew very well if Corry had given Alexa the letter, she wouldn't have been able to keep it a secret and would have steamed it open as a matter of curiosity. Dave on the other hand looked straight at his wife and wondered why she'd never said anything, they never kept secrets from each other, this was new for her but loyalty was one of Karen's strongest points so maybe that was it.

As for Lars, he just smiled, putting the envelope on the table and stating;

"Corry was all about secrets which she had many, this will contain one of her little secrets that she'd give me from time to time and laugh about, it won't be important otherwise she would have told me when I visited the hospital before her death, there I intend to leave it, to open before I go to sleep where no doubt I'll see the funny side of yet another one of her little secrets."

Now that was interesting Alexa and Karen thought because nothing had been said about Lars visiting the hospital and so that was another secret they knew nothing about.

A couple of drinks more as the conversation was now centred on Corry's dry sense of humour, bringing in past memories for them all, but for some reason the expression on Lars's face was tendering towards a more troubled look as the evening went by.

This seemed to bother Karen as she glanced around the room at the others and so like a bull in a china shop she decided to approach the subject of the envelope to be opened in a funny kind of way that would persuade Lars to open that stupid letter as Alexa used to call it for then everything would be out in the open.

"Look, I think you should open that envelope and put us all out of our misery then at least we can have a good laugh and drink to her, you never know the letter may even contain shares to the company as not all of them have been accounted for", she said looking straight over at Lars.

Lars started to laugh as he knew Karen was right and they were all getting worked up over nothing, so open the letter he would, but to his surprise this was no laughing matter for the first thing that came out of the envelope was a Birth Certificate with the name of Duncan Enos Lundqvist.

There were no words to be spoken as Lars tried to make sense of what he'd vaguely read on the birth certificate, the shock on his face told everyone there was definitely something sadly wrong;

"Lars what on earth is the matter, your starting to frighten us, please tell us what's wrong, Alexa said as the shock went round the room like a rocket being fired from the top of a building.

"I have a son, Duncan Enos Lundqvist, Alexa you have a brother".

"What on earth are you on about Lars, how can I have a brother, have you gone mad"

"Afraid not, I have the birth certificate in my hands to prove this, he was born in Scotland", he said in a bewildered tone as he picked the letter up to read, not being able to control himself as the shock ran through his body at the speed of lightening.

"I can't believe it myself but apparently Corry fell pregnant and then went up to Scotland to give birth, and at this very moment, he is being brought up by some trained nanny who has looked after him from birth," was what he'd actually read although nothing really made sense due to the fact that he'd only skimmed through the contents of the letter not reading it properly. Alexa on the other hand was definitely in shock as nothing made sense to what was coming out of Lars's mouth, for there must be some kind of mistake she thought, Duncan Enos, now wait a minute Enos was my grandfather's name, surely this can't be true she thought.

"And you say that my mother had a baby up in Scotland, she never had that much time to be in Scotland, she was always at work, and surely we would have all seen her put weight on if this was true, no you must be mistaken, maybe she adopted a baby up in Scotland and they had the birth certificate changed through the adoption agency as you know what she was like, always taking pity on someone or other" was Alexa's rational answer.

Shock still going round the room with thoughts running in the opposite direction for nobody could understand all this at all; knowing there would have be a simple answer to it in the end before, Dave piped up with;

"Hold on a moment, I can vaguely remember your mother going to Scotland twelve years ago about the time the child was born, she stated that after putting a few extra pounds on, she'd booked into an health clinic to get fit and therefore would be spending time overseeing north of the border companies while residing at that health club which is where all the correspondence came from while she was up there". We never thought anymore about it really as when she came back, she'd lost weight and looked really great, Karen was away in Europe at the time so she wouldn't have had any reason to see her although they were in constant touch".

Now this was starting to make a little more sense but it still didn't tell them where this child was being brought up or even who knew about him. It was a mystery that none of them knew how to go about finding him which would be impossible, before Karen came up with the idea of getting in touch with Peter. As Peter was the finance Director, then he would have to sanction the funds from the company for the upkeep of the child and therefore without another thought, Karen walked over to the coffee table and phoned him.

Luckily it was Peter who took the call thinking there was something wrong for at that time of night it's usually bad news and so when he heard Karen's voice asking; if there was a private bank account that wasn't disclosed on Corry's death or was there a trust that was lodged in Scotland under Corry's name, he was somewhat surprised;

"What on earth are you on about, you were there when the will was read, what's all this about?" was the answer.

"Look we have to know as a matter of urgency if there is monies being syphoned out of the company or even if there was monies going out of Corry's private accounts, and you're the only one we can ask, you being Corry's accountant".

"Just calm down, tell me what's going on as I'm afraid you've lost me, either that or you've had too much to drink at this time of night young lady" was the reply;

Karen took a deep breath before blurting out.

"Look, you are fully aware that Lars is over in York spending a few days with Alexa and Tam, well I was entrusted with an envelope that I had to give him after Corry's death; in this envelope was not only a letter but also a birth certificate.

Which states that Lars is now the father to a twelve-year-old boy that Corry gave birth to in Scotland, so we're now trying to fathom out just where this boy is", she stated as her voice calmed down

"Oh my god was the cry from the other side of the phone, I can't believe what I'm hearing, look just leave everything and I'll fly up to Manchester in the morning".

"And how will that help us find out all the answers" she asked.

"We'll sort it out from there, just don't do anything stupid until I get up there" was Peter's last words before he put the phone down to a deathly silence that filled the room.

That was going to be a long night, they also knew it wasn't going to be easy to find where this child was being kept, if kept was the right word.

What of earth had Corry done to cause all this heartache, no one knew or could even imagined, she must have been at her whit's end to have given her son away although she hadn't really given him away, she had obviously got someone to care for him, bringing him up in a world that was safe for some unbeknown reason.

It didn't matter how they all tried to think these things through, nothing made sense and the only logical person to sort this mess out, would be Tam, him being a Barrister would definitely have the right ideas when it came to sorting all the legal ramifications out or so it was thought. Tam on the other hand was thinking on the same lines as the others, only with a legal brain behind him, knowing he would have to act fast as Scottish law was totally different to that of British law, therefore they'd have to hire a firm of lawyers in Scotland fear things become impossible.

To be honest no one even knew where the child was at this stage, never mind jumping the gun legally, it was just impossible to think clearly and as usual Alexa's impatience kept getting the better of her, wanting to run before she could walk so to speak without any knowledge on how to proceed further.

Appreciating this child was Alexa's blood brother and knowing how impatient she was, they would have to take one step at a time or would miss some vital clue and therefore would have to keep an eye on her as well. Aware that Corry kept secrets close to her chest for fear of burdening others, surely in this case, she would have confided in someone very close, so as to help in organising everything, but there again who on earth was it?

For some reason there was only one person to blame in all of this, oh this man was behind so much heartache, it was unbelievable and even though they got close towards the end of her life, she never trusted or forgave him for the hurt he'd caused both her and Alexa, and whatever decision she'd made was definitely something to do with Jay's selfish attitude.

Being impatient, Alexa couldn't wait for Peter's arrival the next day, even though he'd made it quite clear they shouldn't do anything until he arrived. The only other person that Corry would confide in would be Issa, and although it was now gone midnight a call to her was necessary.

Looking straight at Karen as she blurted out;

"Shall you ring or do I have to make that call".

Knowing what Alexa was thinking, also knowing they wouldn't be able to stop her even if they tried to, the impatience got the better of Karen as she said;

"I think it better if you do the honours this time". was the answer

No sooner had she finished that short sentence before Alexa had the phone in her hand, dialling Issa;

"Sorry to disturb at this time of night but I have to ask did my mother have a baby that she wanted to keep secret, who would be the person that was closest to her, someone that she'd trust and confide above all, was it you? "

"What on earth are you talking about, you're the only child that Corry had, she never had anymore, although she once mentioned you had been hurt so much when her and Jay divorced, she'd never let another child go through that again, so where on earth have you got such an idea" Issa demanded.

"My mother had a son twelve years ago somewhere up in Scotland, we have the birth certificate with Lars being named as the father" was Alexa's reply.

"Have you spoken to Peter yet, for If this mad idea of yours is true as you say it is, then she would have to provide financially for the child's upkeep and Peter as the Financial Director would know of any discrepancies in your mother's accounts over the years", Issa said in a bewildered tone not making any sense of this situation at all.

"Yes spoke to Peter and he knows nothing about it whatsoever, in fact he's flying up to Manchester in the morning, to help try and make some sense of all this as we haven't the faintest where to start looking".

"It's such a mystery and poor Lars is rather shell shocked to say the least" Alexa added with such concern in her voice for a man who could have been her step father should things have been different.

Issa was so shocked at this revelation, that she couldn't get the words out properly, but having a few moments to think about the situation, the answer was quite logical if they'd stopped to think, for who did Corry trust with her every move, someone who always had her back when trouble was around, someone who protected her at all times, someone who would go to the ends of the earth to protect her name.

"There is only one person that will have the answers to what you're looking for if you think about it" Issa concluded;

"Yes we know that, but who the hell could it be outside of the family that she'd trust with such an explosive piece of information is what we want to know?" was Alexa's demanding and impatient attitude.

"That's easy, who was your mother's right hand so to speak, the one that organised everything for her, the one that knew all her secrets yes, I'm afraid to say it was her girl Friday as we used to nick name her, Shelia.

"Oh my god, your right she screamed, and at the moment Shelia is up in Scotland, how convenient." was Alexa's surprised revelation.

As it was getting seriously late, and so it wasn't any good trying to track Shelia down but was considered an early morning call would do the trick even if it wasn't very practical; mind practicality wasn't a word that Alexa was familiar with as she was too hot headed for that. Deciding nothing more could be done at that late hour, the only thing was to retire to bed although it was envisaged that none of them was about to get much sleep with all this going round in their heads.

In all this time, Lars just sat there in a deadly silence, as they wondered just how they would feel, if this had happened to them for they knew that secretly he'd always wanted a child and that's why he'd made so much of Alexa, treating her as though she was his own in some ways.

The vacant look on his hurtful face was a picture that said a thousand words, he may have loved Corry with all his heart but he didn't deserve this, In fact to be honest no man did ever deserve this being done to him, for it seemed to be a cruel act of defiance from an outsiders point of view, but looking at it from another angle, it would have obviously destroyed Corry just the same.

They were to experience the longest night of their lives as they all retired to bed not being able to find any words appropriate to the situation as a condolence to Lars.

Morning came after a sleepless night for all, so to a breakfast of a couple of slices of toast washed down with strong black coffee which for all intense and purpose was, all they could manage which there again was understandable in the situation.

As for Alexa, all she did was clock watch for an hour or so until it would be a sensible time to try and get hold of Shelia, knowing that Peter would be on his way by now.

It wasn't quite eight o clock when Alexa rang Shelia apologising for disturbing her at such an early hour when on holiday or so that was the excuse she'd made when booking time off work;

"Look I'll get straight to the point Shelia, do you know my mother had a baby some years ago and the child has been brought up in Scotland she blurted out" in an arrogant manner.

"Where has all this come from" Shelia enquired in a soft positive voice that Alexa instantly knew she was on the right track.

"To cut a long story short, my mother left a brown envelope in the safe with instructions that upon her death, the said envelope had to be delivered by Karen to Lars personally, in that envelope was a birth certificate together with a letter".

"Alexa, it was me that handed that envelope over and yes I do know what it contained".

"That's not good enough, we need a lot more answers than that, so I think you should open your mouth to what the hell is going on" Alexa shouted down the phone as a chorus of voices around her told her to calm down as it wasn't Shelia's fault.

"Sorry Shelia, but none of us have any idea and it's driving us all mad, Lars is beside himself with worry over the situation and all of us are trying to help the best we can but obviously getting nowhere".

"I'll have a little breakfast and get a plane down to Manchester, whereby I'll do my best to fill you in with what I know, but in the meantime I beg of you not to worry as everything will be alright" was Shelia's reply, knowing she would face a magnitude of questions that was impossible to answer, before adding.

"Look your mother was a good person and this was done for a good sound reason in her eyes" was the only explanation that was given before the phone went dead.

Whether this was intentional or the signal had been lost, no one would ever know as mobile phones had a mind of their own and if it had been in a poor reception area, the signal may have just disappeared which was a good thing in this situation.

It wouldn't be long before they were to collect Peter from the airport as both Alexa and Karen pondered as to how they were to tell him they'd already jumped the gun by getting in touch with Shelia that morning, knowing full well, Shelia would be joining them that evening to throw a little more light on the situation.

Lunchtime came as Tam and Dave collected Peter, when he arrived and then Alexa and Karen would collect Shelia later on, yes they'd got that sorted out knowing full well it was Shelia who would have the information as to the child's whereabouts if anyone. No, they were no fools, knowing that if anyone knew the whereabouts of the child then it had to be her and that's why this was arranged, you don't need detectives, all you need is a woman's intuition, especially when they have a notion that something is going on they don't know about, it's called a personal built in radar.

Time seemed to drag at first but it was when Peter arrived that the situation had calmed down somewhat to his thinking, and with a meal already waiting for him, it was a pleasant surprise not to have to deal with Alexa's multitude of questions, but what he wasn't aware of at that time was Shelia was already on her way down from Scotland. Alexa was no fool and therefore wasn't going to break the news that her and Karen was leaving Peter in the hands of the men while they collected Shelia from the airport, so quietly excused themselves for the time being with an excuse of having to collect a friend from down the road which was pretty feeble in the circumstances.

It was when all three of the females walked in a couple of hours later that the penny dropped, for Peter realised they'd a head start on information about the child but really he shouldn't have been that surprised as Alexa was the daughter of one of the most intelligent women he had ever met and therefore wouldn't let sleeping dogs lie so to speak. Yes, they were clever but the one thing in all of this they'd missed, was the question of what Corry had put in the letter that had accompanied the birth certificate, or had they missed it on purpose as a mark of respect to Lars and Corry's memory knowing eventually Lars would give it them to read.

After making both Peter and Shelia comfortable whereby staying in the guesthouse, arrangements were made for dinner and the discussions to follow over drinks in the lounge due to having been such a traumatic day throughout.

Lars on the other hand played his part by agreeing to wait for discussions to be put in place to find his son. And so it was after a beautiful three course meal where everyone sat down to enjoy the Yorkshire hospitality, before retiring to the lounge for drinks, Shelia now seeing the anxiety in the faces of all, before she started to tell what she knew;

"Look before I start and tell you what happened, I'd like to say this, Corry was a good woman with a heart of gold, she not only did the best for her family but also did something that hurt her immensely, as you are all aware she never had a bad bone in her body and therefore you can't judge her before putting yourselves in her shoes, for at that time it was thought, this decision was to be the best solution for all, so with this I will tell you what I know and why she entrusted me to do this for her".

Chapter 27

"It happened one morning when Corry arrived at work and as usual I brought her coffee.

Sorry Shelia I just can't face that this morning, I think I'm coming down with something as been sick since the early hours, it's as though my stomach's on fire and feel quite dizzy, just rang the doctors, made an appointment to see him in half an hours' time, so if you could cancel all my appointments until I return it would be appreciated. She said

No problem with that but I'll get you something light for lunch when you return as it sounds like you've picked up a bug that's going round.

It was some two hours later that Corry returned appearing as white as a sheet;

You shouldn't really be in work, what did the doctor say I asked being rather concerned that she'd been overworking recently and not looking after herself as usual.

Being ill is the last thing on my mind was the reply as she slumped down in her chair adding.

I'm pregnant, five months gone, was her shock announcement.

To be honest I was speechless, well what could I say as words wouldn't come out of my mouth for what seemed ages.

It was as Corry gathered her composure she went on to say;

This is what I want you to do for me; I don't want anyone to know about this and am relying on your integrity as always.

Firstly, I intend to work as long as possible before anyone notices changes in my body which I'll put down to stress and irregular eating, after that I'll make excuses, telling them I'm going to Scotland to have a few months at a health spar where I'll run the company north of the borders from there if need be.

Secondly, when the time comes for the baby, I'll contact you whereby you'll arrange time off with maybe some excuse whereby a family member is ill, travel up to Scotland to help finalize arrangements for a suitable nanny who will then take over duties in looking after the child.

I realise I'm asking an awful lot to keep this secret but must stress its vital that no one knows about this especially those that are close, she said with a sadness in her voice.

If that's what you really want, then I'm quite prepared to go through this helping you in every way possible I replied, not realising what was to happen after she'd hired the nanny whereby informing me that she intended to purchase a property up there where the child would be brought up in secrecy.

The next few months were hard as Corry often struggled with her conscience but I was there whenever she needed a shoulder to cry on as she'd been there for me when I was in need of her help, oh so many years before.

Time passed by so quickly although she struggled to hide not only the bump but also the tiredness she had to endure without anyone suspecting there was anything wrong and so it was into her eighth month that she complained about not feeling well with the weight she'd rapidly gained, therefore without hesitation stated to those close to her, it wasn't any good just dieting it would have to be more of a drastic action and book into a health farm.

This had to be a snap decision, for she rang one night from the station and politely informed me she was on her way up to Scotland, not to worry as she'd already informed the powers that be of her intentions, i.e. Peter, Alexa, Issa and Karen.

Having made it clear to everyone that she needed a rest and therefore intended to book a health spar to lose a little weight and tone up for a few months, no one suspected anything other than what she'd been on about weeks previously.

A few weeks went by when one morning the phone rang at the break of day; Corry was on the phone asking would I be able to fly up to Aberdeen as she wasn't feeling too well and maybe it was time for the baby to make an appearance.

With bags already packed for such an anticipated journey, all I had to do was phone the airlines and book the next flight to Aberdeen, then a taxi to the hotel she'd been stopping since she'd arrived in Scotland.

But before leaving London, a phone call to Peter had to be made informing him that my aunt was very ill, and that I'd had a call from Scotland to fly up there straight away, her being my only living relative.

Peter had said words to the effect; look if you're needed then that's where you should be for family comes first in situations like this.

Arriving late that afternoon, I was asked to attend the hospital straight away as my friend had been rushed in as an emergency an hour before.

Dropping my cases, I took a taxi and arrived just in time to accompany Corry into the labour ward where it was my privilege to be with her for the next couple of hours before she produced the most beautiful little boy with a mass of black hair and blue eyes weighing 7lb3oz and looking just like his father".

Taking a deep breath, Shelia caught a glimpse of Lars's face, a face of pride and yet there was sorrow as tears rolled down his cheeks with the emotions that were now welling up inside of him as she asked politely;

"Would you like me to stop for a while"?

"No that's all right, please carry on he said with a lump in his throat while the rest of the room was in utter silence."

Shelia looked around the room once more before continuing her story.

"Corry had lost a lot of blood in childbirth and therefore had to stay in hospital for nearly a week, bonding with the baby, which in a way, was to make handing him over so much harder than she anticipated when the time came, but never the less she knew in her heart that was the right thing to do as she didn't want him to suffer the pain that Alexa suffered, he said.

The name she chose for the little one was Duncan, as it was a name that reminded her of being free as a bird, it was also a name that the child's father always liked; Enos was her grandfather's name who she idolised till the day he died and adding Lundquist as a surname would be proof of the father's name in later years.

Upon her release from hospital, it was decided, we would both look after Duncan until Corry finalised the interviews for a mature lady to bring him up whereby she would visit him every month until his education had been completed and then he would take his place in the company alongside his sister.

A property had already been purchased out in the highlands to accommodate all of this, with things being done professionally through lawyers, a trust fund and separate accounts had also been opened with an unknown private share in the company which would last for a number of years or in the case of her death, then they would be handed over and held in a trust by the child's father, all this was done through lawyers in Scotland".

It was at this point that Shelia had to pause as you could see the distress it was causing just telling the story, for although she didn't agree with Corry and also told her after the child was born, it wasn't her place to say anything to the family as she'd been sworn not to.

The room still silent when Dave spoke up and said;

"It's about time we all had a break for coffee, let Shelia have a little time to settle, you can all see the pain this is causing her, having to relive this nightmare in front of all of us".

Shelia smiled a smile of gratitude for what Dave had said was perfectly true, she felt drained but also knew it all had to be out in the open and laid to rest before they could all move on with their lives and so after the coffee she would continue;

"You wouldn't believe how it broke Corry's heart to hand young Duncan over to be brought up in a strange place and thank god, he was too young to know this.

To hand your child over to a stranger, she must have gone through hell, they all thought.

The lucky thing about handing him over to this stranger was, she was such a good old fashioned lady that reminded Corry of her own grandmother, with the same values that she'd been brought up with, when she was young and therefore Corry would respect the life that he would be shown.

Yes, it was hard for her to give her son away to a stranger and only she would suffer the heartache at that decision but having her reasons wasn't for us to make judgement on, as spending time with him, was like spending time with his father in her eyes, an honourable man that she walked away from.

As Duncan grew up into this handsome young gent as she often called him, you could see the hurt in her face every time she had to kiss him goodbye knowing that he was her secret son who only one other person knew about.

Don't get me wrong Duncan never wanted for anything, he had the love of his mother and nanny, her sister and I myself visited whenever possible and was brought up to know that his father was a pilot in Sweden and his mother had to work to provide a good education for his future which he readily accepted.

Whenever he asked questions about his father, he was told the truth, a warm handsome man who put family before everything and that one day in the future, he would be reunited with both of his parents either in England or Sweden, to this, no further questions were asked realising his parents loved him dearly and like many of his friends who were brought up by grandparents due to divorce, he accepted this was a normal situation.

He was such a bright child who came on in leaps and bounds at school, hungry for education with a passion for learning languages at the top of his list, sport again was another thing he had to try for every time he mastered a particular sport, he went in for another, no he never lacked in anything.

Being such a well-mannered young boy it was a pleasure to have around, with such a loving nature, that whenever you came into contact with him, you just felt so at ease".

By this time there wasn't a dry eye in the room for a secret had been kept all this time and there was a young boy that had just got on with life being a happy little soul not even knowing that all these good people were his family and yet he'd missed out on the one thing that would have made his life complete and that was the love of his father. Shelia sat back for a few minutes awaiting the response from everyone when all of a sudden Lars spoke up in a weakened voice asking the vital question that was on everyone's lips;

"Where is my son now?"

"Don't worry he's safe and well cared for, living in a small highland village in Scotland" was the reply;

The look on Lars's face now started to brighten up as he asked:

"As you obviously know where he is, would it be too much to ask for your help in taking me up to see him, I know we have to sort all the paperwork out for him to be reunited with the family but to explain what I have gone through this last twenty four hours would be impossible and therefore I'm begging you to help me see my son" he pleaded.

Shelia smiled as tears rolled down her face; answering;

"I think the best thing for all of us to go to Scotland, taking one step at a time as Corry knew that one day this would happen and therefore made me promise to help you reunite with Duncan".

"Oh my god" Alexa screamed, "were all going to Scotland in the morning and I won't take no for an answer" as she looked over at Lars who was grinning like a Cheshire cat by now knowing there wouldn't be any stopping her even if he'd wanted to for Duncan was her flesh and blood too.

Lars looked emotionally drained but very happy, Alexa and Karen was just on cloud nine as everything was now coming together while Tam and Dave had other ideas as they walked out of the room for a quite talk together.

A quite talk was more of a legal discussion, with Scottish law they could see complications and so something had to be worked out beforehand otherwise there may be a lengthy battle in the courts, this they wanted to avoid at all costs as there would be a lot of private matters come to the fore which wouldn't help anyone. Tam being the Barrister and therefore legal mind in all of this came up with a plan they should all go to Scotland, talk with this lady who had virtually brought Duncan up single handed and propose a package whereby she wouldn't be able to refuse.

The proposal in mind would consist of, a pension; signing over the property into her name as a gift for all that she had done with an allowance, which would enable the lady to lead a comfortable life without having to worry about working again, this would be for all the loyalty she had shown Duncan over the years. None of this would be mentioned to Lars at this stage as he had enough to think about , but this package would work for all to benefit, and so leave it until the situation became a little clearer whereby should any obstacles arise then they could be sorted out accordingly.

With exhaustion overtaking them all it was a night's sleep they needed as tomorrow was going to be a long day for them, not even trying to imagine what was going to be the outcome at the end and so as they climbed the stairs to the thoughts of what may lay ahead. Afraid dreams wouldn't come so easily that night only problems looking into the foreseeable future for a young man that was going to give them so much joy and pleasure.

As the morning broke over the skyline there was a fresh beginning in the air with a smell of freshly roasted coffee and a hearty Yorkshire breakfast to welcome them to start the day, a day that was full of promises of the unknown in which an army of people was ready to fight for their rights should this become necessary.

Leaving Jilles wasn't an ideal situation but with luck they would be returning with an uncle, so the pain of parting would be short lived in Alexa's eyes as they set off for the airport.

Arriving at Aberdeen airport they were to collect a couple of Land Rovers which had been pre-arranged before they set off and would accommodate the seven of them being the larger vehicles and with a lot of luck it was anticipated there would be an extra little guest on the return journey. But there again that was all depending on what would happen when they reached their final destination which only haven knows where it was as they had no idea, it was all in the hands of Shelia.

But It was on the plane after they'd all settled that a surprise request came about, for Alexa decided to brave the storm so to speak and approach the question of what her mother had put in that fateful letter that was addressed to Lars, she knew only too well, if she approached the conversation in a way that gradually got round to it, there would be a chance Lars would tell or even go as far as letting her read the letter. The only problem was, Alexa was never very tactful when she wanted something and therefore with bated breath just came out with;

"Maybe I shouldn't ask and maybe it's the wrong time to ask but I'm left with no alternative as its killing me over what my mother has done to you, so Lars, please tell me what excuse she gave for causing us all this heartache".

Lars looked over with a vacant expression before saying;

"You're on about what your mother put in the letter aren't you, sorry Alexa but I can't really tell you, I didn't read it properly, when the birth certificate fell out I knew deep down what it meant and what she'd have gone through to keep this a secret, you see, your mother and I shared a love that was never destroyed by two people. It was destroyed by one man who let her down badly, that badly she never got over it. That's why she could never trust any man again, for as soon as they showed any emotional attachment, she'd walk away, I understood her but I couldn't change her in that respect".

I know where your coming from" Alexa replied as a tear rolled down her face.

"I know he's your father but he never loved her the way that I did, he was far too selfish for that, and didn't realise she was a woman that cried out for love and respect, and for this, he just hadn't the capability to fulfil her needs for the only person he really loved was himself. It's a pity really for when he woke up to his true feelings, it was far too late as she'd lost all respect for him and would go on to the end of her days with no forgiveness in her heart, yes one man made her and then he destroyed her, not understanding what real love was until it was too late".

Everyone listened but said nothing because what Lars had said was true in more ways than one and now was the time to make things right, there would be no more secrets as far as he was concerned as he reached down into his briefcase, taking the brown envelope out and with a deep sigh of relief before handing it over to Alexa saying:

"I may be wrong but I would like you all to read that letter before you make any judgement about the only woman that I ever really loved and although I haven't read it properly myself, I know in my heart what she will have written, for there wasn't a more honourable woman that walked the earth than Corry".

Sitting back in his seat, Lars left everyone to absorb what had been written in Corry's moment of pride and torment, the heartfelt letter that would have broken her heart while doing it.

THE LETTER

My dearest Lars, The love of my life in the true sense,

As you read this, I pray that you won't judge me too harshly for what I have done, you will now realise what I did was to protect the ones I love so much and it's with regret that it had to be this way for our son Duncan was conceived in love and will bring you as much happiness as he's already given me in his short life, I know you will cherish him as will Alexa, and hope that you'll forgive and understand the reason as to why I chose to take this path.

Not being able to see Duncan go through what Alexa went through when Jay and I split, the hurt she still suffers within is heart-breaking, although she'll never admit to, but although I feel her pain, I'm helpless to comfort her. I know this would never have happened where you were concerned but just couldn't take that risk yet again.

The times I've tried to bring myself to tell you about our son but at last minute relived the heartbreak of the past and just couldn't bring myself to face that period of time yet again and therefore sure you will understand.

Having maintained that Duncan should know about his real family and background and therefore putting everything in place for that special day when you will be able to claim your rightful place in his life. You don't have to worry over him as he's been well cared for and brought up by a trained nanny in the highlands, who was not only a friend to him but also a surrogate mother in many ways which I'll be eternally grateful for. I would also state that a trust fund set aside for any eventuality should one arise.

I thank you with all my heart for the acceptance and love that you showed Alexa and have faith, this will always be the case knowing you have loved her for many a year like your own.

You will now be aware, what some would call a reconciliation between Jay and myself, this was brought about mainly by the fact that, as we got older it was a way of making peace but never did he mean to me what you did, also I never forgave him for the painful time he caused to both Alexa and myself in Berlin, for you was always in my thoughts from the first time we met and will be until the day I die.

Ours was a love born from the first moment we met, unfortunately you came along at the wrong time in my life when I'd been emotionally damaged to the point that couldn't be repaired, yes we had good times and those memories I will take to my grave leaving a memory for you, being our son whom I know you will cherish with every bone in your body, giving him the same respect and love that you showered on me.

Our times were together as one, our hearts were beating in the same direction, our love was unbelievable, our strength was for the future, yes we had everything but still the shadow that Jay left hung over me, left me with a weakness in which I couldn't fight as doubts clouded my every move leaving me with thoughts that I wasn't allowed happiness.

I only hope that one day you will find it in your heart to forgive and believe that we'll be reunited in another life where there is no pain just the love that we share, that made us altogether one.

Don't judge Jay too harshly for deep down he is a good man who doesn't know how to show emotion's like the rest of us and should you look at it from another angle, we would never have met if circumstances had been different.

You will find with the documents I have left relating Duncan, a share certificate in your name; this has been done for one reason and one reason only, to bind you to the company which Alexa now is majority shareholder so it will keep you as part of the family that we all hold dearly to our hearts.

As I leave you, I leave you with my heart, body and soul forever until we may meet again in another life that was made for us alone. Please don't be sad for this was meant to be and as I leave you, I leave with just your love, where as I have left you part of me in Duncan.

My love forever Corry

Alexa said nothing as the tears flooded down her face, she passed the letter on to Karen who after reading it was choked just as much, what more could be said, it was all in that letter, a letter written from the heart that touched everyone, a sacrifice you'd never believe made in the name of love, but there in black and white was the proof of such an emotional sacrifice.

The rest of the flight was left in silence for no one could find the words to follow.

Aberdeen airport, touching down was smooth and without a problem, the vehicle hire was waiting for them and so it was a matter of offloading what few overnight clothes they had into the vehicles, setting off for the ride of what was to be an unknown journey of unexpected joys and sorrows.

Luckily there was a sat navigation fitted, for travelling in the highlands was going to be a journey of a lifetime with Dave driving and Shelia accompanying him in the first vehicle as it was the first time he'd been that far up north before, and with the others following in close proximity over these lonely road, yes this was the real Scotland he'd heard about.

A beautiful land with tranquil fresh air that put you at peace with all your troubles for the scenery was just magnificent to say the least. They'd been travelling some four hours before they reached their destination which was a small village with individual dark grey cold looking stone houses and bungalows and yet giving a feeling of friendliness set in a picture like post card, you could well imagine in the heat of the summer, the flower blossom falling from the trees, honey suckle filling the air and with a view to die for as you gazed over the fields with cattle roaming at their leisure.

It was when Shelia interrupted Dave's train of thought by saying;

"Just pull onto that drive at the end of the road, there's plenty of room at the back where the summer house is and I'll do all the talking to start with as Duncan will no doubt be at school."

This is where Shelia would come into her own for she'd been up here so many times before, even to the point of spending a few holidays in the past and therefore it made sense for her to take the lead in conversation as the others pulled up in the vehicle behind, not knowing just what to expect at this stage.

Walking up to a large solid wood door and taking a few knocks, to be heard as the loud thunder seemed to sound in an airy tone when the door opened with a surprised greeting that was so welcoming to a stranger, putting them all at ease in such comforting surroundings.

"Why hello again Shelia was the voice in a slight Scottish accent, my name is Molly and who are these lovely friends of yours that's come to see our little village, now you must all come in and be having a nice cuppa tea with a drop of whisky as no doubt you will all be weary"

Looking at this lady, they would all agree, Corry couldn't have chosen anyone better to look after Duncan. Yes, Molly seemed to be such a warm, inviting character, slight of accent, pleasing to the eye, smart but casual lady which at a guess would be around late fifties to early sixties, had a hard time somewhere in her life, never been blessed with any children of her own but with a personality of outgoing strength that you would trust your life with.

"You will all have to be excusing me but my sister Maggi has come to stay with us for a few days, she gets so lonely since her husband died, so therefore comes up from the city to stay, it's all right as this is a happy house where we welcome all visitors so feel free to have a wonder about if you wish while I get hot drinks for you all", yes this woman was one in a million and I'm sure if you'd have searched the country over you wouldn't have been as lucky to find someone like her again.

Making themselves at home in such relaxation came naturally and it wasn't before long that Tam stood up to stretch his legs looking out of the window at the huge garden neatly laid at the back in which an extension had been added to the four bedroomed property;

"What a beautiful place you have here Molly, it's so tranquil and yet mystifying, a place you've lived all your life is it" he enquired.

"Oh no I came here some twelve years ago with my foster son, well that's what I call him although that's another story and yes your right, it's so serene and beautiful, that's why my sister comes here so much, to get away from the hectic noise of the city life in Aberdeen".

Serving tea, scones sandwiches and fairy cakes washed down with a malt whisky for each of them just seemed to come natural to Molly even though Shelia did offer to help with a slight refusal as she was the guest which Molly politely put.

"Now I don't know if your all up in these parts of the highlands on business or pleasure, but you'll all be welcome to stay, it may be a bit of a squeeze but we'll manage as we welcome all guests that come to stay don't we Shelia"

"No it's alright, we can book a hotel, I saw one a couple of miles down the road" Tam insisted with a friendly smile as the hospitality was overwhelming.

"Look I will be having none of that in my house, you will be staying, what will folk be thinking of my hospitality if I let you go paying good money to stay at one of those fancy hotels, when I can be putting you up here, I'll not be taking no for an answer so be told" Molly said in a sharp Scottish tone that you didn't argue with.

"We have dinner in this house about eight sharp so when my sister gets back from picking Duncan up, it will be time to start preparing, while Shelia tells you a little about the place, then there will be time to get to know each other a little better don't you think".

It was then, the door opened to a smart looking young man who was a younger looking version of Lars together with Molly's sister Maggi who was the double of Molly in fact they were like two peas in a pod and could have been taken for twins.

"Now say hello to these good folk that have blessed us with their company" Molly said to Duncan as like many a young boy of his age rushed to the kitchen as a matter of hunger.

Yes, food goes before anything at that young age with growing so fast, it's all they think about and Duncan was no different to any other youngster.

The room was quite, Lars holding his head down not to show feeling too soon although cutting him up inside, now trying to keep his composure as Duncan rushed past him to go upstairs without a word, but then minutes later he appeared back stood in front of Lars with a look of apprehension before saying;

"I'm sorry sir, for ignoring you like that, it was very bad mannered of me, you're my father aren't you" as the tears rolled down his little face.

Not being able to control his feelings, Lars stood up, flung his arms around Duncan and cried uncontrollably;

"Oh my son, you don't know how I've longed for this moment, you really don't".

This moment was for Lars and therefore no one could take it away, others looked on with pity and happiness for a father and son to be reunited in this way was a miracle that happens only once in a lifetime and that had to be savoured for as long possible.

It was then that the two sister appeared from the kitchen door to smiles that lit up the room, they knew one day that Duncan's father would come to claim his son but hoped against hope they would see him grow up to the age where he wouldn't forget them, for they knew the possibility of him turning up was near since Corry had passed away, but never expecting how near it would be before it became inevitable.

With tears in their eyes Molly was the first to speak;

"I'm so happy for you all but I must say, I knew this time would come sooner or later and now my work is done, for you have a son to be proud of, someone who has not only brought us happiness and joy but also a family life in which we never thought we would ever experience." She said wiping her face with the tea towel she was holding at the time.

"I think you'll have time to catch up now while my sister and I get on with making the dinner or you may go away starving" she added with a few tears rolling down her face. And although tearful, Karen piped up with:

"Is it still alright if we stay here overnight as you suggested before or should we ring and book the hotel down the road, we don't want you to feel uncomfortable with the situation"?

"I'll be having none of that talk here, you will all be staying and that's final" Molly said quite firmly as she and her sister walked into the kitchen giving everyone time to get fully acquainted.

Things started to settle down with everyone talking amongst themselves which mainly consisted of Duncan asking questions relating to his father's work on the airlines which he found so interesting like any teenage boy would, before the meal was served. The food went down a treat, this being old fashioned good wholesome cooking which no one in their right mind would turn their nose up at, and of course being in Scotland there was always the whisky to end the meal before retiring to the lounge.

Through all of this Lars sat quietly holding his son while Tam did all the talking, wanting to get the situation cleared up before any legal battles became an issue.

Starting off in a relaxed speech Tam thought it best to get business out of the way seeing how they could all be able to proceed without going through the legal ramifications, for that would not only take time but it would also be rather hurtful to all concerned and with this in mind he started to suggest what he thought as an amicable arrangement should all parties agree;

"Now this is only a suggested proposal and as we all think about it, we'll be able to adjust for all parties so that it won't cause any inconvenience or litigation "he started;

"First of all this property will be signed over in its entirety to Molly, she will be able to do with it as she wishes, either sell to purchase another smaller property or keep it to do whatever she desires, this will be her decision and hers only.

Secondly, As Molly is not of a retiring age, the company will pay a salary together with full pension rights as though she was employed by the company from the day Corry hired her

Thirdly, Molly will be entitled to statutory holidays consisting of, six weeks with her sister to travel at her leisure paid for by the company; this may be anywhere, as to her wishes.

All perks that she received from Corry will continue such as a new vehicle every three years

Both Molly and her sister will have access rights to see Duncan whenever they wish due to them being part of the family he'd grown to love and cherish, this will of course be at Duncan's discretion taking into account that he will be adapting to a new lifestyle, but under no circumstances will anyone put any obstacles in the way of such requests.

Now in my opinion, I think this is a fair deal all around but am open to any other proposals that any of you may suggest, this, I hope will be amicable and if so will start as soon as were back in London to put into processing legally.

I now speak for Lars, and this is for a personal request for I realise it's a delicate subject but wish to have the answer before we all retire for the evening having seen the pain he has had to endure these last seventy-two hours.

Duncan to travel back with us tomorrow whereby we can formulate all the documentation and introduce him into a life he will no doubt adjust to in time, getting to know the family he didn't realise he'd got".

Of course there was a deathly silence, this was to be expected, for on one side a child of the family was being taken away and on the other side a child was entering the family he rightly belonged to. But Silence has to be broken sooner or later and obviously it was Molly who spoke first to the delights of others who'd been put on the spot, not realising how Tam was going to approach that request;

"Doing what I was paid to do, with love and compassion, Duncan has been my world and will always have a special place in my heart but he isn't my flesh and blood and therefore I knew one day I'd have to say good bye to him as his father would come and now that day's arrived where I can't stand in his way, for he has a brilliant future to look forward to been the son I never had.

I realise how hard this has been on all of you and thank you for being so kind as not to involve the legal system for they only make things worse and to be honest it would break my heart to go through such proceedings knowing how much we all love Duncan" and with tears in her eyes she carried on the proposals that had been suggested;

"The financial offer; this is beyond a dream but can't accept for it's far too much, the offer of the vehicle I would accept gratefully together with a time period that I will be able to find new accommodation".

Oh no, Alexa wasn't having any of this, she was Corry's daughter and believed in what was right and Tam's proposal was a way of putting a wrong to right, that's what Corry would have done if she'd been in this situation although it was her that caused all of this and so.

Getting to her feet and with a look on her face that told you how stubborn and defiant she could be when she wanted her own way, she politely said;

"There will be no argument over this agreement, it will be just as my husband has stated for he is the legal brains with the compassion that I love so much and what he thinks is fair, will be an acceptance of the matter, is everyone in agreement" she asked looking round at everyone before taking a seat again, knowing that's what Corry would have done.

The echo around the room was definitely in favour as Molly and her sister started to cry;

"I was only doing my job and loved every minute of it, for that I am grateful, for what you are all doing for me is a gift from heaven, one beyond belief" she whispered.

"Well that's settled, I would also add on a personal note that you will always be welcome in my home in York should you ever wish to come and visit with us "was Alexa's last remark.

"Now it's time we all celebrated with a toast, a drink to the future" Tam requested as he walked over to the drinks cabinet where a selection of whiskies were on show, this being his tipple he'd enjoyed on celebratory occasions.

"And now for a toast of the evening "as Molly piped up with a satisfactory smile;

"To a wonderful lady who gave me an opportunity that was sent from heaven, and now she looks down on us all with peace in her heart knowing that everything has turned out right, I always suspected her heart was broken in pieces but no one could ever deny the love she had for others and the talents she possessed."

No one could argue with that speech and so glasses were raised in her honour.

"TO CORRY, WITH ALL OUR LOVE AND RESPECT FOREVER".

Chapter 28

Yes that night was a night of change for everyone.

With a night in the highlands, sleep came at a price as they slept so deeply with all their worries behind them, although the two sister did find it a little difficult knowing their lives were to change, in some ways for the better but all the same they were looking at a lonely road without Duncan.

He had been their life for so long, but not to fear too much as they hadn't lost him completely, they would still have a relationship that would go on for the rest of their lives seeing him whenever they wished, which is more than they could have dreamed in the circumstances.

Morning came with a sudden light and a hunger that even surprised them, there again it must have been the fresh air, but never the less with the smell of fresh coffee, porridge, a full breakfast, toast and fresh fruit to help on their way, and with enough to feed an army so to speak as they chatted over the breakfast table with a feeling of contentment, which they'd not experienced for a while now, but then came the crunch where it was time for their goodbyes.

Putting a brave face on, Molly and her sister flung their arms around Duncan in such a loving way it was like a mother saying goodbye to her young one, going away on a trip of a lifetime as they hugged him so tightly hoping beyond hopes he wouldn't forget them as he left for his new life. Seeing the tears rolling down his face, knowing the pain of leaving the nearest thing to a mother over his short lifetime would be breaking his heart and yet knowing it was the right thing to do without prolonging the agony of the legal situation, it was goodbye.

All packed up and ready to leave it was Duncan who was the last to get into the vehicle with his father, as Molly shouted;

"Now don't forget your manners when you meet everyone and we promise we'll be coming down to see you in the big city before you know it, if there's anything you've forgotten we'll bring it down with us".

To see the hurt in Duncan's face went through Molly but not as much as the hurt she experienced in her heart as the vehicle drove away out of site leaving her standing by the roadside with her sister, a memory that you will never forget having ever been in that situation.

The journey back to Aberdeen airport was pretty solemn until Duncan started to ask questions, firstly about where he would live, what he would be doing about school, where was he going and then came the more personal question which was fired at Lars.

These he answered the best he could but was more interested in his son as the conversation got round to Duncan's likes and dislikes, what he'd done through school and places he'd been or would like to visit, just the conversations that we all get into when getting to know someone for the first time.

And now to see the thrill on Duncan's face as they approached the airport was magical as he'd never been on a plane before, yes this was a new experience for Lars who was in his element explaining with all the technical details thrown in from a pilot's point of view as his son listened with such enthusiasm and awe.

Boarding the plane, the thrill of flying was another great for Duncan as by then he couldn't stop talking, involving everyone else with the inquisitive side of him emerging as it does for a young boy, especially one who had led such a quiet and sheltered life.

This was Lars's special time with his son but on the other hand, Alexa was just as eager to get to know her new brother, but for now she was willing to take a back seat letting time take its course, knowing that should she rush things it may overwhelm him and there would be plenty of time over the next few weeks, to lavish her attentions on him while others sorted the legal ramifications out satisfactorily.

Arriving at Manchester and then onto York was a dream come true for all of them as what they'd set out to do a couple of days earlier, was to put in place plans to reunite a father and son, to accomplice this would have been short of a miracle which no one even dreamt they would accomplish and yet now, they were all together arriving back where they'd all started from and that was to a warm welcome at Alexa's home.

There was another surprise in store that he'd not anticipated and that was a small bundle of trouble in the shape of a two-year-old little boy who had become an instant uncle, this being Jilles who now gained a new playmate. Oh the experiences just got better and better for him.

Everyone settled in to a few days whereby getting to know Duncan, showing him parts of Yorkshire, the Viking centre in York, the railways museum, a multitude of shops where he was kitted out in new trendy clothes that he could pick himself, the introduction of many a new thing that he'd never imagined, and now appreciating all the experiences one by one

Having talked it over with everyone, it was decided that Duncan would stay up in York with Alexa and Karen while the others travel back to London where they'd put in place all the legal documentation i.e. passport, papers to take him out of the country such as guardianship documents, then there were the share certificates that was in the safe in Corry's office and maybe other stuff that they weren't aware of which may take time.

Lars had also decided to purchase a small apartment in the city where both Duncan and he would stay when they came over rather than infringe on others hospitality. Yes, all of this was to take time but then again time was now on their side as Lars wasn't in any hurry now he'd got the most precious thing in his life and as all his business interest back in Sweden would be managed by those he employed, no it was important that everything was done correctly so he could take his son back to his family home.

As most of Lar's business holdings were tied up in Sweden, that's where they would live for the present, he'd already got a large house situated on the riverbank in Stockholm so it only made sense that they settled there and with a place in London which would be appropriate to keep in touch with the family.

A few weeks went by with everything eventually falling into place when Alexa, Karen, Duncan, and Jilles accompanied by the nanny travelled back to London, leaving the vehicles in York while travelling down by train. Now this may have seemed a little strange but as Duncan hadn't experienced travelling by train before, the thrill of yet something new, left him with an uncontrollable excitement not realising that when he arrived at Kings Cross station it would be his first glimpse of London and a new world would open up to him.

To see the young boy's face as he stepped from the train was quiet a picture, for having never ventured far from that a village in Scotland; he now found such a hectic carry on which took his breath away, yes this was the big city alight and for the next few weeks his father would take him on the biggest site seeing tour he'd ever imaged.

"Would it be possible to invite both Molly and Maggi down for a few days to show them round London, before we leave for Sweden". Duncan asked;

Oh, such a polite request, from someone who'd obviously been brought up well mannered, Lars thought.

"Of course we can, phone and ask them if it's alright, while I book them into our hotel and I would also suggest that they stay for at least five days in which we can act as their tour guides if that's all right with them" was the reply to Duncan's request.

The beaming smile on this young man's face was a picture, he felt so grown up making a decision all by himself, now this had never happened before as all decisions had been taken by his elders and therefore with great pride phoned Scotland with the news which was to make his day, with a feeling of being so grown up

Oh it was so lovely to hear Mollie's voice on the other end of the phone, for secretly Duncan had to admit he'd missed her immensely but time has to move on and with the news that she and her sister would love to accept such an invitation, all that was left to do was book seats on the train as soon as possible. But with this, there was yet another surprise with a suggesting, it would be far better if they flew down to London. Now this was an invitation they couldn't resist having never been on a plane before and so with such eagerness, packed and arrived in London some two days later where both Lars and Duncan greeted them with a bouquet of flowers, then whisking them off to the hotel in the heart of the city.

The next four days was so hectic as Lars and Duncan showed the two sisters round London's finest, visiting everything from Buckingham Palace, to Tower Bridge, even taking in the Zoo as Duncan had never seen anything like that before. Having wined and dined at the best restaurants, even taking in a show one night seeing the Lion King, and although Lars had taken Duncan to see that show a few weeks before they knew it was the most impressive show in the West End and that the two sisters would be amazed.

These were memories that they could all treasure in the future, memories they would all look back on over time, but like all fairy tales they have to come to an end as Molly and Maggi said goodbye on the return journey to Scotland with a promise that when Duncan was settled, Lars would arrange for them, to visit Sweden, all expenses paid.

Now this was family time, with a few more days in London which was spent at Alexa's apartment whereby they could just sit back and relax, doing the things that come natural to a family before it was time to say their goodbyes Knowing it wouldn't be long before they were reunited in whichever country, as everything had been finalized with all the appropriate documents in place for the return to Sweden for Lars and Duncan.

Time was now drawing to an end, as the last day in the country for Lars and Duncan before they flew out to a new venture of father and son and so to spend the last evening together where the family would gather for one last meal at a local restaurant before their goodbyes. Yes, a lot had been achieved in such a short time since that night in York when Lars opened what Alexa called, an unforgiving letter, but then that night was to put everything into prospective as the outcome had now reached a happy conclusion for all concerned.

The parting was sad for both Lars and Duncan the next day as they left London airport flying to their new life in Sweden but in a way it was a happy ending to a journey that Lars could never have dreamt existed, bringing him to a future without the one he'd lost and yet it was a future that without that love, he would never have experienced the new love which was now in his life, something of herself that would last his lifetime, the love of his son.

Reaching Sweden was a little unsettling for Duncan for being in a strange land there was a language barrier and a new way of schooling that seemed very strange at first but within a short period of time and people his own age who spoke English, he soon overcame that obstacle and settled in nicely, while also keeping in touch with Scotland at the same time.

Alexa and Tam spent as much time as possible in York running the business from Alexa's office that had now been built especially for her needs, so she wouldn't have to live in the city all the time although being the CEO she did have a strong interest in ruling the company from there, not being able to take a backseat just like her mother.

She also started an official charity to help local children who needed surgery abroad, this brought her tremendous satisfaction in her personal life making her realise and come to terms with what her mother had done and the reasons why she did it.

Tam decided that his family was more important than working himself to death and therefore cut his workload down as their passion for each other grew stronger, although he never forgave his father and only suffered his presence for the sake of Alexa and Jilles.

It also came to pass, that Karen and Dave cut their workload down and travelled more with each other, having purchased the house in York and another one in Spain which would give them more time to spend with their grandchildren.

Time passes so quickly and before you realise, it's either taken your good years away or you lose them altogether.

Peter; well work was in his blood and he was in head office most days with a wife that would have agreed to anything as long as he was happy and content, and they too would travel but being a workaholic all his life, time just couldn't change him as he stood in for the family with the thoughts flowing back many a time to the earlier days when times were hard.

The same with Issa and Rob, happily married to her true love but still kept her side of the business running and with a house in the country and a place up in York she was in her glory doing a little charity work from time to time whereby she'd design sensual underwear for the less fortunate than herself as a payback for the success she'd achieved, she also went on to do lectures on rape for young girls having experienced the trauma herself.

Shelia, she never got over Corry's death but one day quite by accident while visiting Molly in Scotland on a short break, happen to sit on the train when a man stopped in the isle and asked if the seat next to her had been taken and from that day on they were inseparable, finding happiness which no one would deny them.

Maggi decided to sell her property in Aberdeen and move in with her sister up in the Highlands, visiting Duncan at least twice a year, the two sisters lived a comfortable life with Molly having a private pension from the company, money wasn't an object, enabling them to travel far and wide visiting countries they'd never even heard of a few years ago.

It was believed that Maria finally married her prince charming after their long courtship but still kept both properties and therefore lived six months a year in each.

Marcus, now that was one Greek God so to speak who never got over his love for Corry and unfortunately died of a broken heart leaving all his wealth to the daughter of the love of his life, yes Alexa inherited all Marcus's wealth.

Now the person who we would all wonder about was Jay.

He visited his, Daughter, Son and Grandson whenever he could although Tam would always remain distant;

Alexa tolerated him so that Jilles would grow up with a grandfather. His days were occupied by playing the stock exchange and dabbling in new business ventures which were profitable but then that was Jay, his position meant more to him than anything for he had lost the thing that should have made him happy but that was the past, his only regret was that Corry never forgave him leaving her TO WALK ALONE.

To many this was a love story but to others it was heartbreak of a woman that deserved to experience true love and who gave her all for what she believed in, the united power of preservation.

Printed in Poland
by Amazon Fulfillment
Poland Sp. z o.o., Wrocław